An **Organ** Miscellany

85 attractive pieces

Kevin Mayhew

We hope you enjoy *An Organ Miscellany*.
Further copies of this and our many other books are available
from your local music shop or Christian bookshop.

In case of difficulty, please contact the publisher direct by writing to:

The Sales Department
KEVIN MAYHEW LTD
Buxhall
Stowmarket
Suffolk IP14 3BW

Phone 01449 737978
Fax 01449 737834

Please ask for our complete catalogue of outstanding Church Music.

First published in Great Britain in 2000 by Kevin Mayhew Ltd.

ISBN 1 84003 523 4
ISMN M 57004 660 7
Catalogue No: 1400231

0 1 2 3 4 5 6 7 8 9

Cover designed by Jonathan Stroulger.

Printed and bound in Great Britain

Contents

VERSET

Alexandre Guilmant (1837-1911)

ALLEGRETTO con GRAZIA

Edward John Hopkins (1818-1901)

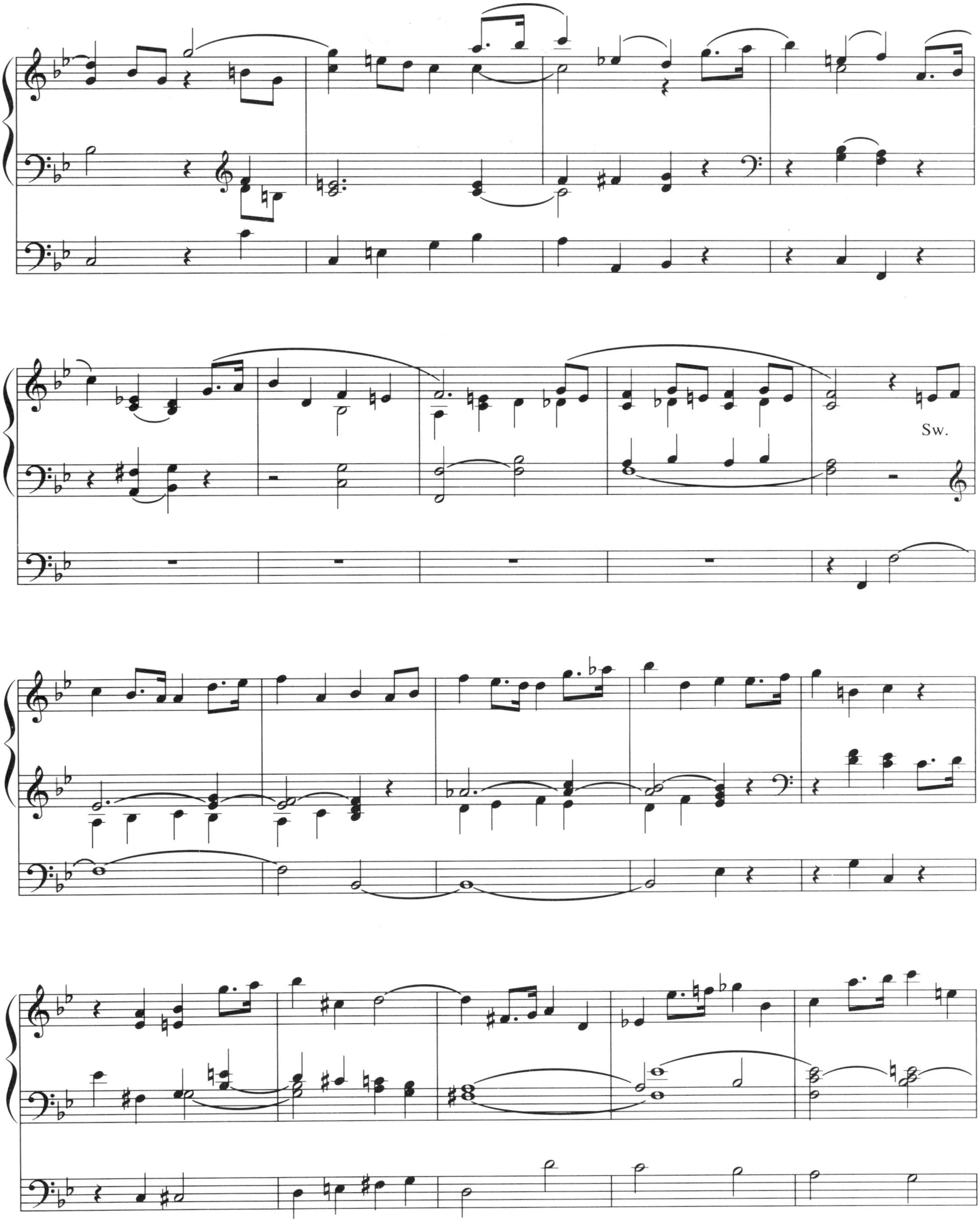
Sw.

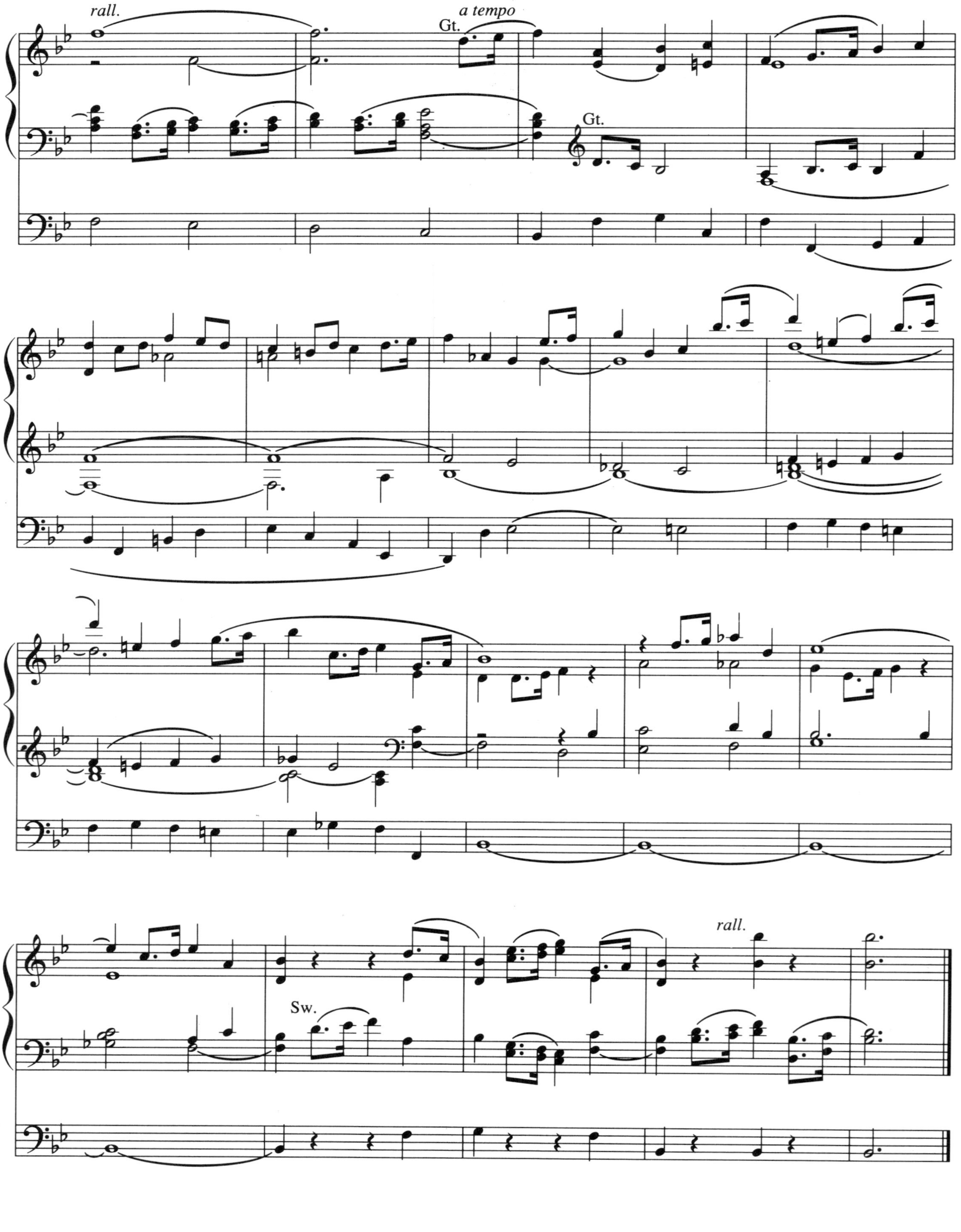
rall.
a tempo
Gt.
Gt.
Sw.
rall.

CHORALE PRELUDE on 'ROCKINGHAM'

Hubert Parry (1848-1918)

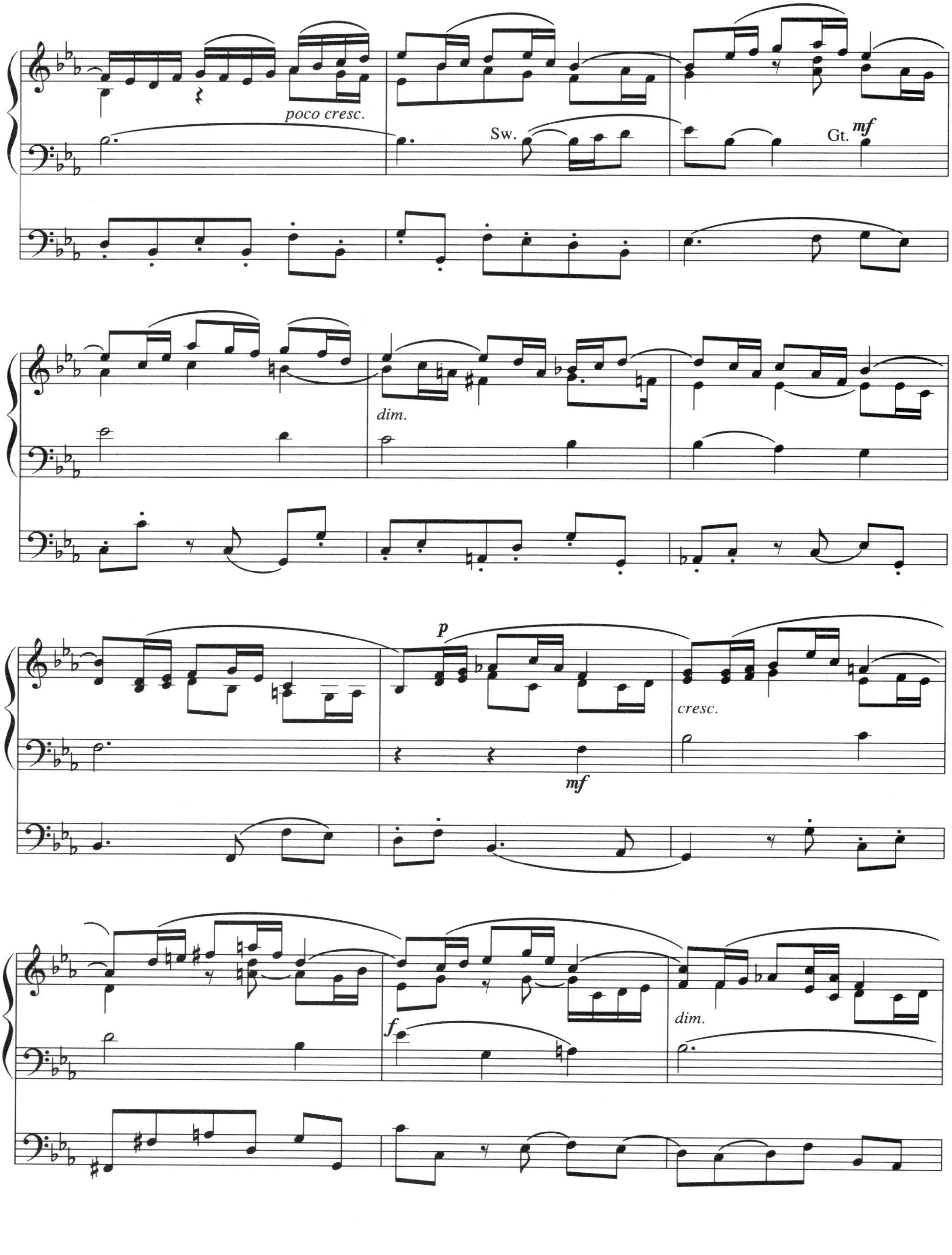
poco cresc.
Sw.
Gt.
mf
dim.
p
cresc.
mf
f
dim.

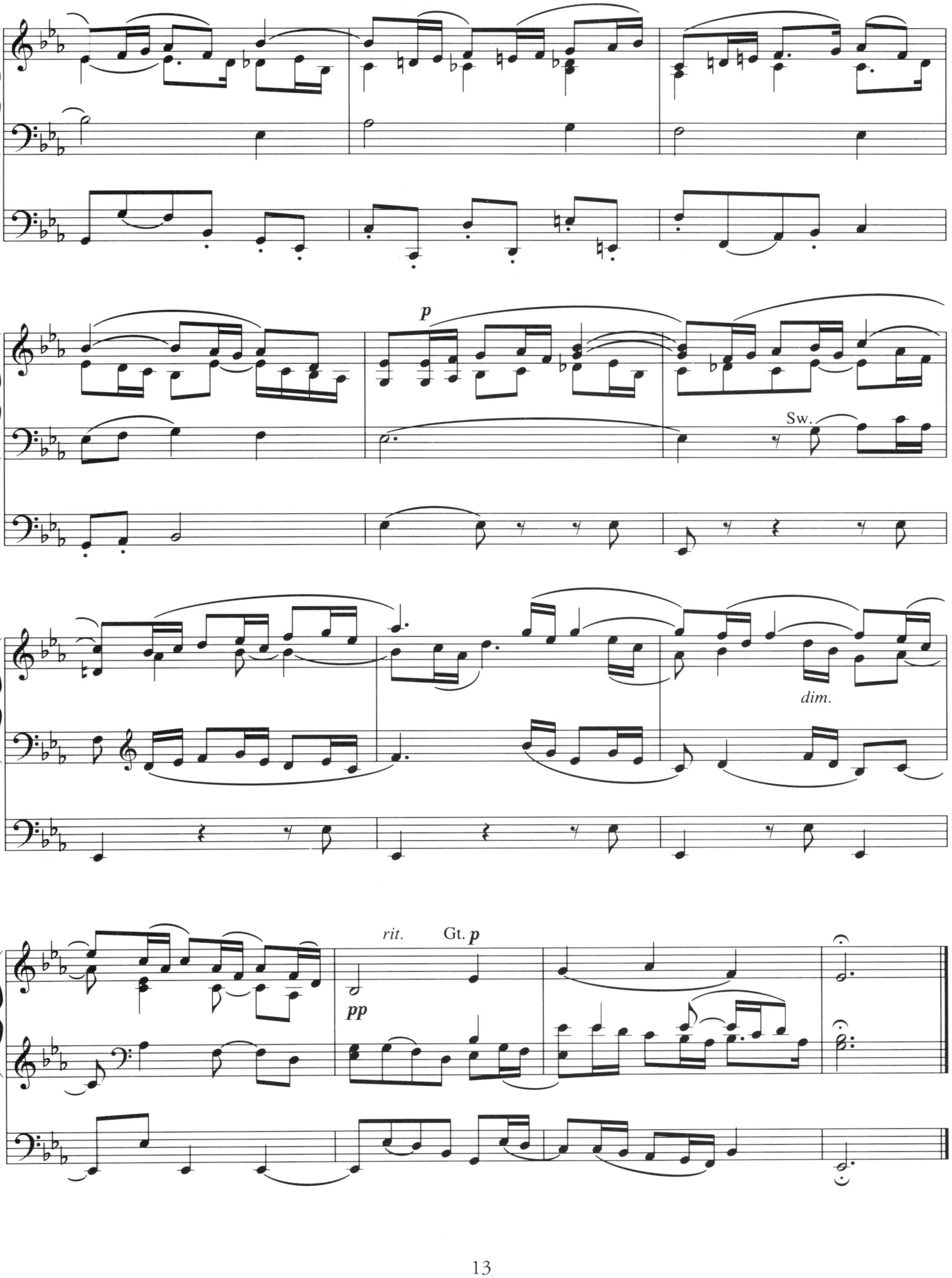
p
Sw.
dim.
rit.
Gt. p
pp

For Mary

FANFARE and SCHERZO

Christopher Tambling (*b*.1964)

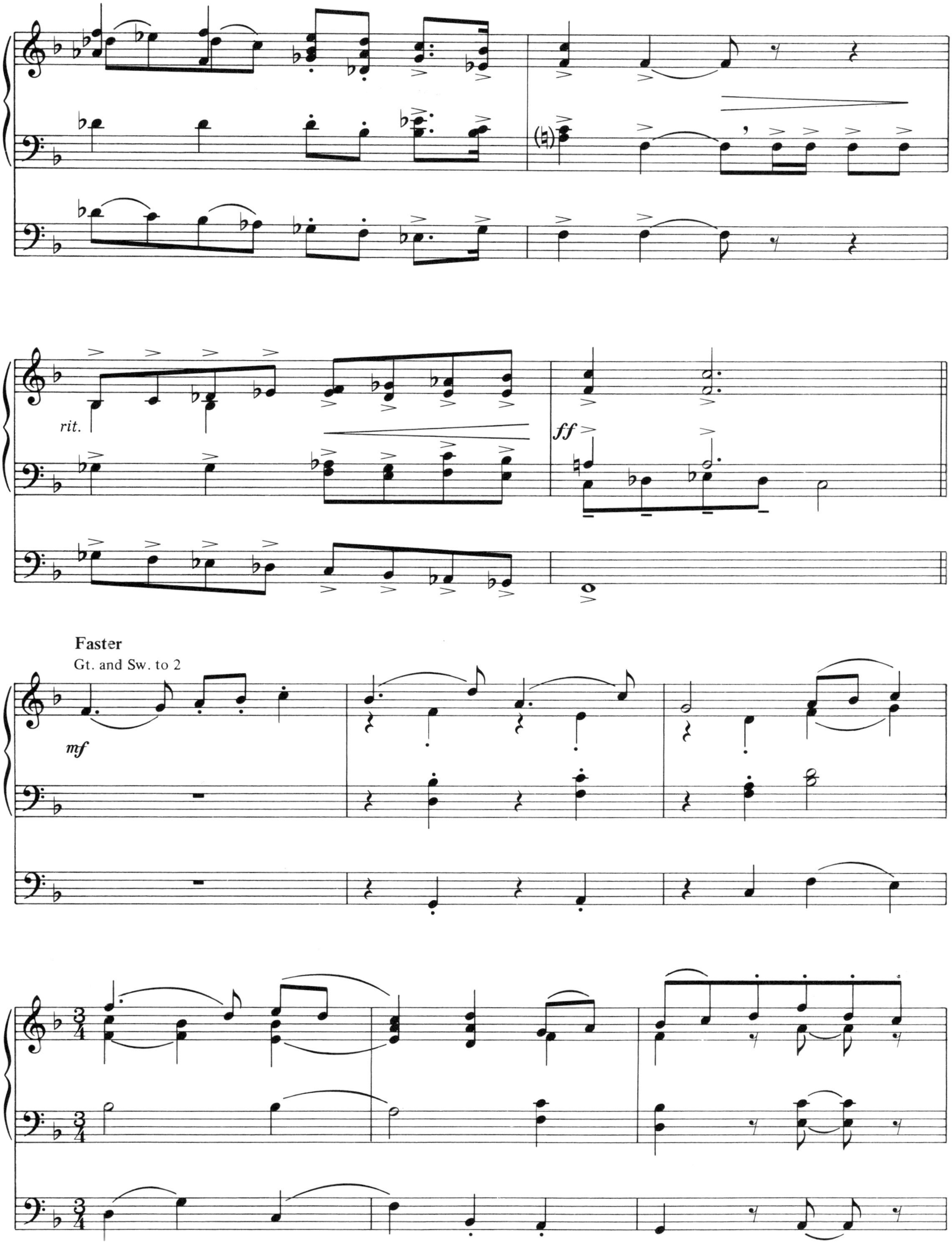
rit.
ff
Faster
Gt. and Sw. to 2
mf

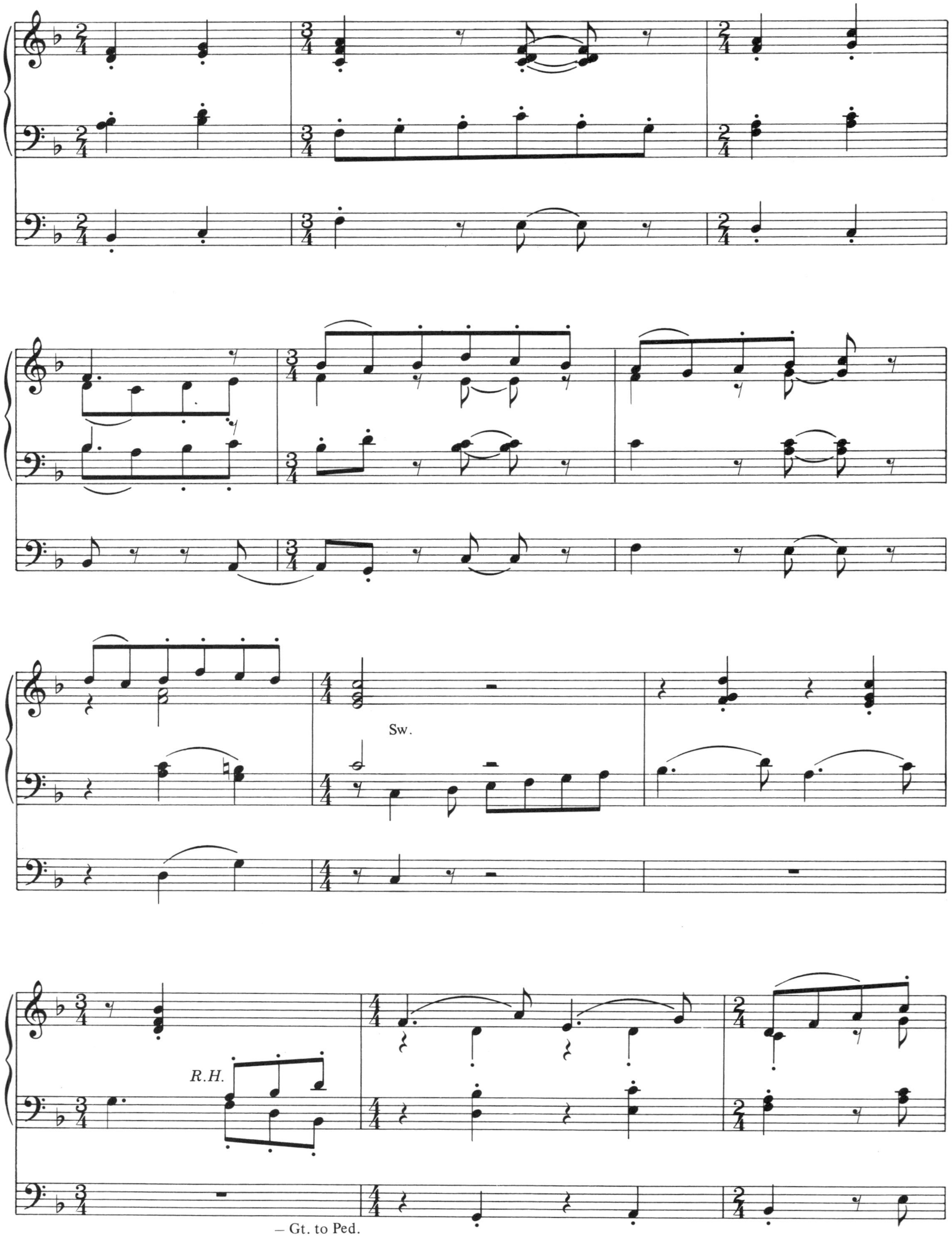
Sw.
R.H.
– Gt. to Ped.

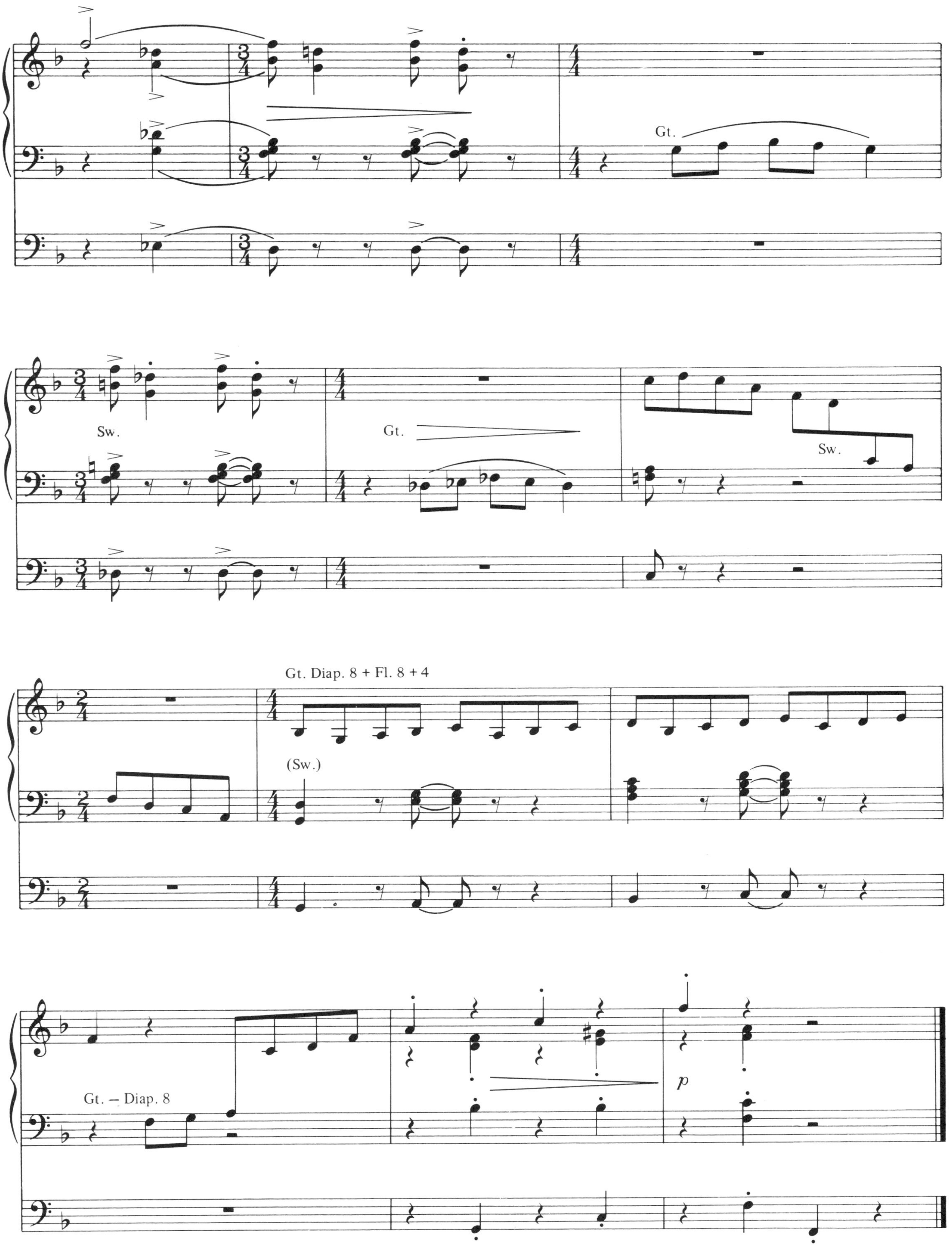
Gt.
Sw.
Gt.
Sw.
Gt. Diap. 8 + Fl. 8 + 4
(Sw.)
Gt. – Diap. 8
p

PRELUDE in C

Johann Rinck (1770-1846)

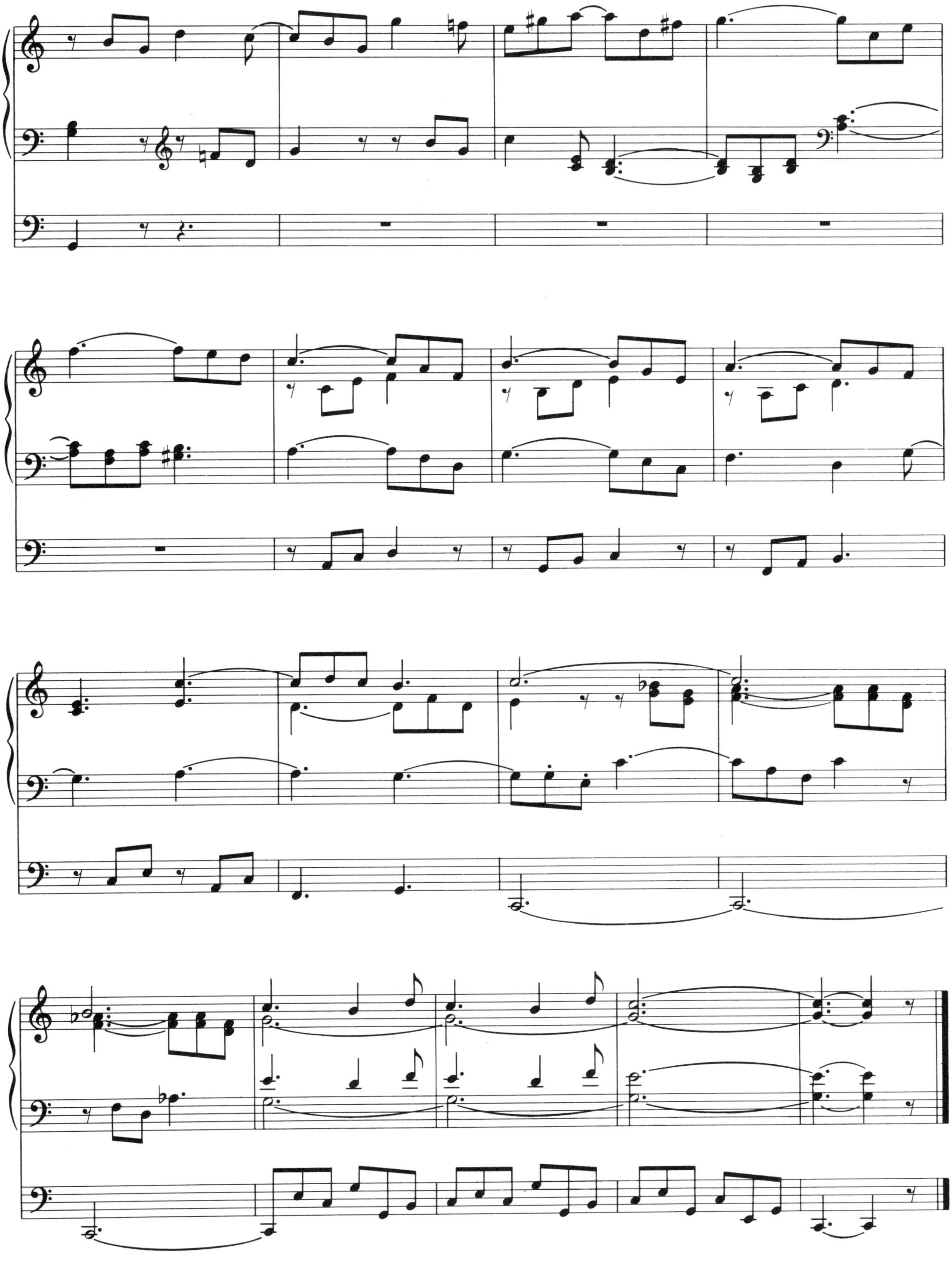

For Mavis Murphy

BLUE PROMENADE

Alan Ridout (*b.*1934)

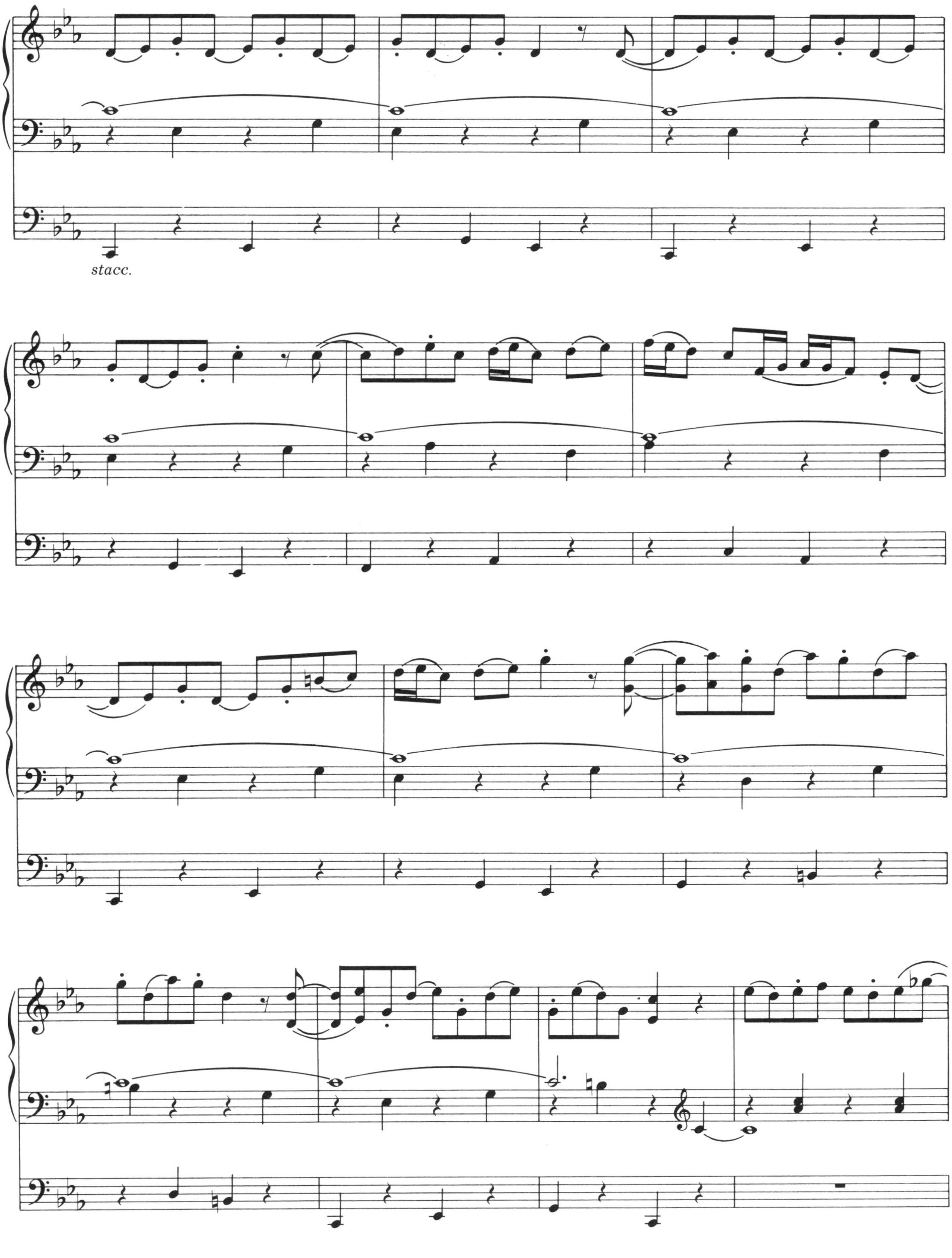
stacc.

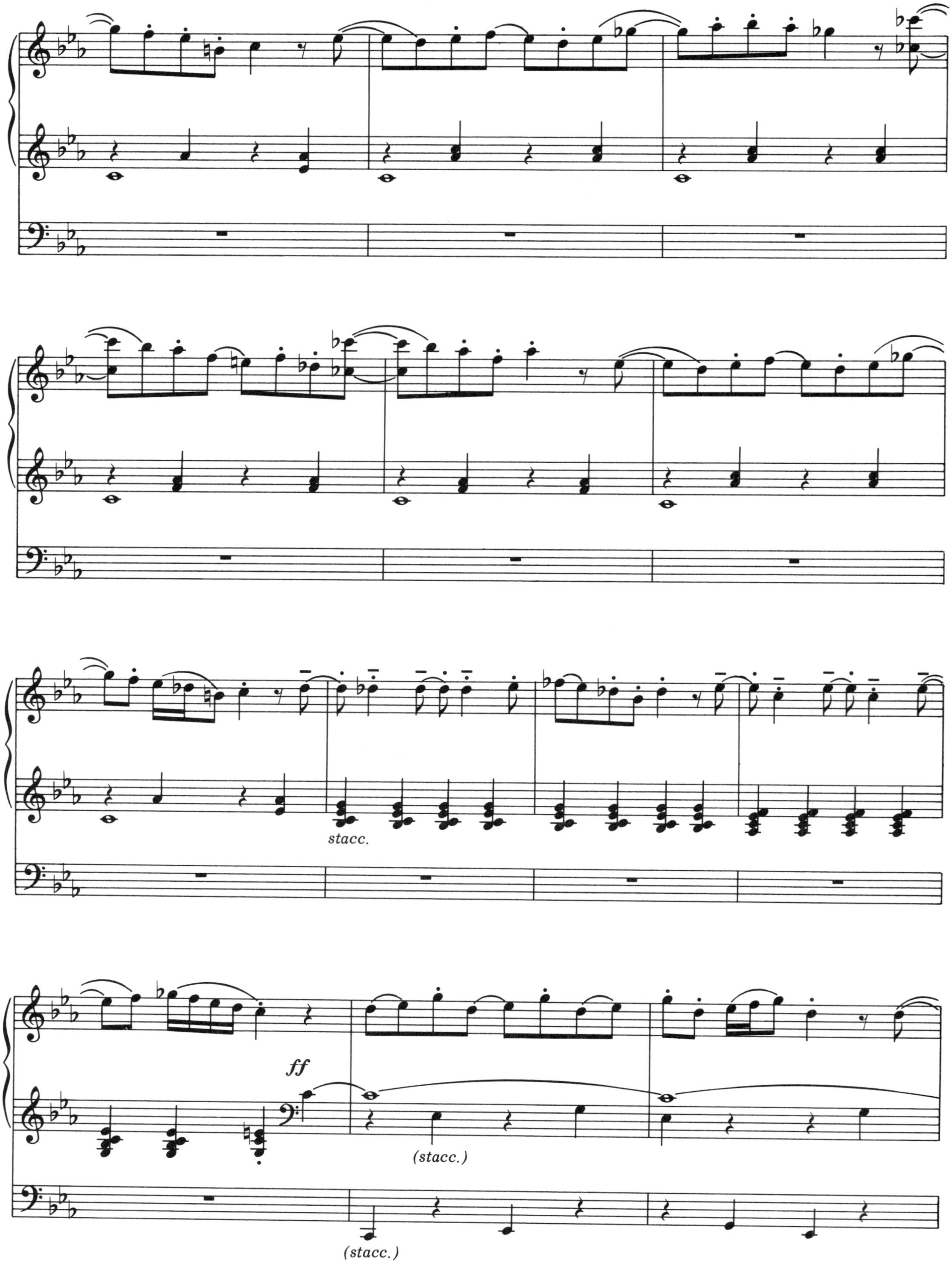
stacc.
ff
(stacc.)
(stacc.)

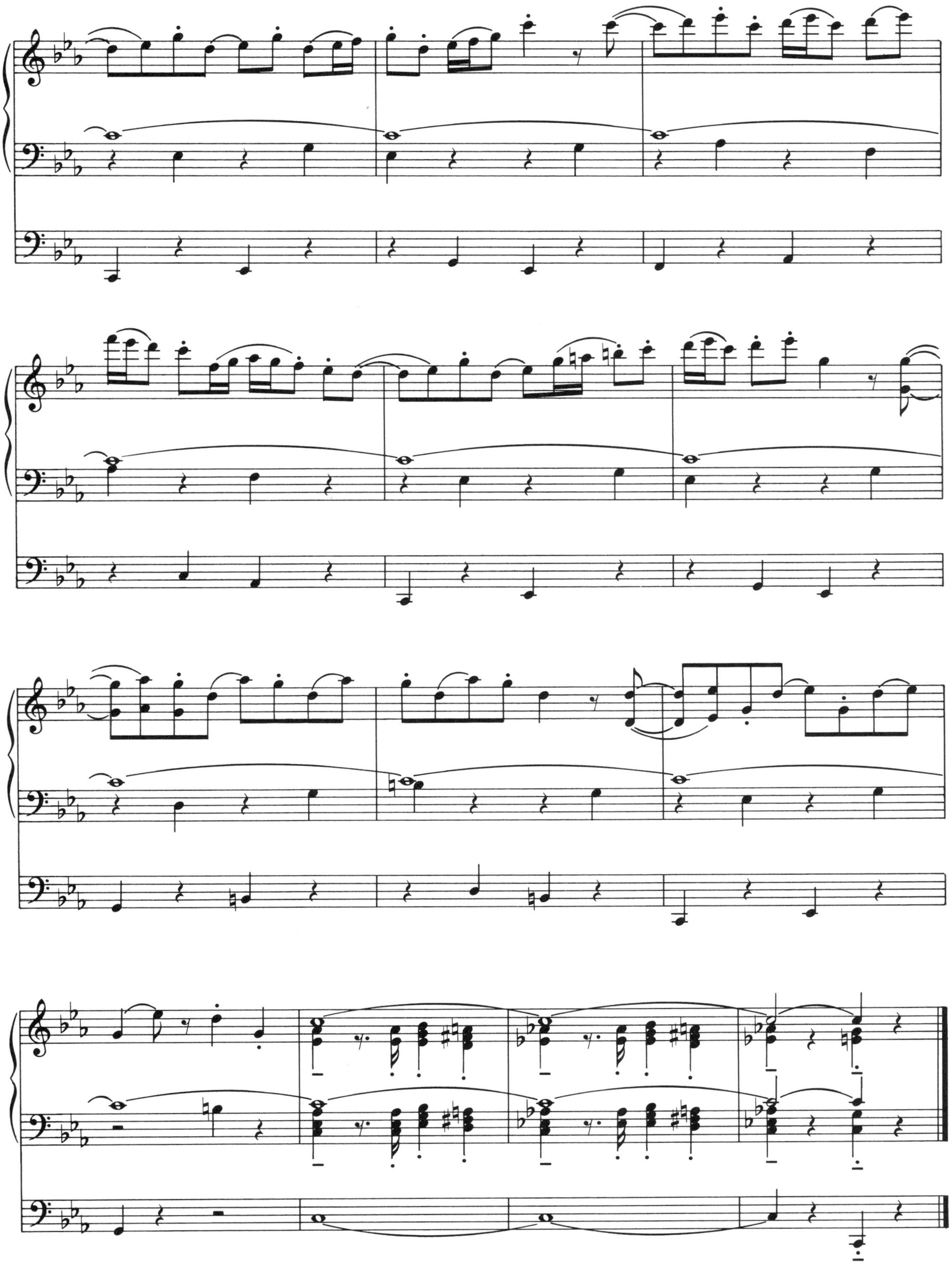

GRAND CHOEUR in G

Théodore Salomé (1834-1896)

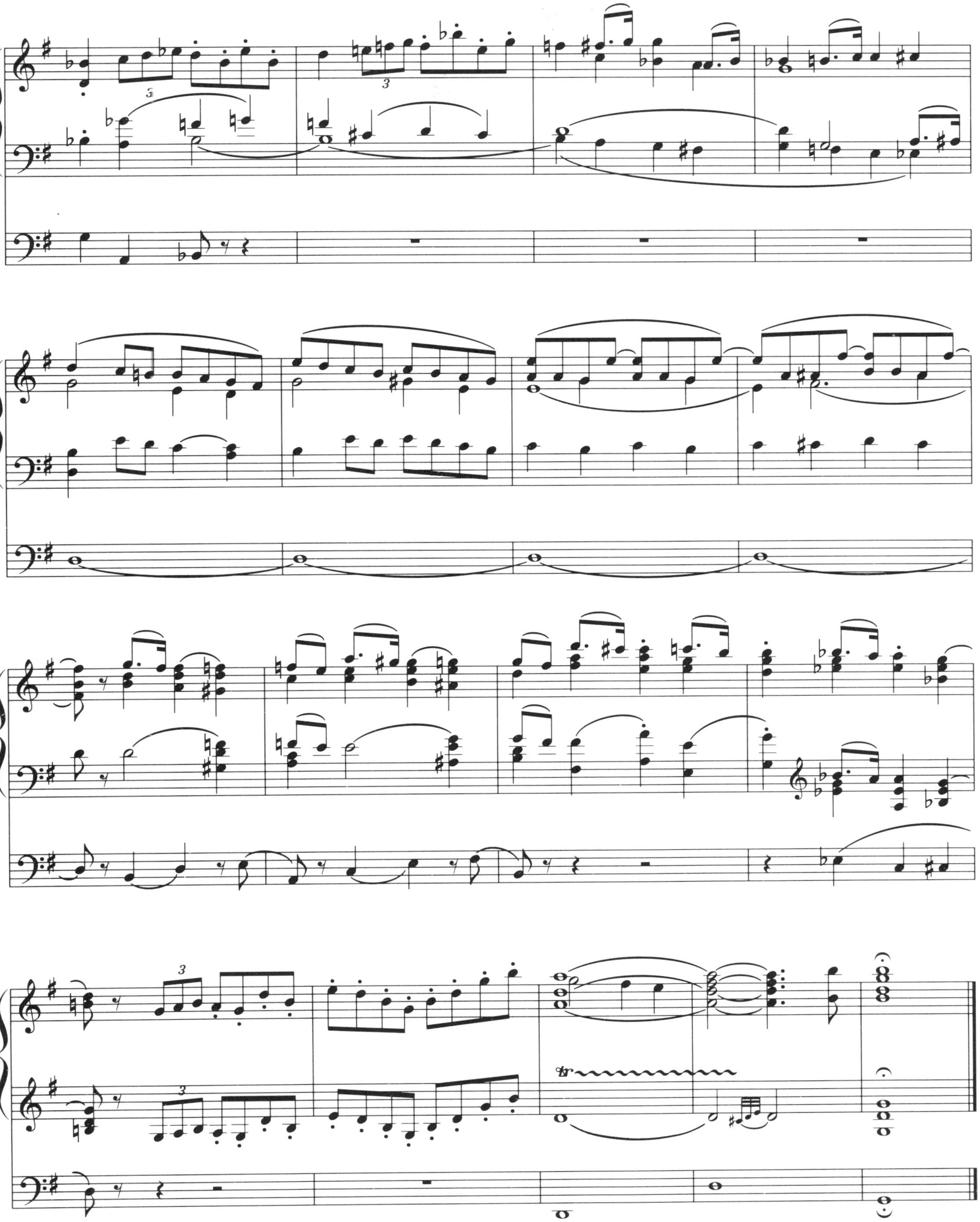

MEDITATION in B MINOR

Alexandre Guilmant (1837-1911)

Andante quasi adagio (♩ = 50)

Gt. **p** *sempre legato*

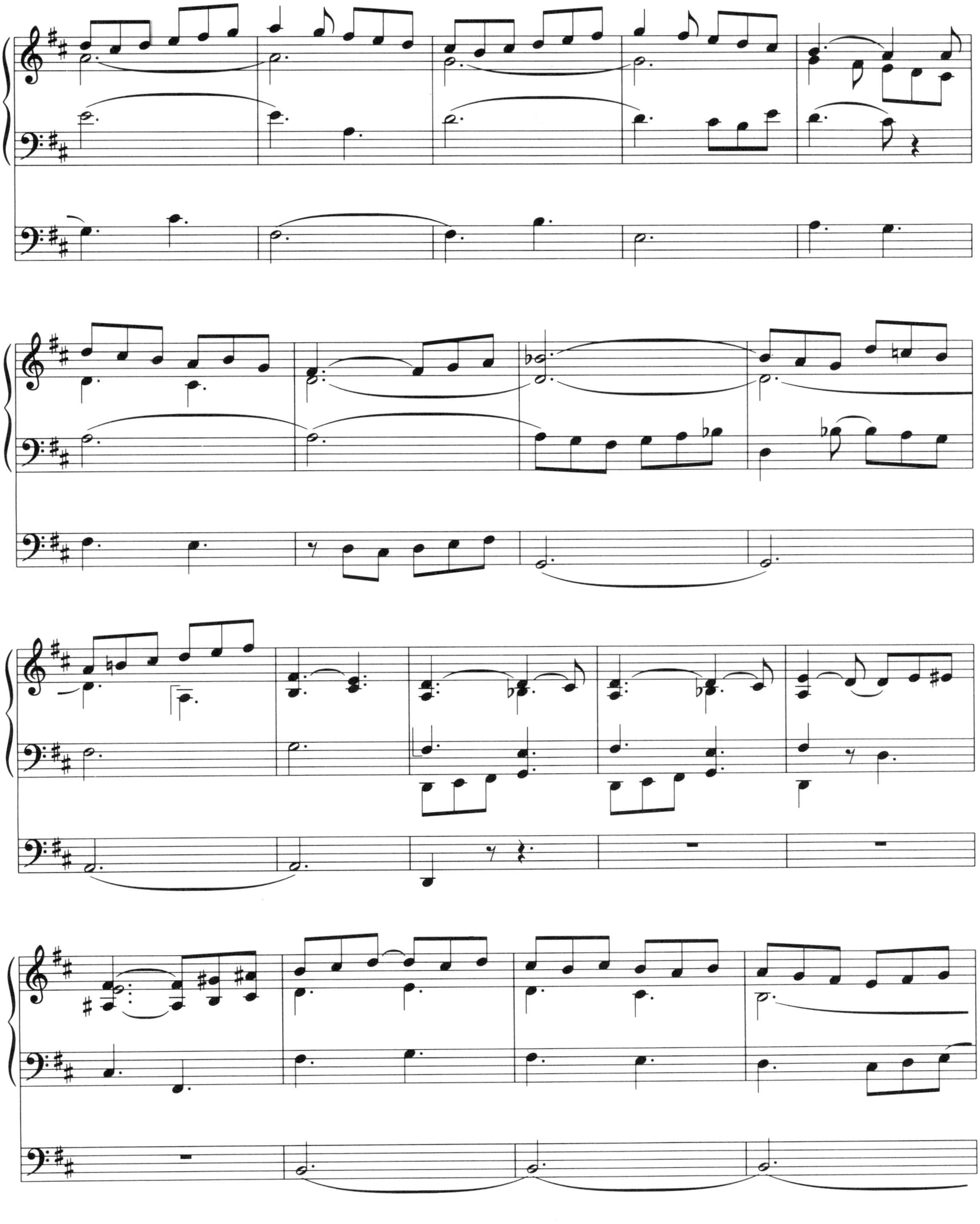

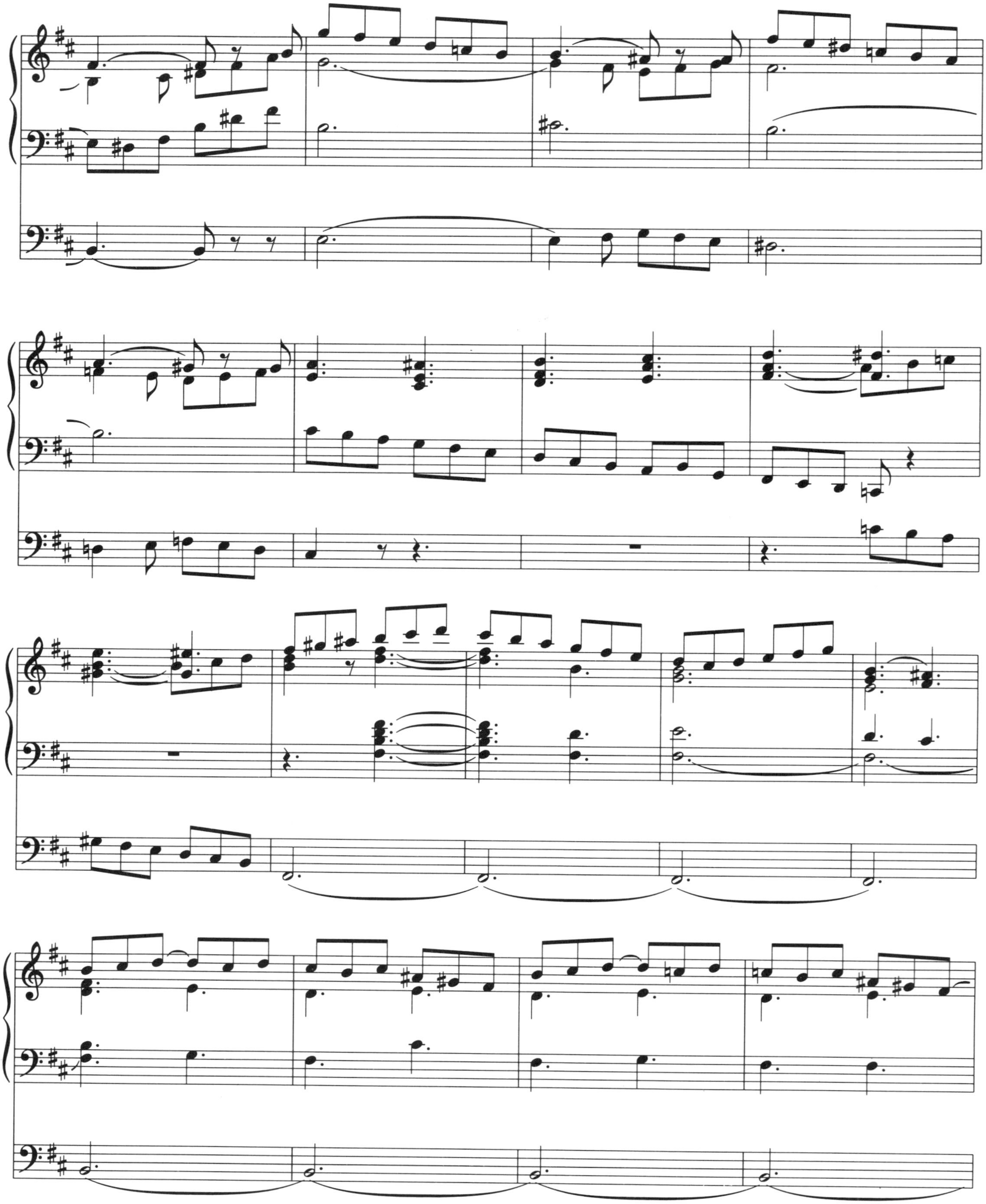

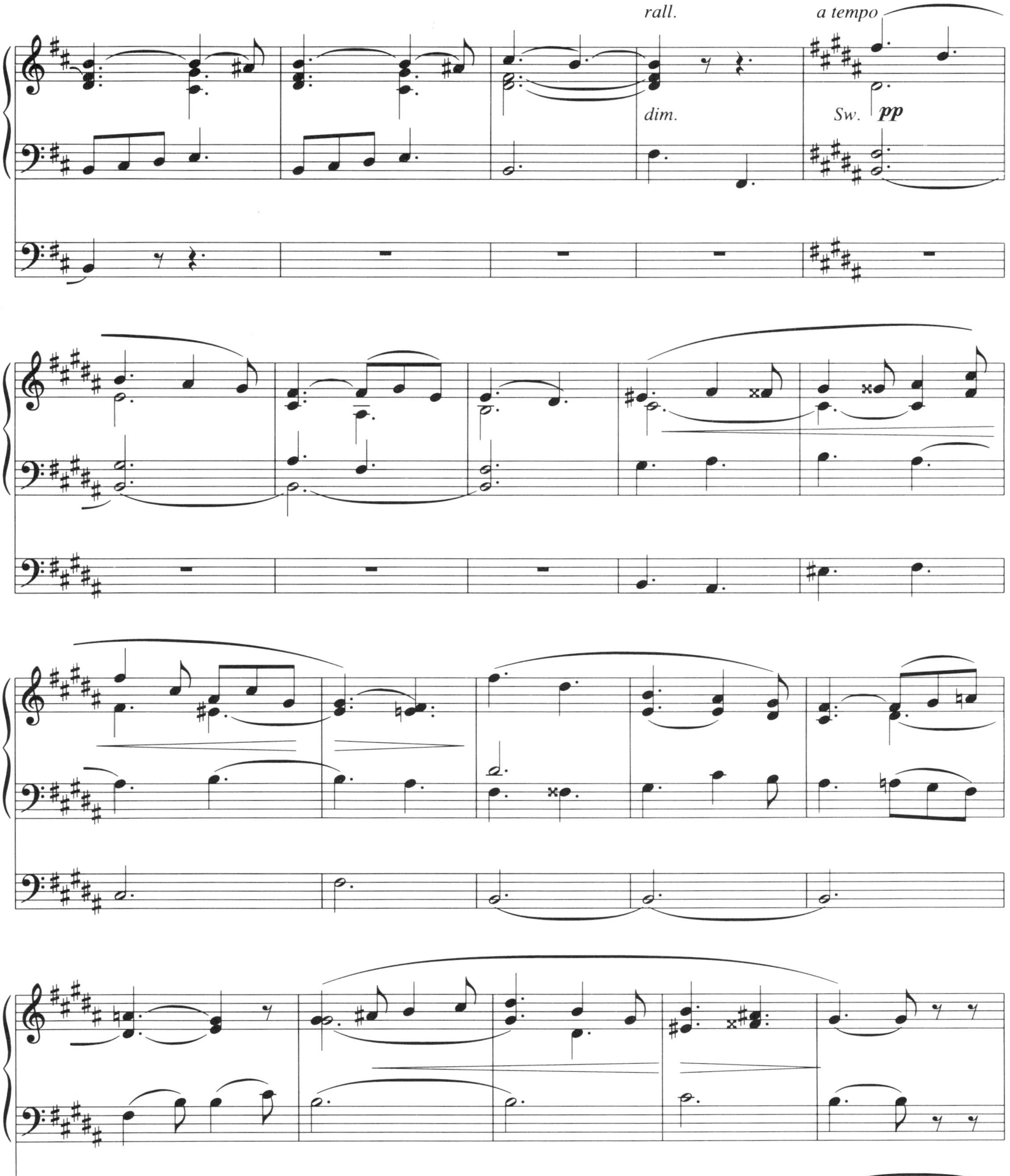
rall.
a tempo
dim.
Sw.
pp

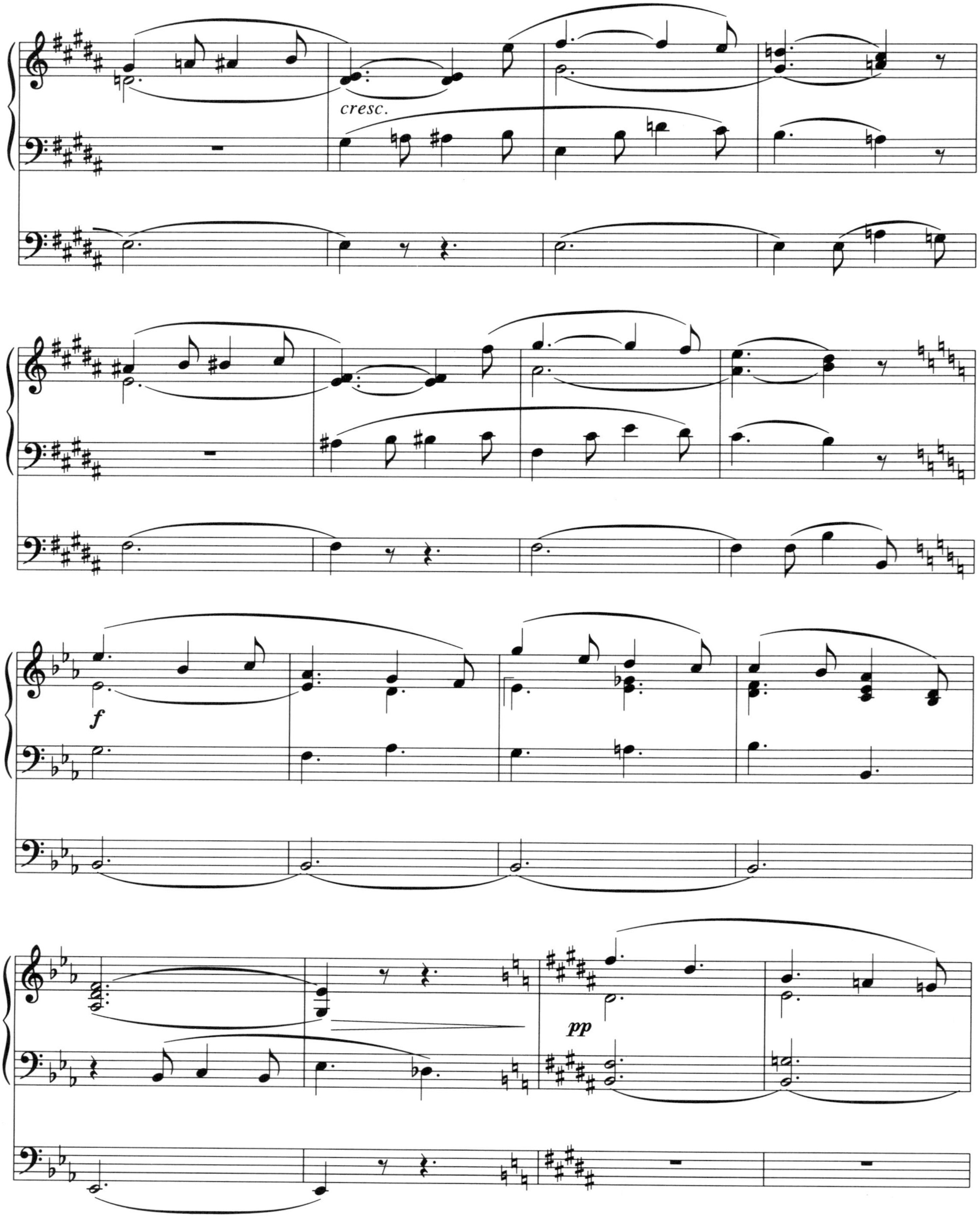
cresc.
f
pp

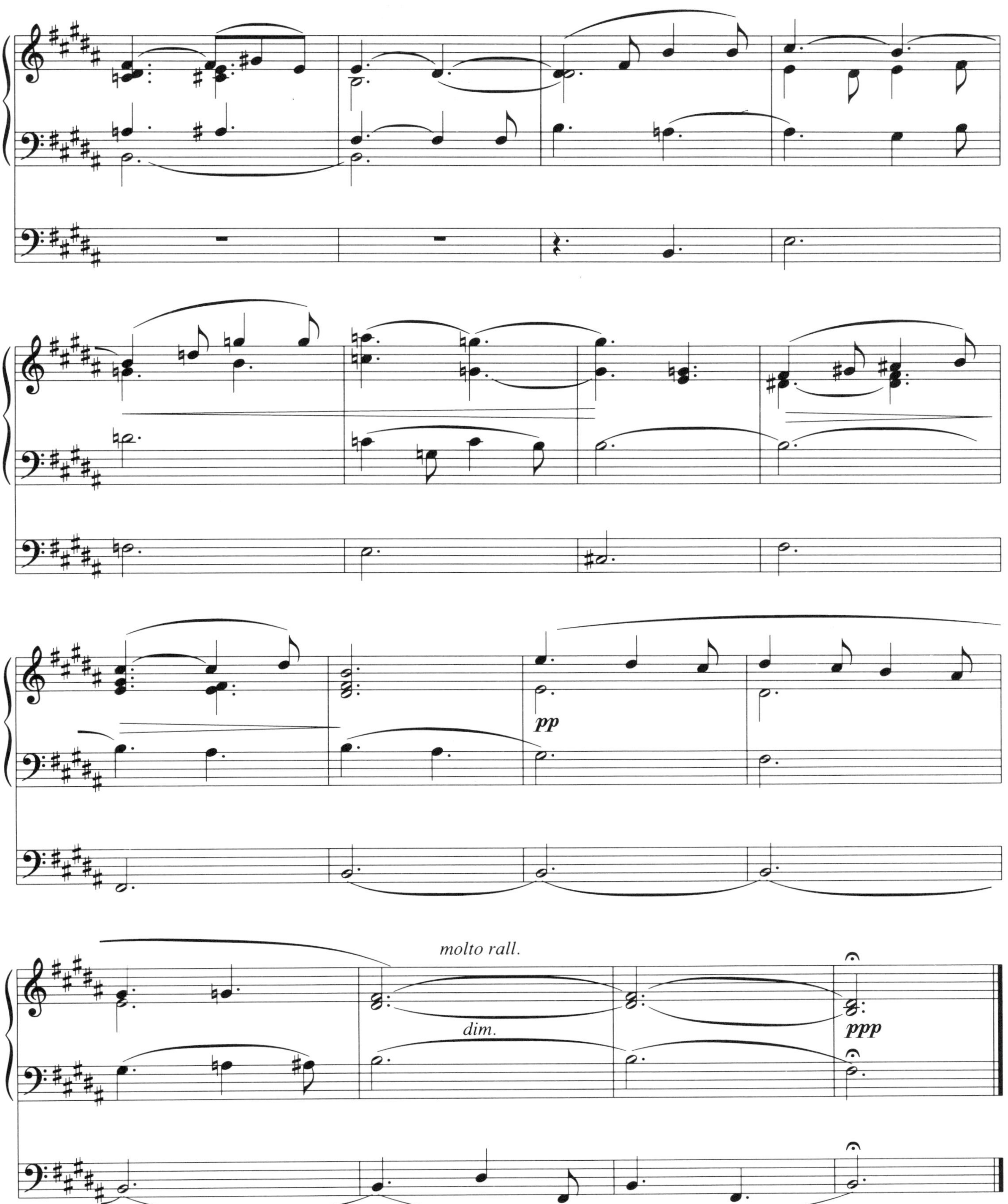
pp
molto rall.
dim.
ppp

EVENSONG

Cuthbert Harris (1870-1932)

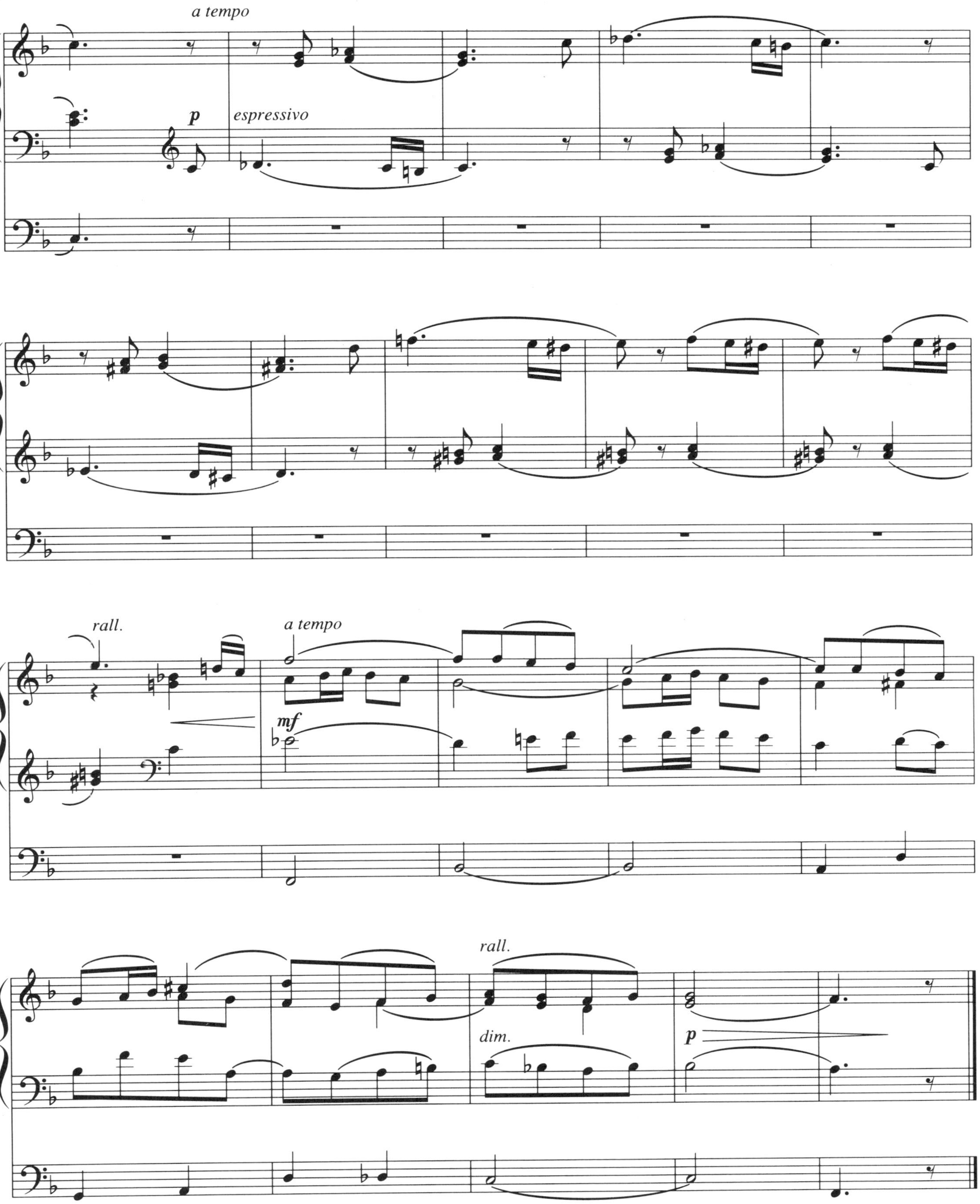
a tempo
p
espressivo
rall.
a tempo
mf
rall.
dim.
p

PRELUDE in D

Edouard Silas (1827-1909)

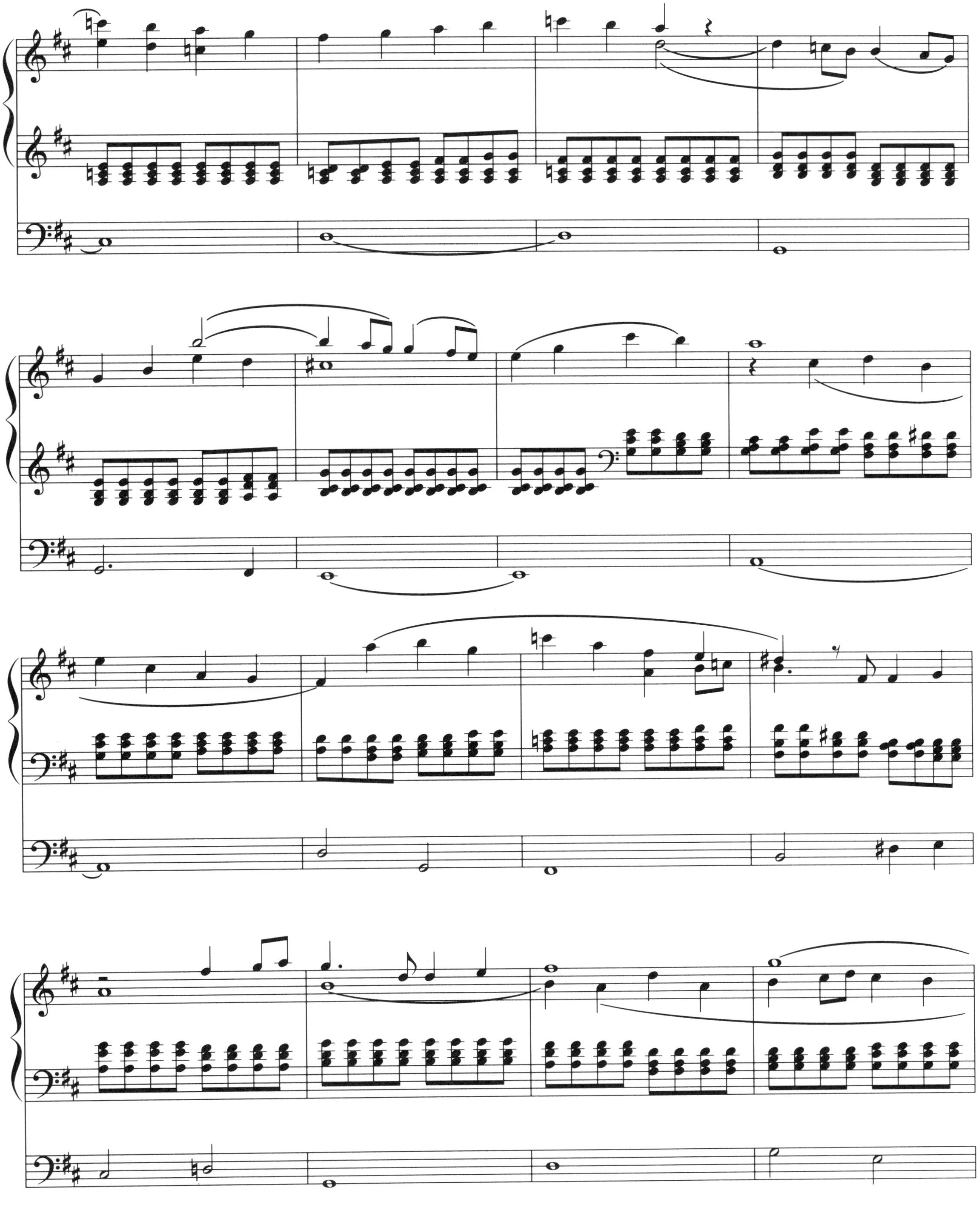

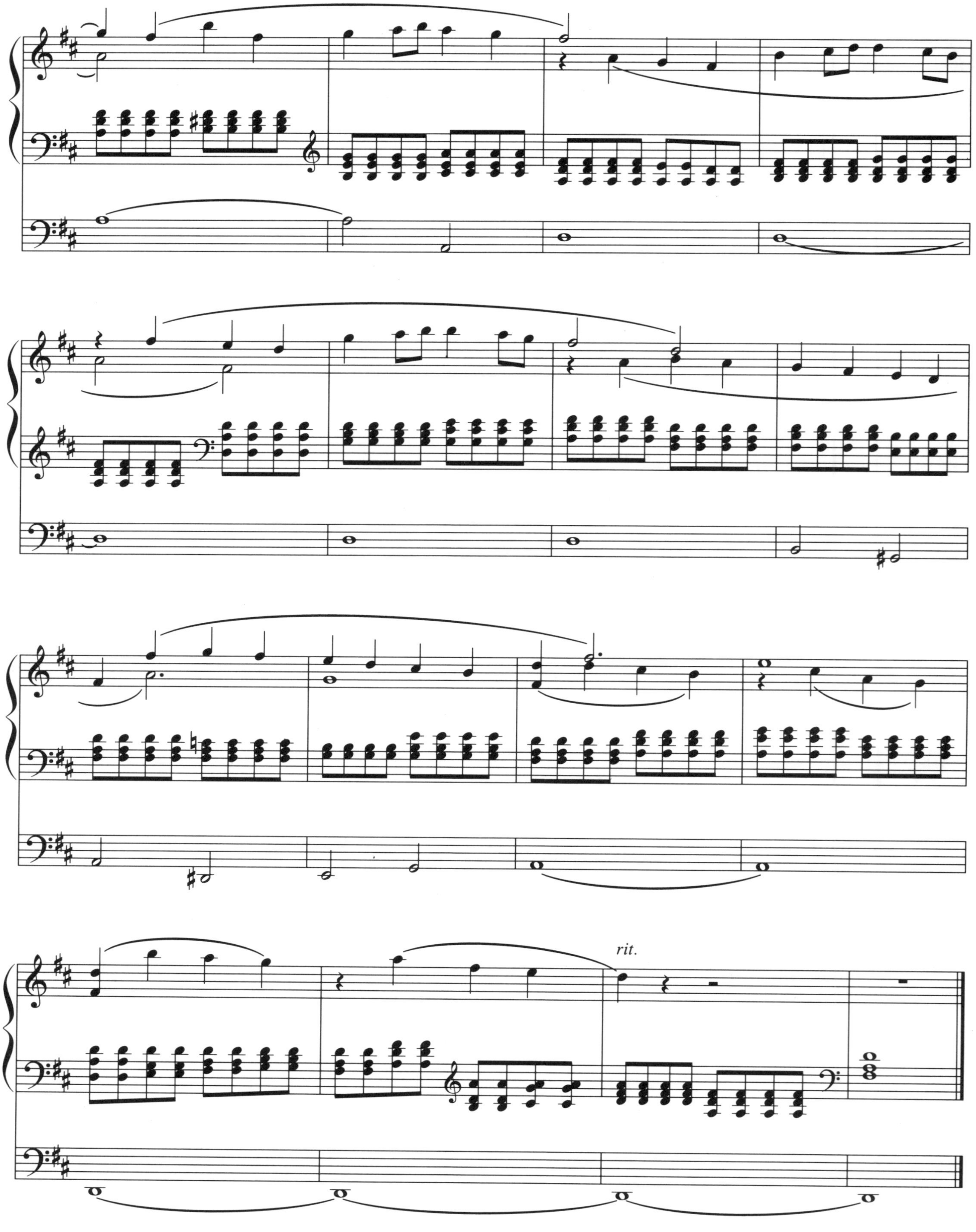
rit.

For Rupert, Tim and Amy

CHORALE

on 'York' (Scottish Psalter, 1615)
Christopher Tambling (*b.*1964)

Gt. to Mixtures
Sw. to Mixtures

With spirit

Gt.

detached

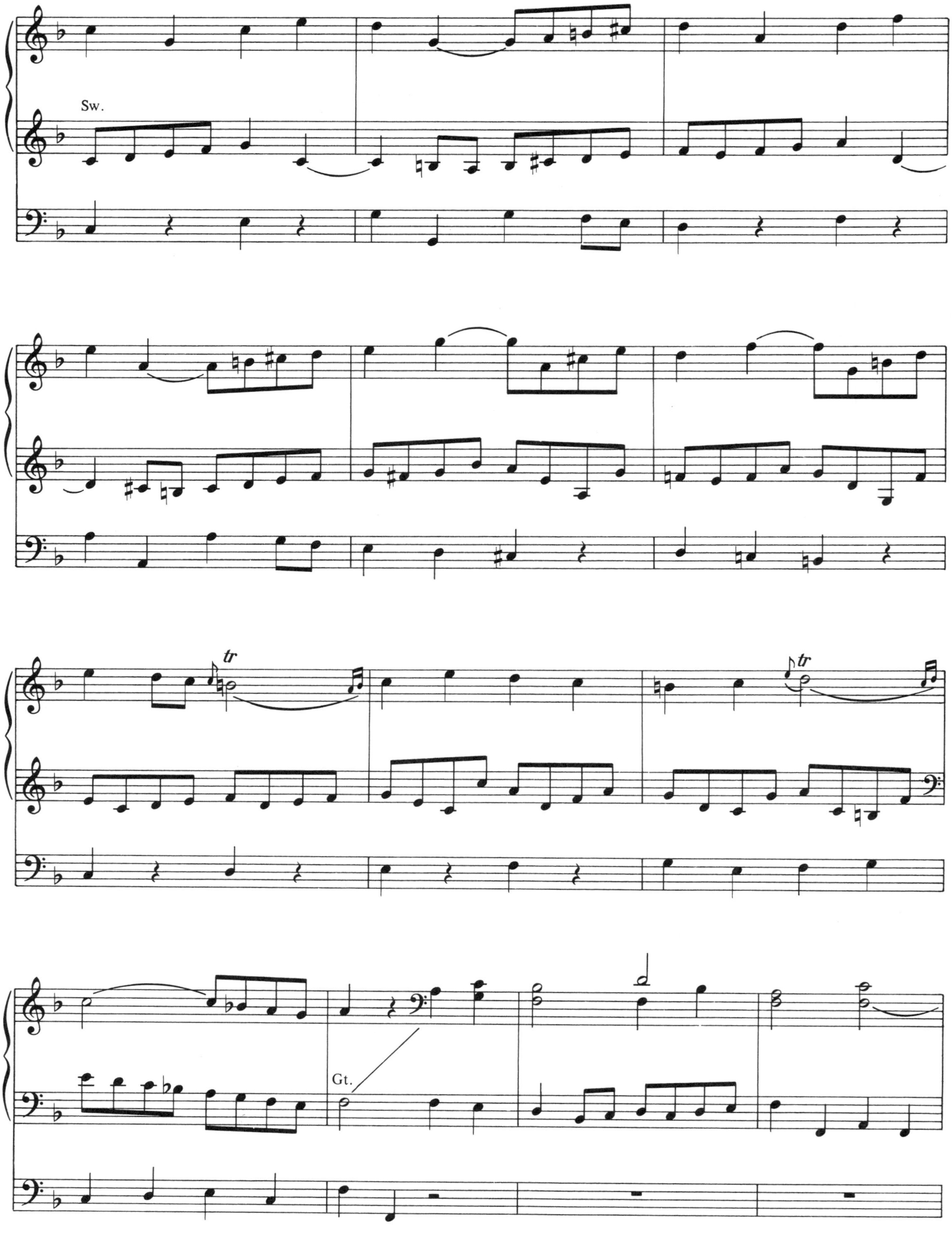
Sw.
tr
tr
Gt.

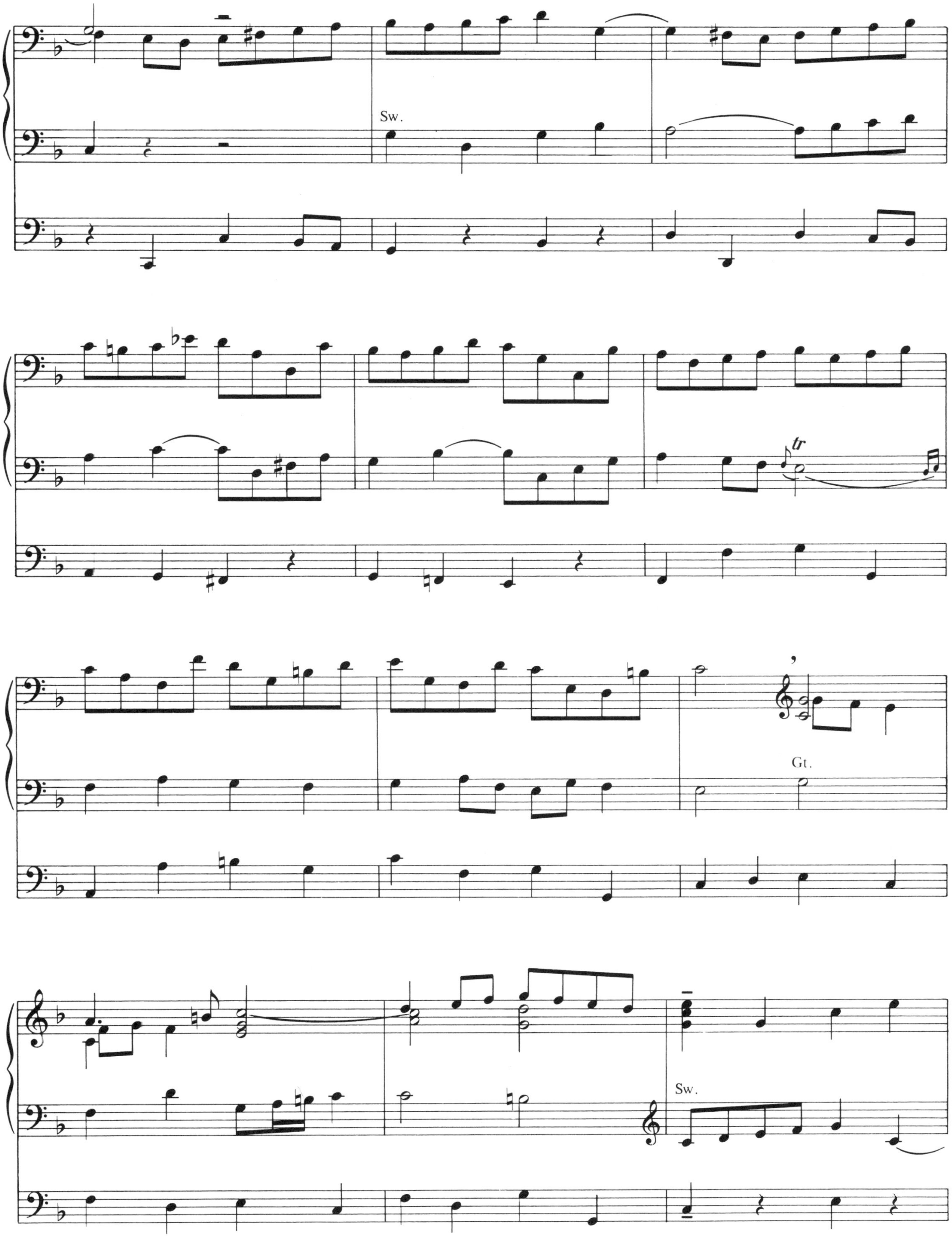
Sw.
tr
Gt.
Sw.

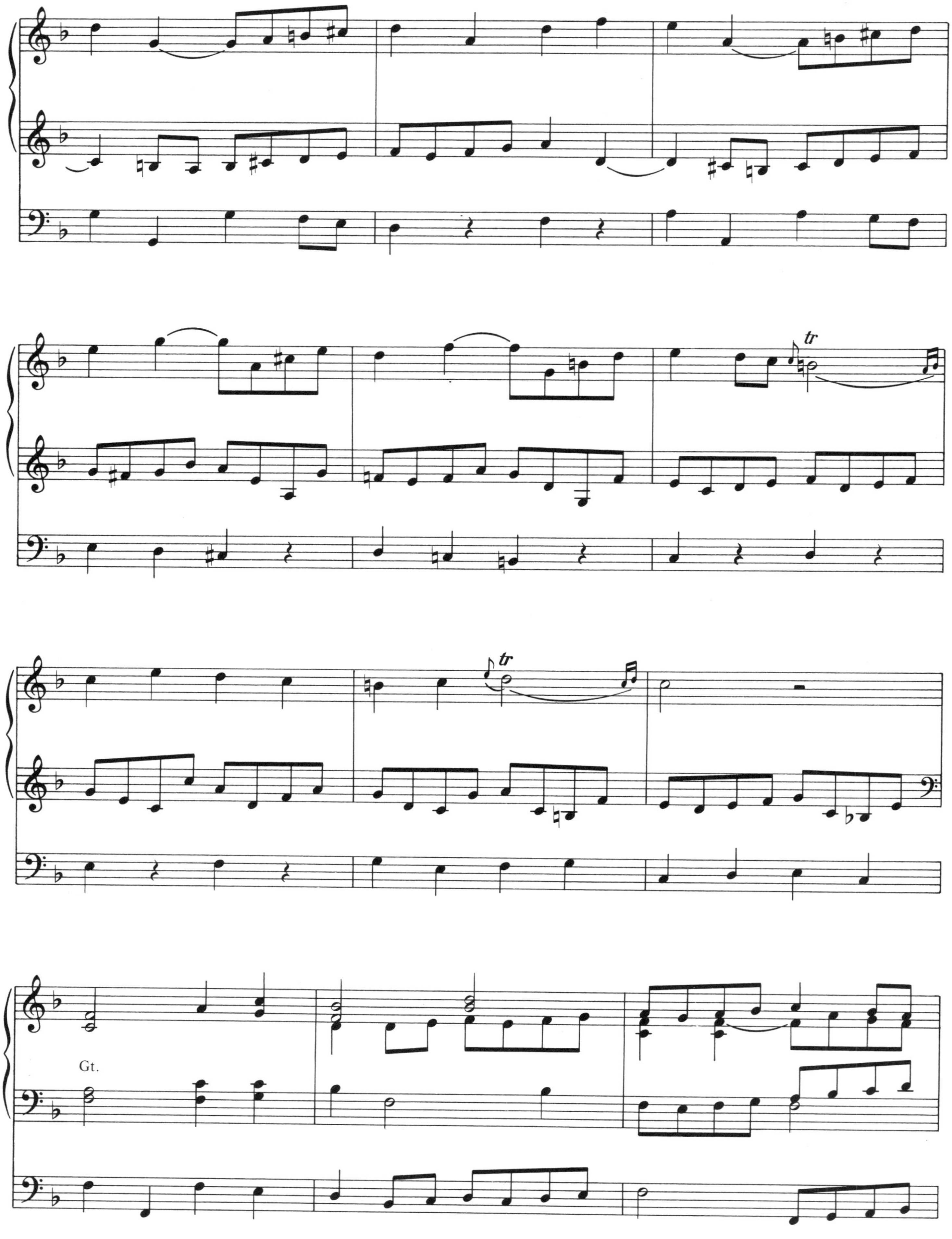
tr
Gt.

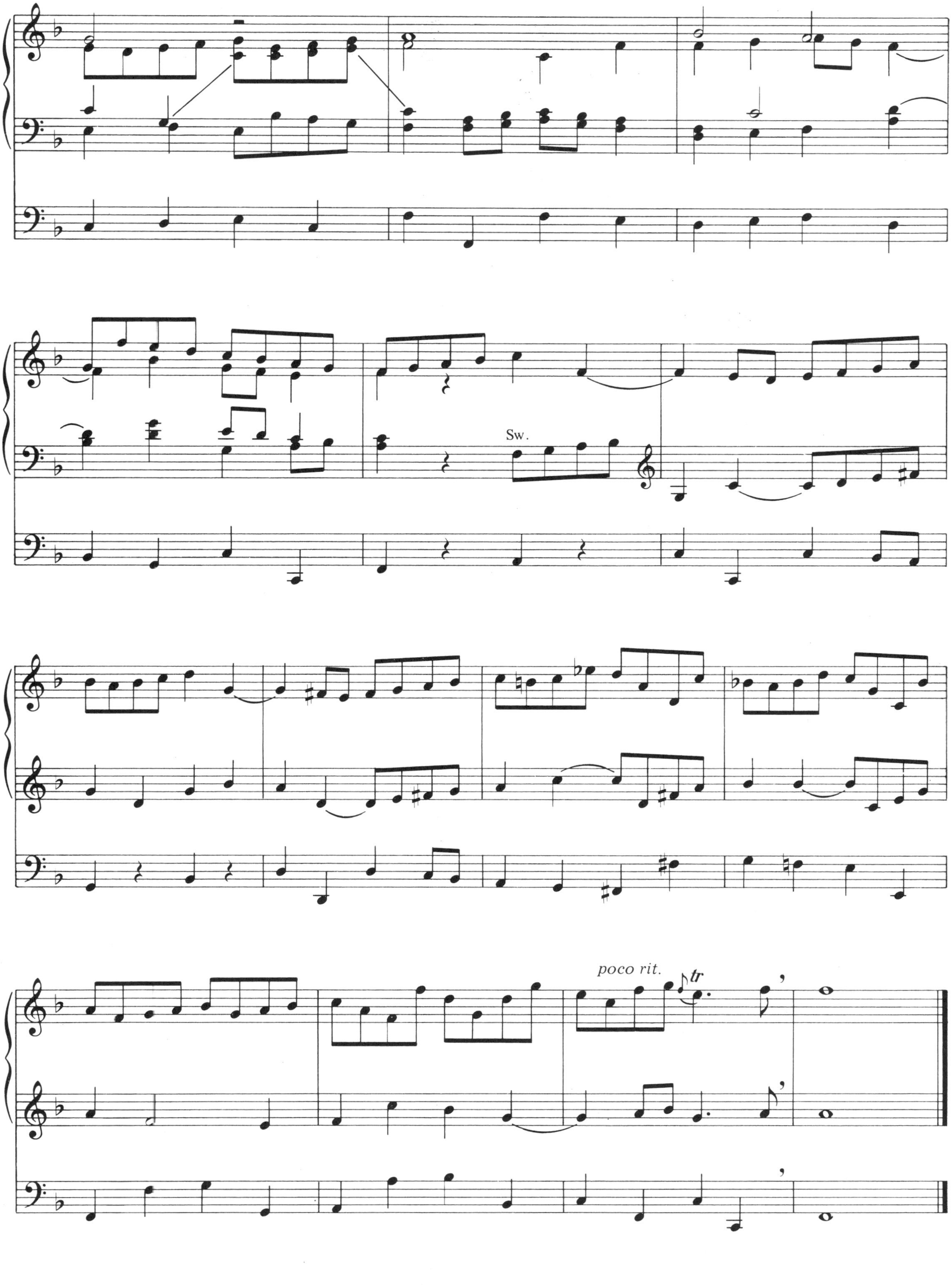
Sw.
poco rit.
tr

DIVERSION

Richard Lloyd (*b.*1933)

Tempo, dynamics and phrasing at the player's discretion

poco rall.   *a tempo*

poco rall.

a tempo

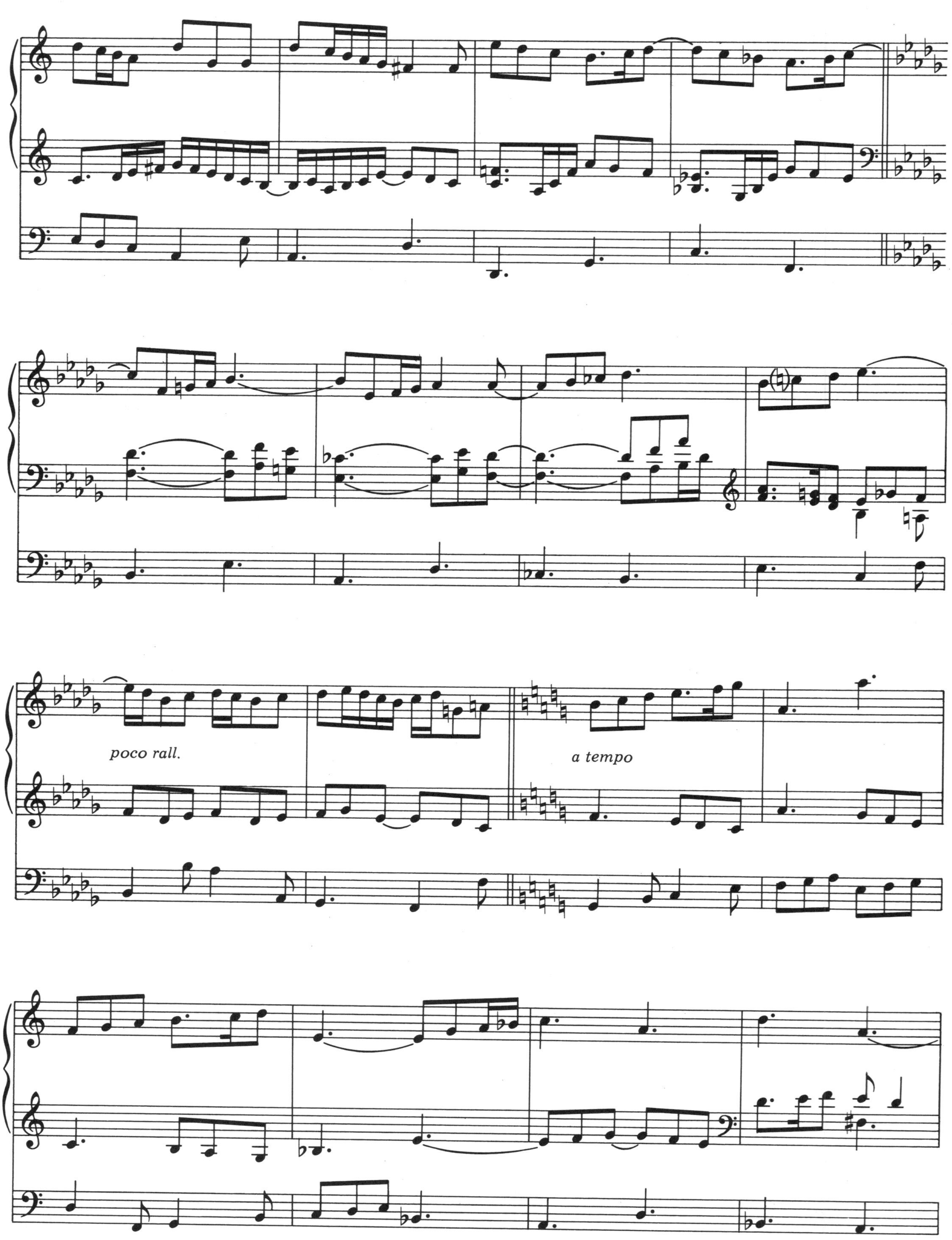
poco rall.
a tempo

rall.   *a tempo*

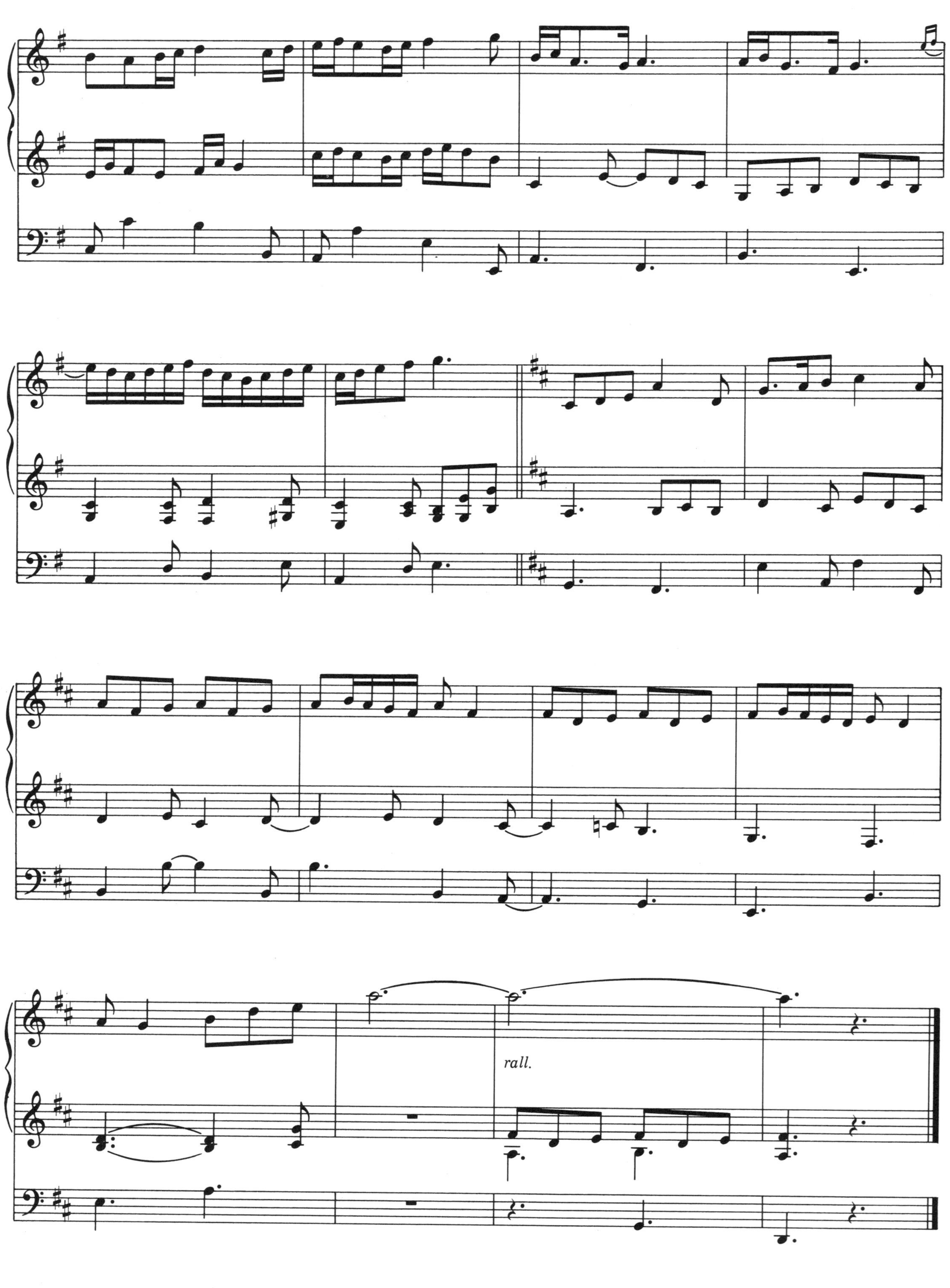
rall.

INTERMEZZO in D MINOR

Alan Gray (1855-1935)

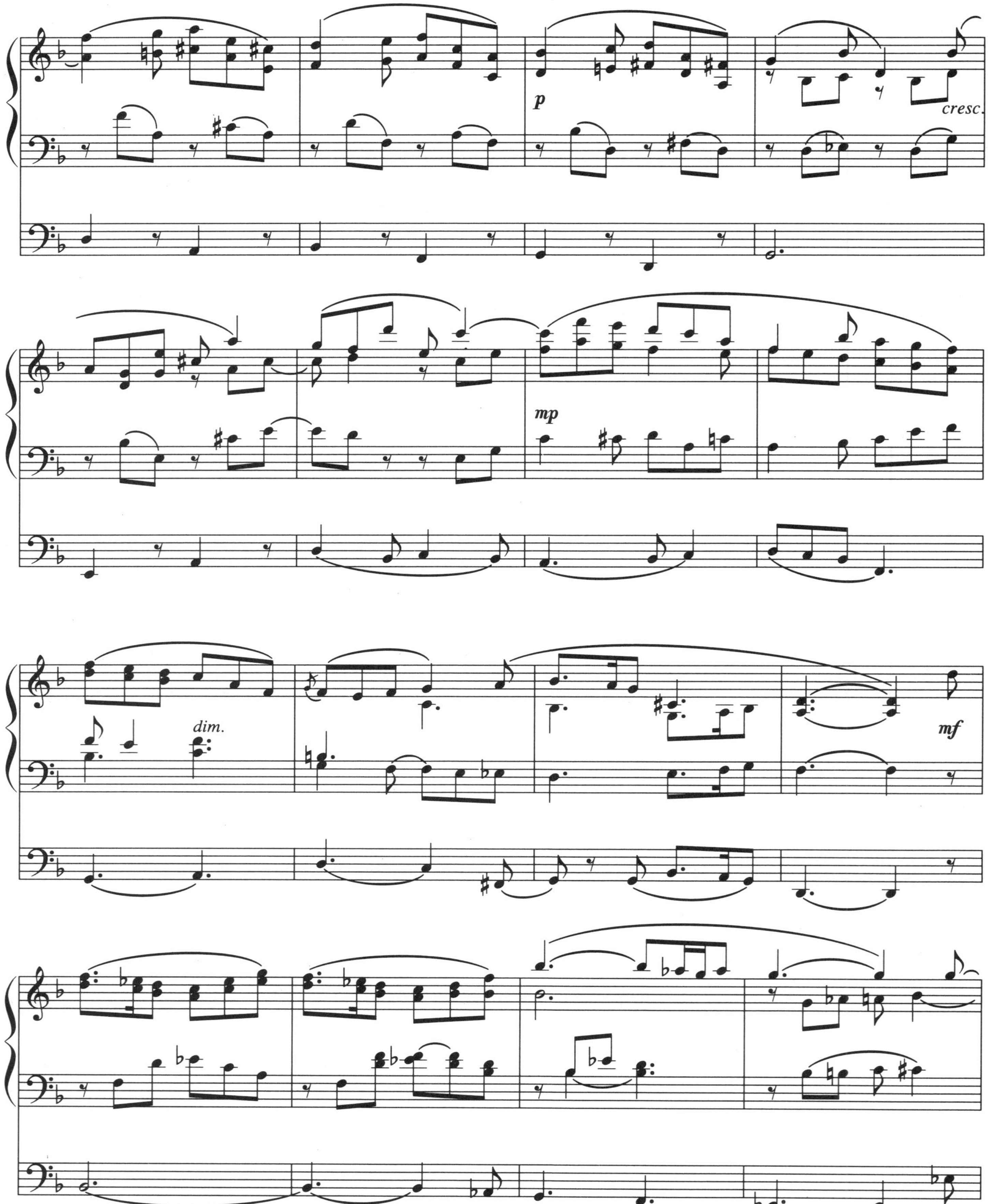
p
cresc.
mp
dim.
mf

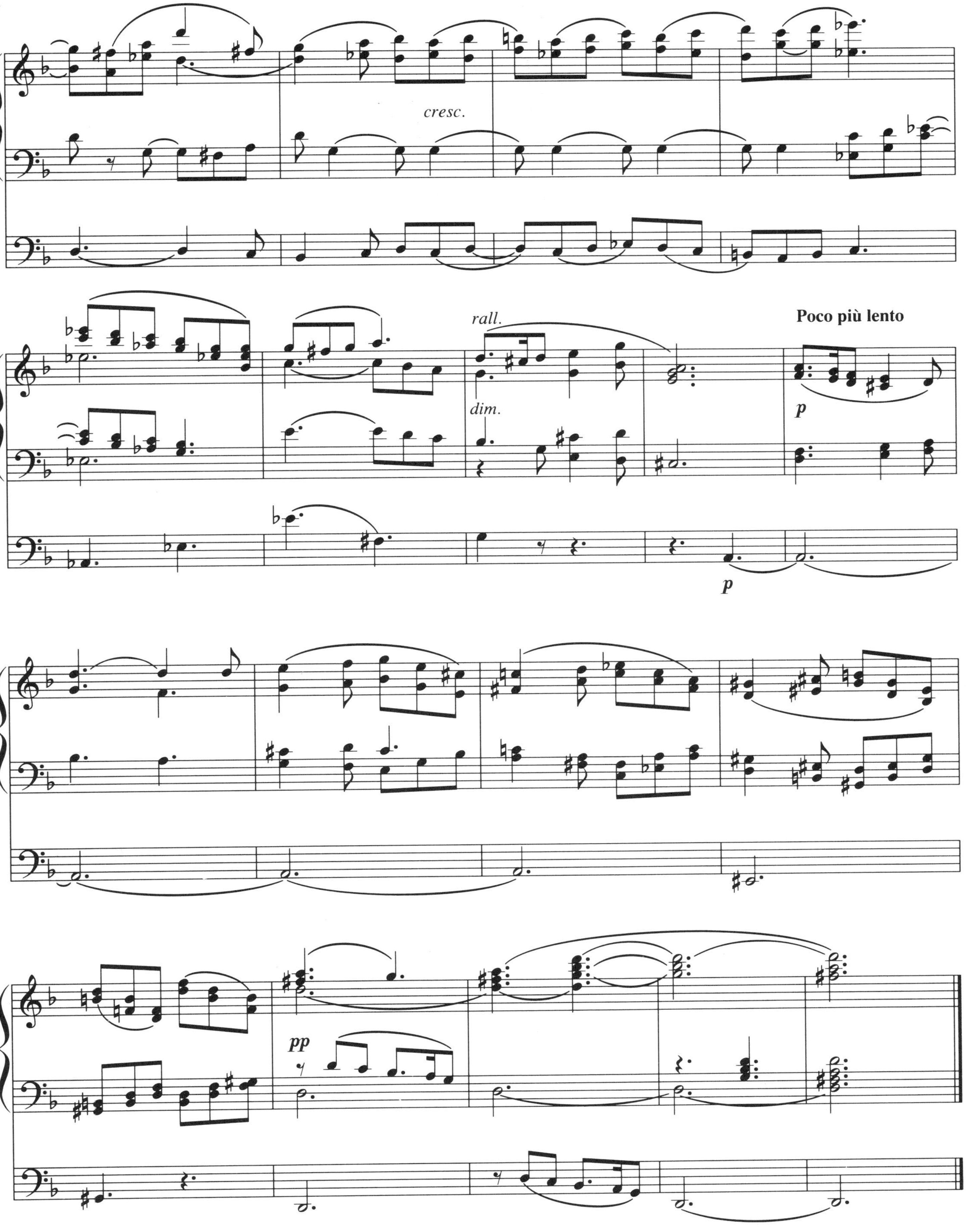

cresc.
rall.
dim.
Poco più lento
p
p
pp

PRELUDE in C MINOR

Johann Rinck (1770-1846)

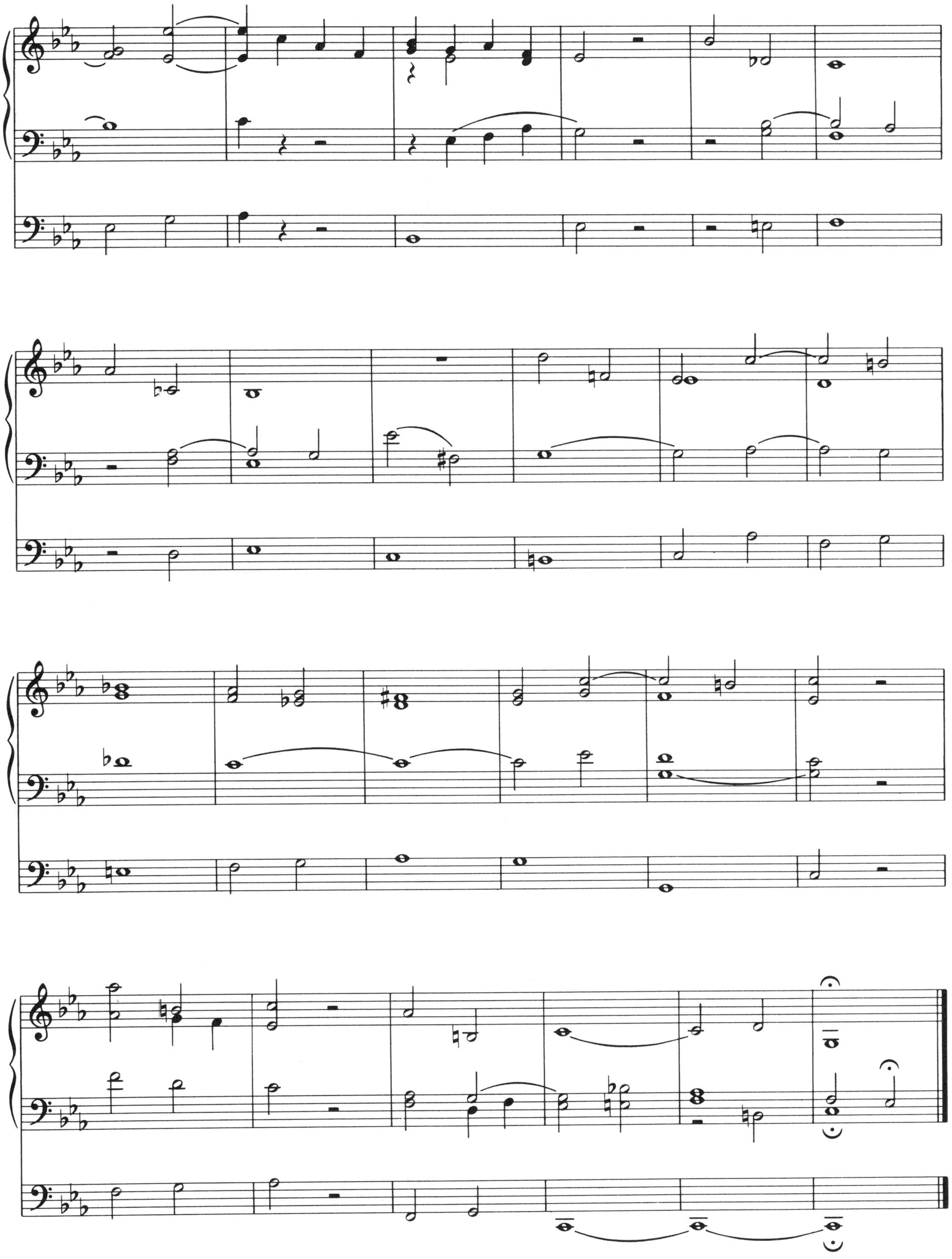

BOURRÉE I

Charles Wood (1866-1926)

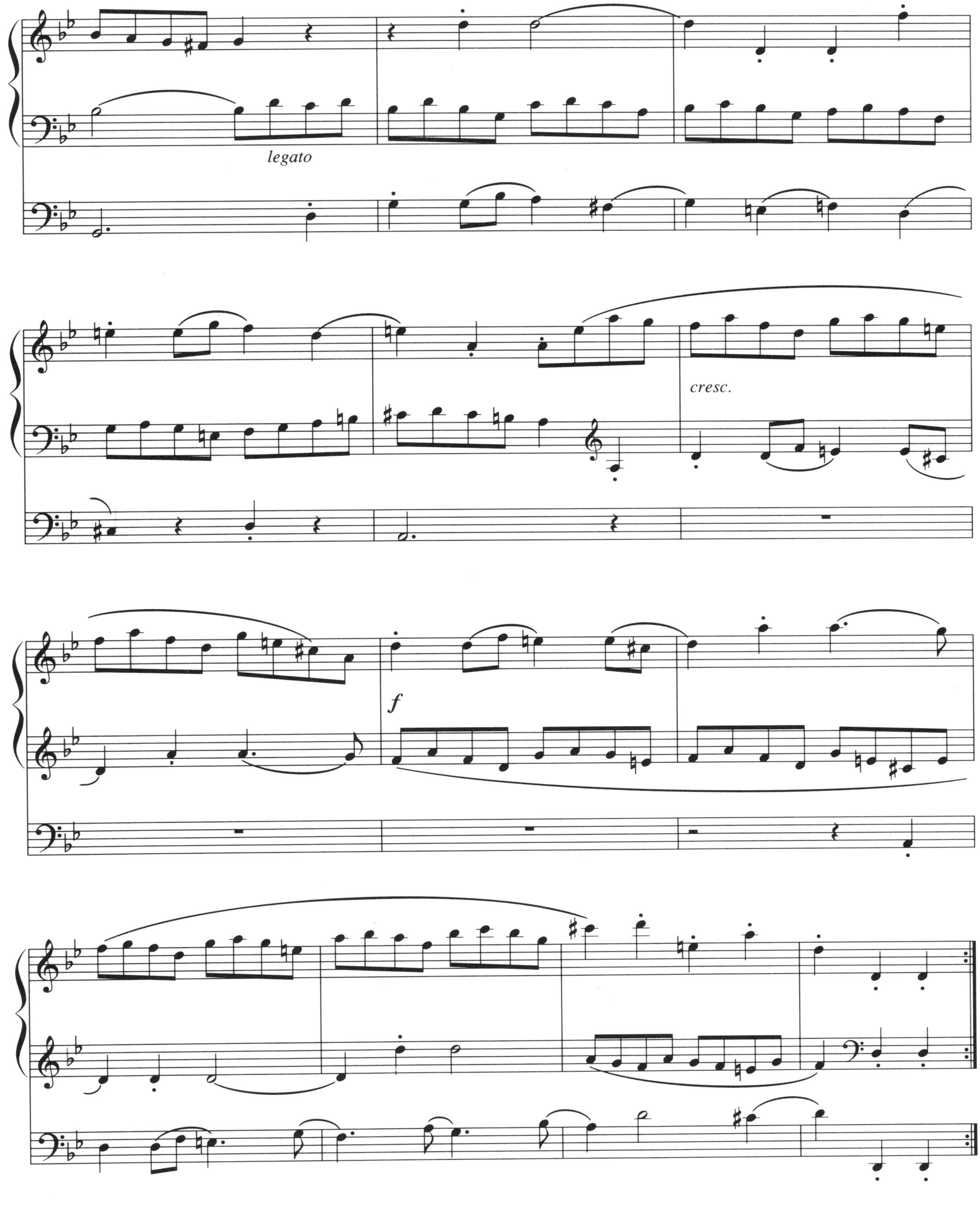
legato
cresc.
f

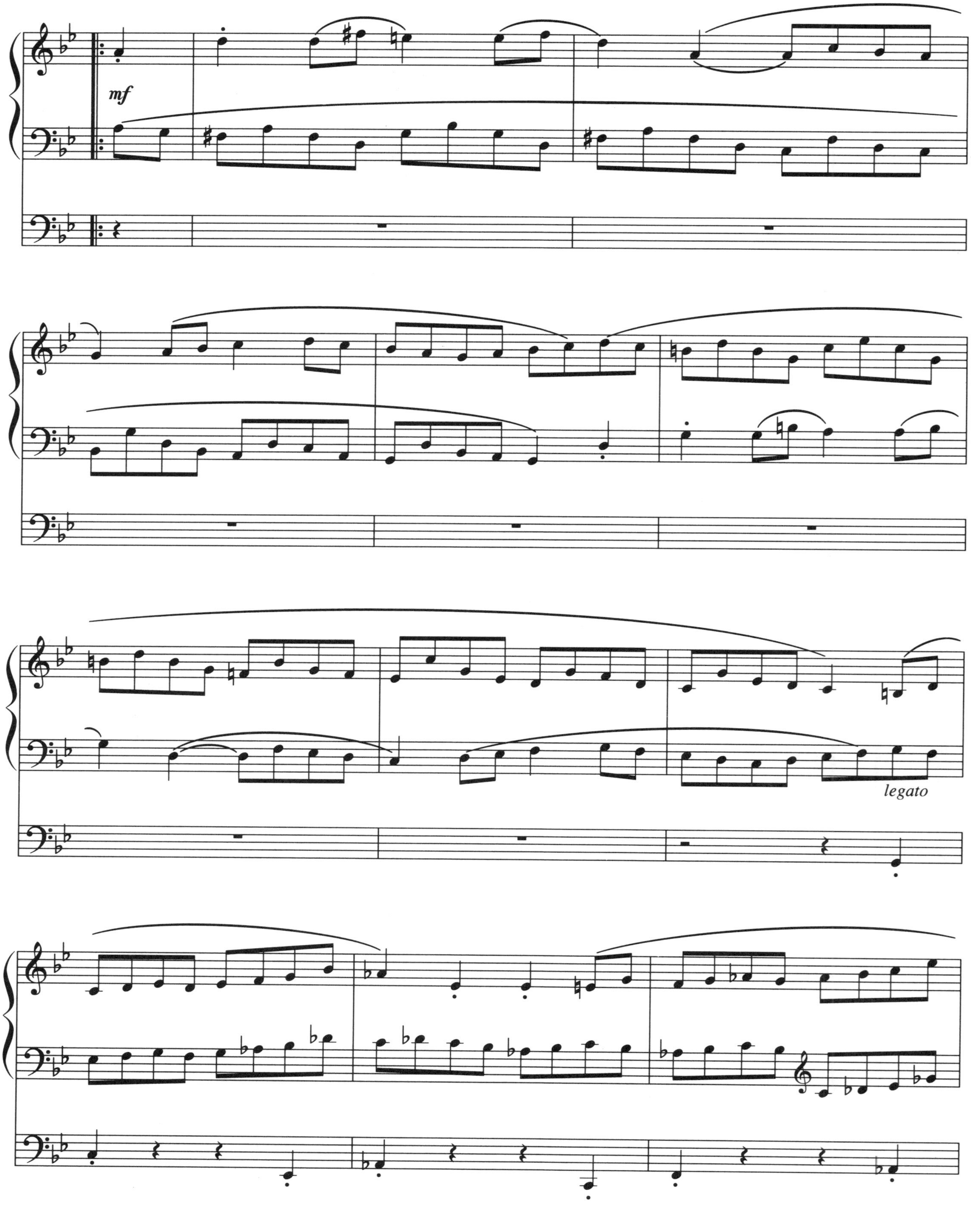
mf
legato

(to Bourrée II)

BOURRÉE II

Charles Wood (1866-1926)

*(Bourrée I D.C.
senza ripet.)*

For Benjamin

TOCCATINA for FLUTES

Christopher Tambling (*b.*1964)

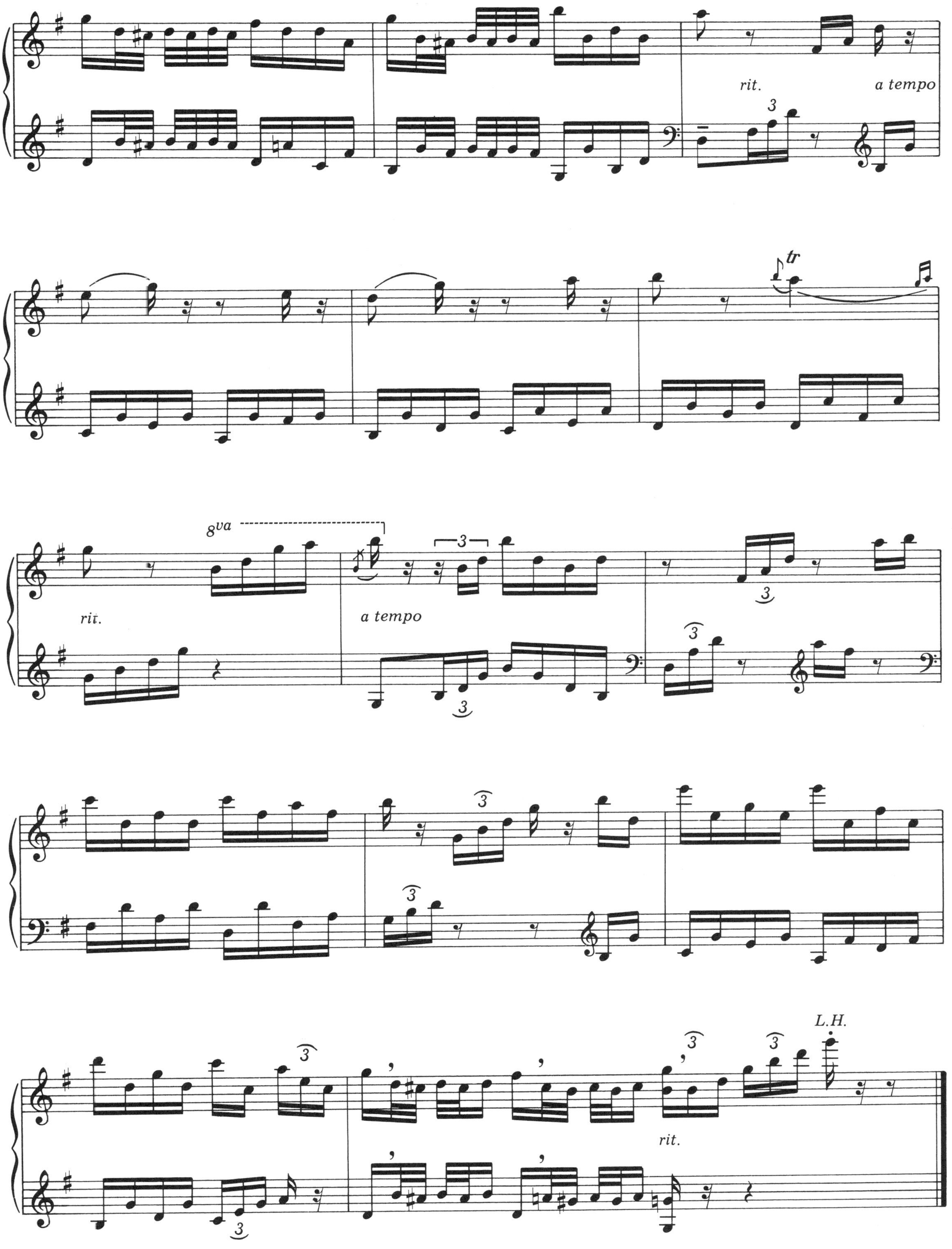
rit.
a tempo
tr
8va
rit.
a tempo
L.H.
rit.

BALLINARIA

Adrian Vernon Fish (*b*.1956)

Appassionato, poco mosso (♩ = 98)

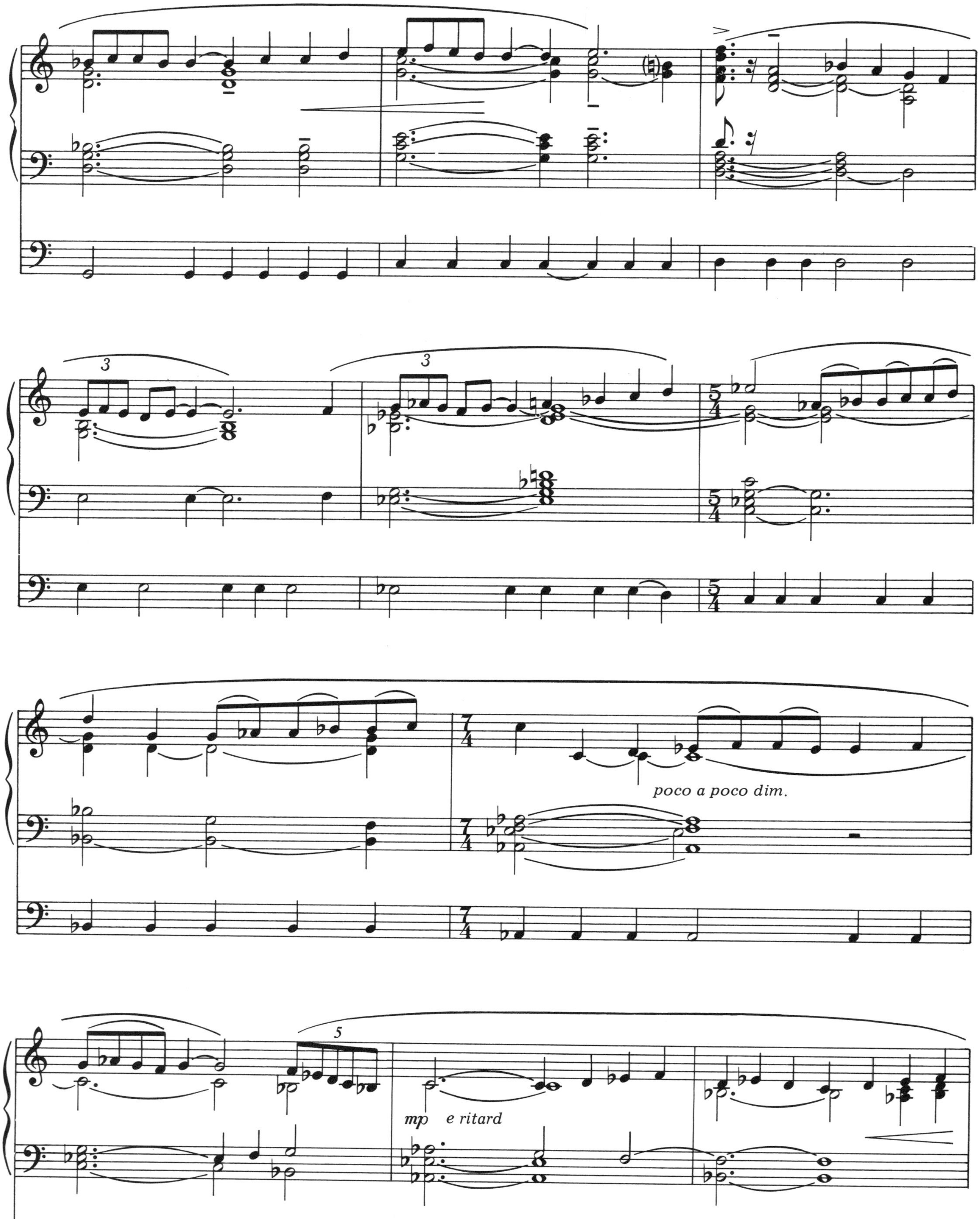
3
3
5
4
poco a poco dim.
7
4
5
mp e ritard

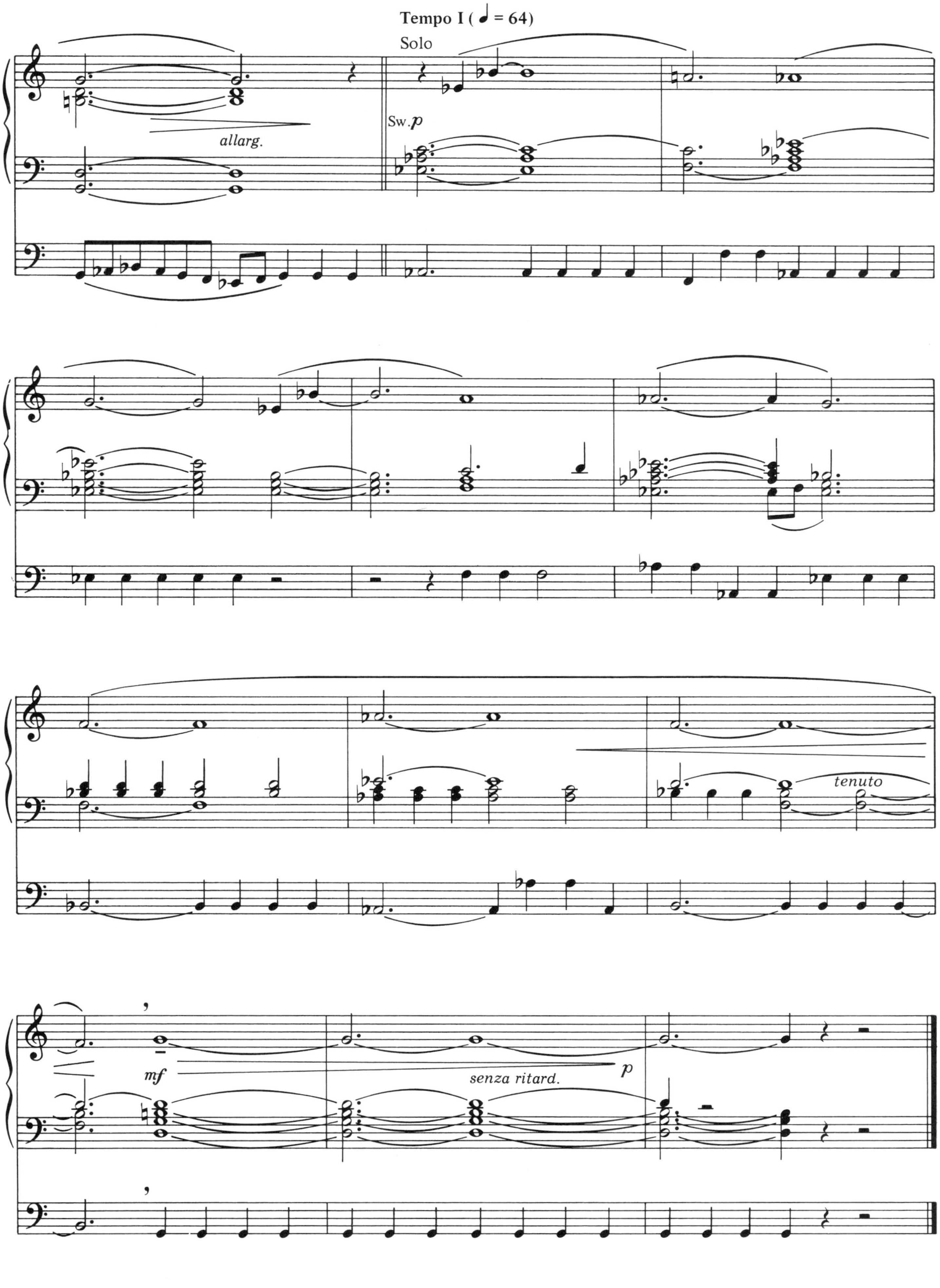

Tempo I (♩ = 64)
Solo
allarg.
Sw. p
tenuto
mf
senza ritard.
p

COMMUNION in G

Alexandre Guilmant (1837-1911)

+ Gt. to Ped.

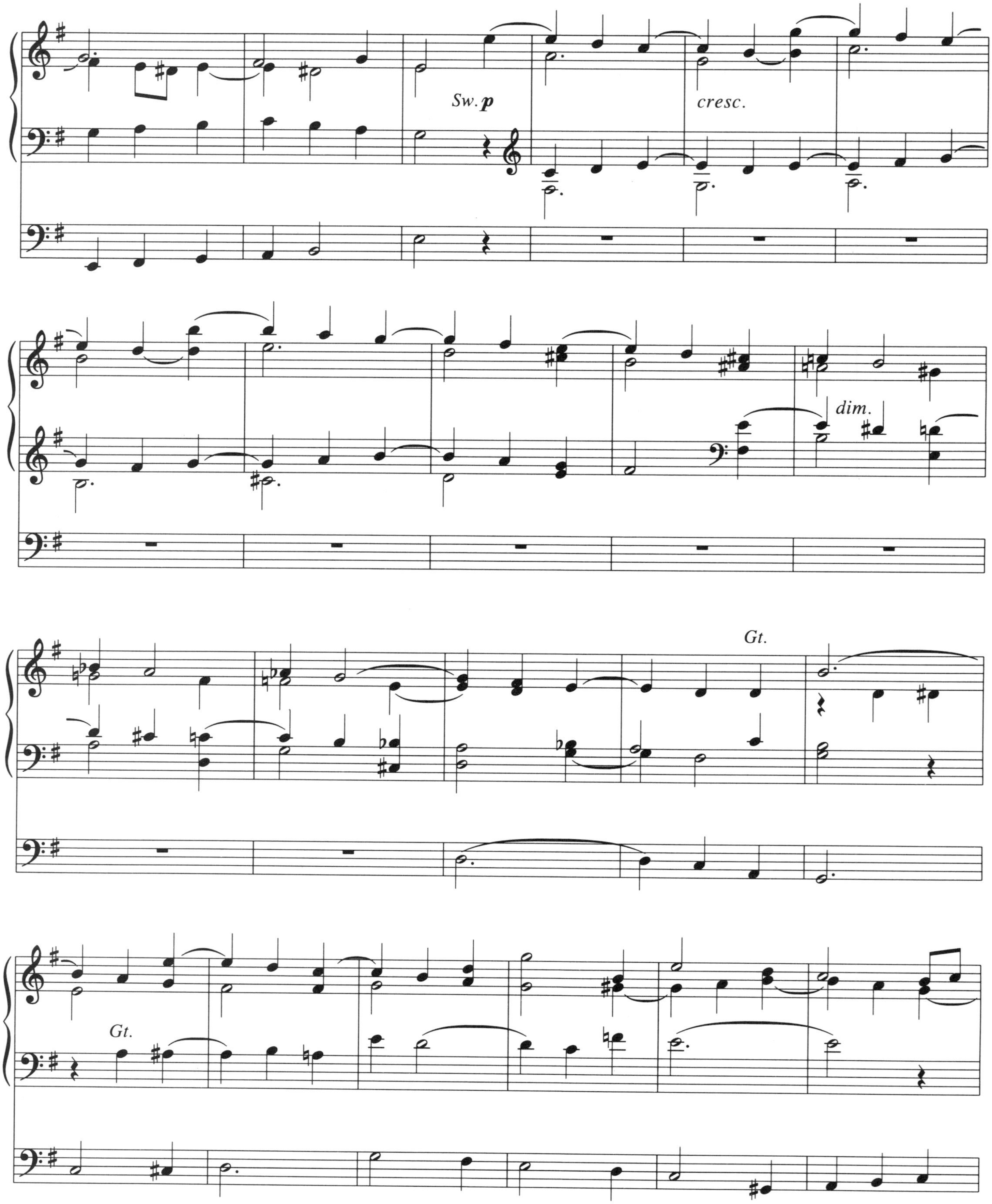
Sw. p
cresc.
dim.
Gt.
Gt.

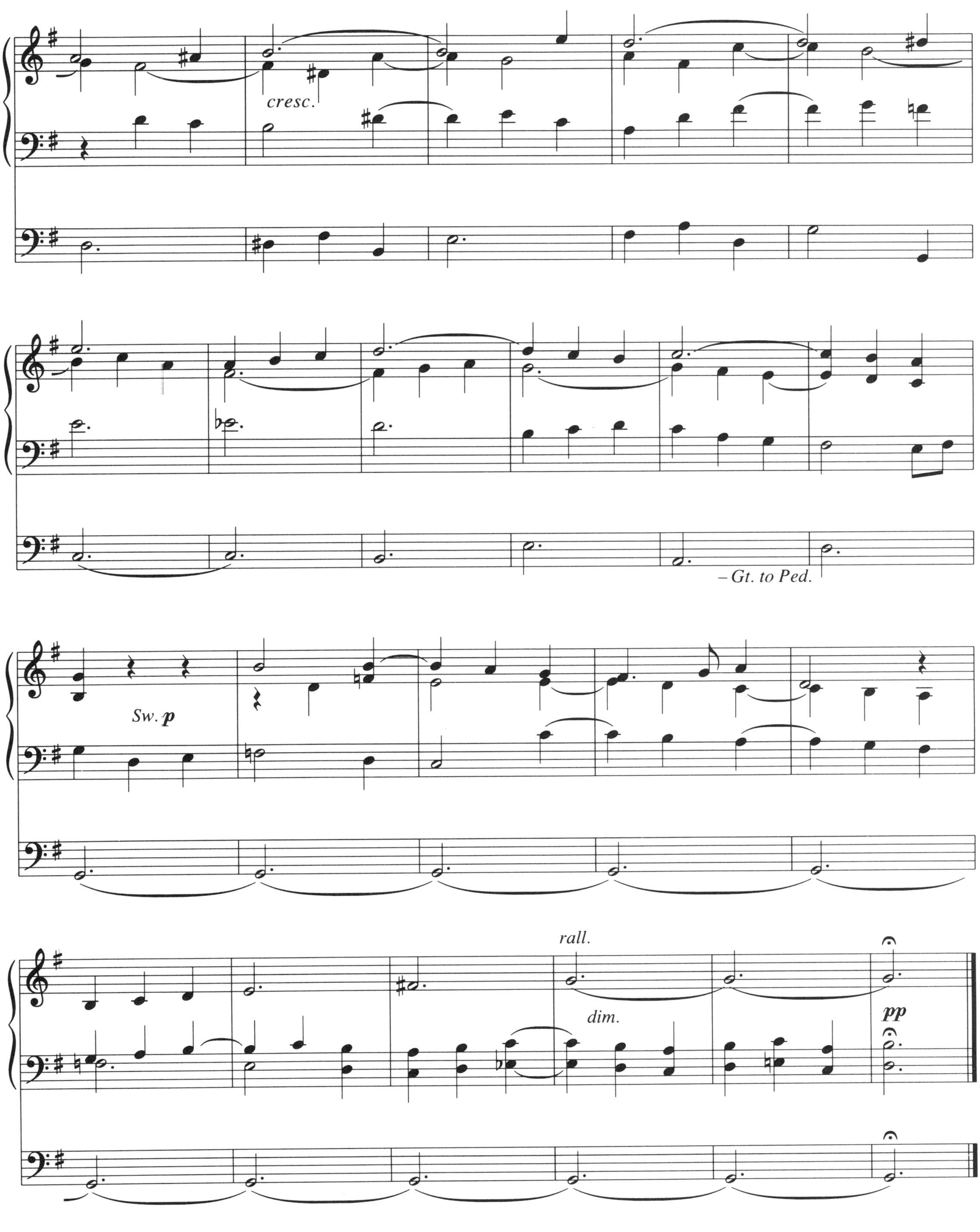
cresc.
– Gt. to Ped.
Sw. p
rall.
dim.
pp

PAX VOBISCUM

Henry Elliot Button (*d.*1925)

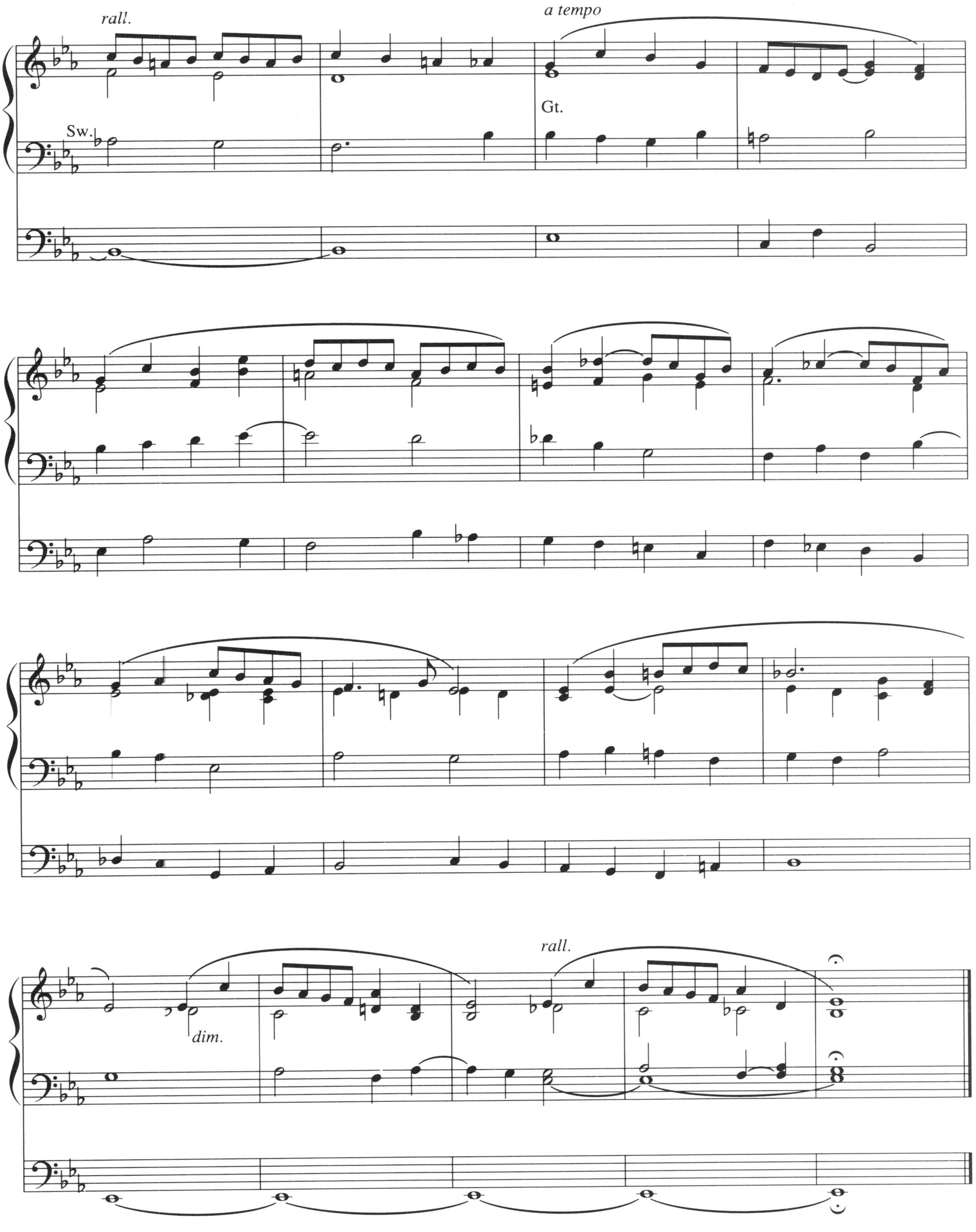
rall.
a tempo
Sw.
Gt.
dim.
rall.

PRELUDE in G

Johann Rinck (1770-1846)

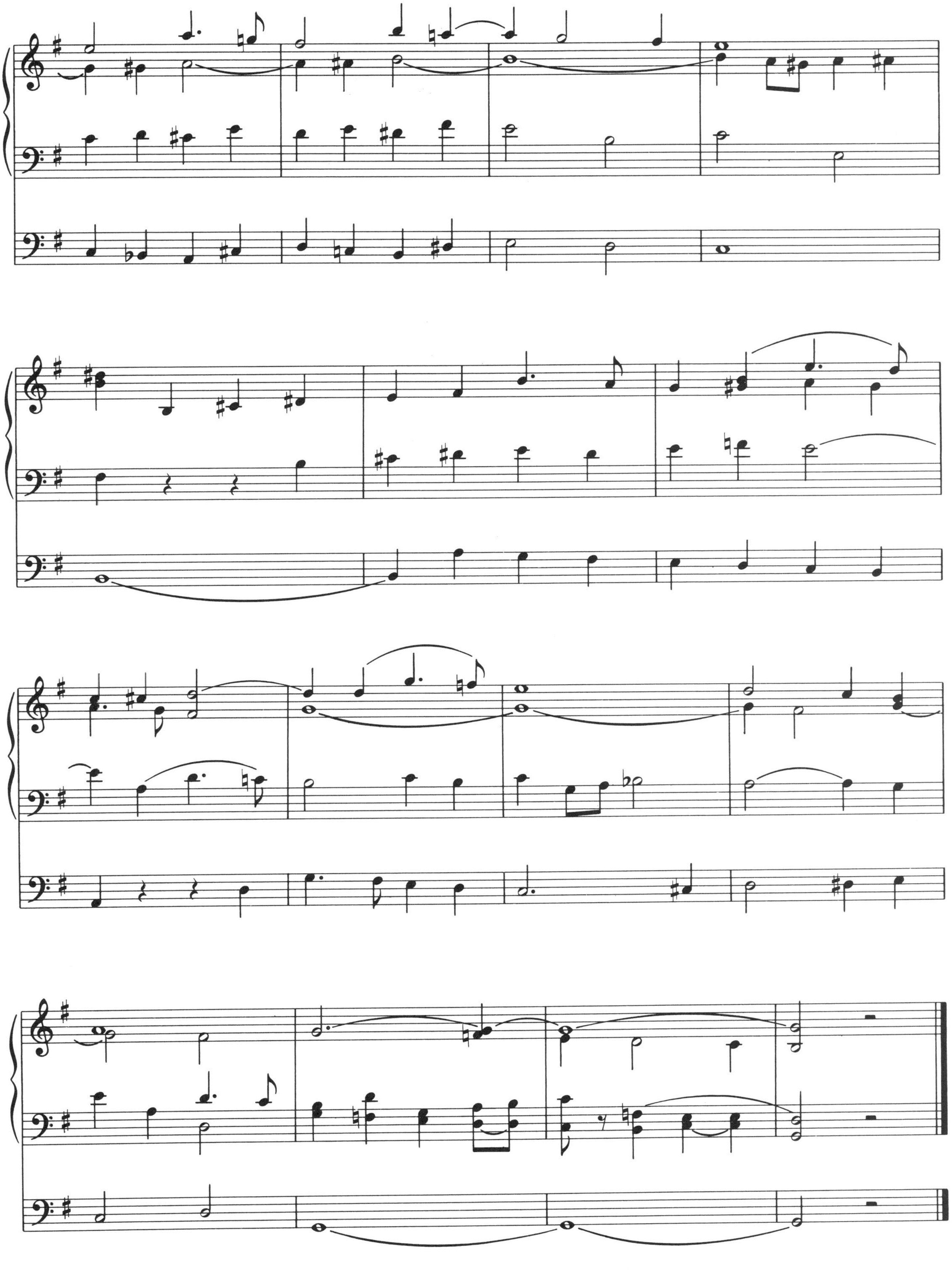

For Meirion Bowen

ROMANZA

Simon Clark (*b.*1975)

Tempo adagio ma rubato (♪ = *c.* 72)

* G octave lower, if necessary.

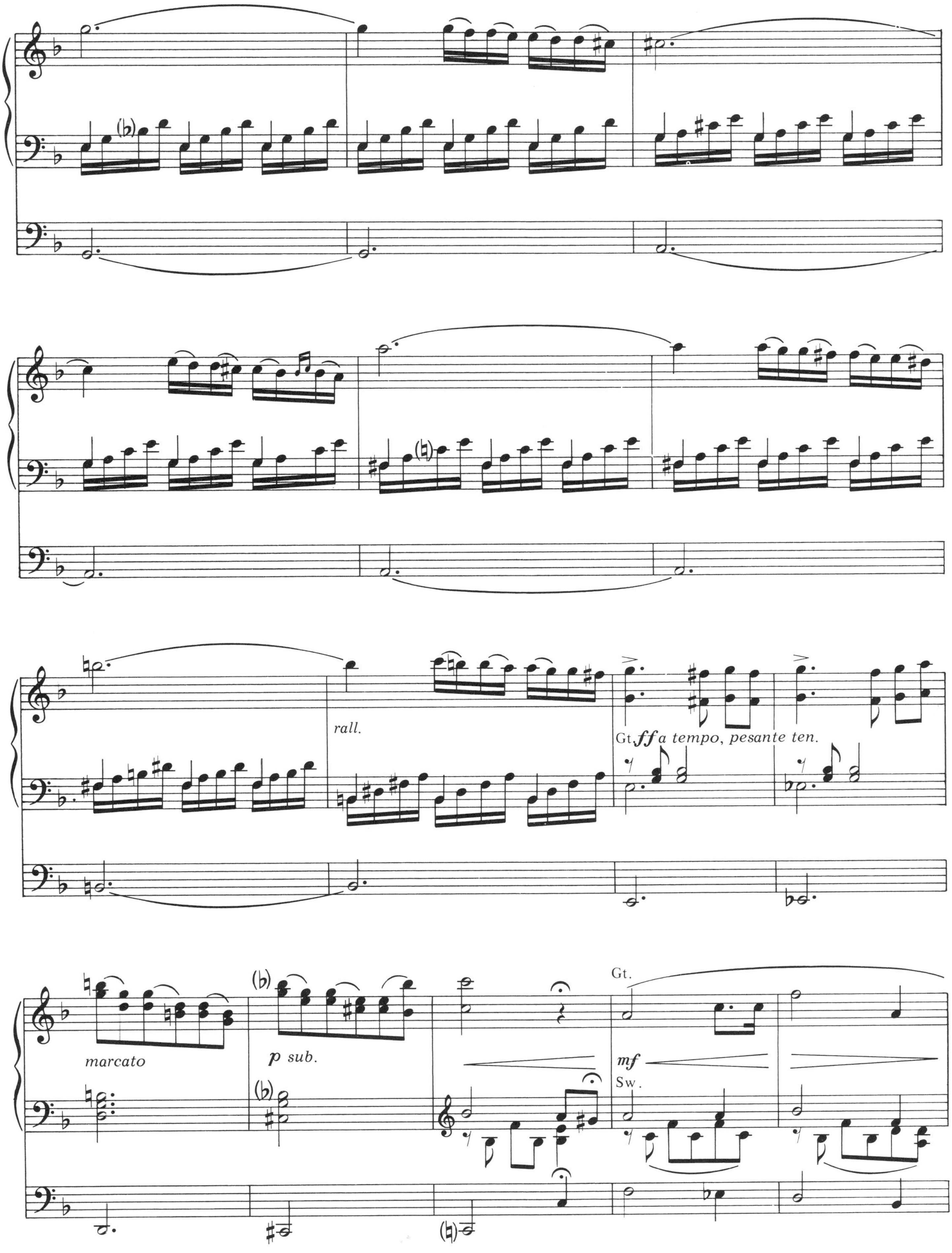
rall.
Gt. ff a tempo, pesante ten.
marcato
p sub.
Gt.
mf
Sw.

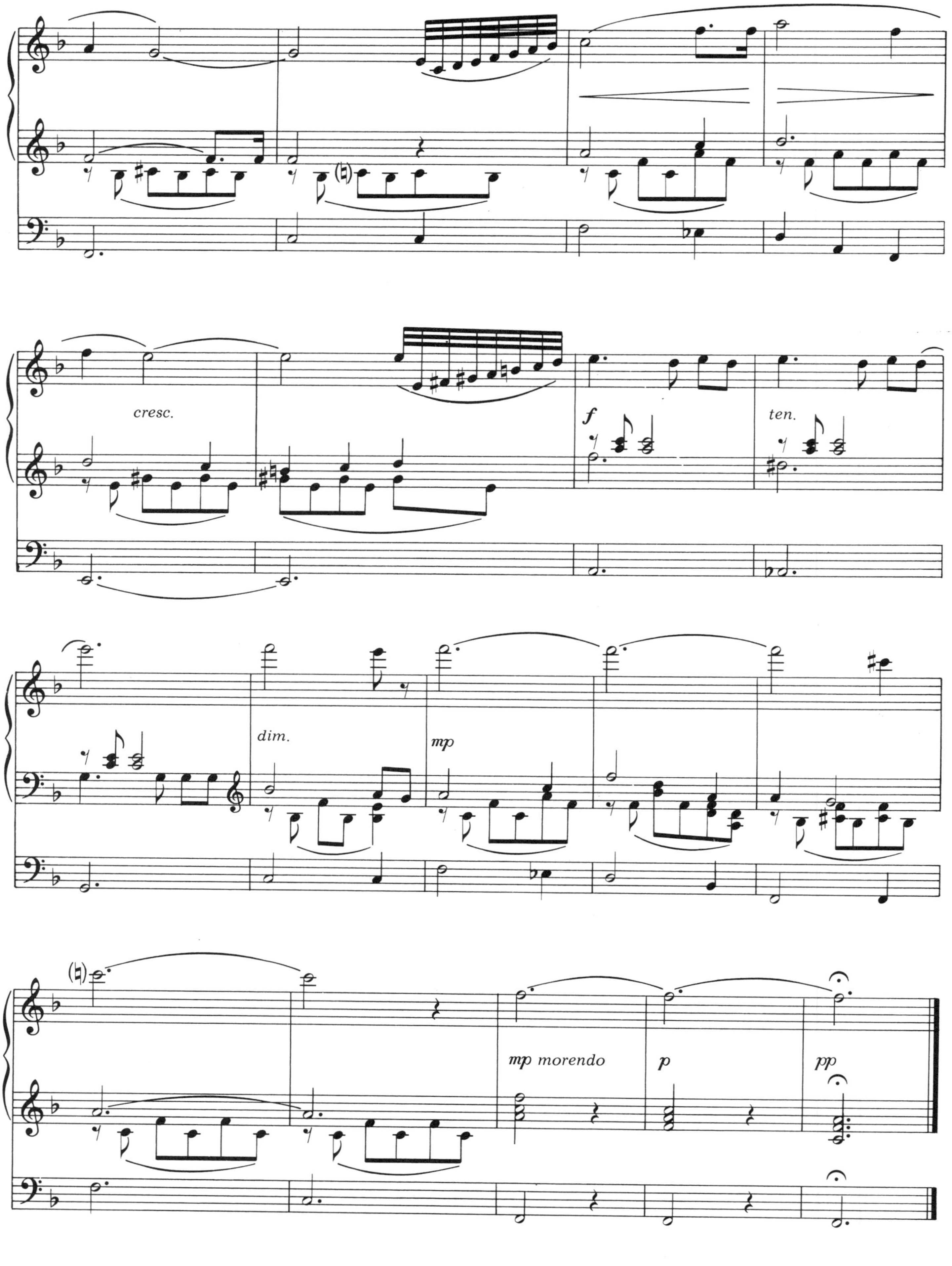
cresc.
f
ten.
dim.
mp
mp morendo
p
pp

ELEGY

Charles Harford Lloyd (1849-1919)

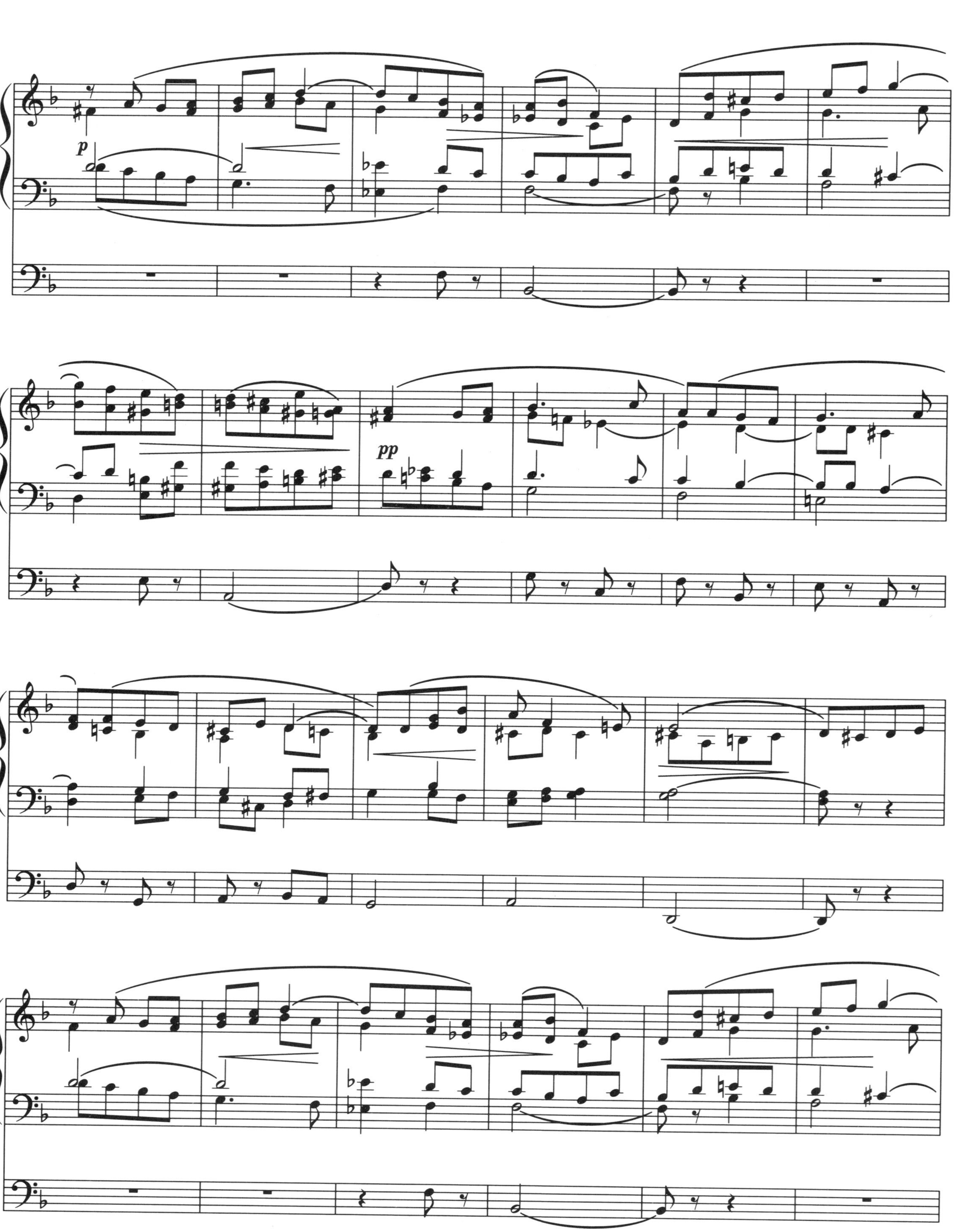
p
pp

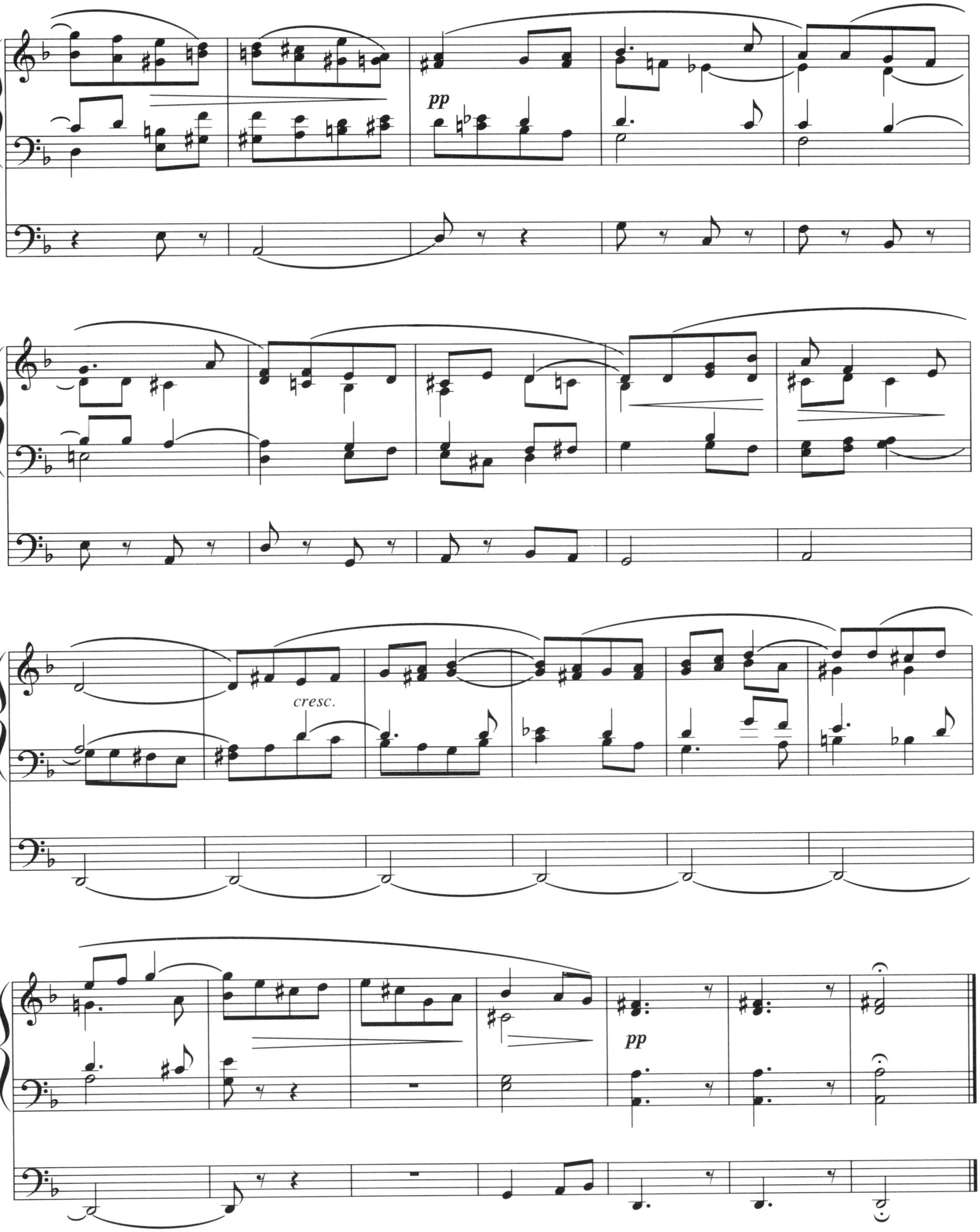
pp
cresc.
pp

For Mum and Dad

FUGUE and CHORALE

Christopher Tambling (*b.*1964)

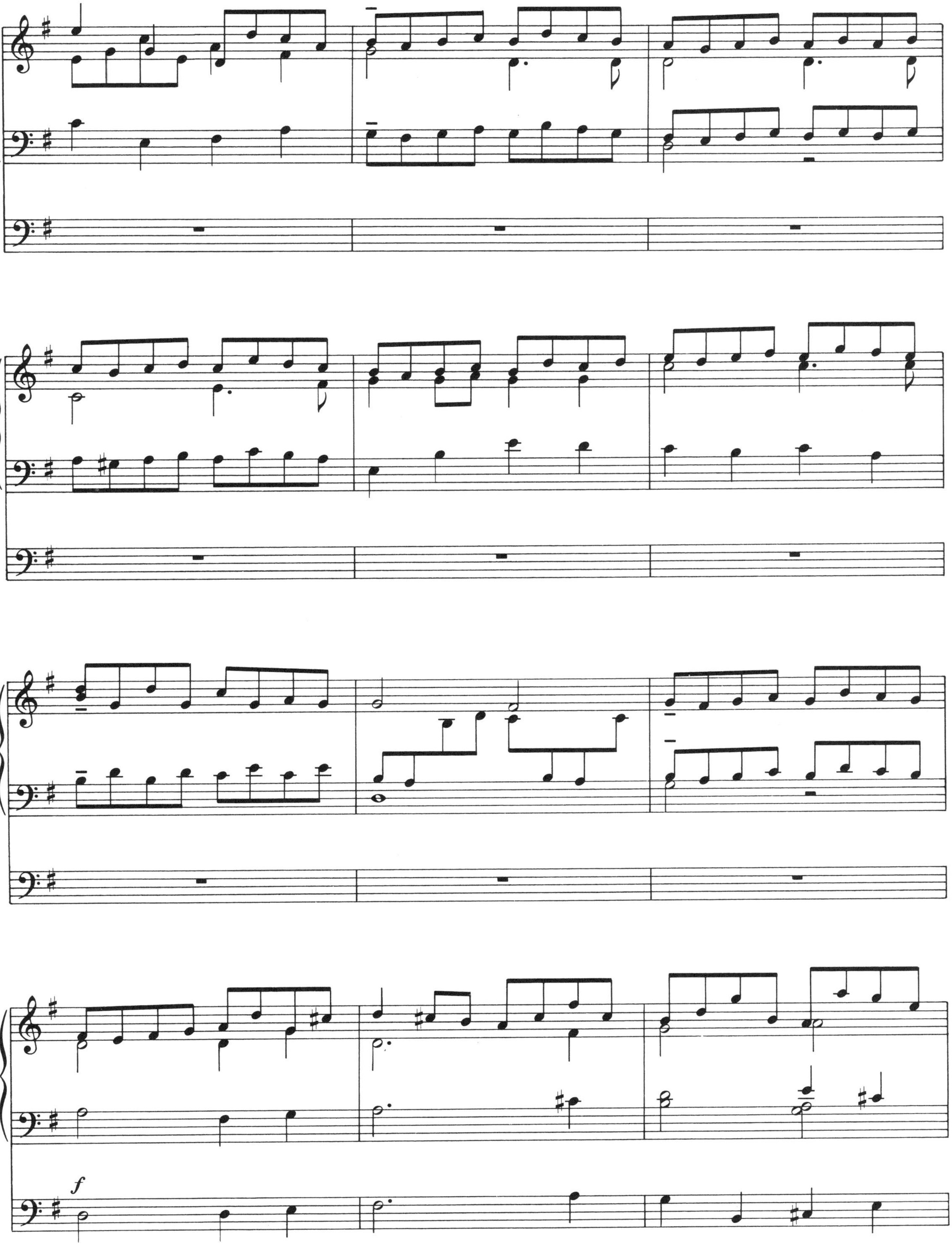
f

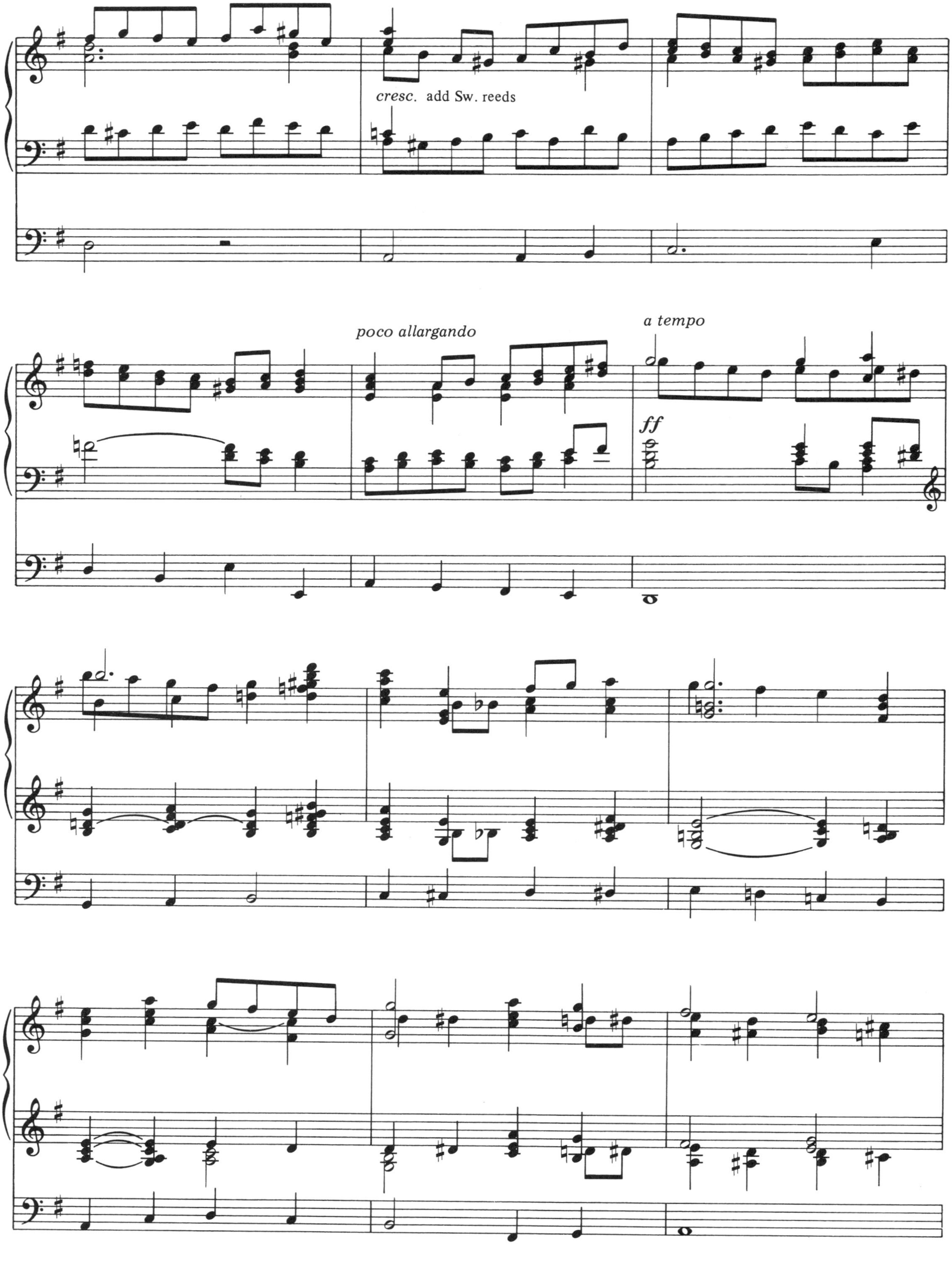
cresc. add Sw. reeds
poco allargando
a tempo
ff

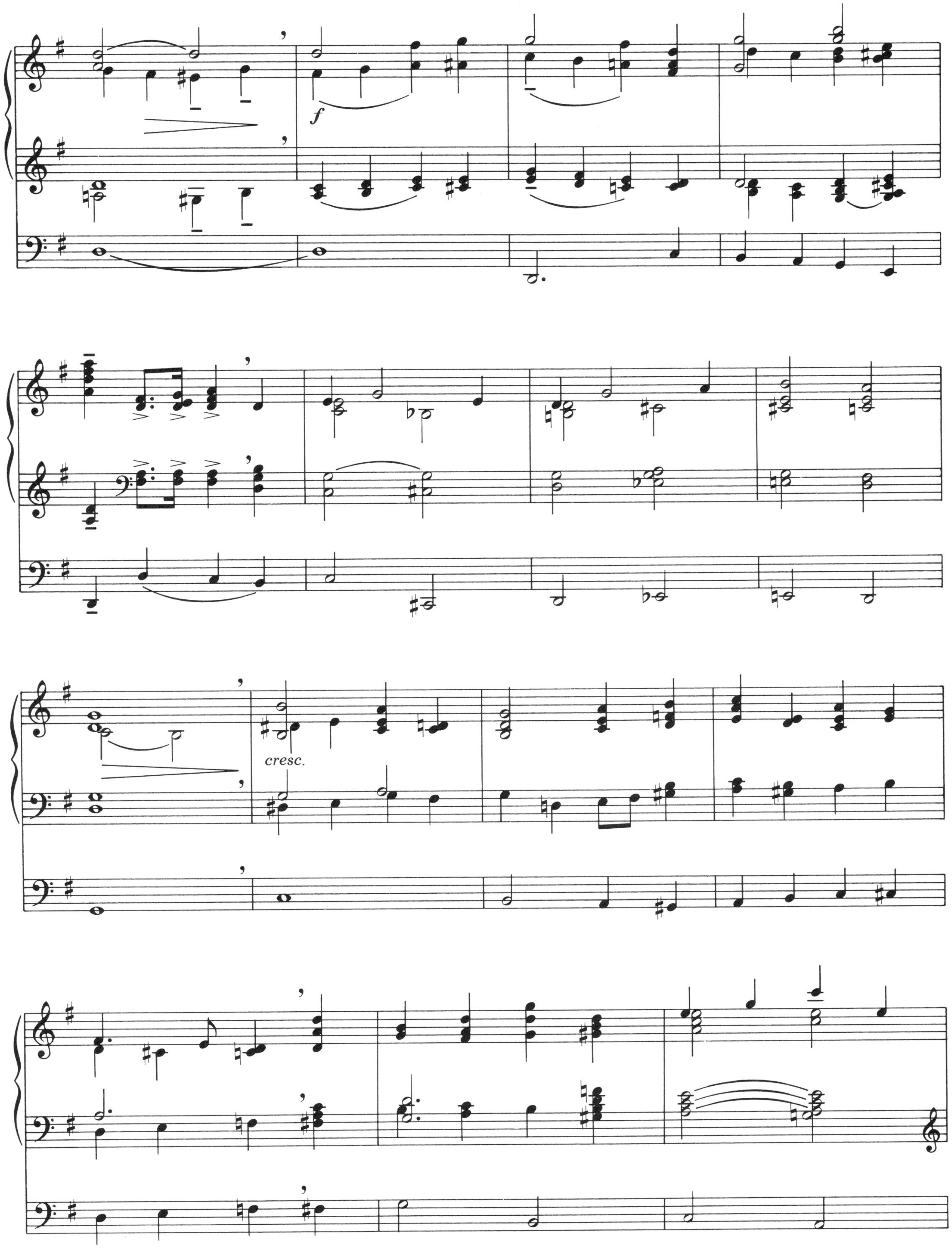
f
cresc.

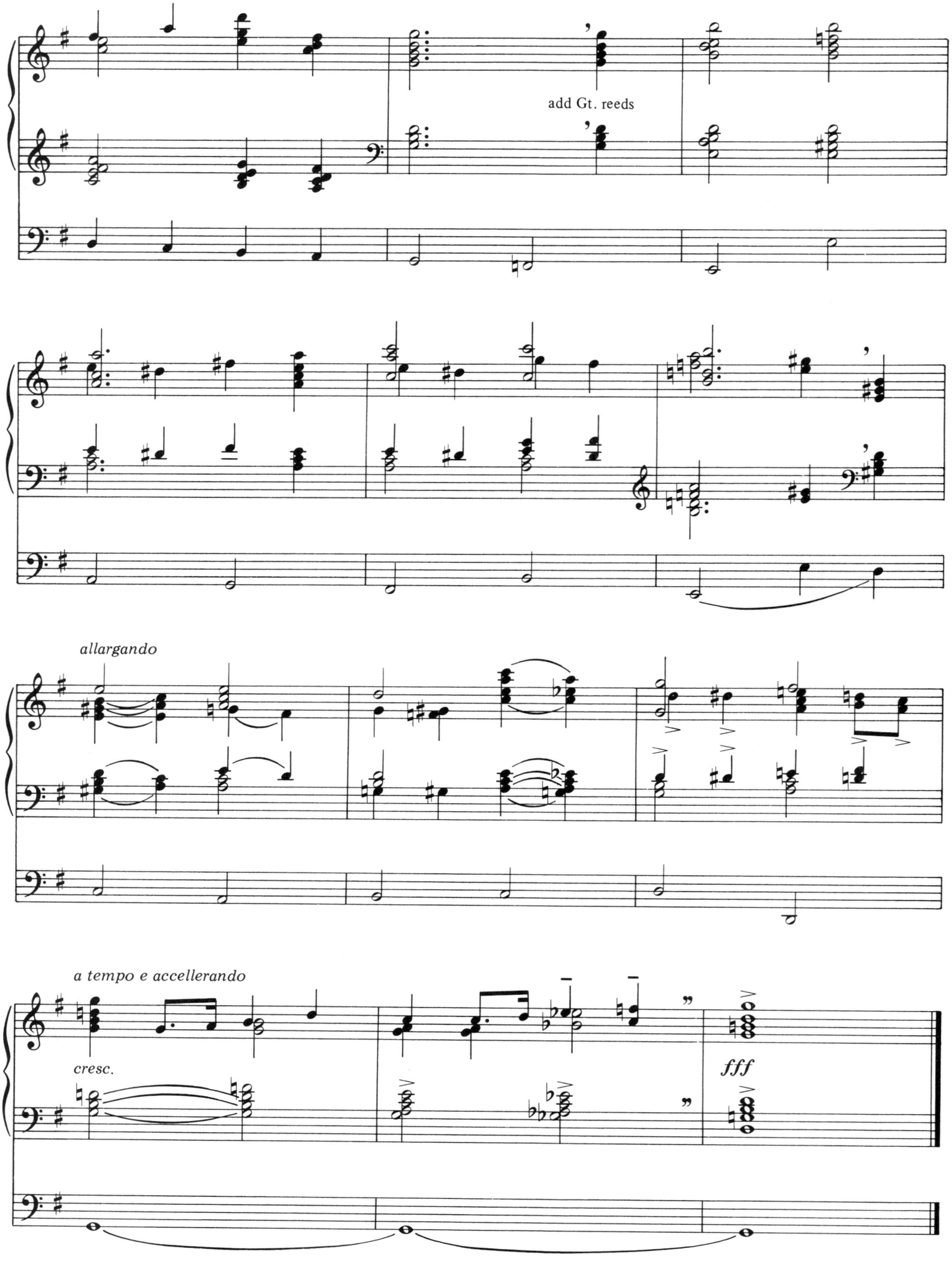
add Gt. reeds
allargando
a tempo e accellerando
cresc.
fff

MELODY

Alexandre Guilmant (1837-1911)

L.H.

+ *pedal couplers*

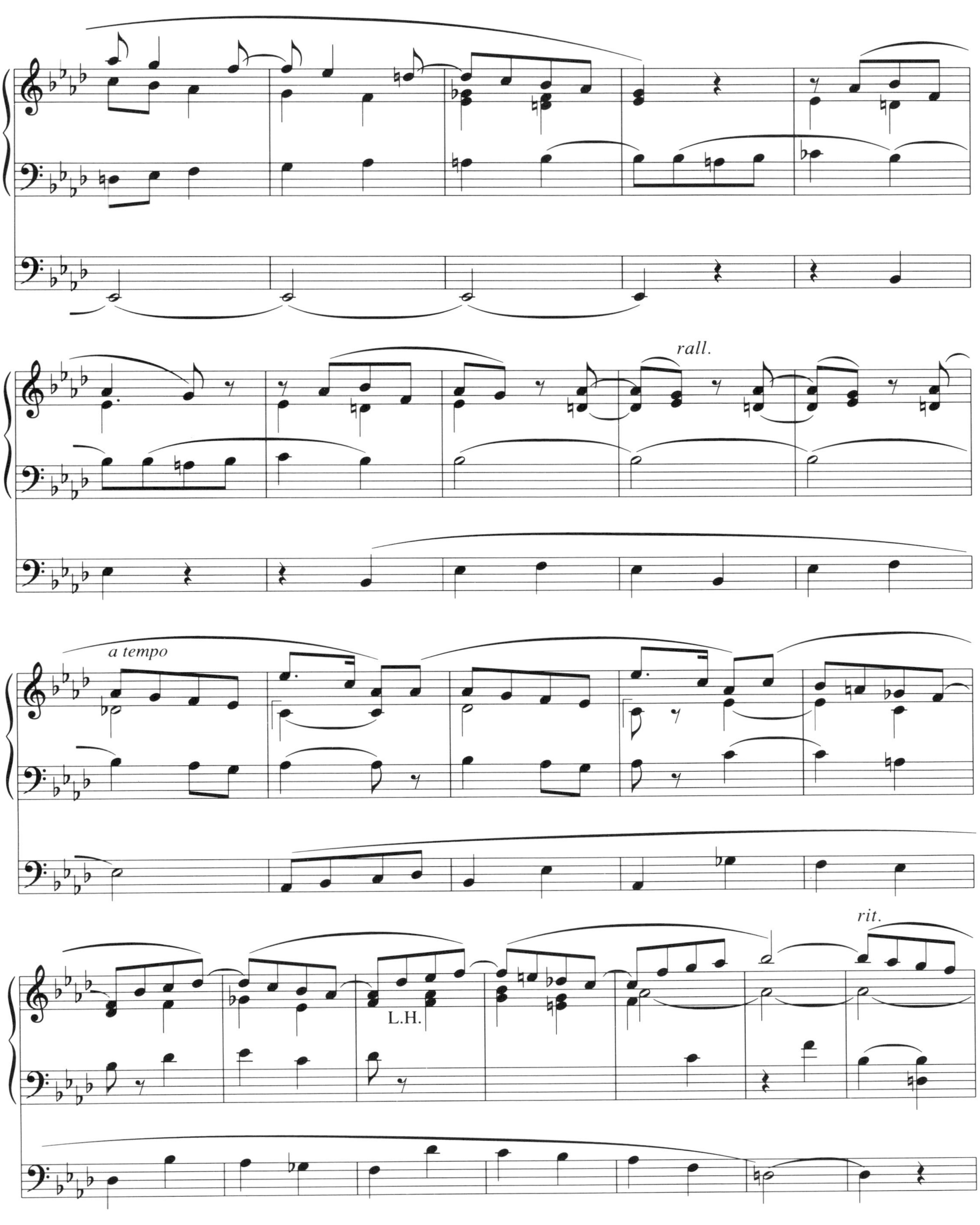
rall.
a tempo
L.H.
rit.

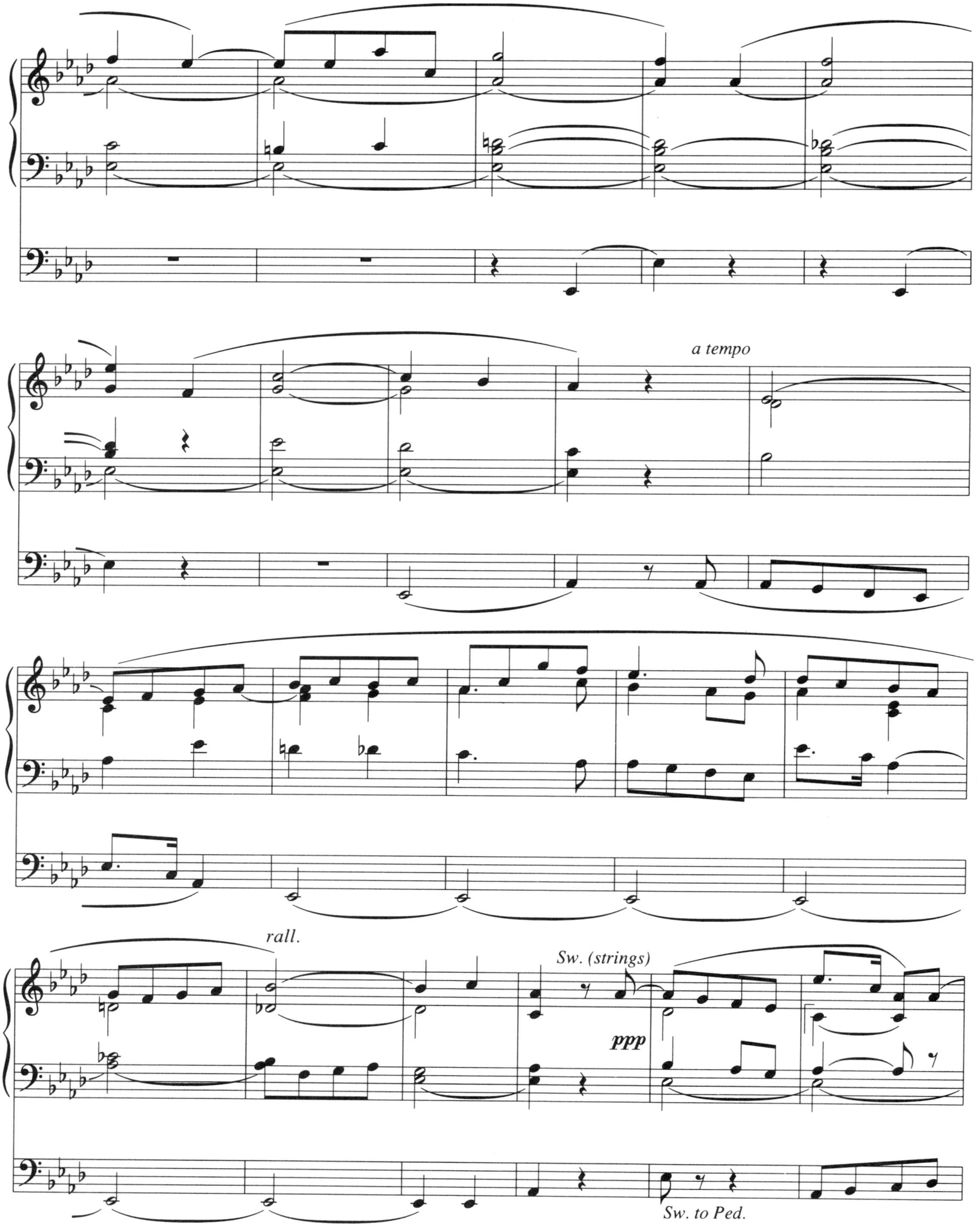
a tempo
rall.
Sw. (strings)
ppp
Sw. to Ped.

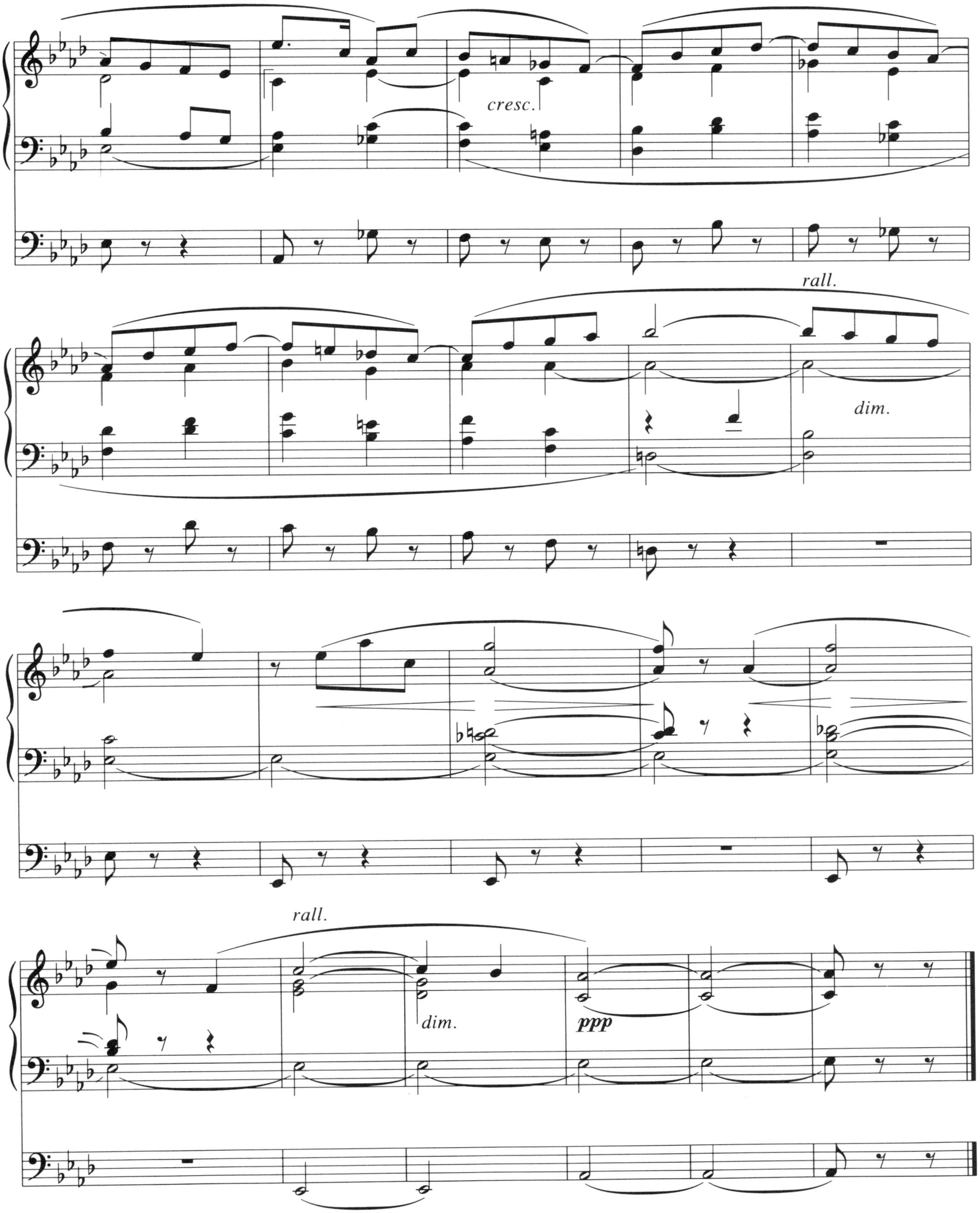
cresc.
rall.
dim.
rall.
dim.
ppp

PRELUDE in E MINOR

Johann Rinck (1770-1846)

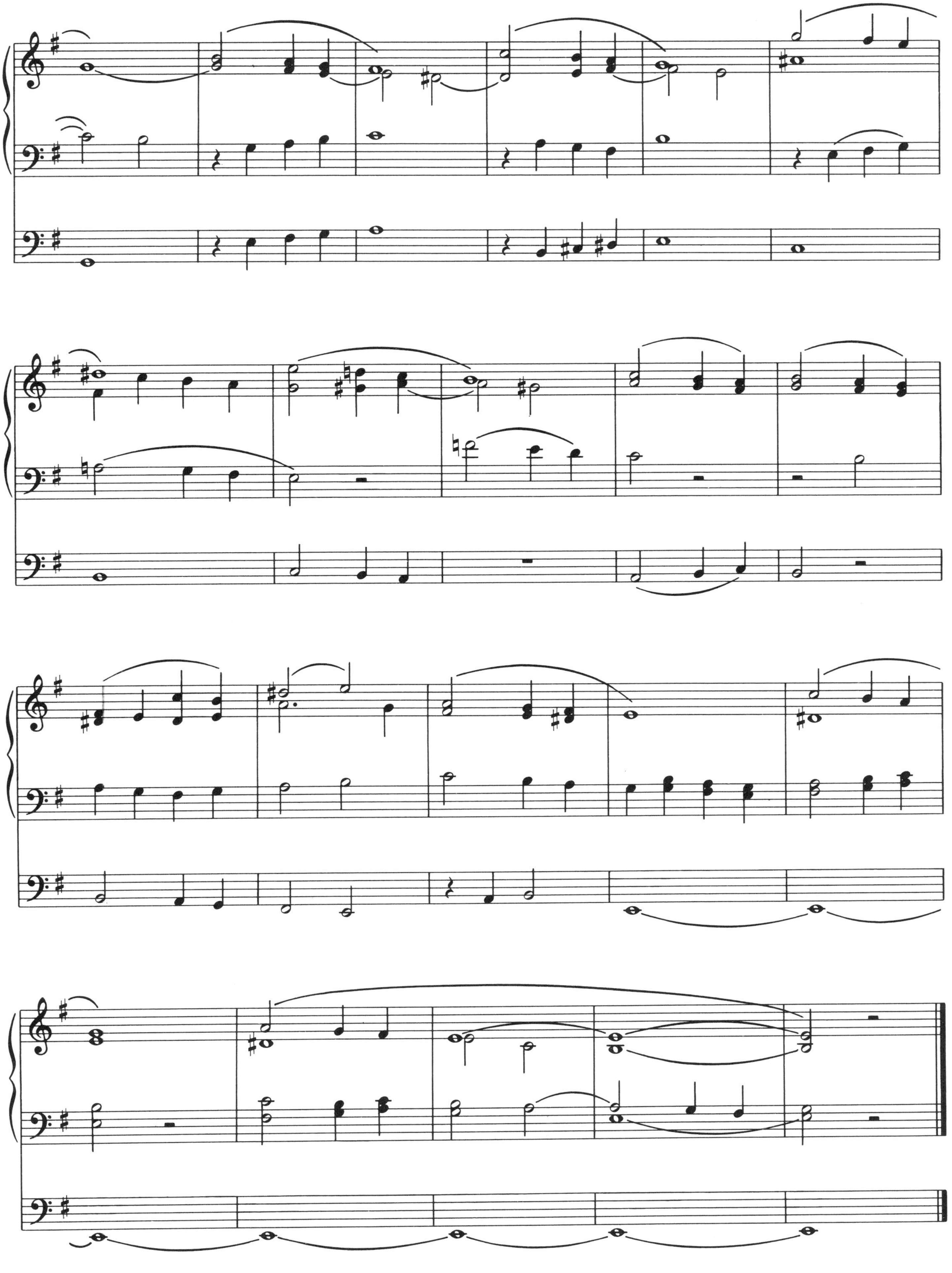

For Matthew Wall

A CHEERFUL PRELUDE

Donald Hunt

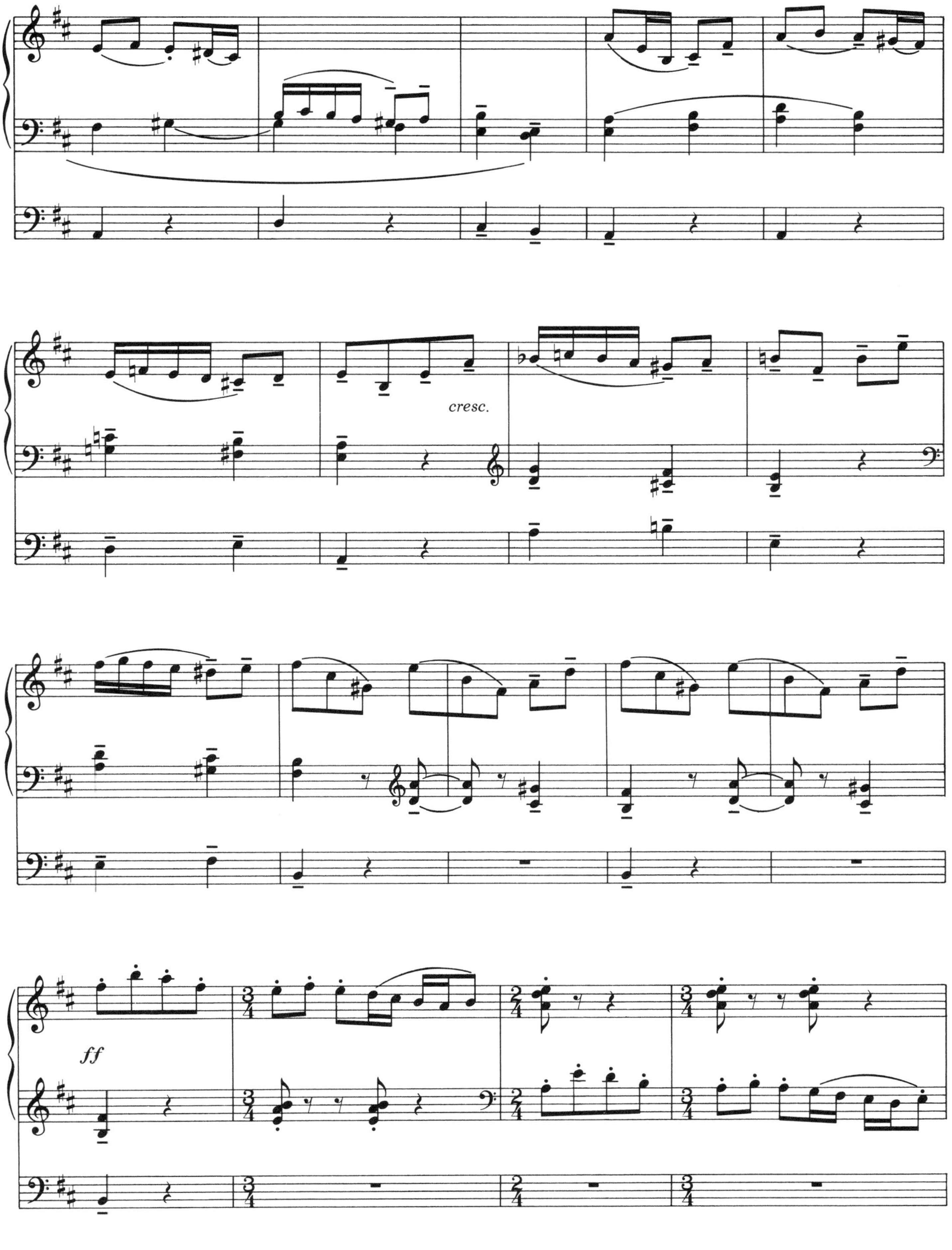

cresc.
ff

becoming broader

+ Reed

mf Gt. 8' and 2'

in time
p Sw.

sfz

Gt. to Ped. off

Gt.

Sw. *mp marc.*

mp marc.

Reed off

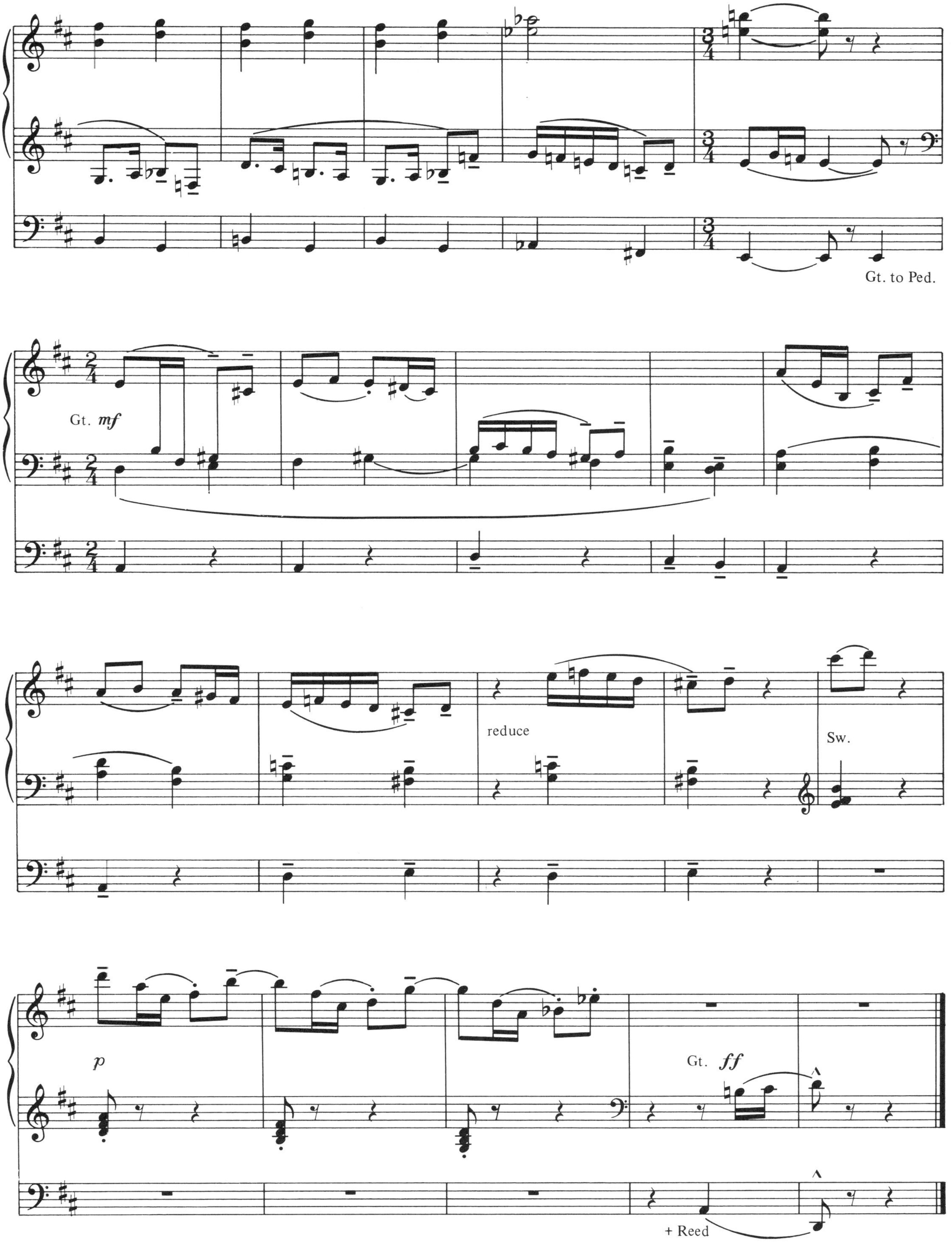
Gt. to Ped.
Gt. mf
reduce
Sw.
p
Gt. ff
+ Reed

For Paul and Judith

AGNUS DEI

Christopher Tambling (*b.*1964)

Freely flowing, but slowly (♩ = 60)

a tempo
cresc.
mf
Gt.
Sw.
dim.
mp
Gt.
cresc.
Sw.
mf
3
mp
Gt.
poco rit.
a tempo
Sw.
rit.

PRELUDE in D MINOR

Johann Rinck (1770-1846)

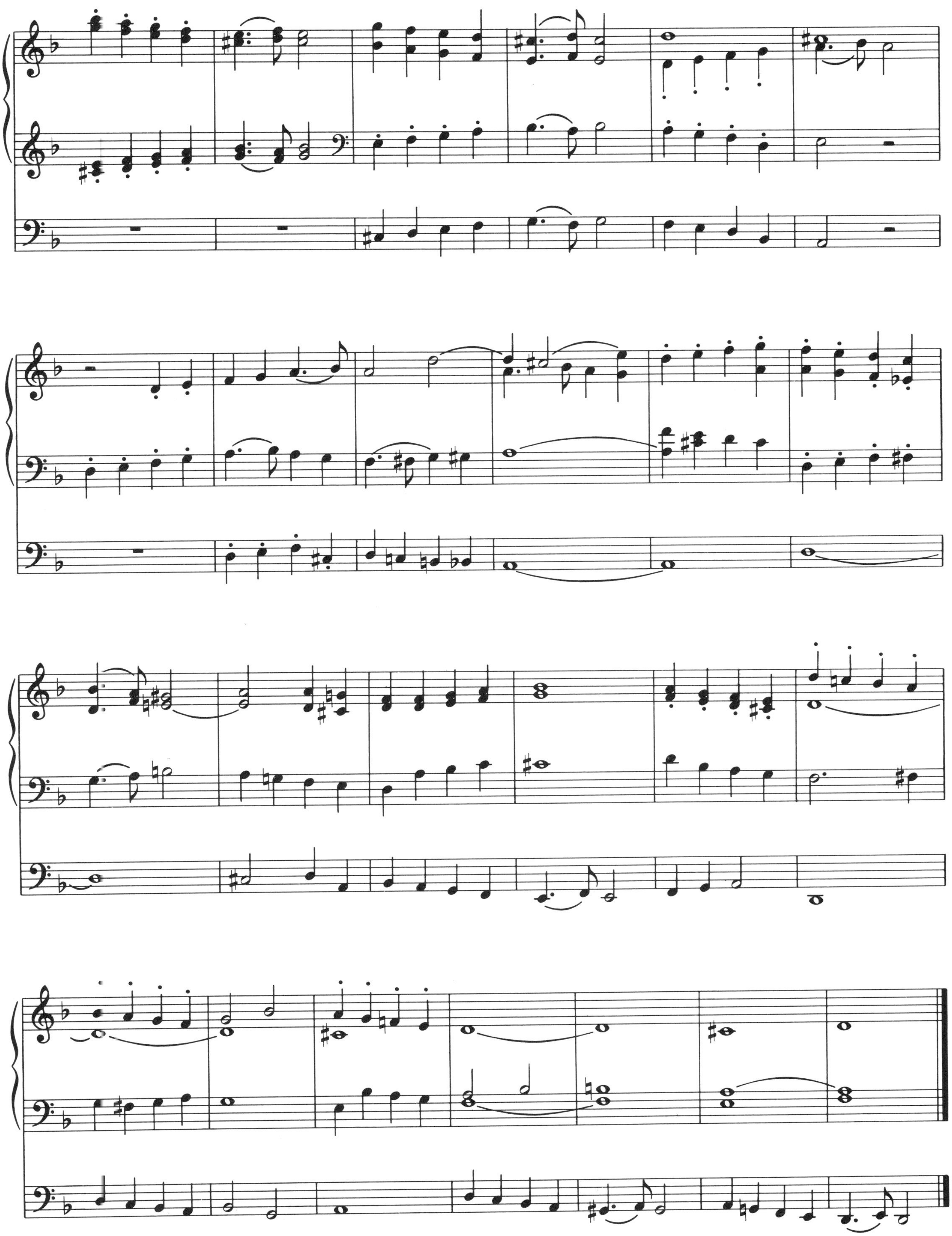

ALLA MARCIA

Thomas Adams (1785-1858)

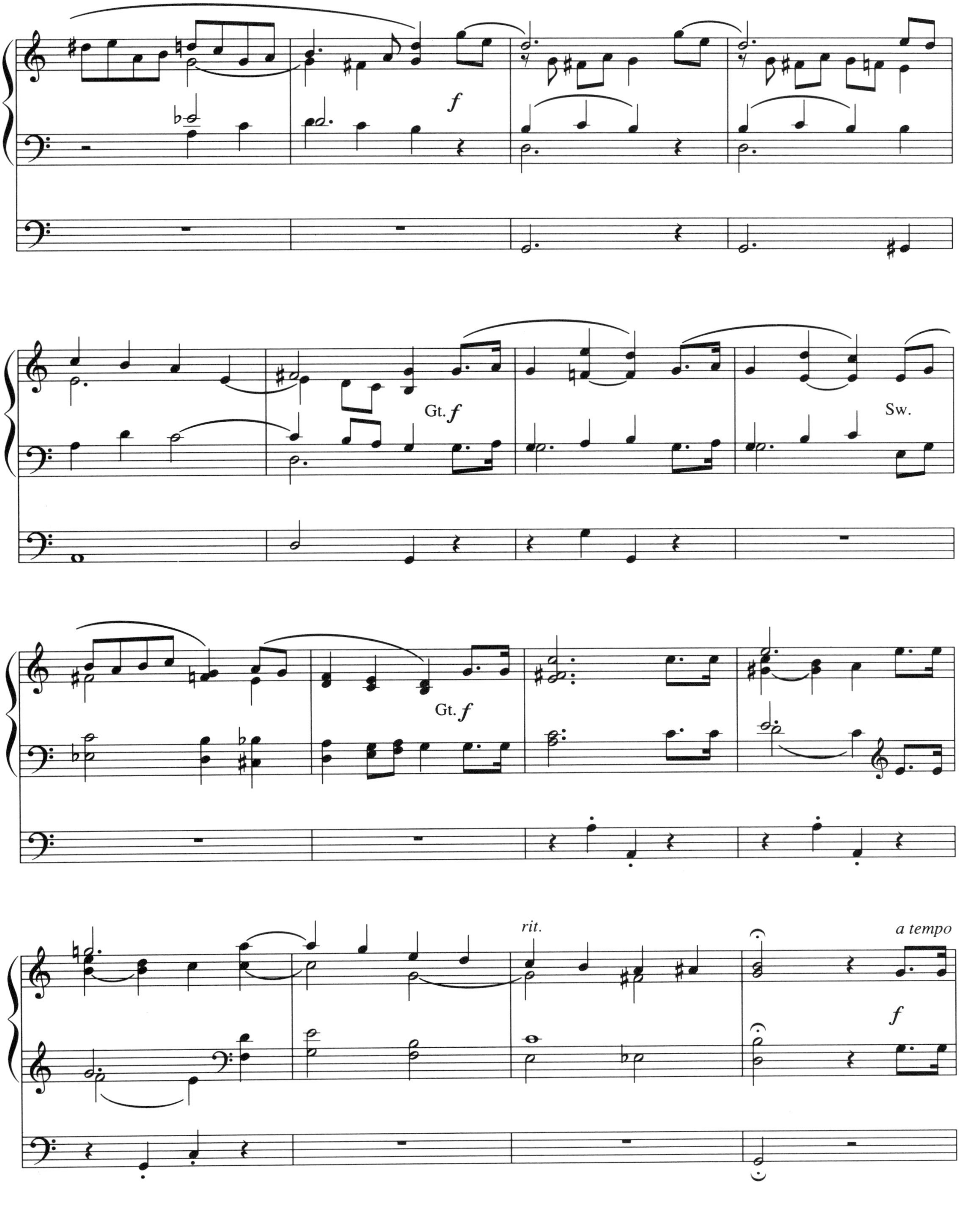
f
Gt. f
Sw.
Gt. f
rit.
a tempo
f

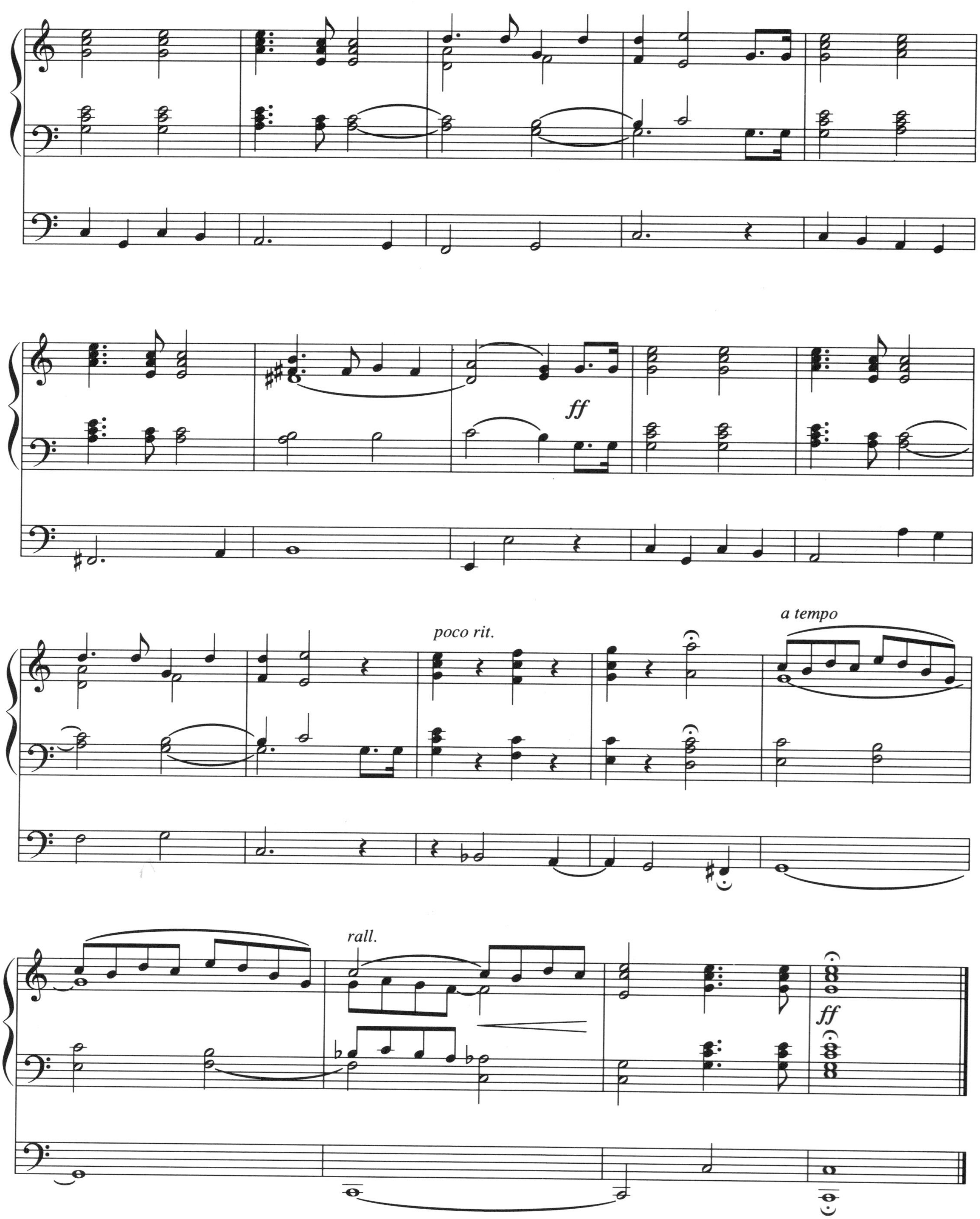
ff
poco rit.
a tempo
rall.
ff

For the Hon. Mrs Pleydell-Bouverie on her ninetieth birthday

PROCESSIONAL

Christopher Tambling (*b.*1964)

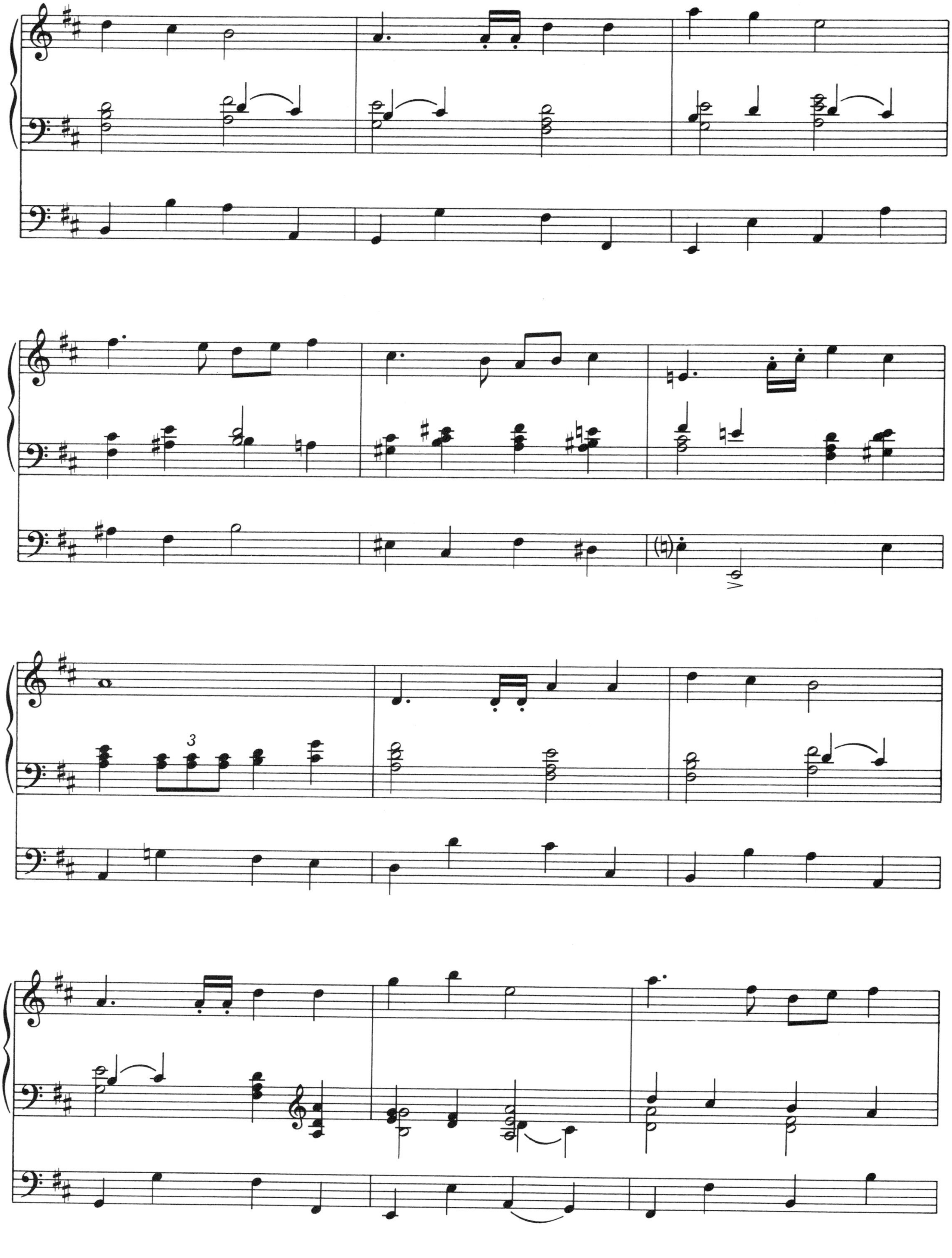

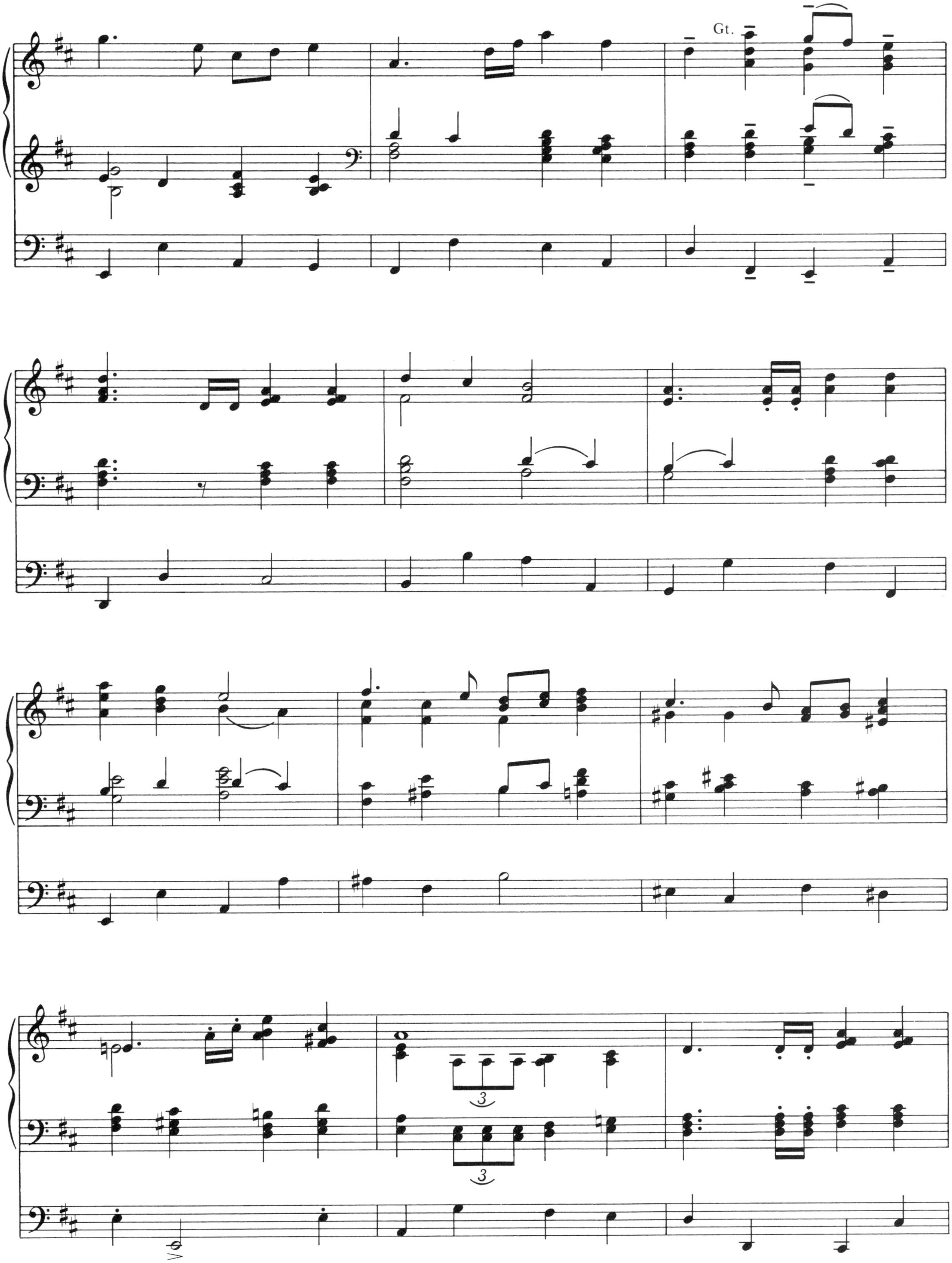
Gt.

second time
to Coda ⊕

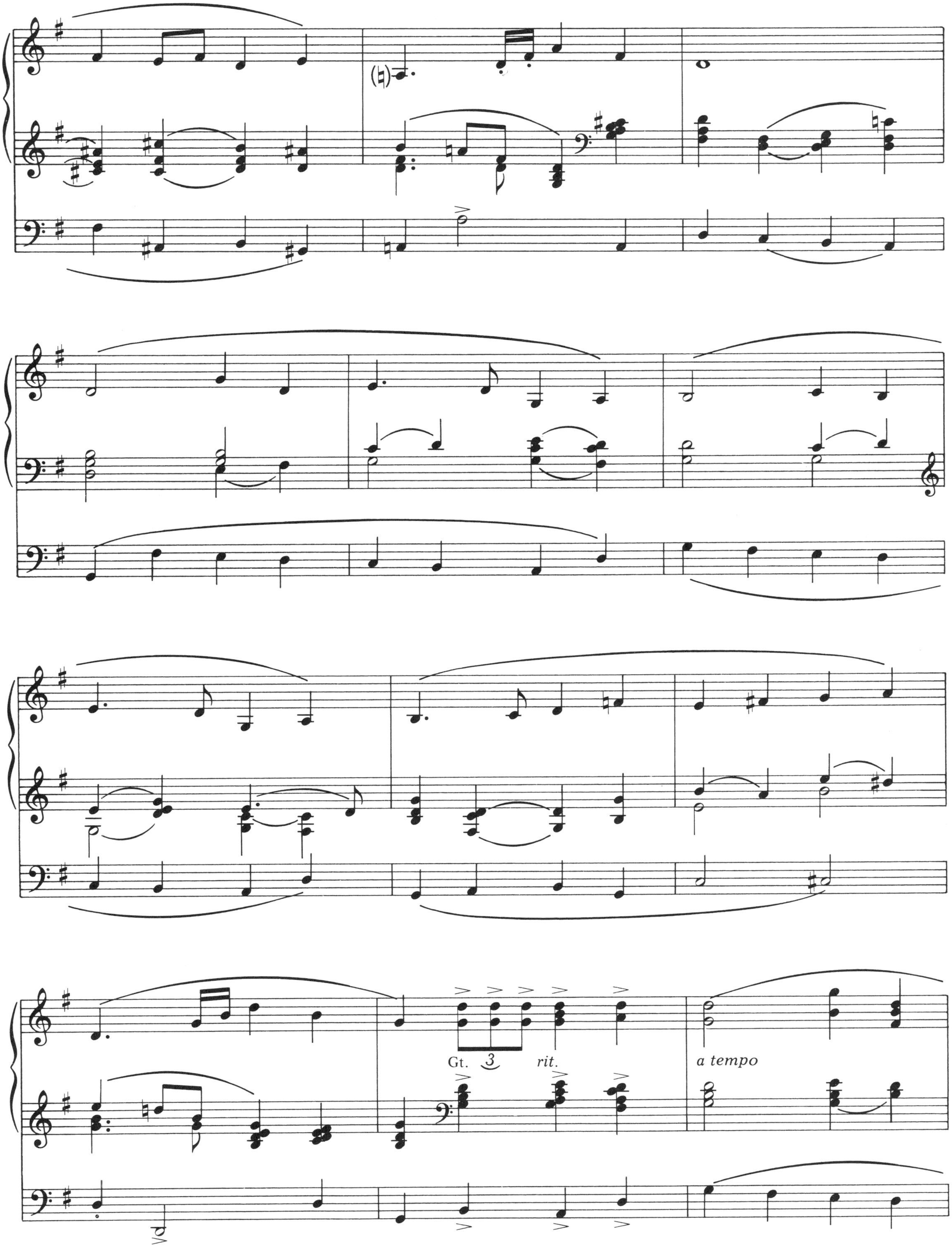
Gt.
3
rit.
a tempo

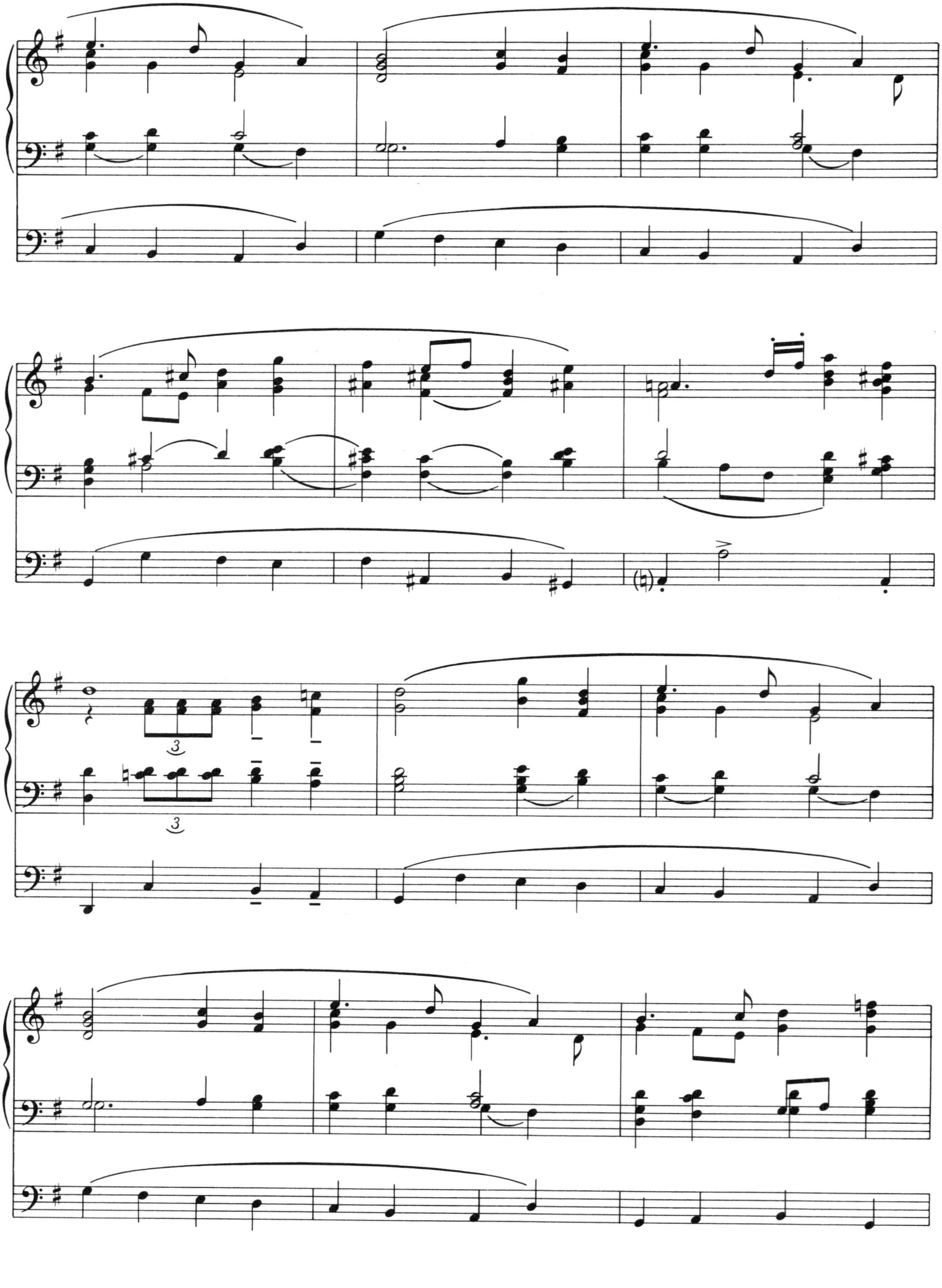

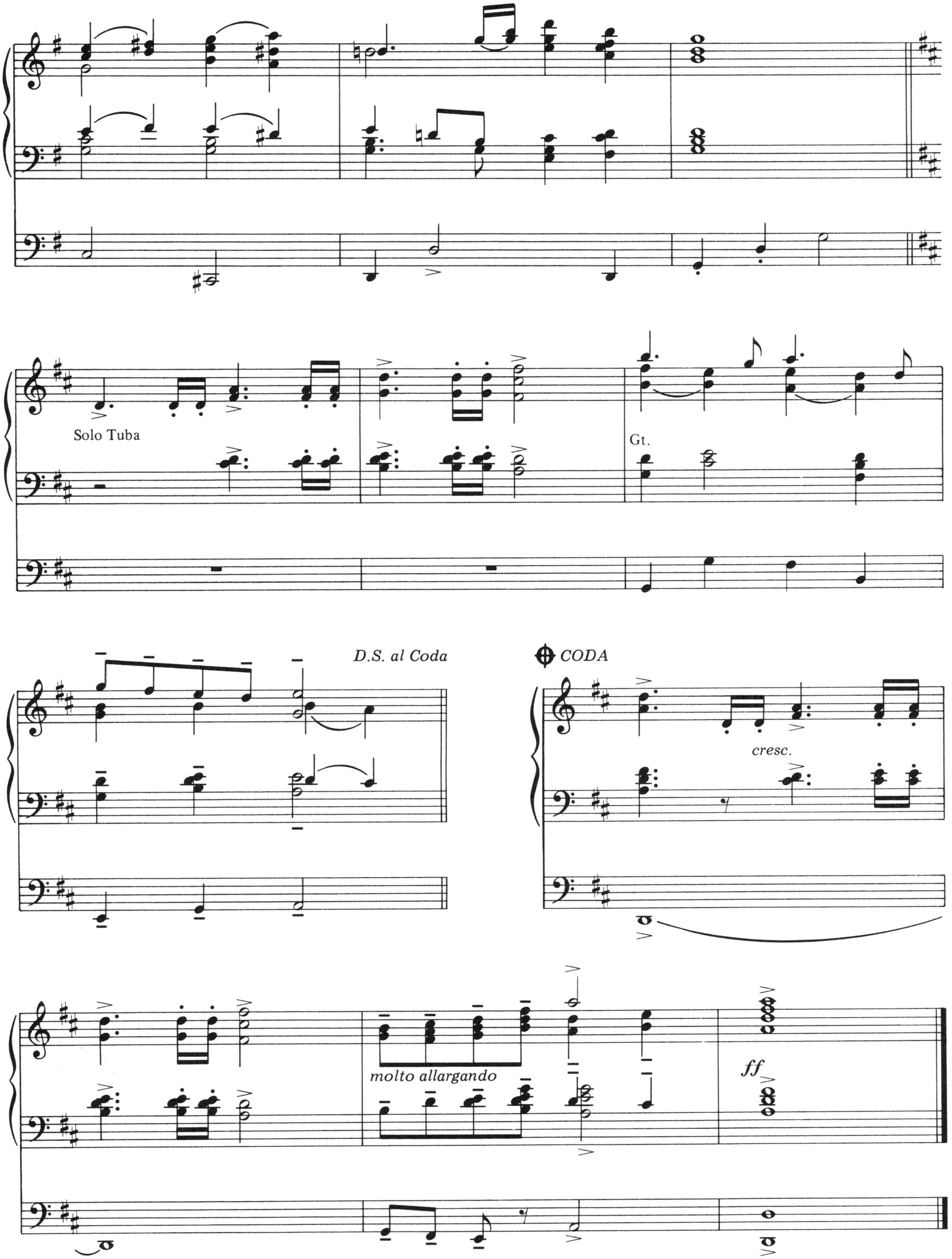
Solo Tuba
Gt.
D.S. al Coda
CODA
cresc.
molto allargando
ff

BERCEUSE

based on a French Noël
Alexandre Guilmant (1837-1911)

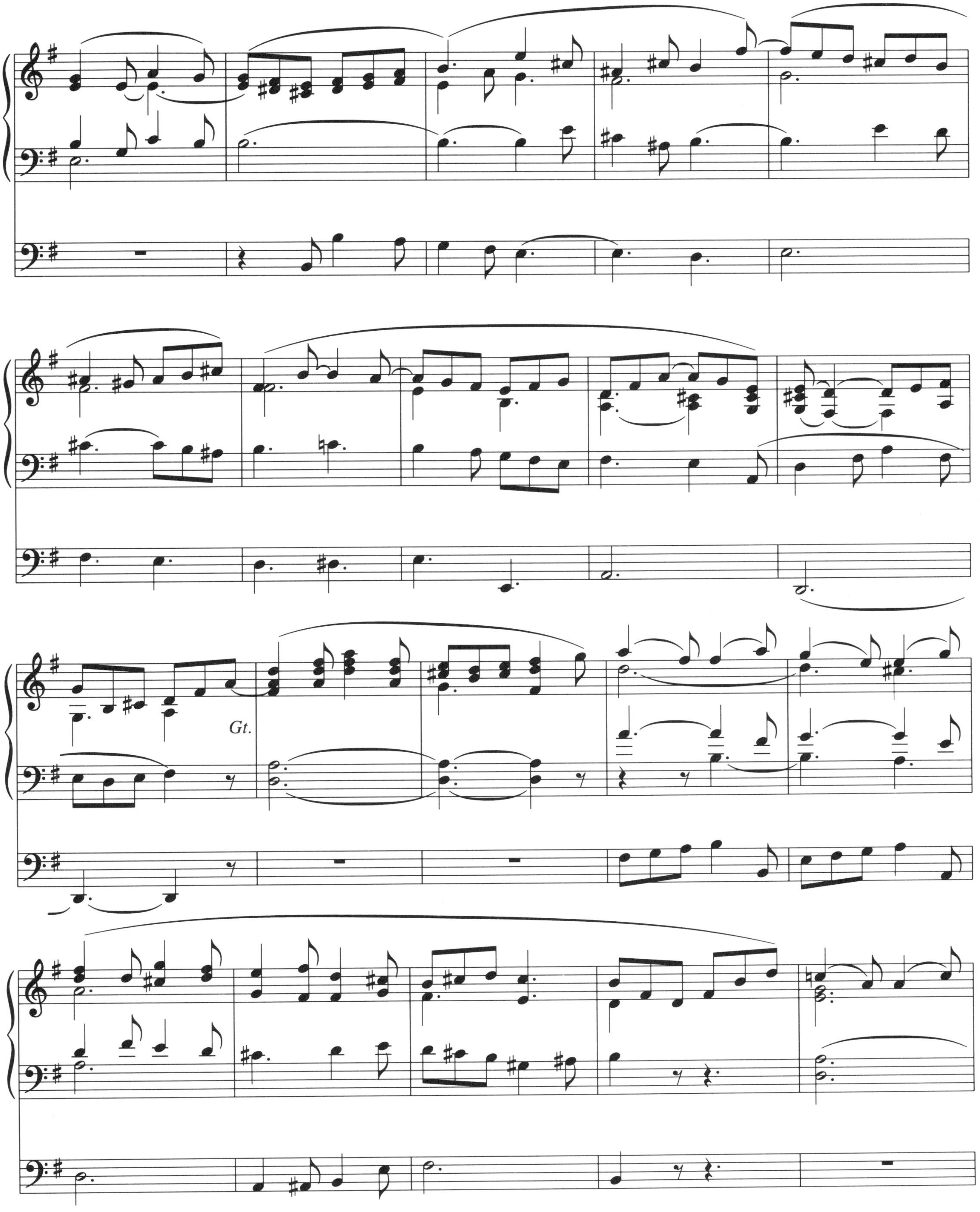
Gt.

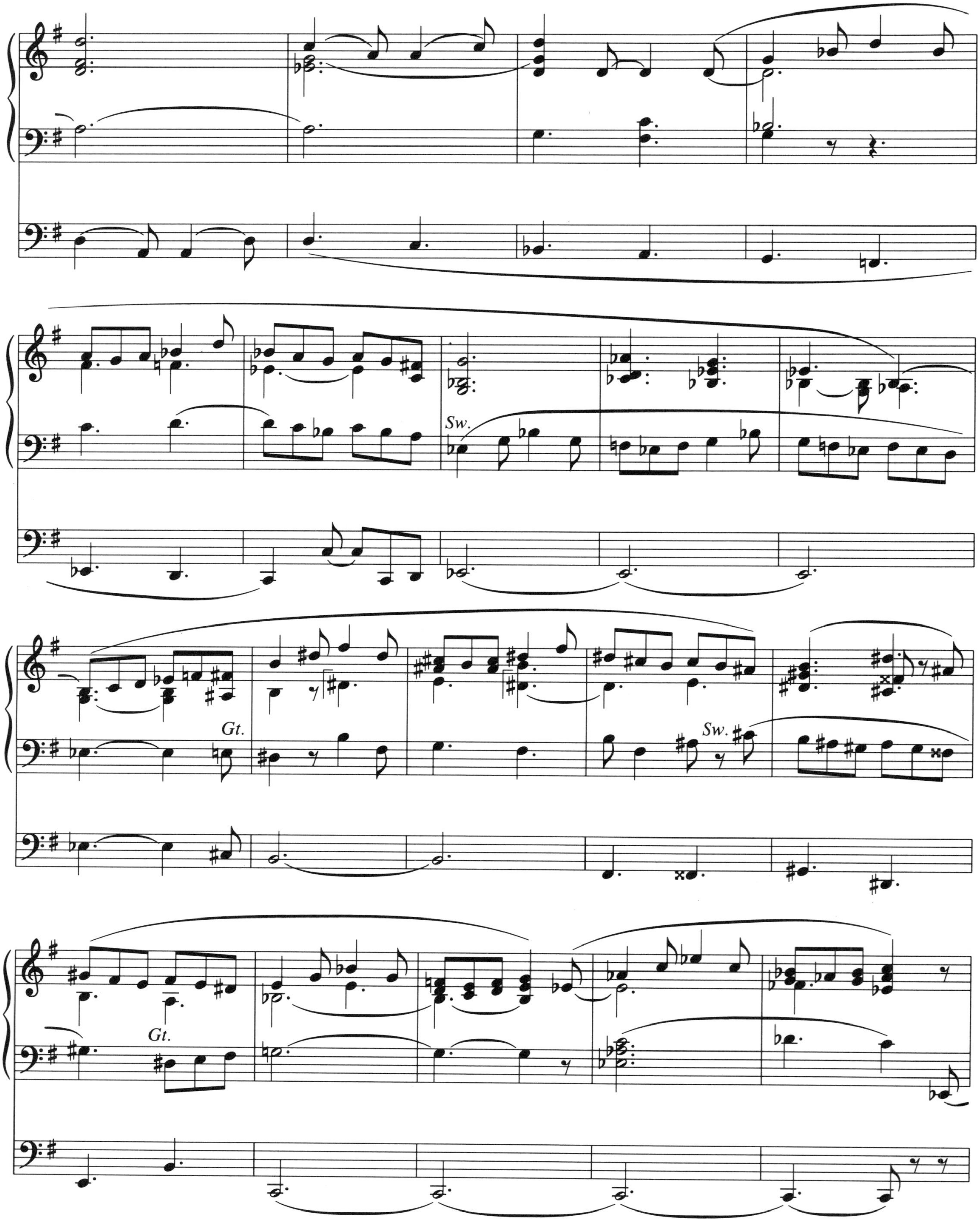
Sw.
Gt.
Sw.
Gt.

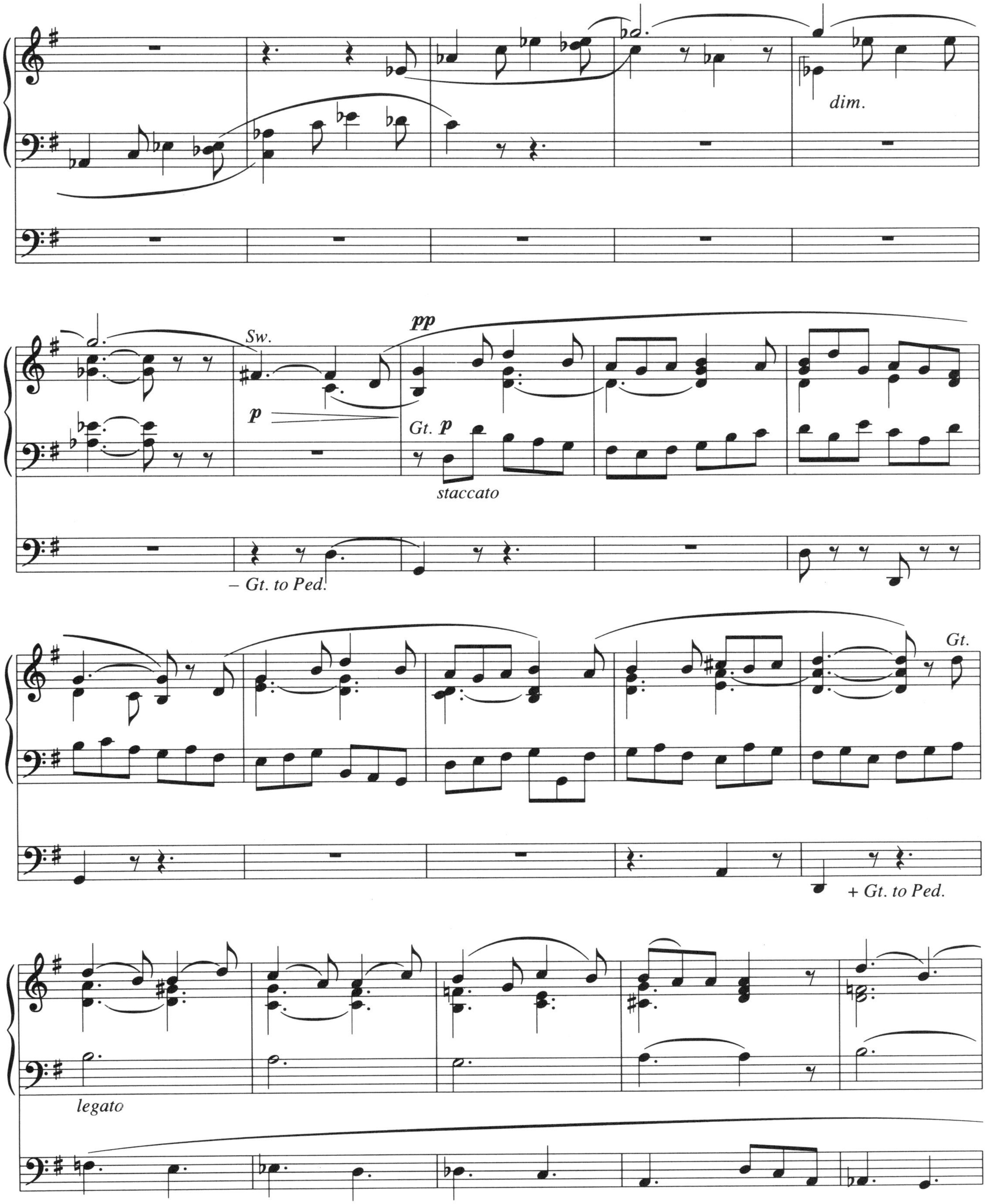
dim.
Sw.
pp
p
Gt. p
staccato
– Gt. to Ped.
Gt.
+ Gt. to Ped.
legato

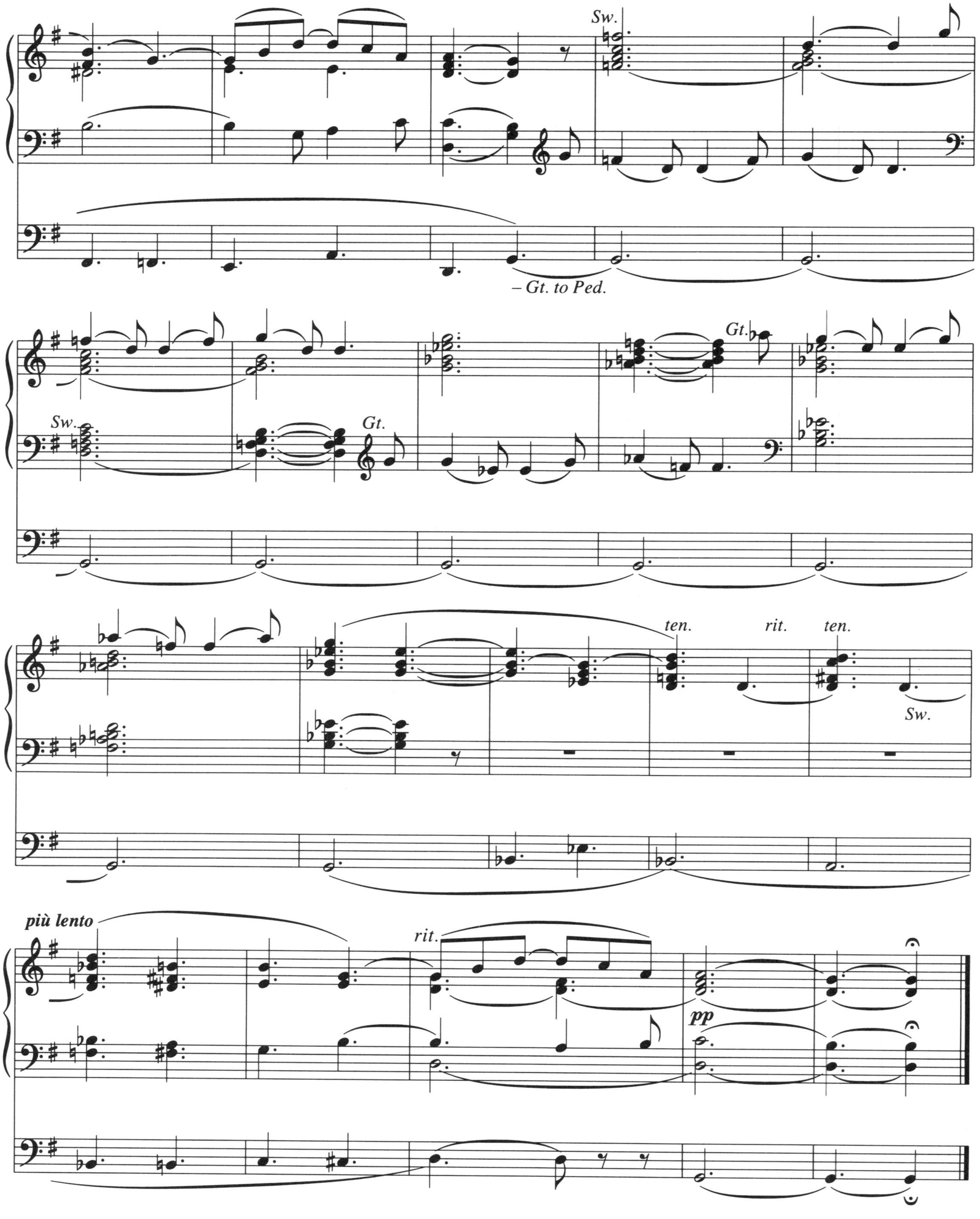
Sw.
– Gt. to Ped.
Sw.
Gt.
Gt.
ten.
rit.
ten.
Sw.
più lento
rit.
pp

PRELUDE in E♭

Johann Rinck (1770-1846)

LARGHETTO

Thomas Attwood Walmisley (1814-1856)

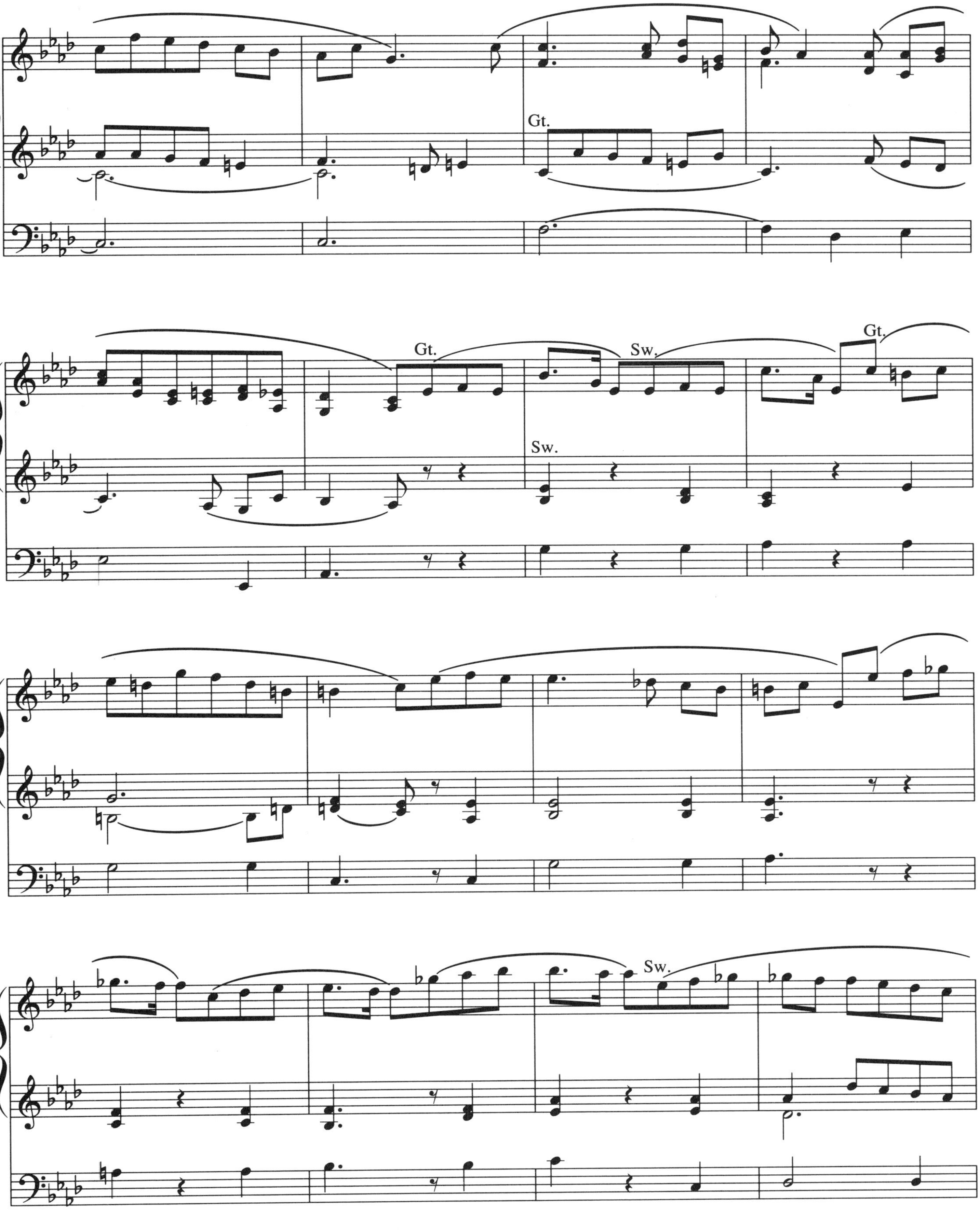
Gt.
Gt.
Sw.
Sw.
Gt.
Sw.

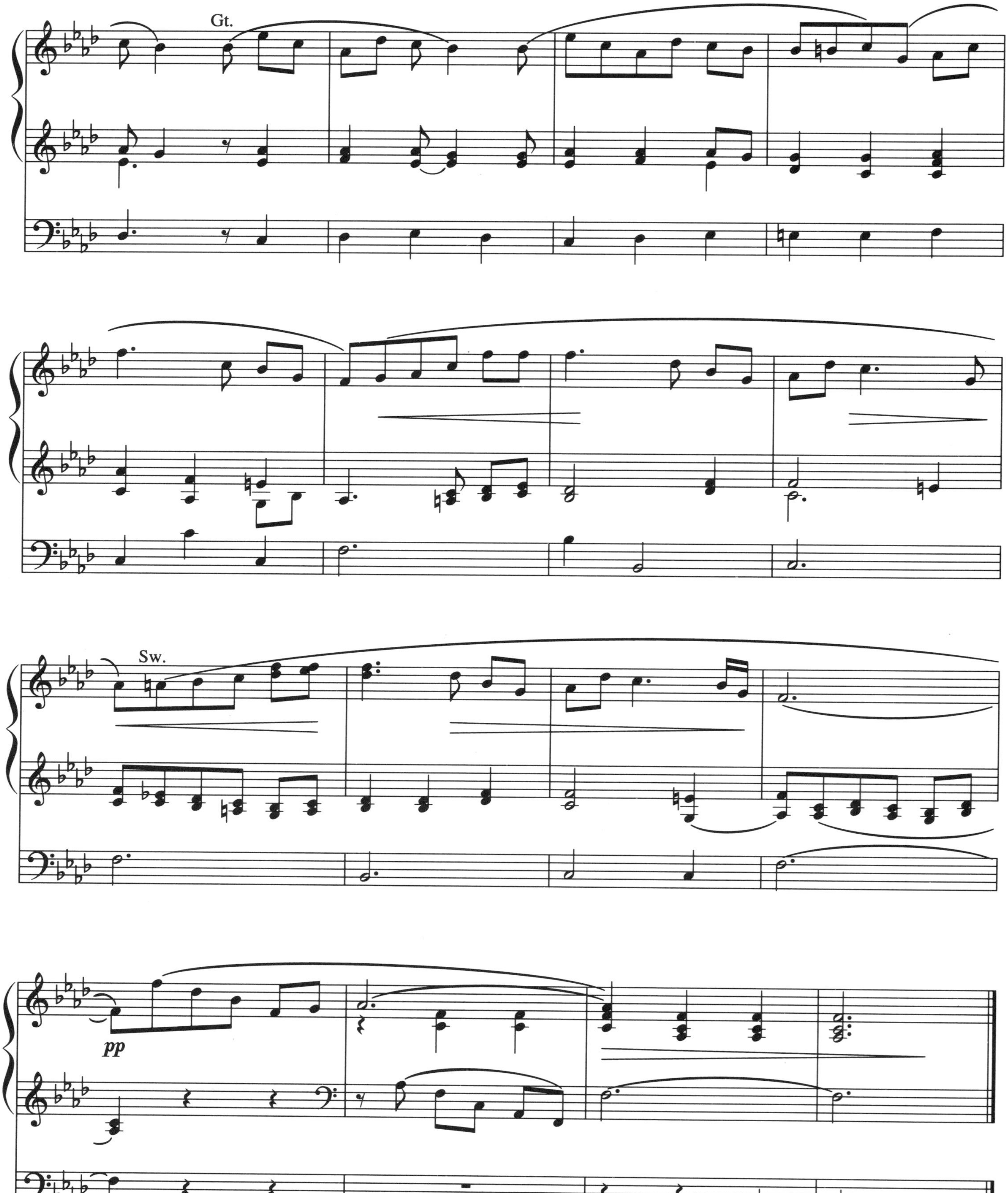
Gt.
Sw.
pp

For Edward

TUBA TUNE

Christopher Tambling (*b.*1964)

1st time: Gt. Solo
2nd time: Sw. at pitch
Both times: Sw.
Both times: Gt.

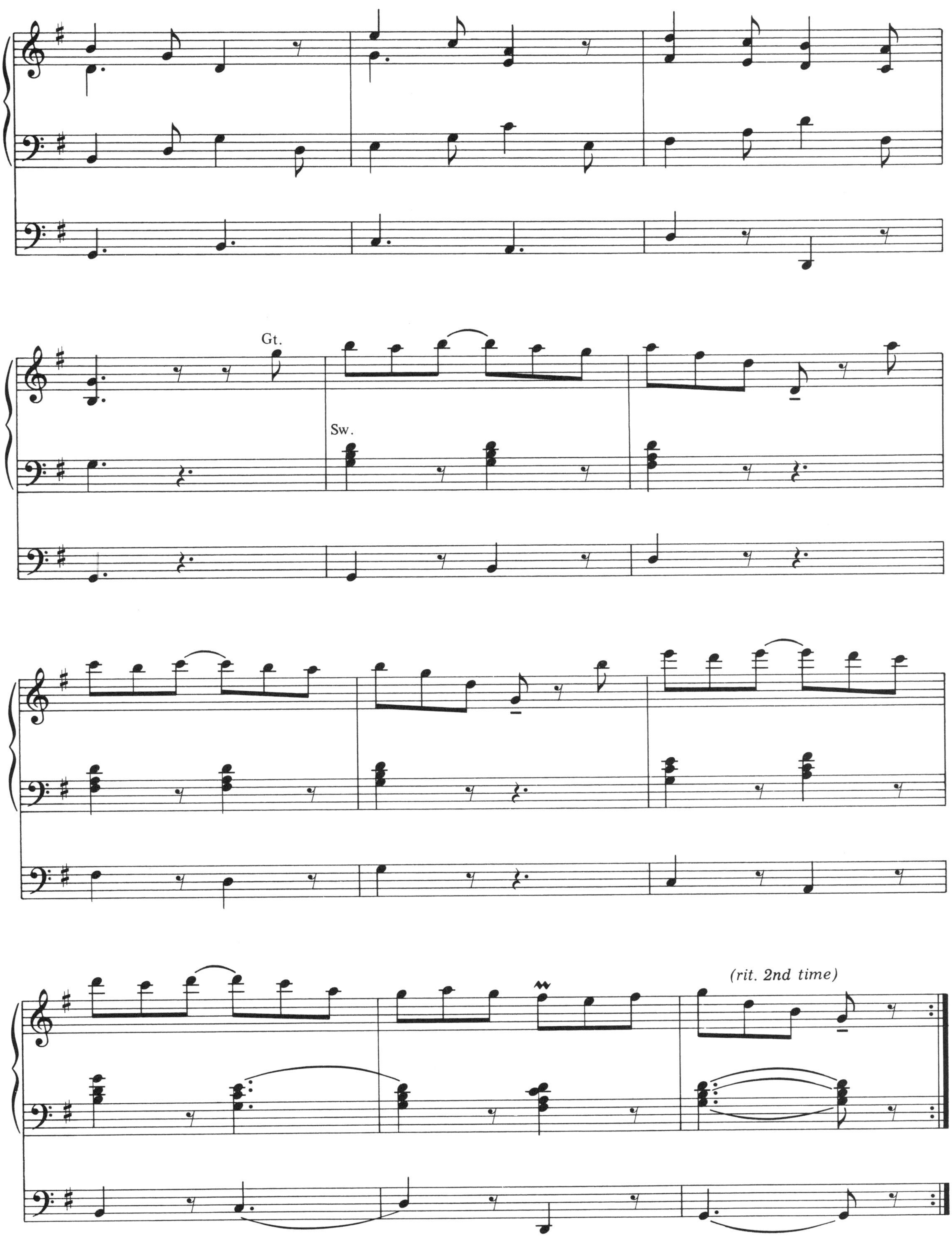
Gt.
Sw.
(rit. 2nd time)

ALLEGRO ben MODERATO

Frank Bridge (1879-1941)

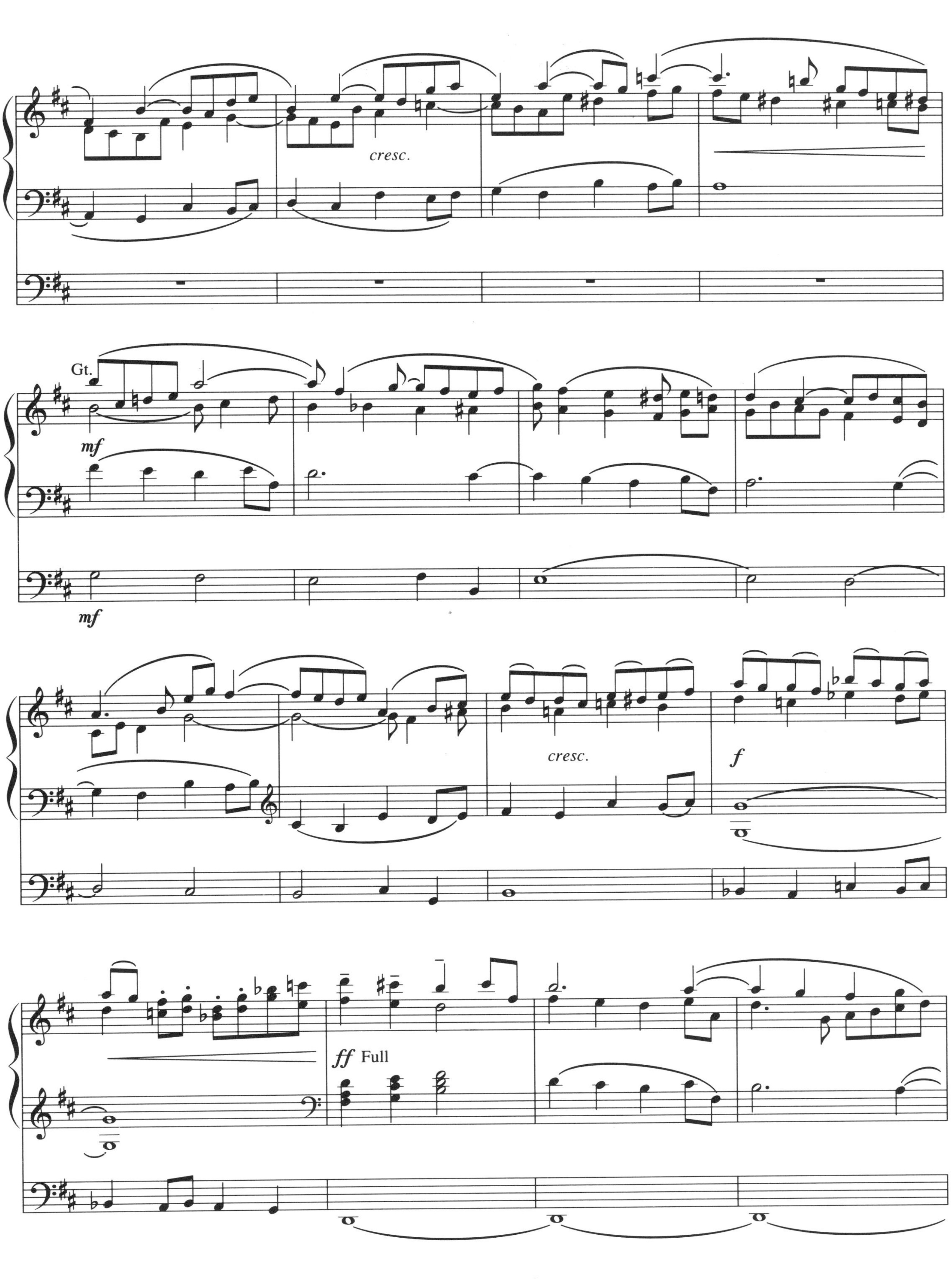
cresc.
Gt.
mf
mf
cresc.
f
ff Full

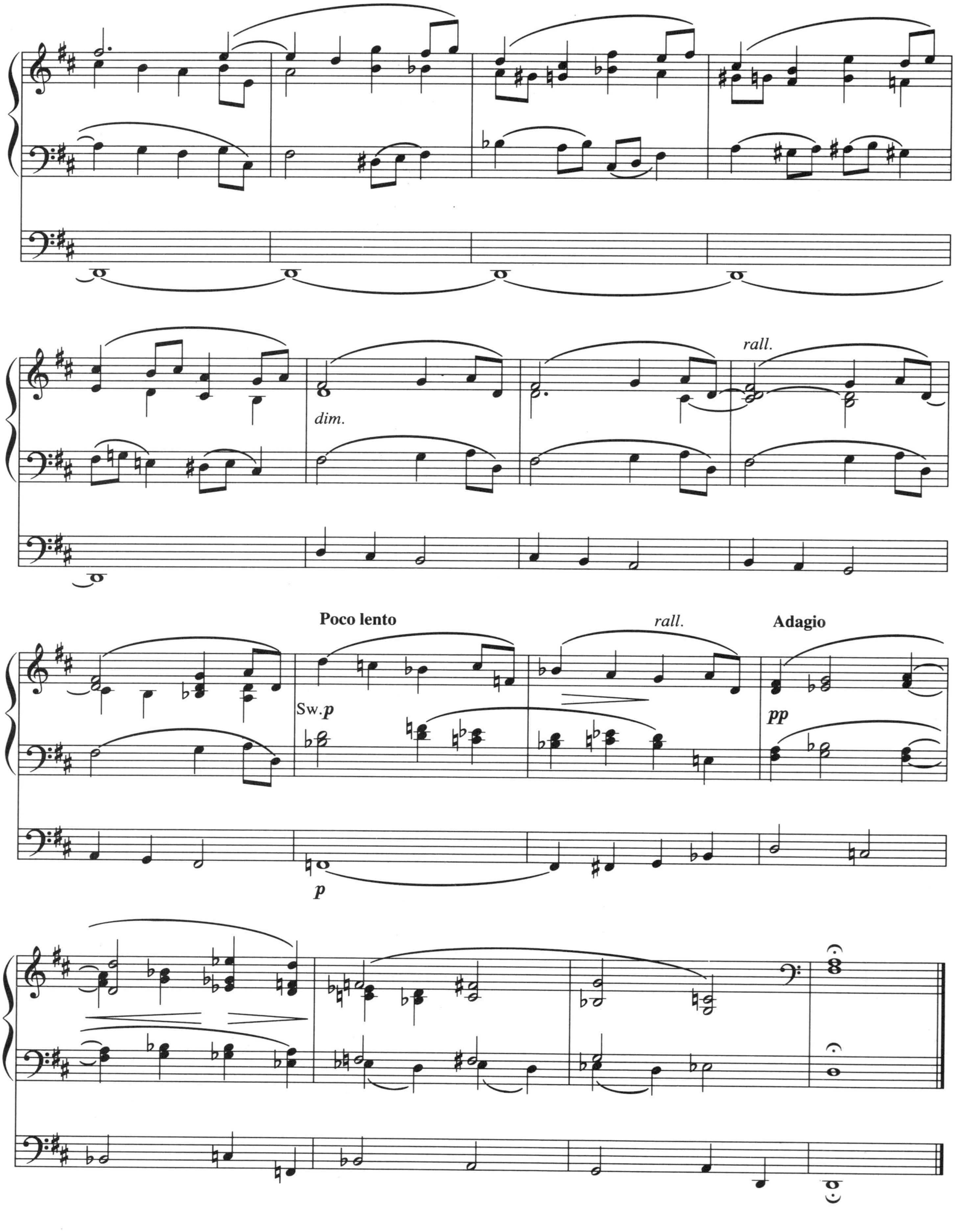
dim.
rall.
Poco lento
Sw. p
p
rall.
Adagio
pp

ANDANTE

W. Warder Harvey

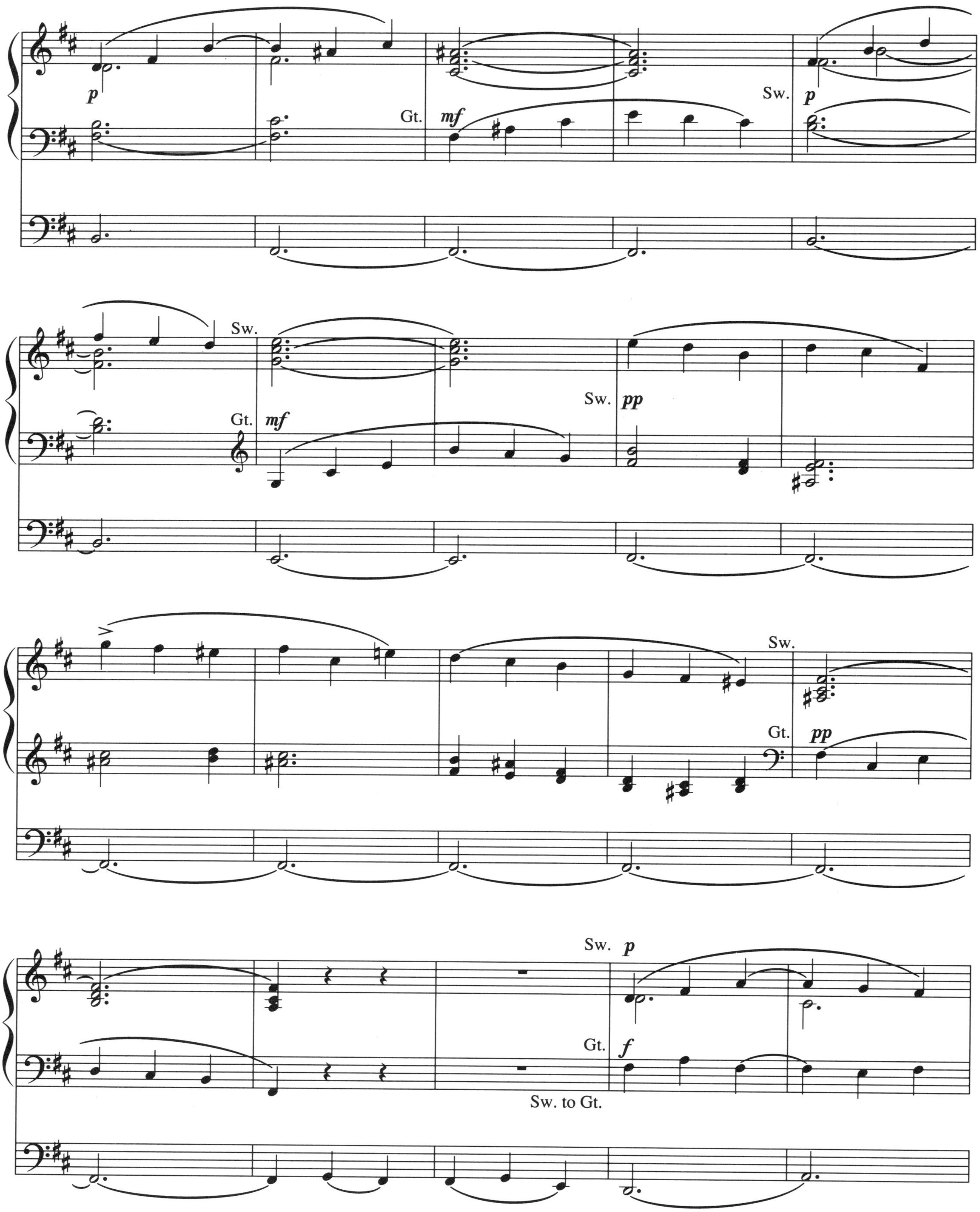
p
Gt.
mf
Sw.
p
Sw.
Gt.
mf
Sw.
pp
Sw.
Gt.
pp
Sw.
p
Gt.
f
Sw. to Gt.

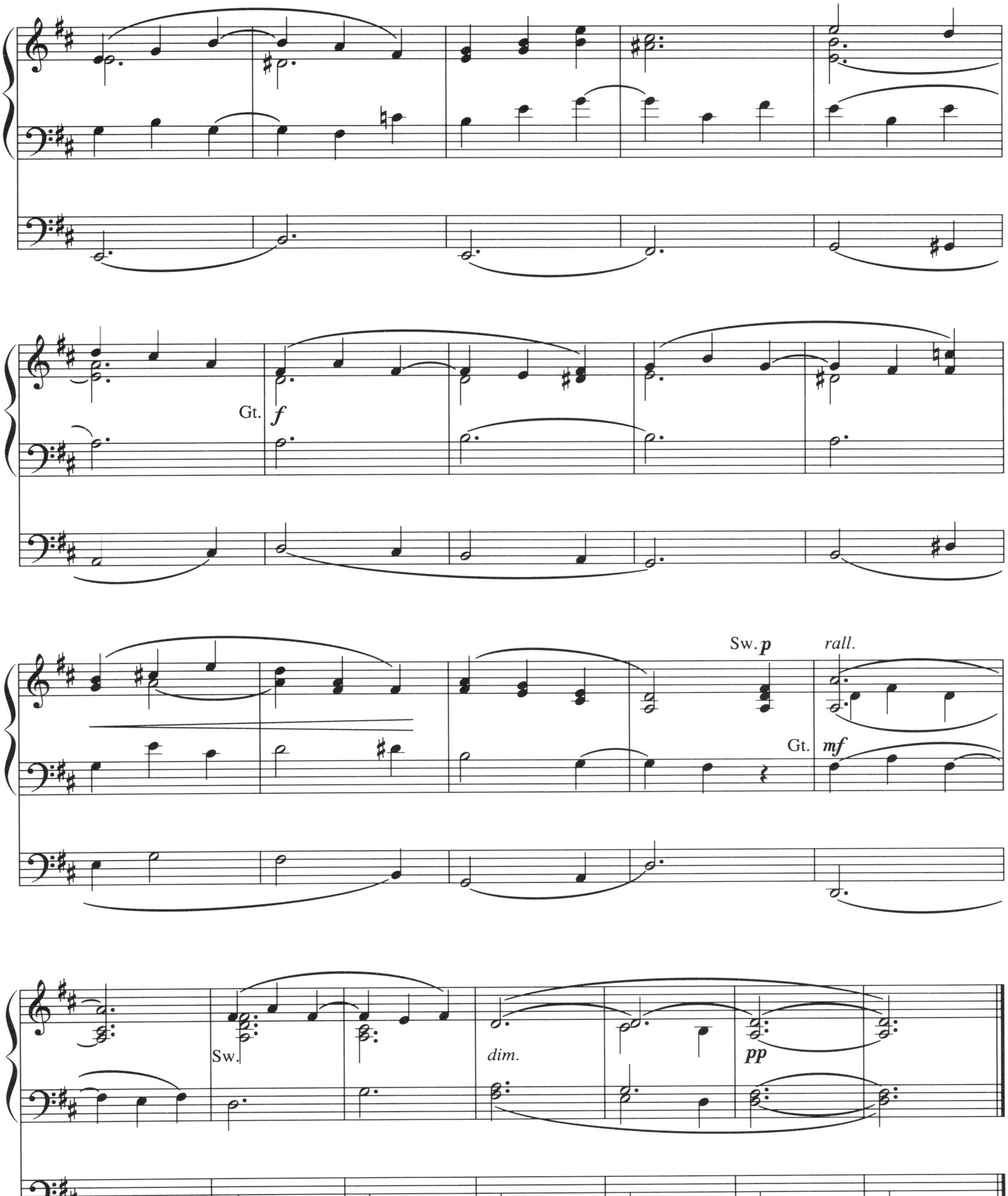
Gt.
f
Sw.
p
rall.
Gt.
mf
Sw.
dim.
pp

PRELUDE in B♭

Johann Rinck (1770-1846)

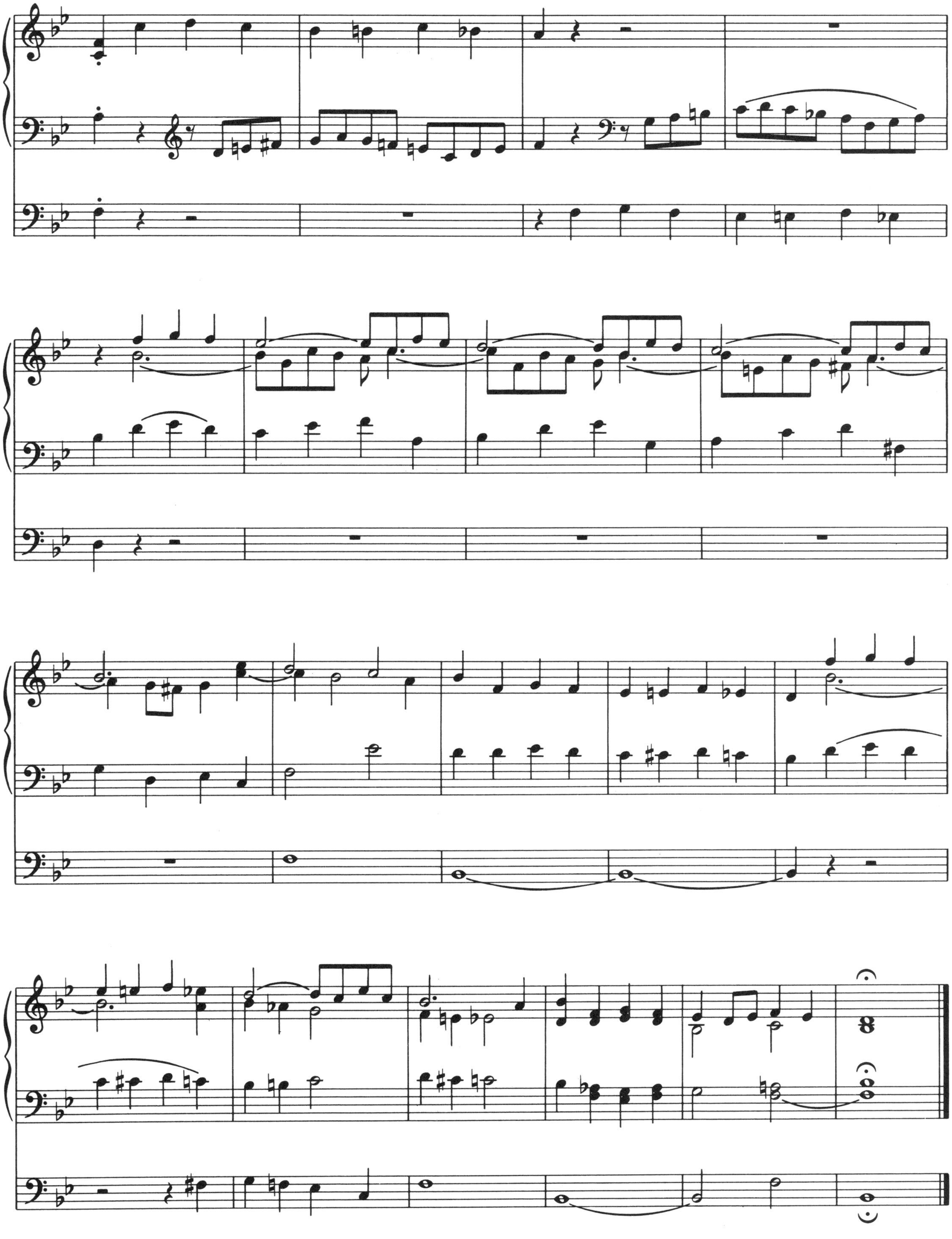

A POPULAR MEMORY

Quentin Thomas (*b.*1972)

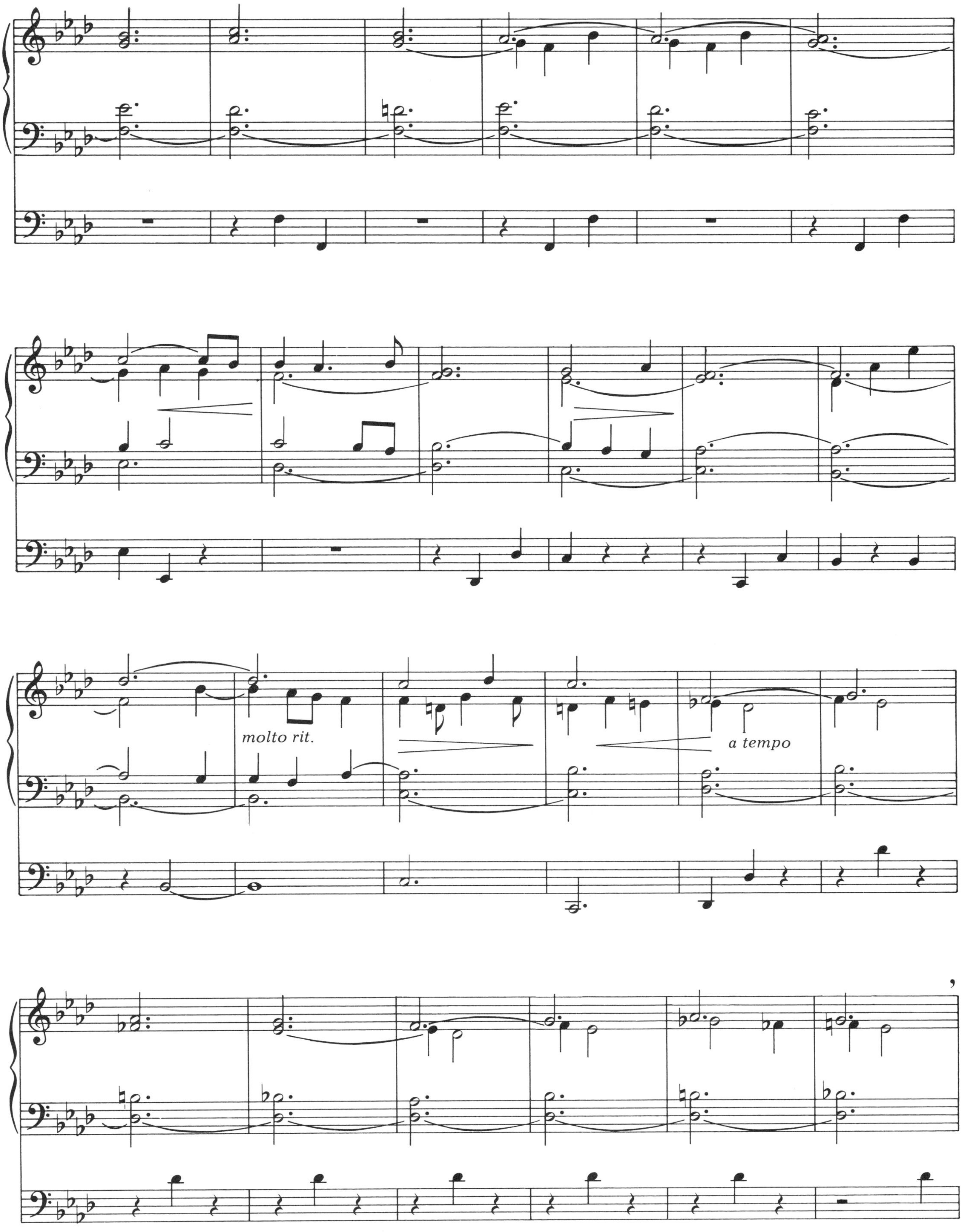
molto rit.
a tempo

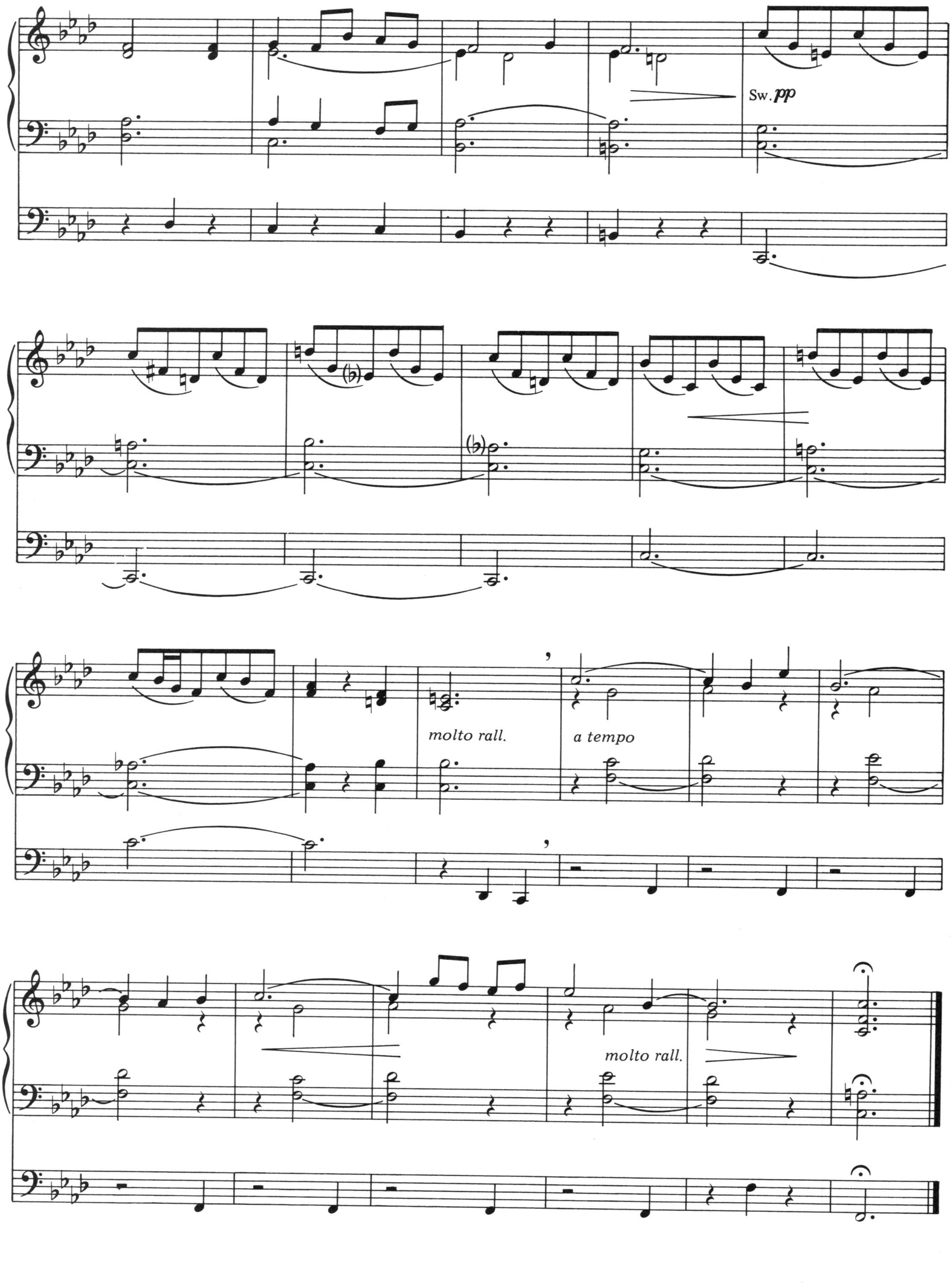
Sw. pp
molto rall.
a tempo
molto rall.

RIPOSO

Joseph Rheinberger (1839-1901)

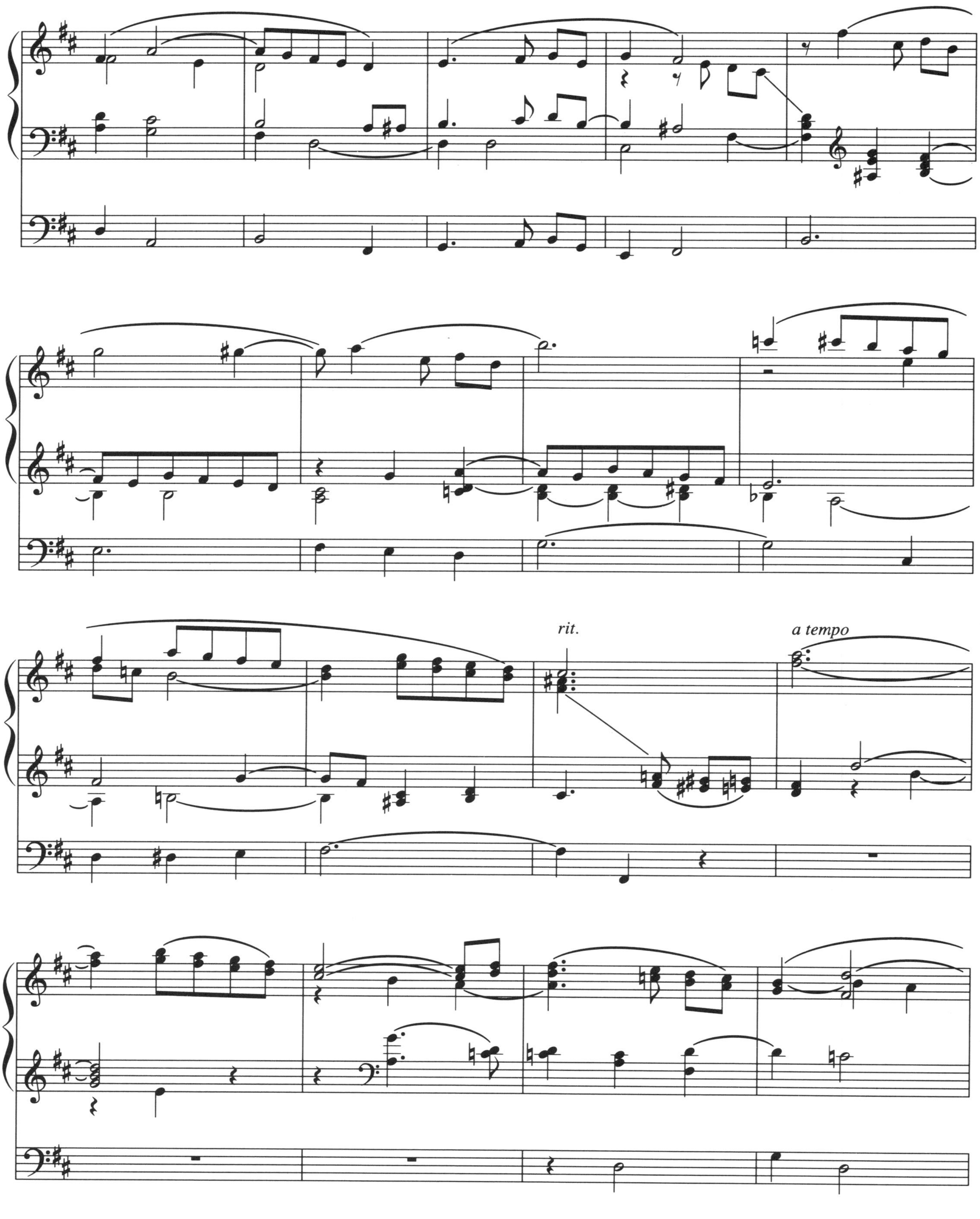
rit.
a tempo

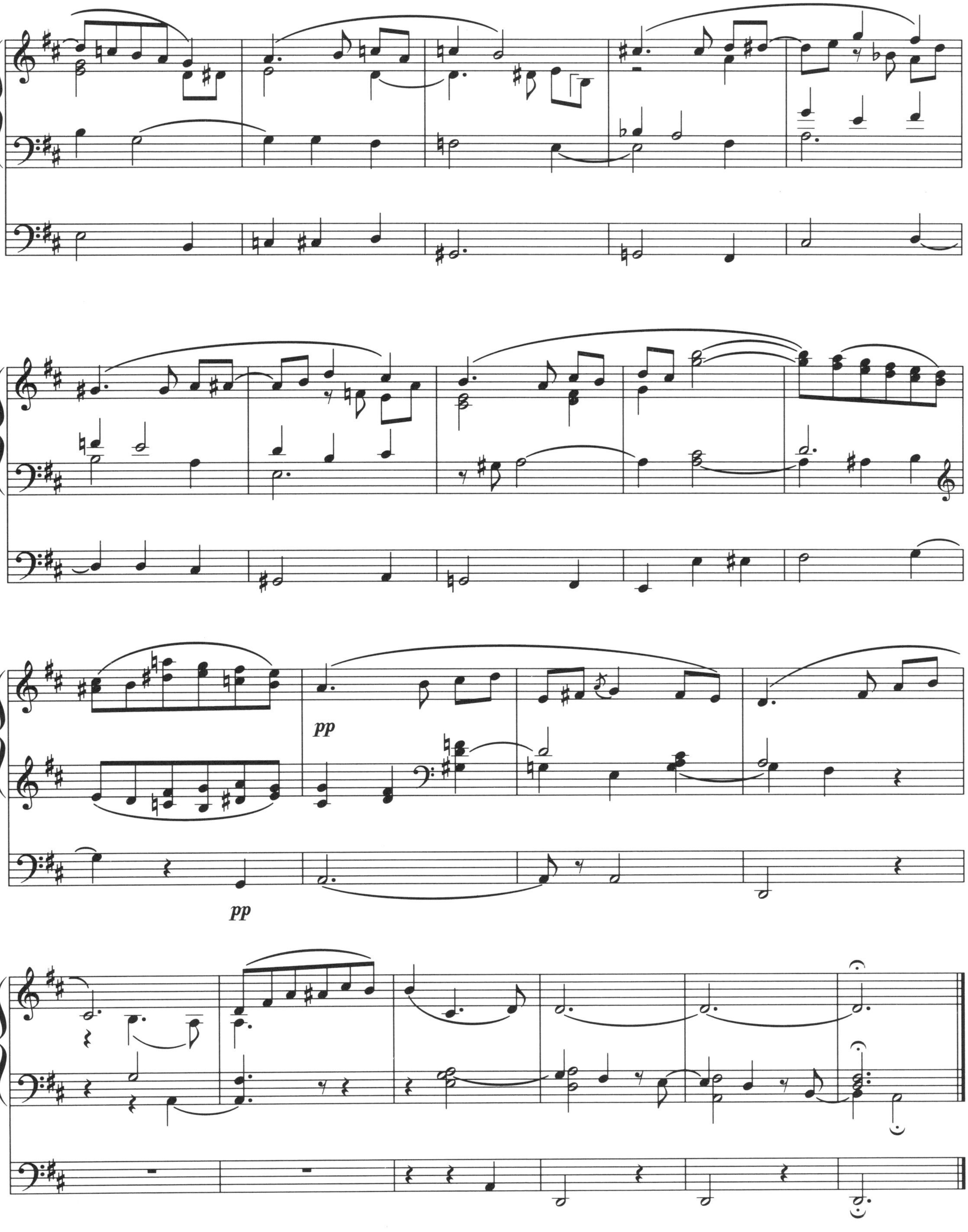
pp
pp

PASTORALE

Alexandre Guilmant (1837-1911)

It is illegal to photocopy music.

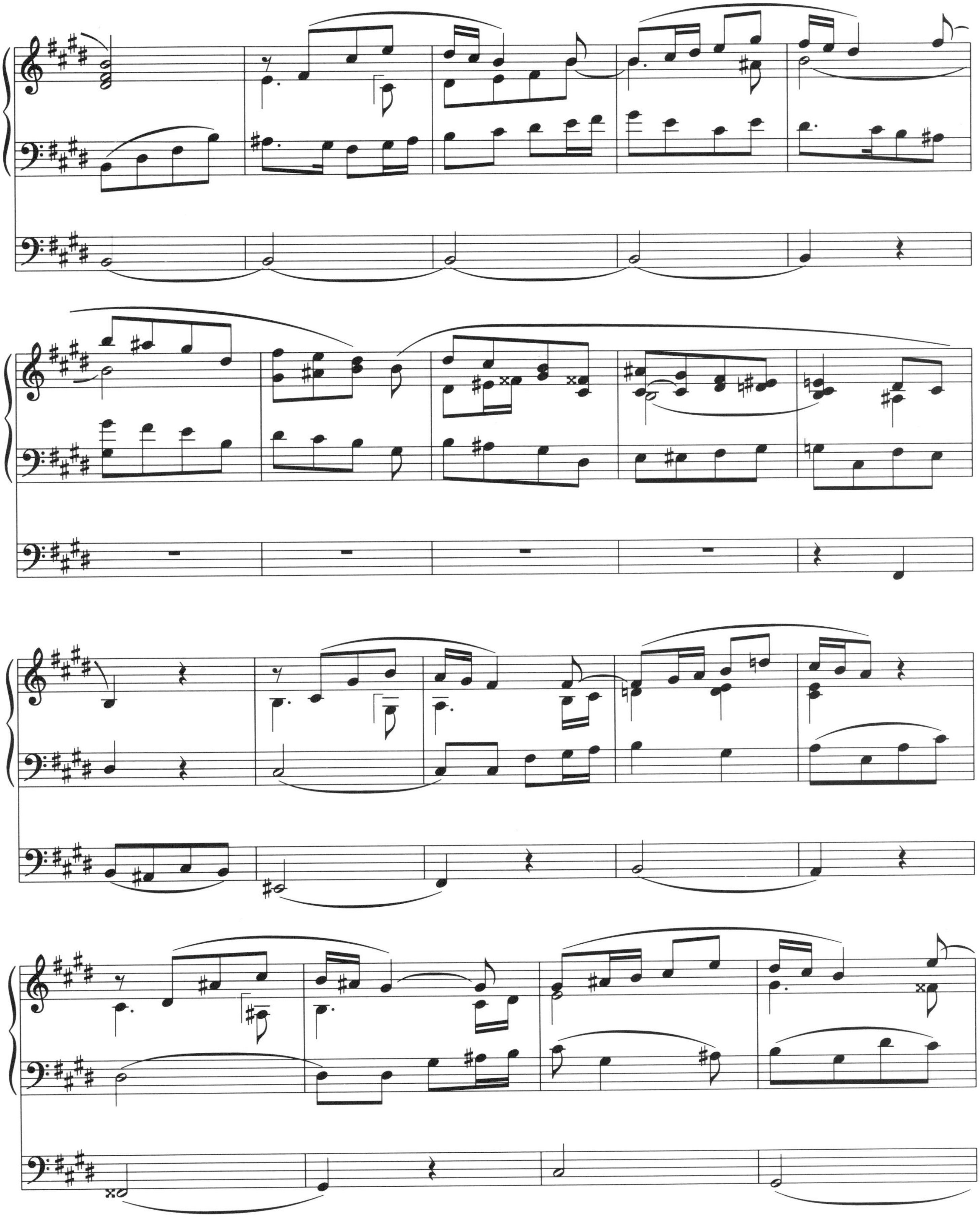

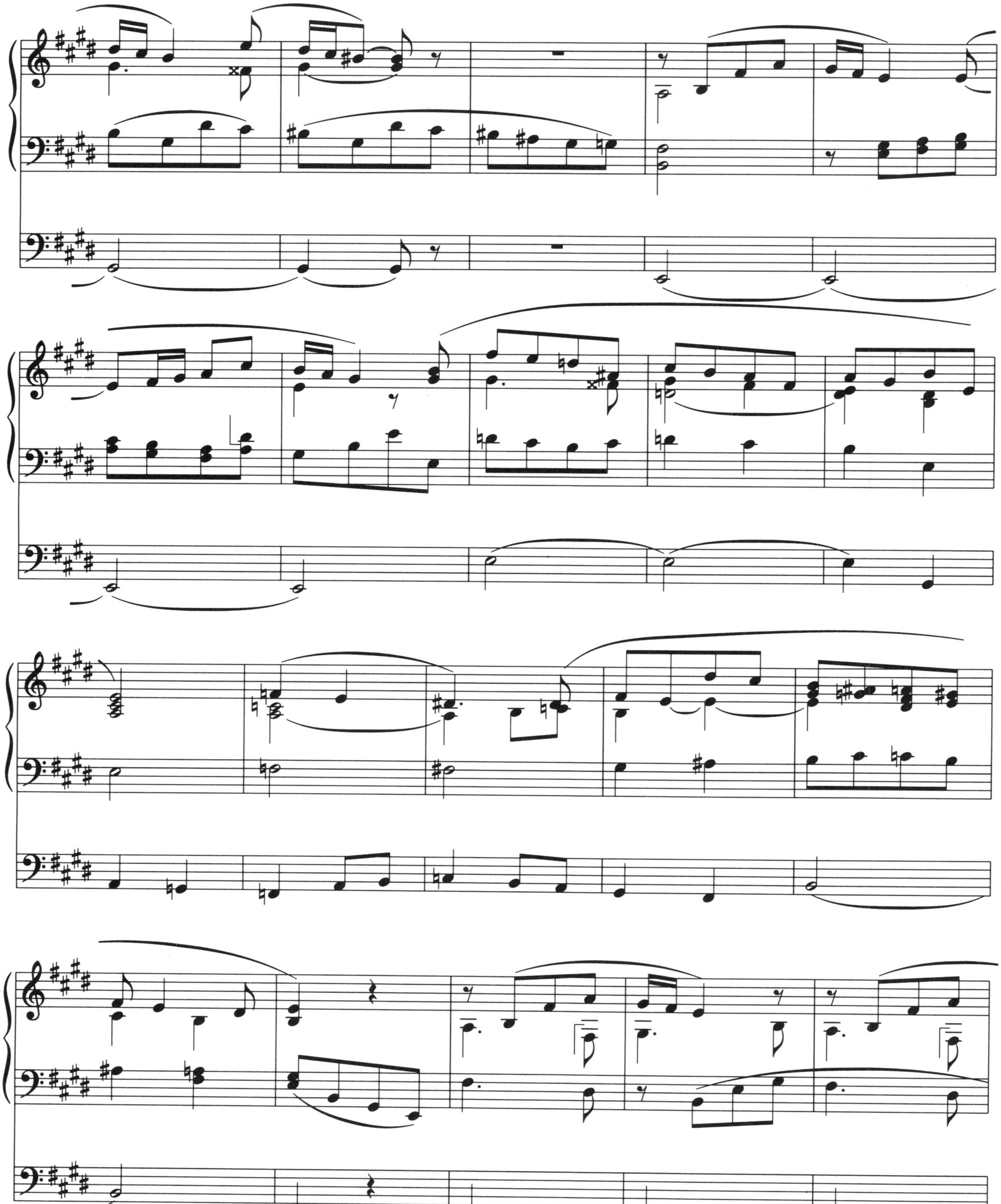

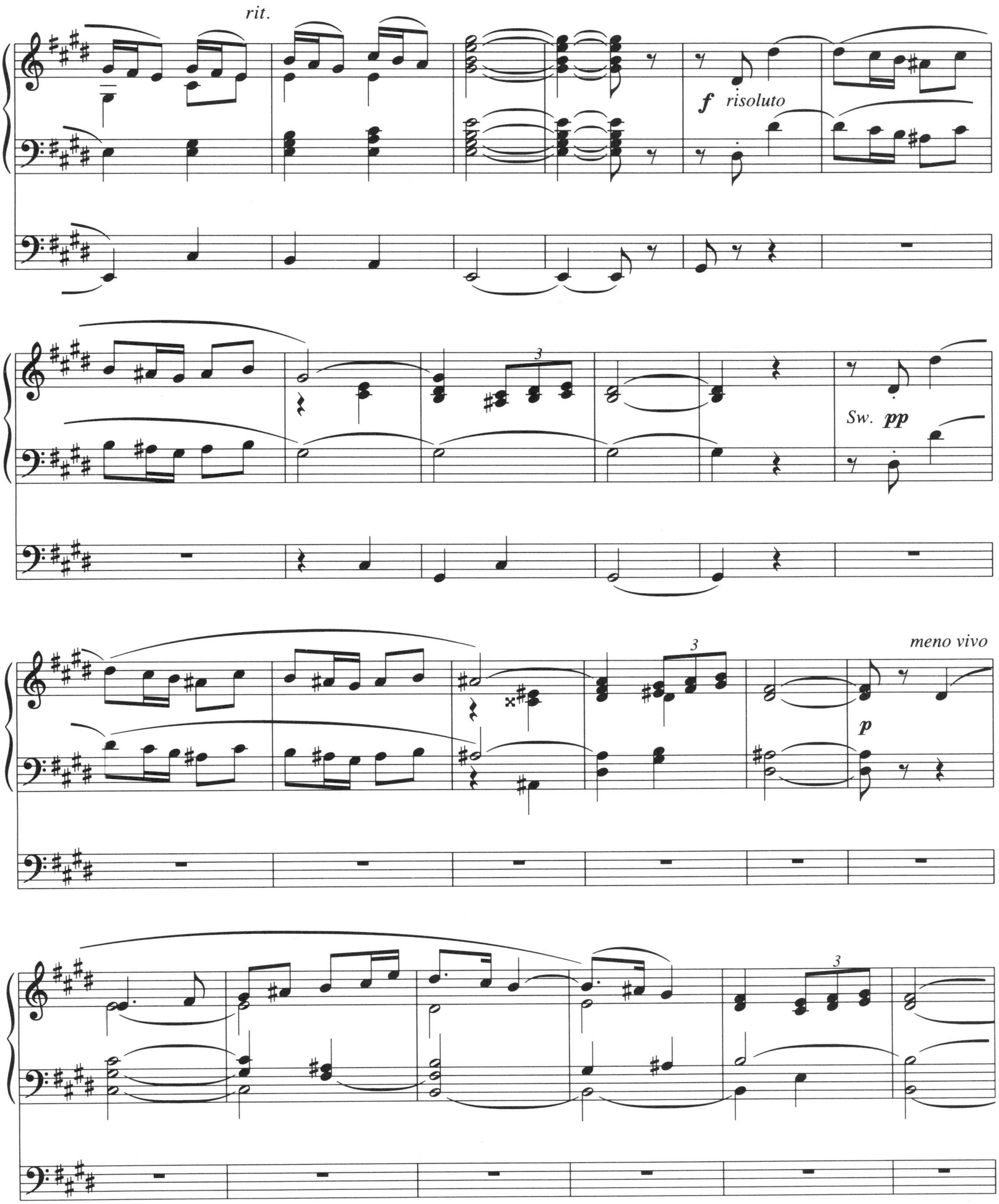
rit.
f risoluto
Sw. pp
meno vivo
p

Tempo 1
Gt.
f
risoluto
Sw. + reeds
3
3
p
tranquillo
– reeds
più lento
pp
rit.
Gt.
+ Sw.
reeds
a tempo
f

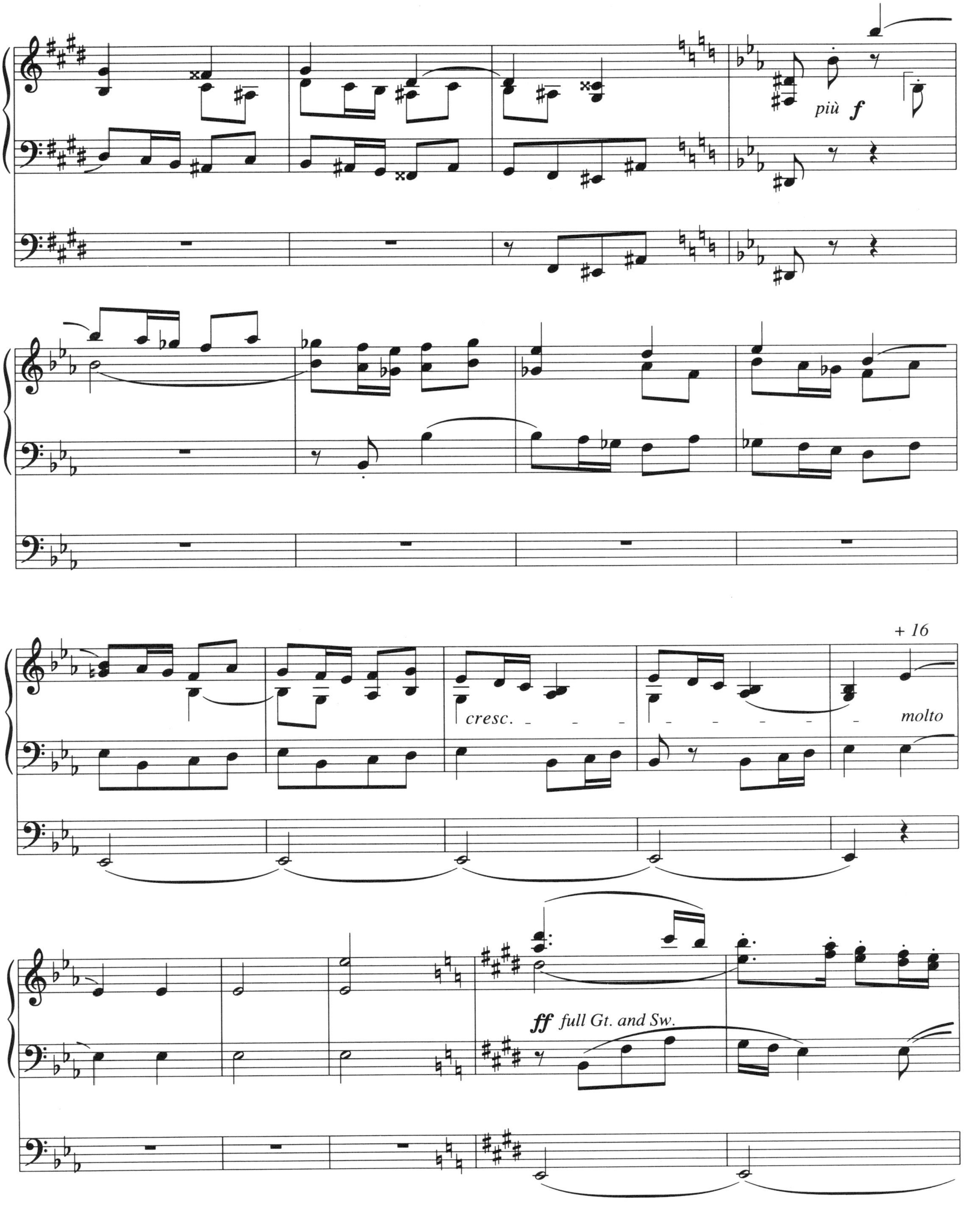
più f
+ 16
cresc.
molto
ff full Gt. and Sw.

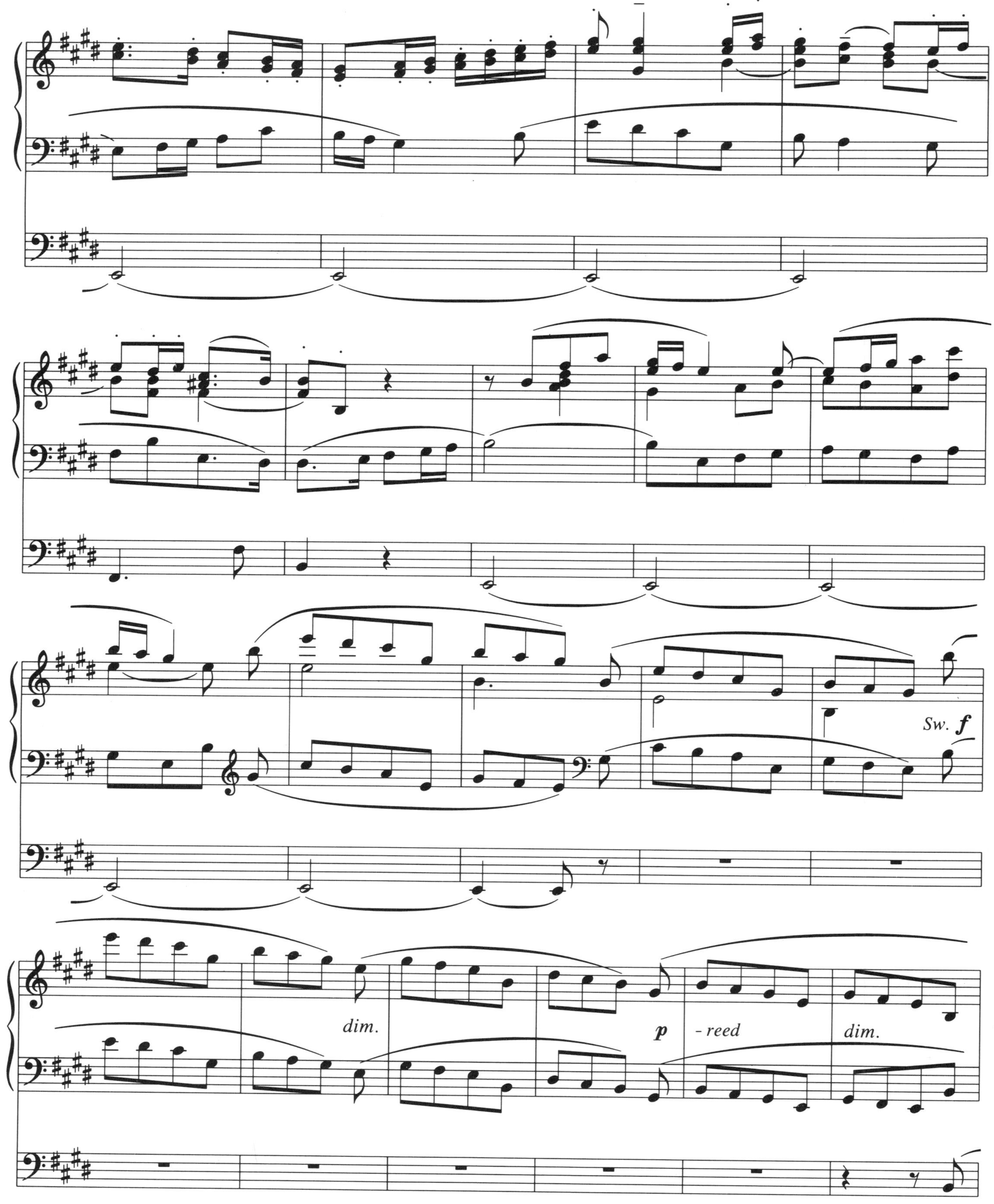
Sw. f
dim.
p
- reed
dim.

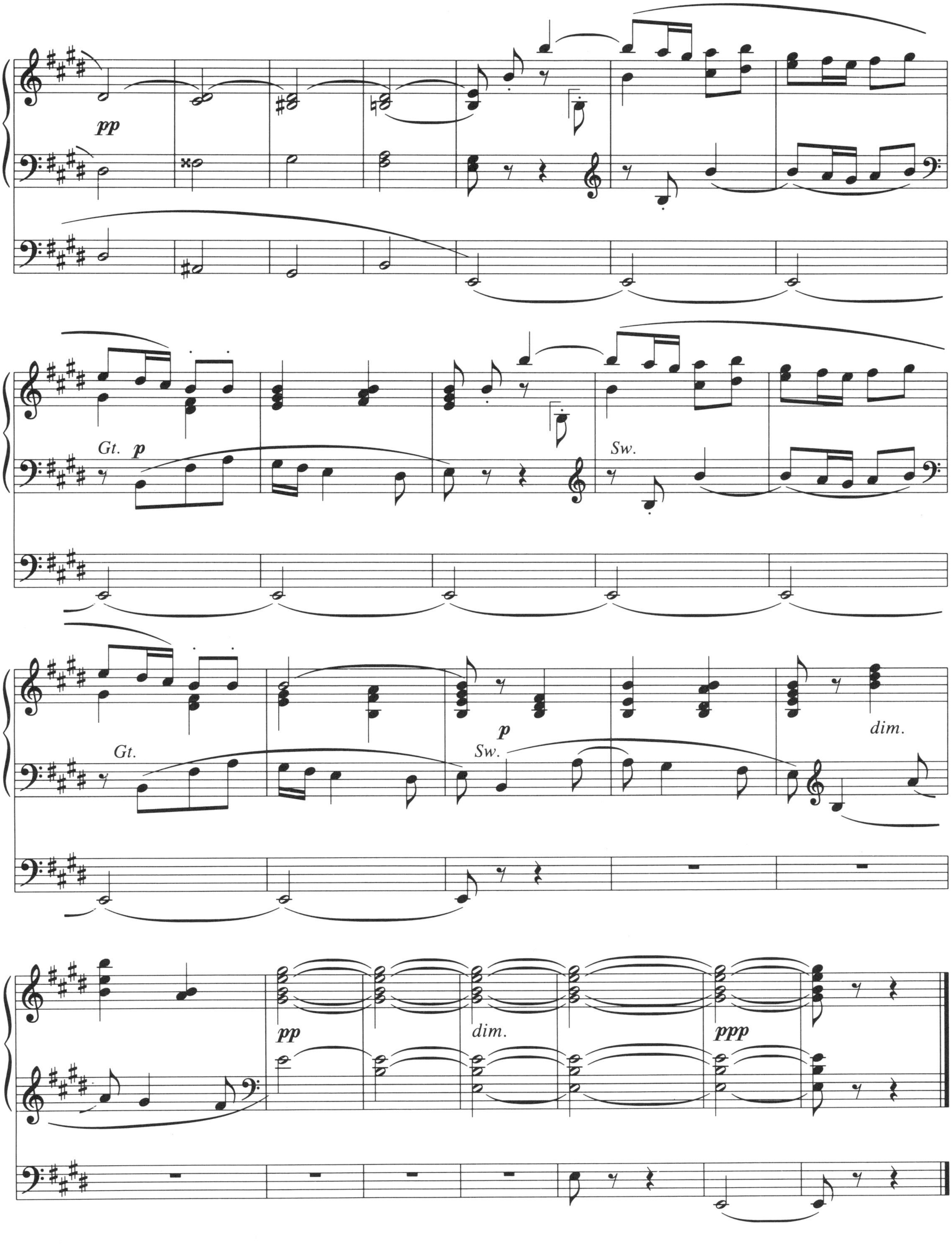
pp
Gt. p
Sw.
Gt.
Sw.
p
dim.
pp
dim.
ppp

For Andrew and Mavis

FOLK TUNE

on 'Dream Angus'
Christopher Tambling (*b.*1964)

Gt. Flutes 8 + 4
Sw. Diaps. + Oboe 8

Never hurrying

+ Gt. to Ped.

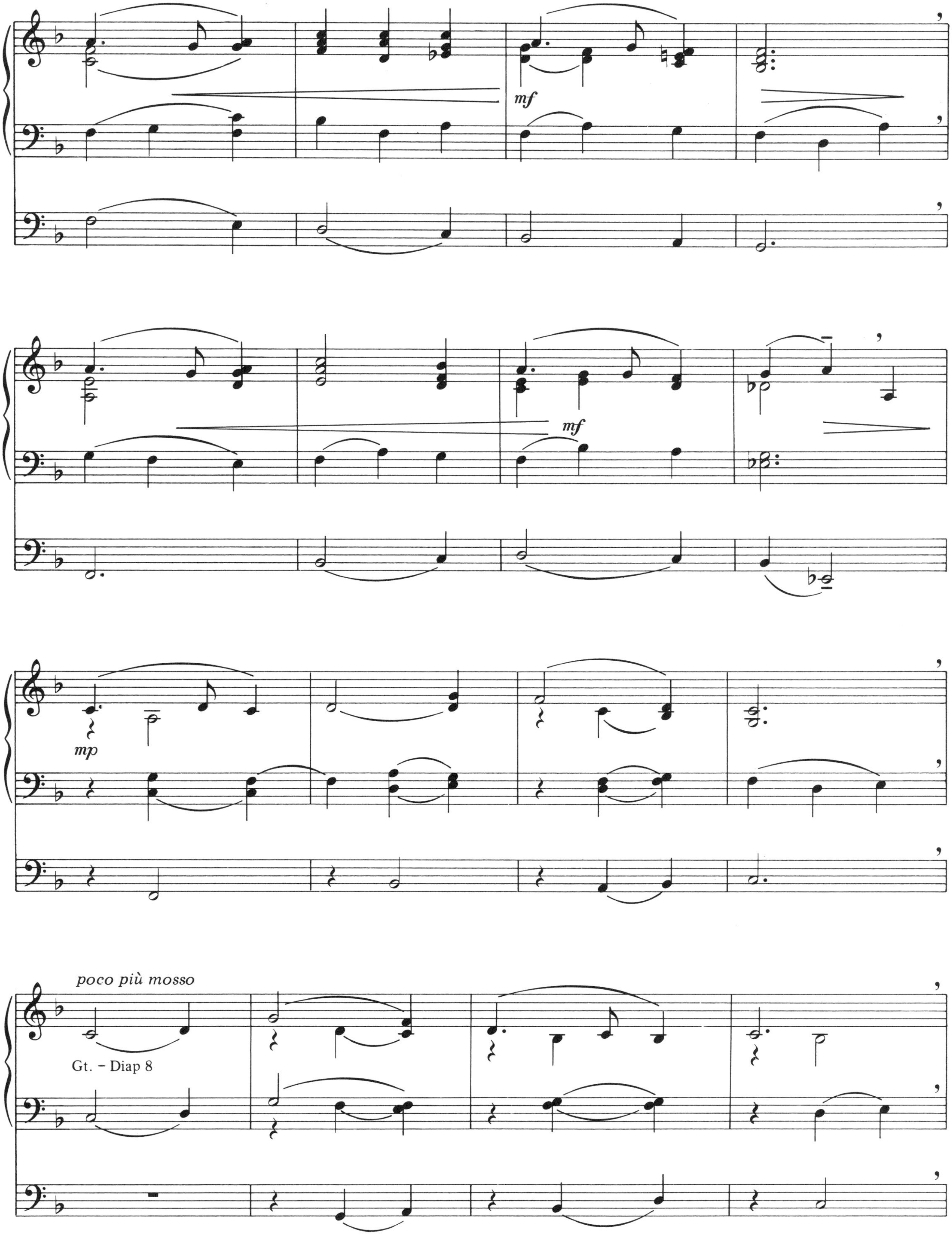
mf
mf
mp
poco più mosso
Gt. – Diap 8

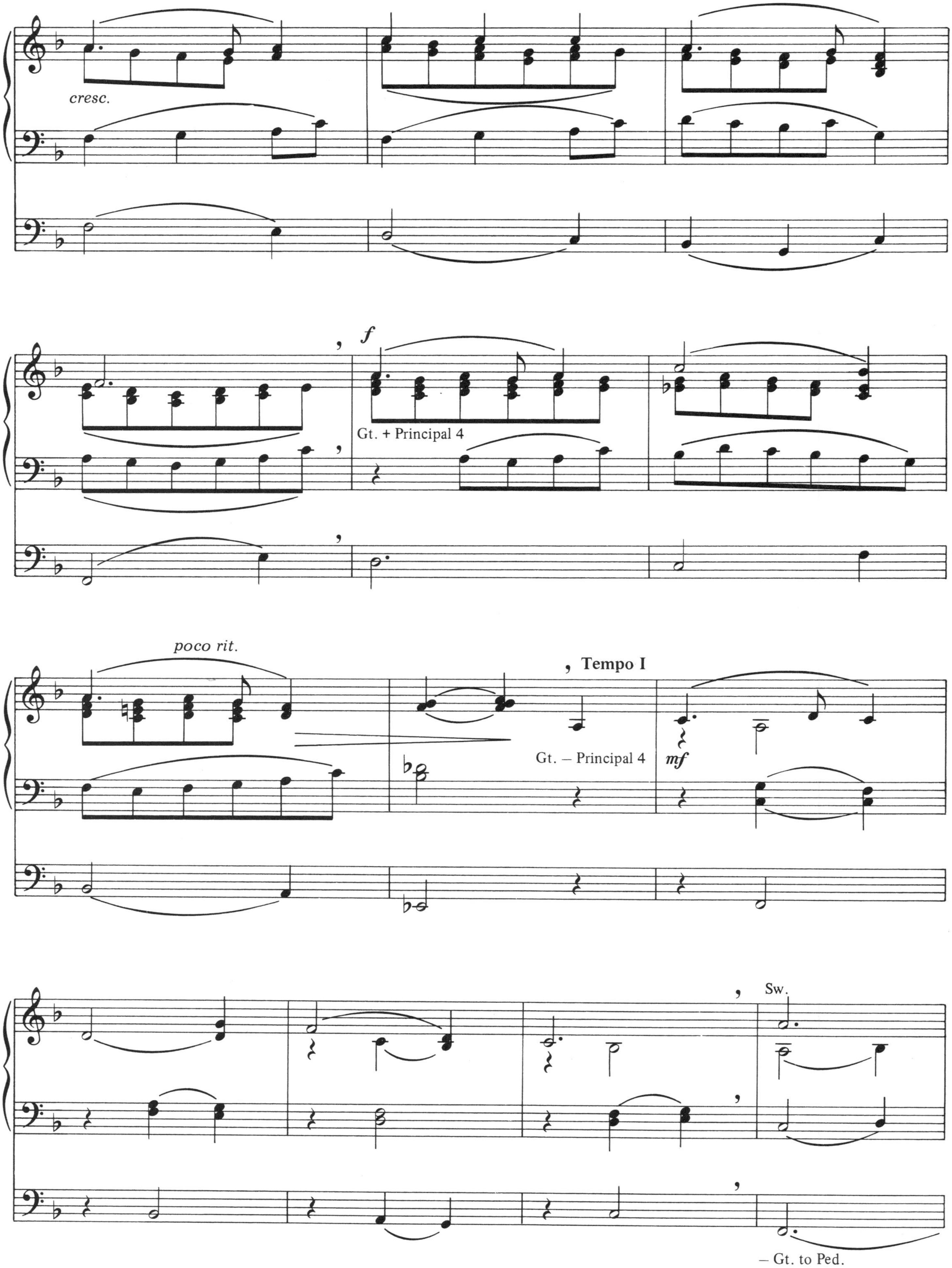
cresc.
f
Gt. + Principal 4
poco rit.
Tempo I
Gt. – Principal 4
mf
Sw.
– Gt. to Ped.

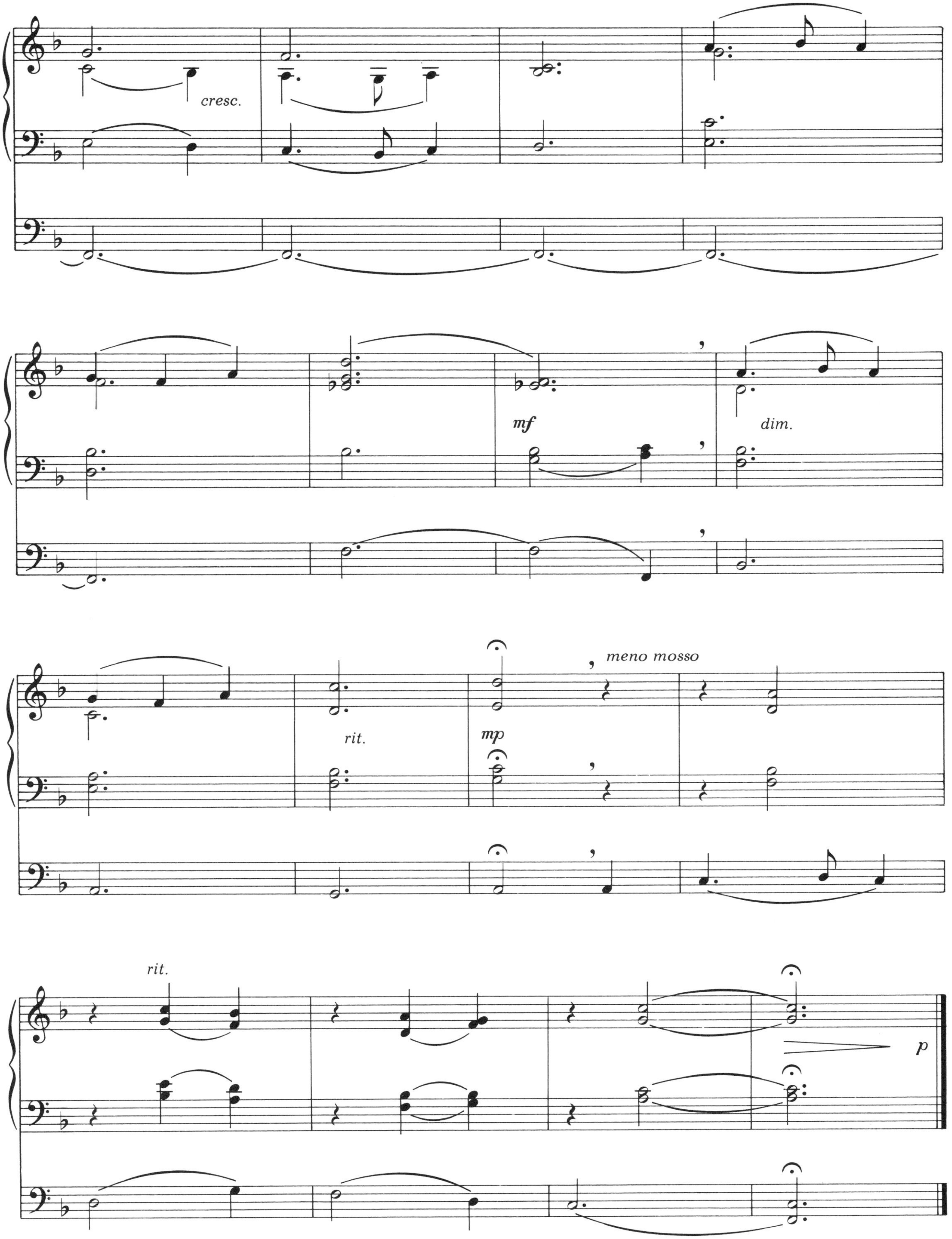
cresc.
mf
dim.
meno mosso
rit.
mp
rit.
p

SECOND PRELUDE in C

Johann Rinck (1770-1846)

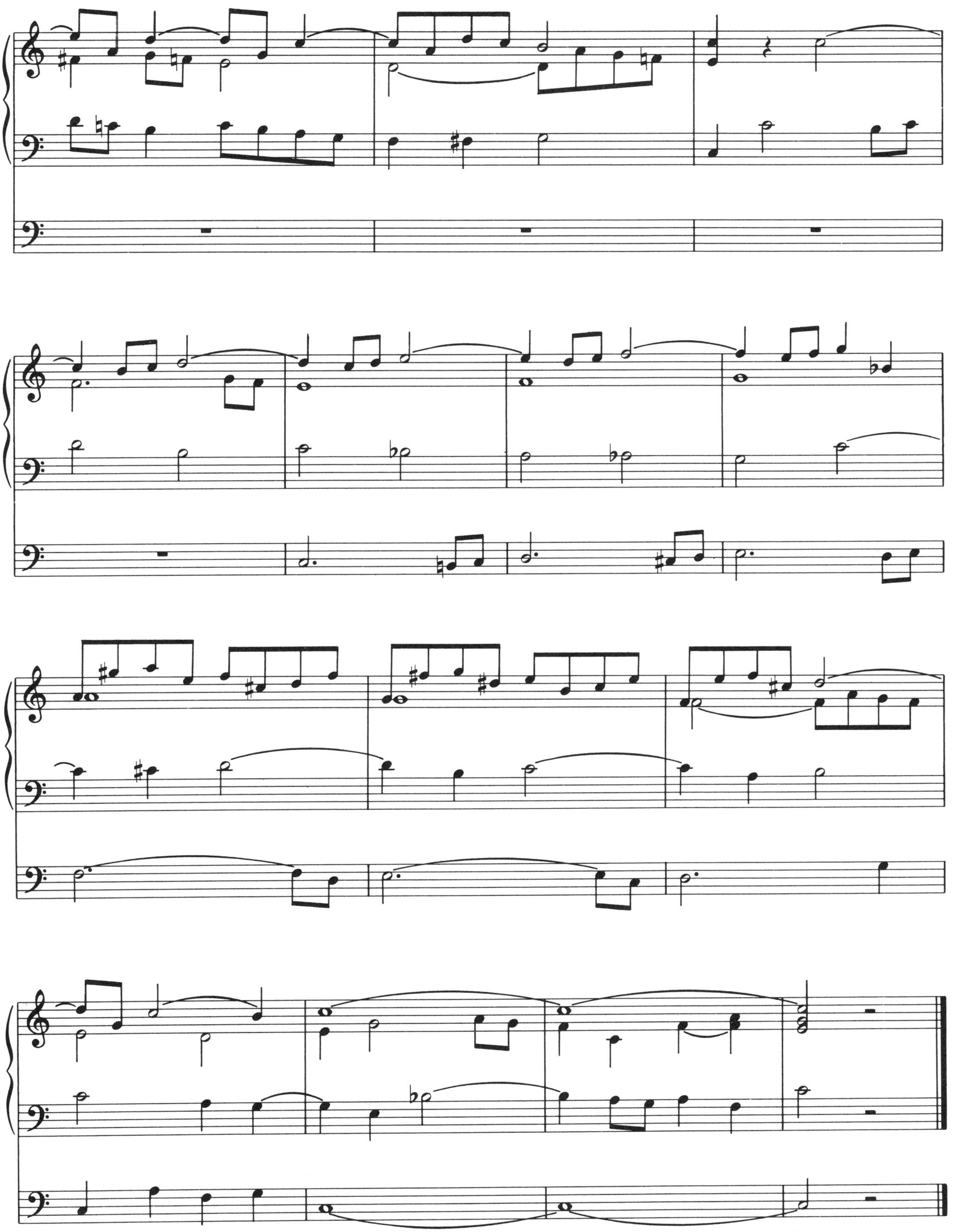

PRELUDE in A

Eugene Thayer (1838-1889)

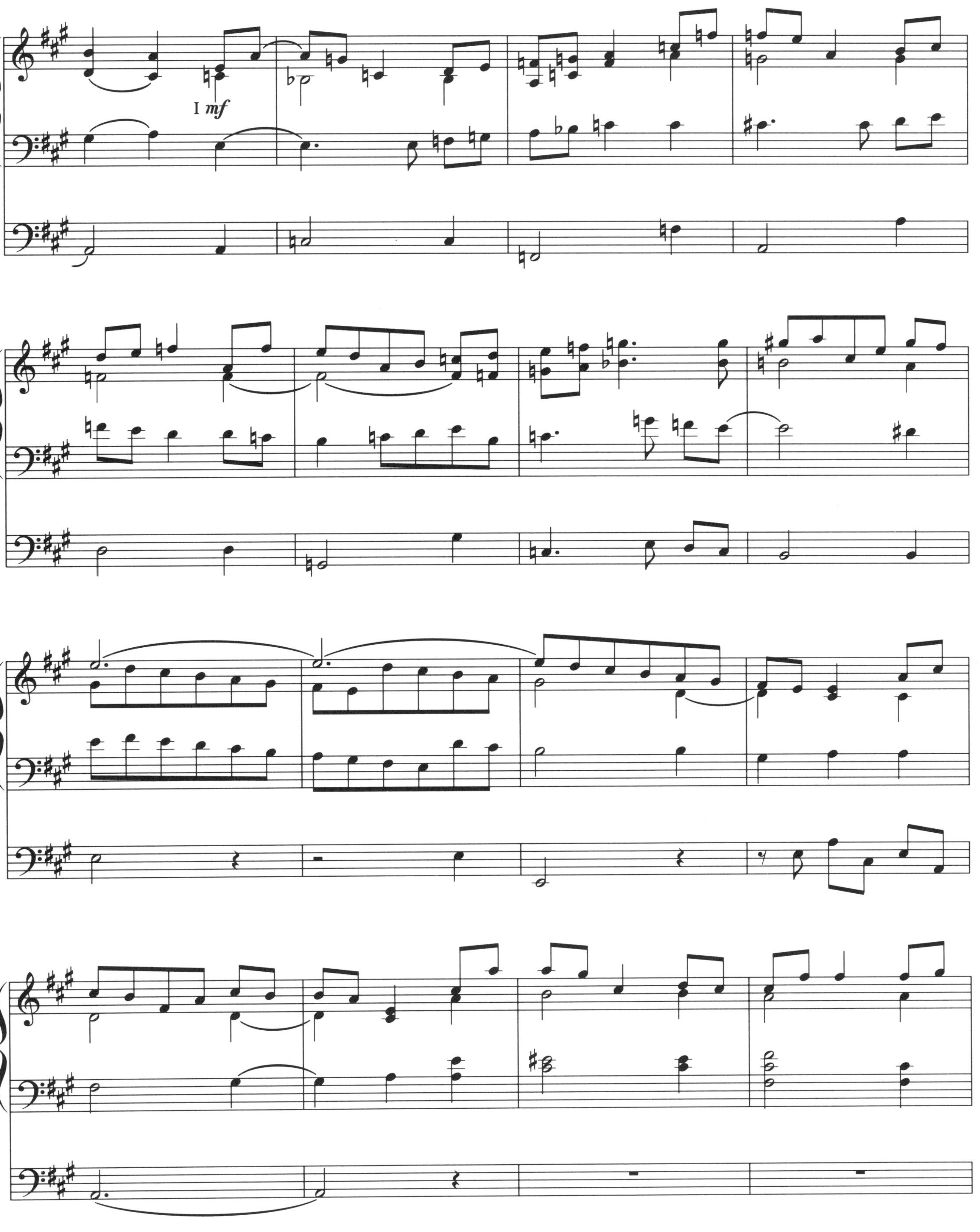
I mf

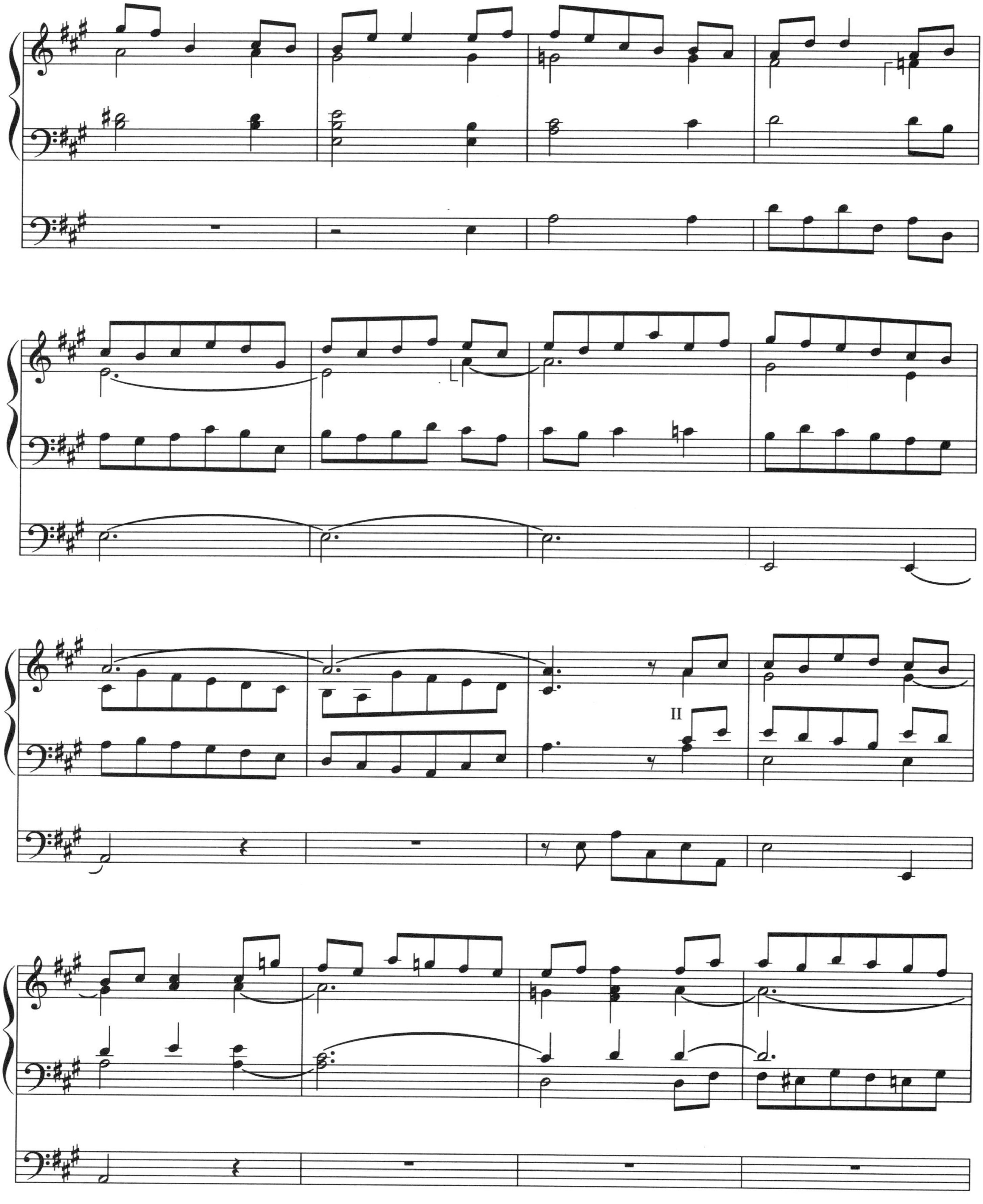
II

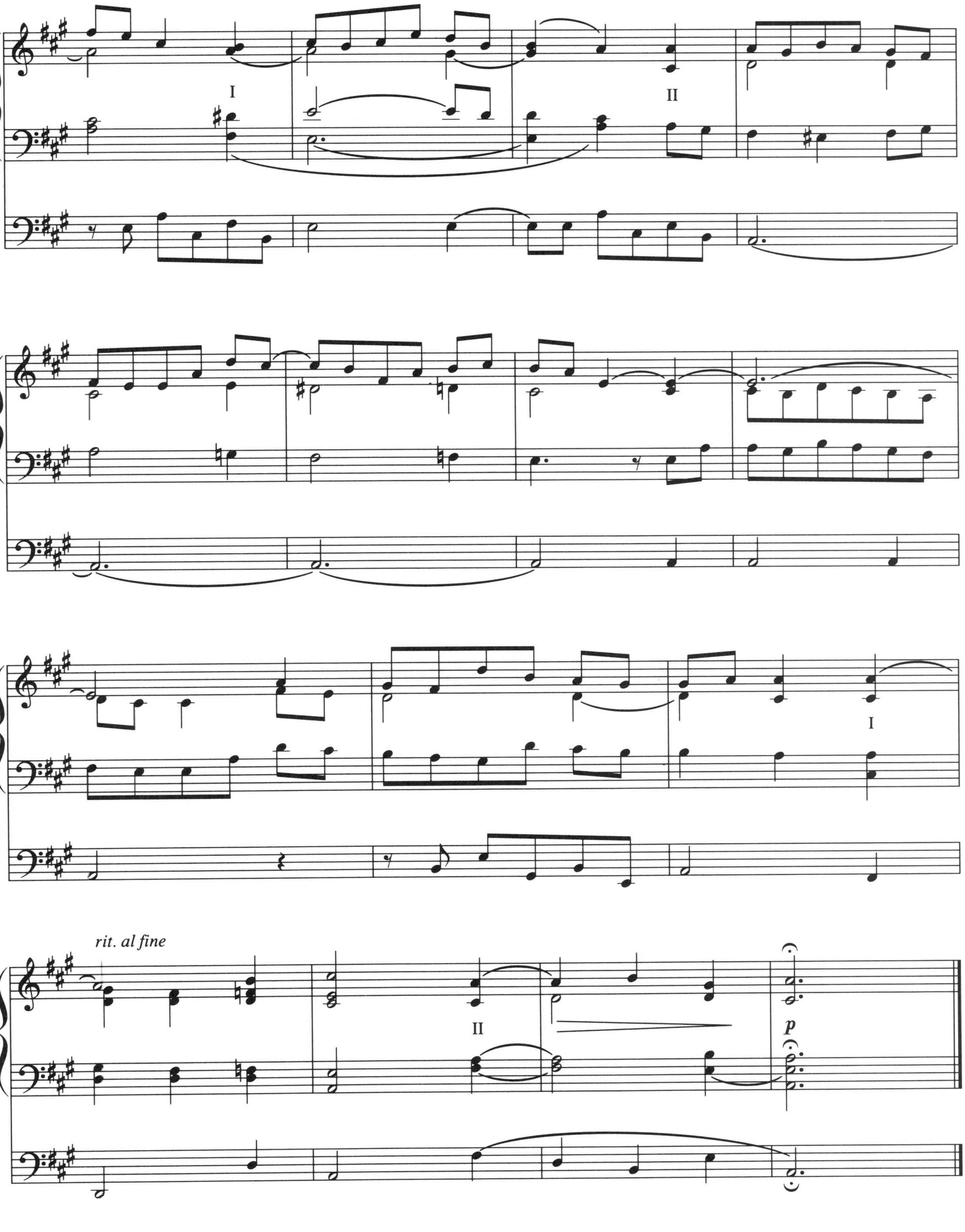
I
II
I
rit. al fine
II
I
p

ELEVATION

Alexandre Guilmant (1837-1911)

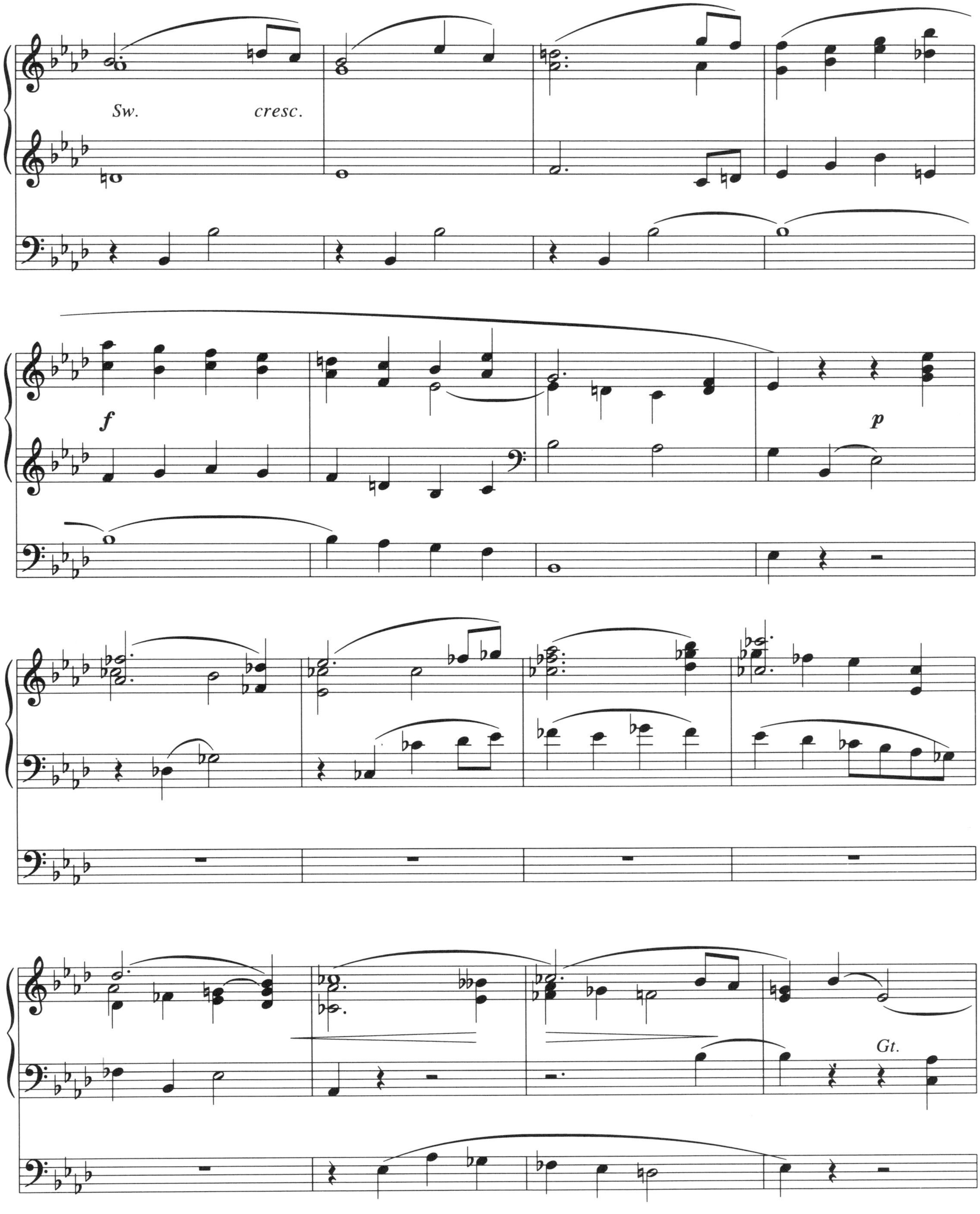
Sw.
cresc.
f
p
Gt.

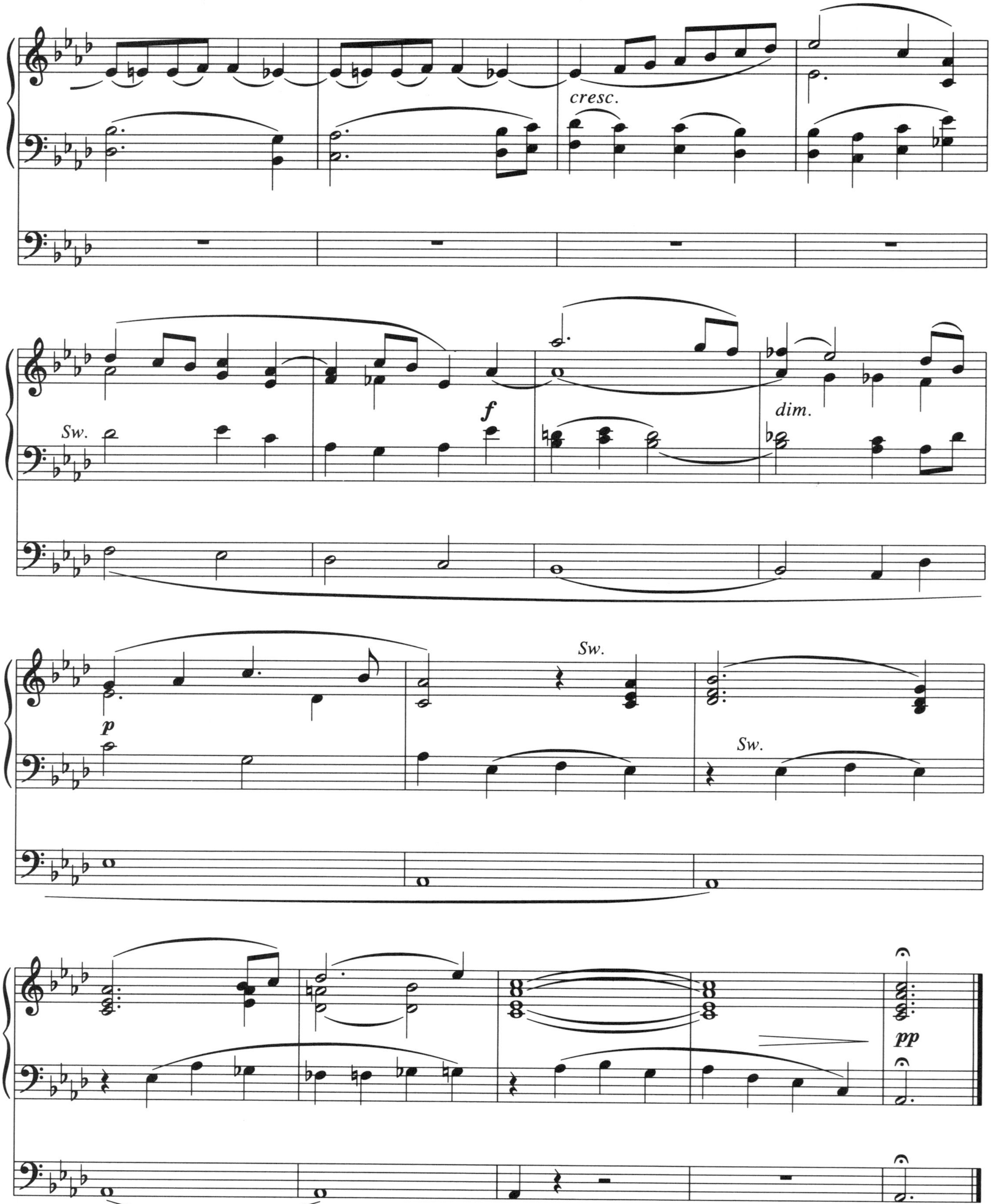
cresc.
Sw.
f
dim.
p
Sw.
Sw.
pp

MELODY

Horatio William Parker (1863-1919)

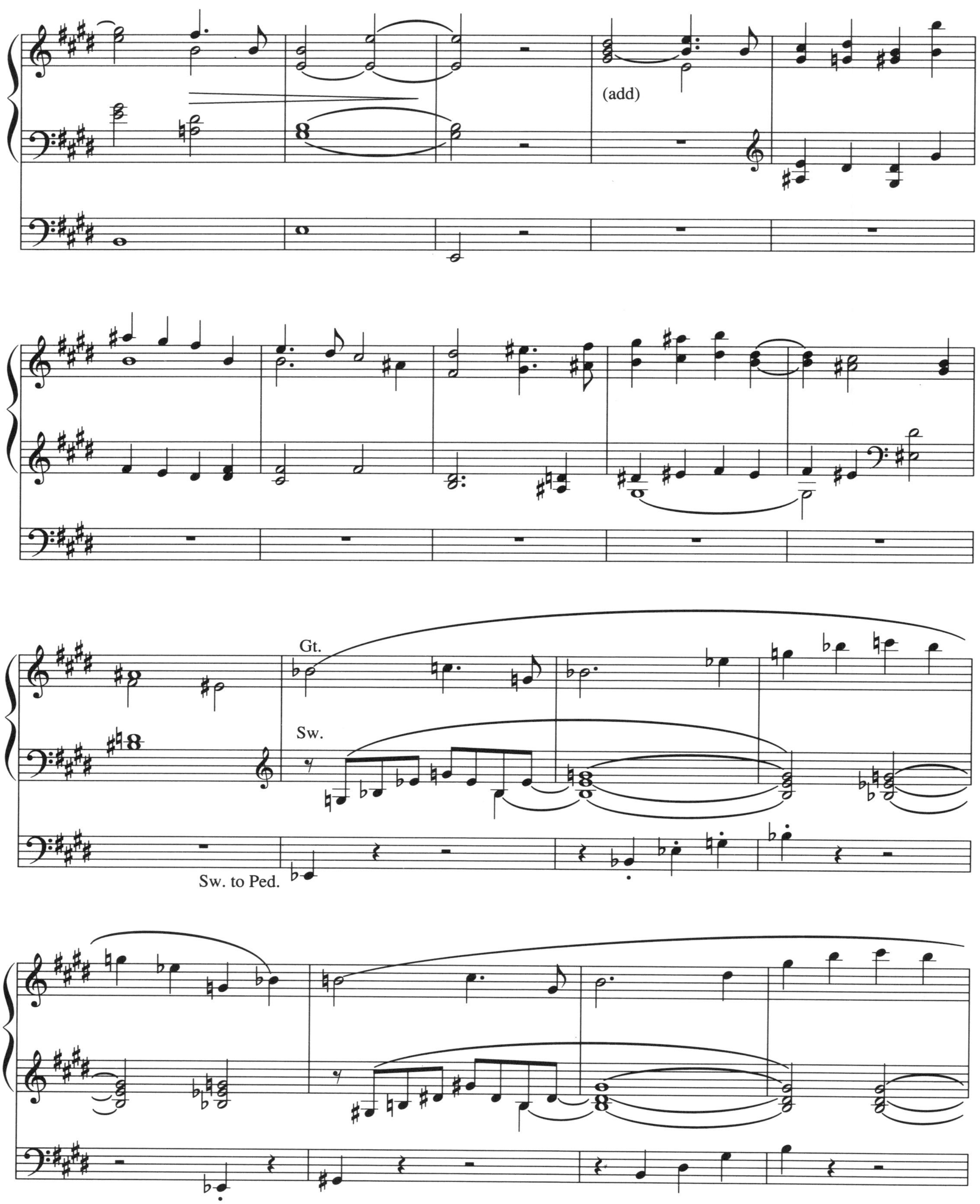
(add)
Gt.
Sw.
Sw. to Ped.

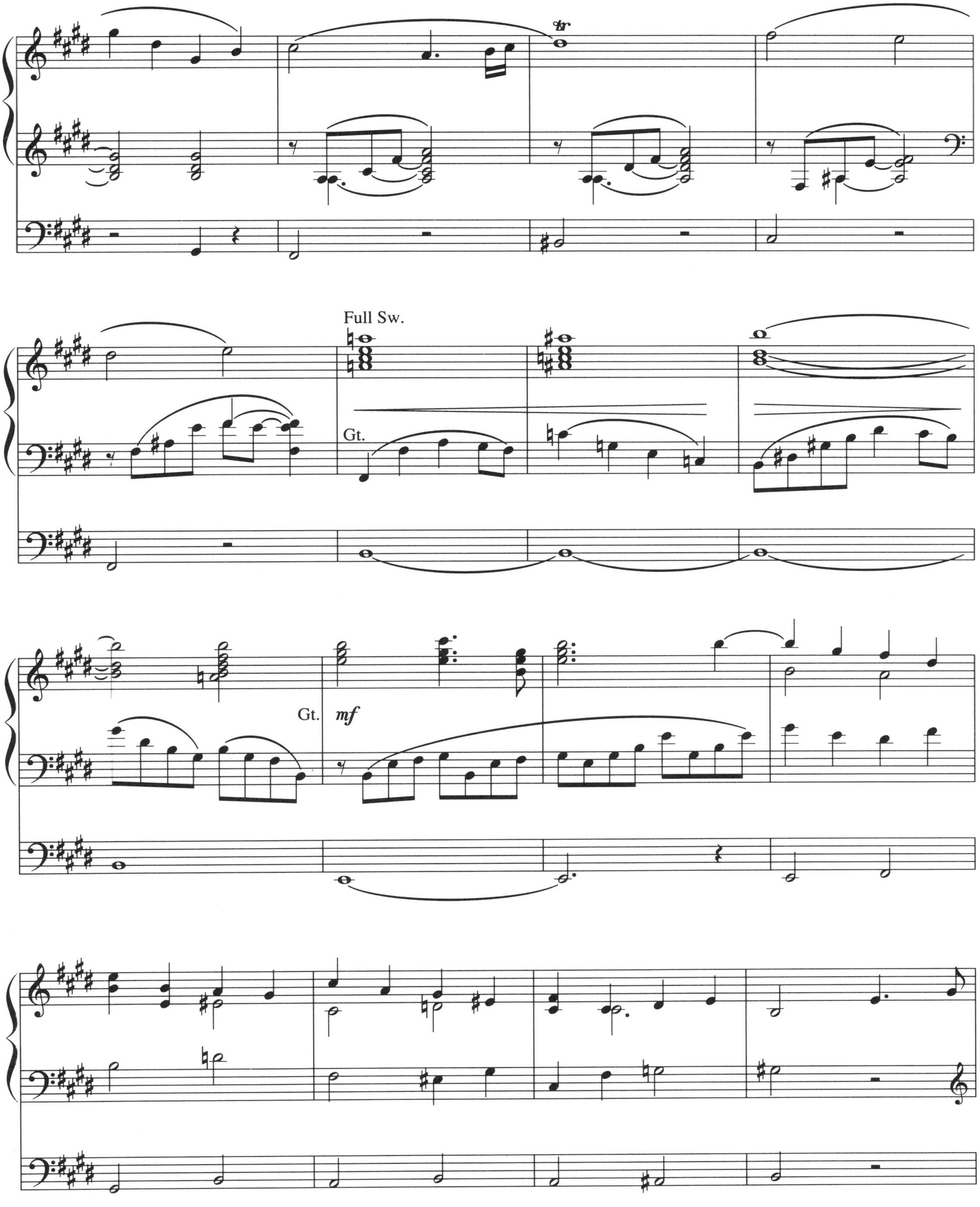
tr
Full Sw.
Gt.
Gt.
mf

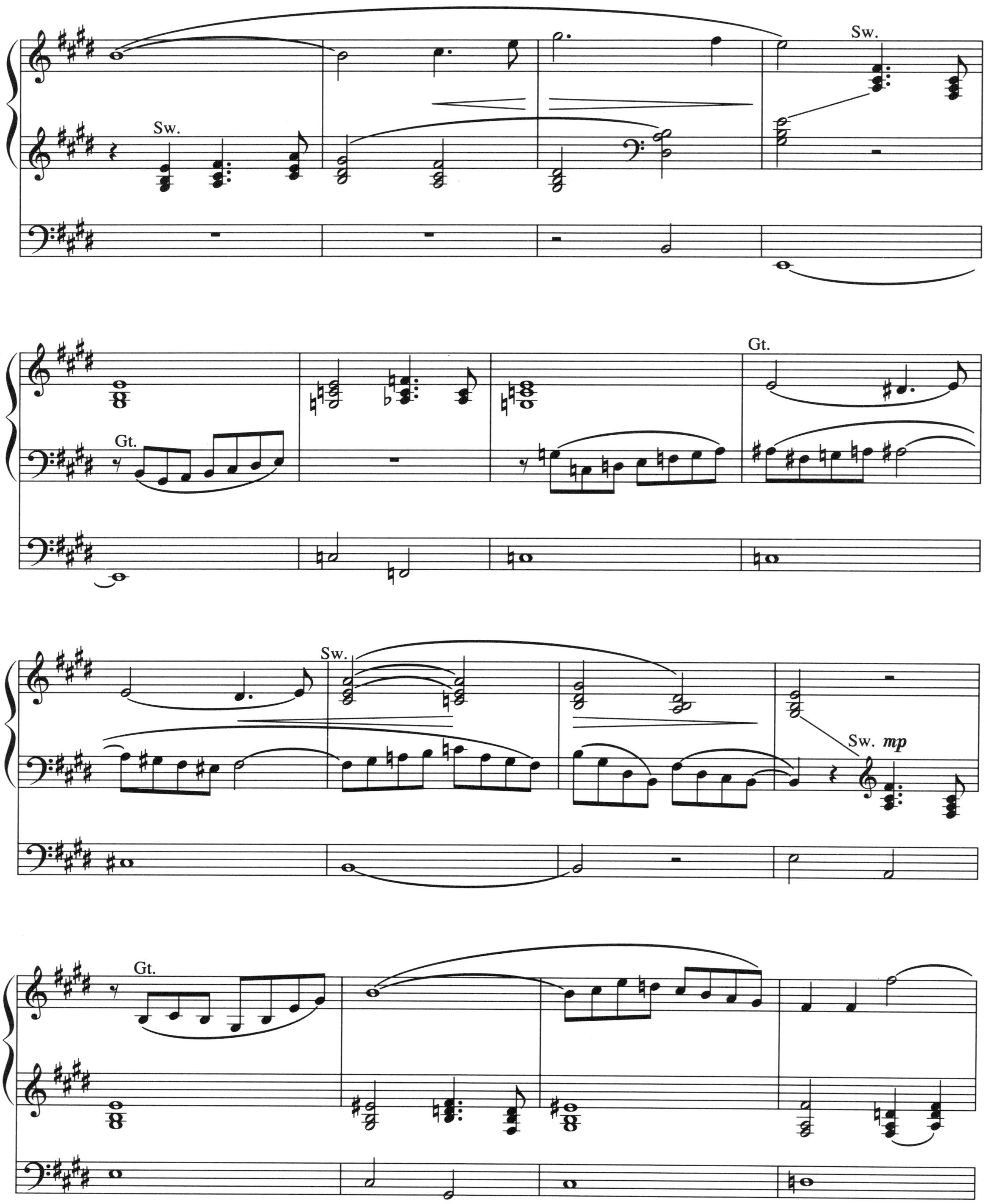
Sw.
Sw.
Gt.
Gt.
Sw.
Sw. mp
Gt.

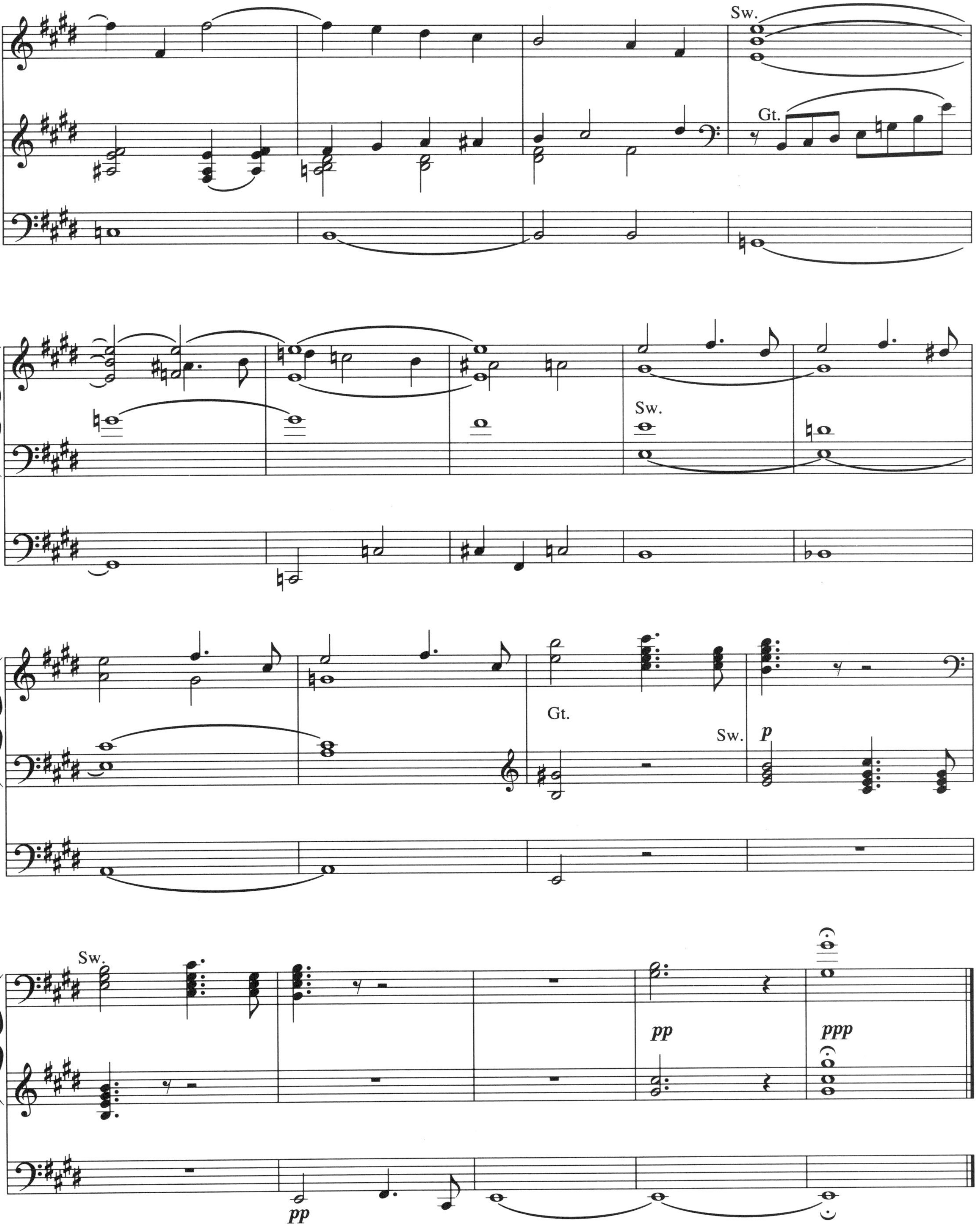
Sw.
Gt.
Sw.
Gt.
Sw.
p
Sw.
pp
pp
ppp

PRELUDE in F♯ MINOR

Johann Rinck (1770-1846)

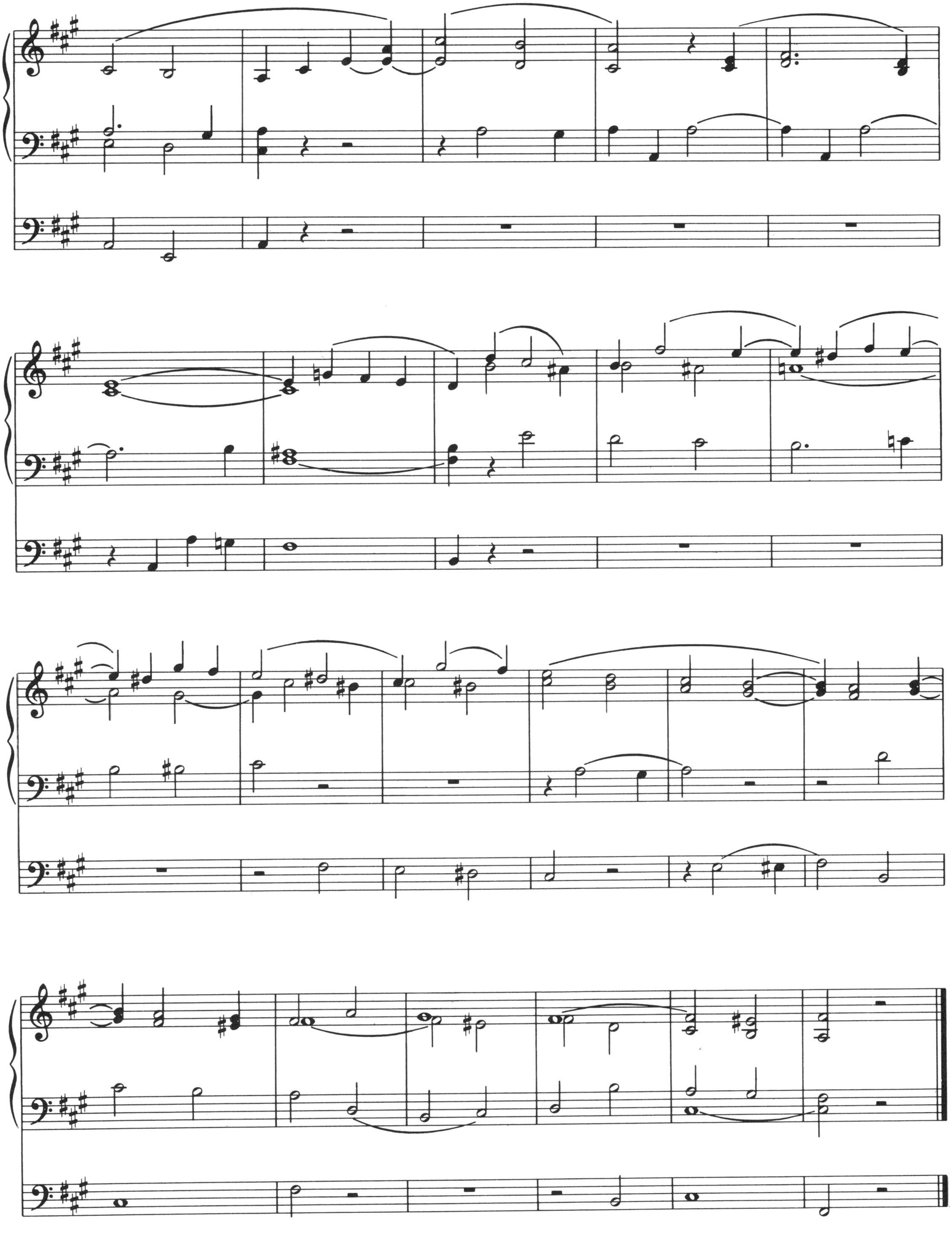

INTERMEZZO in F

Alan Gray (1855-1935)

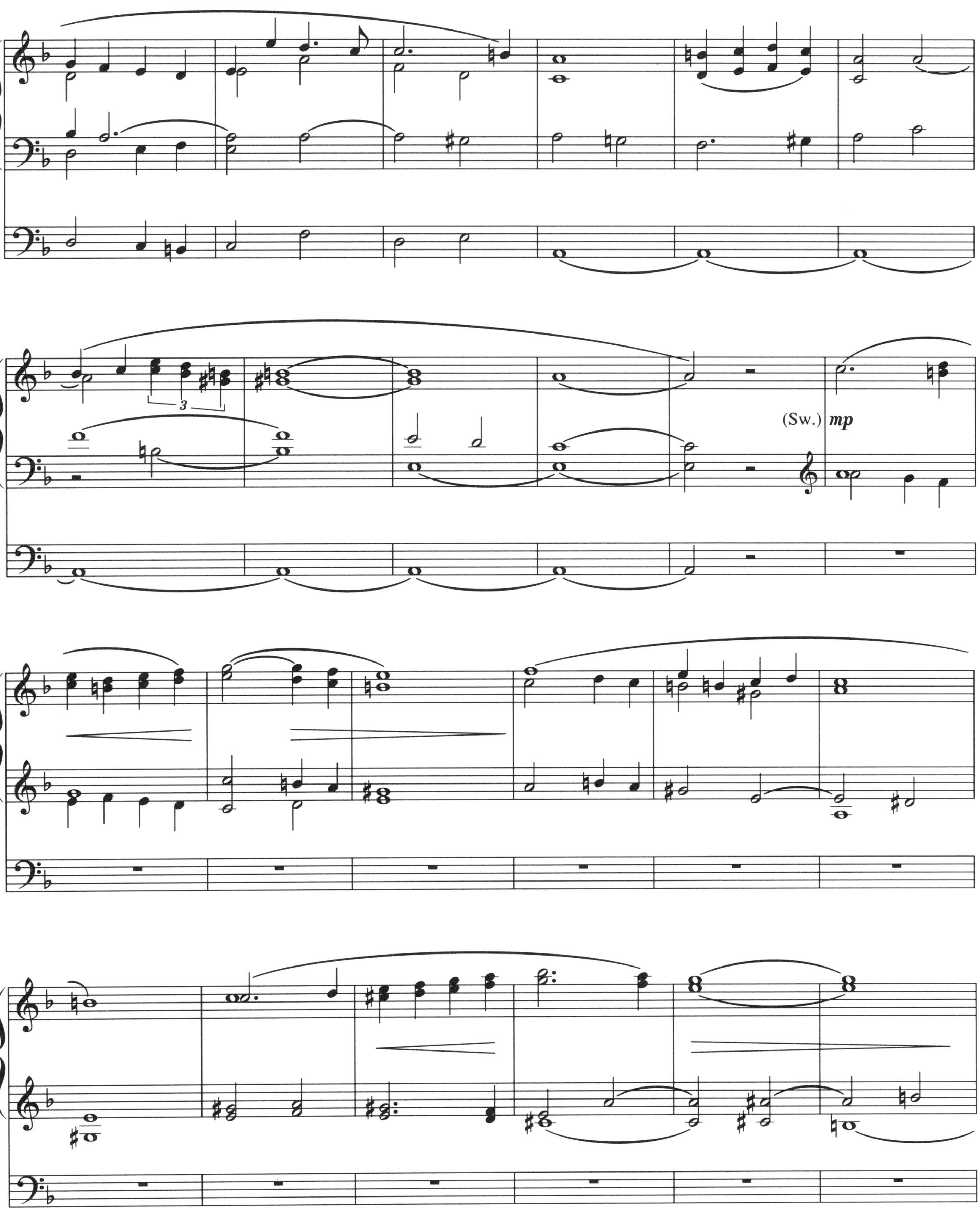
(Sw.) mp

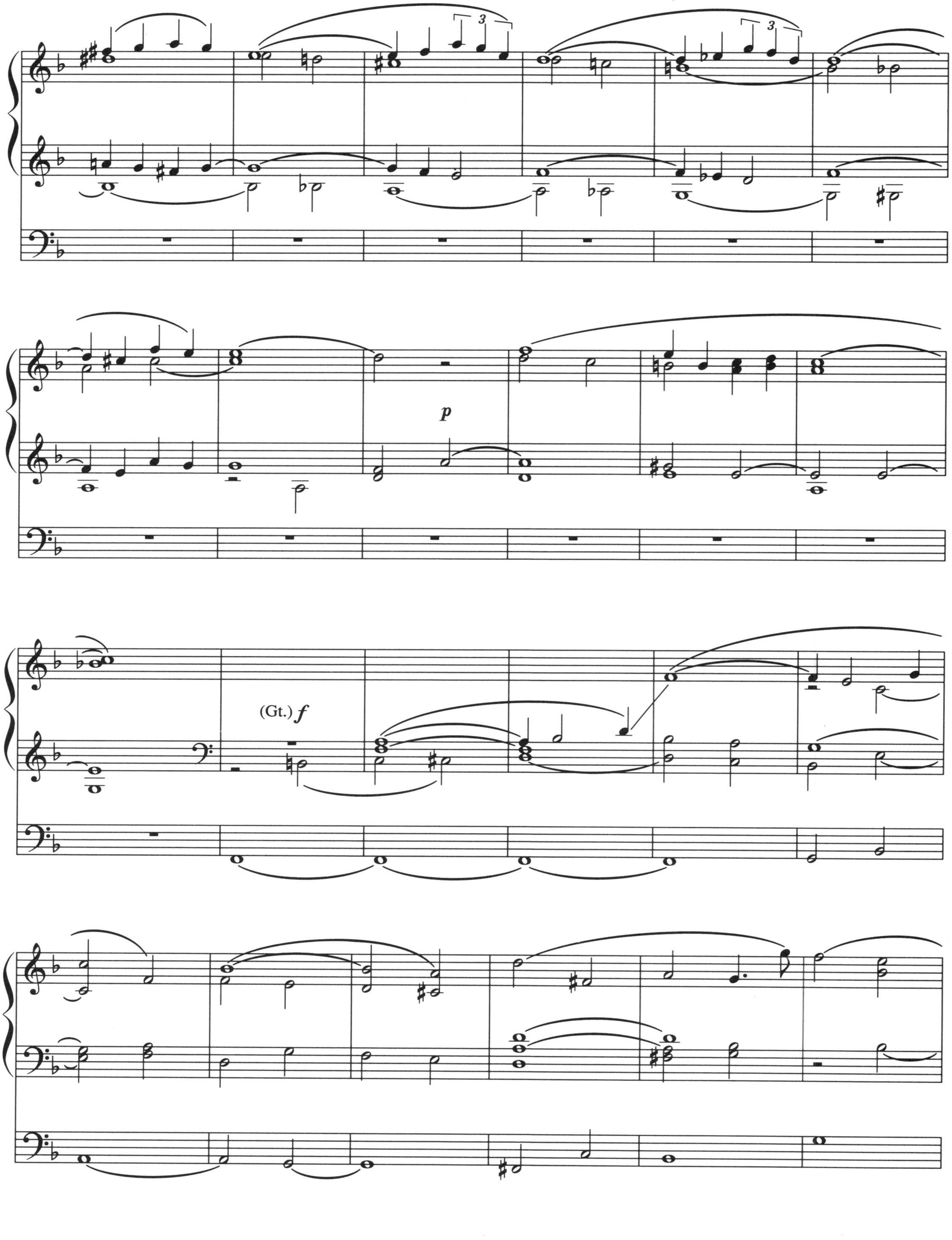
3
3
p
(Gt.) f

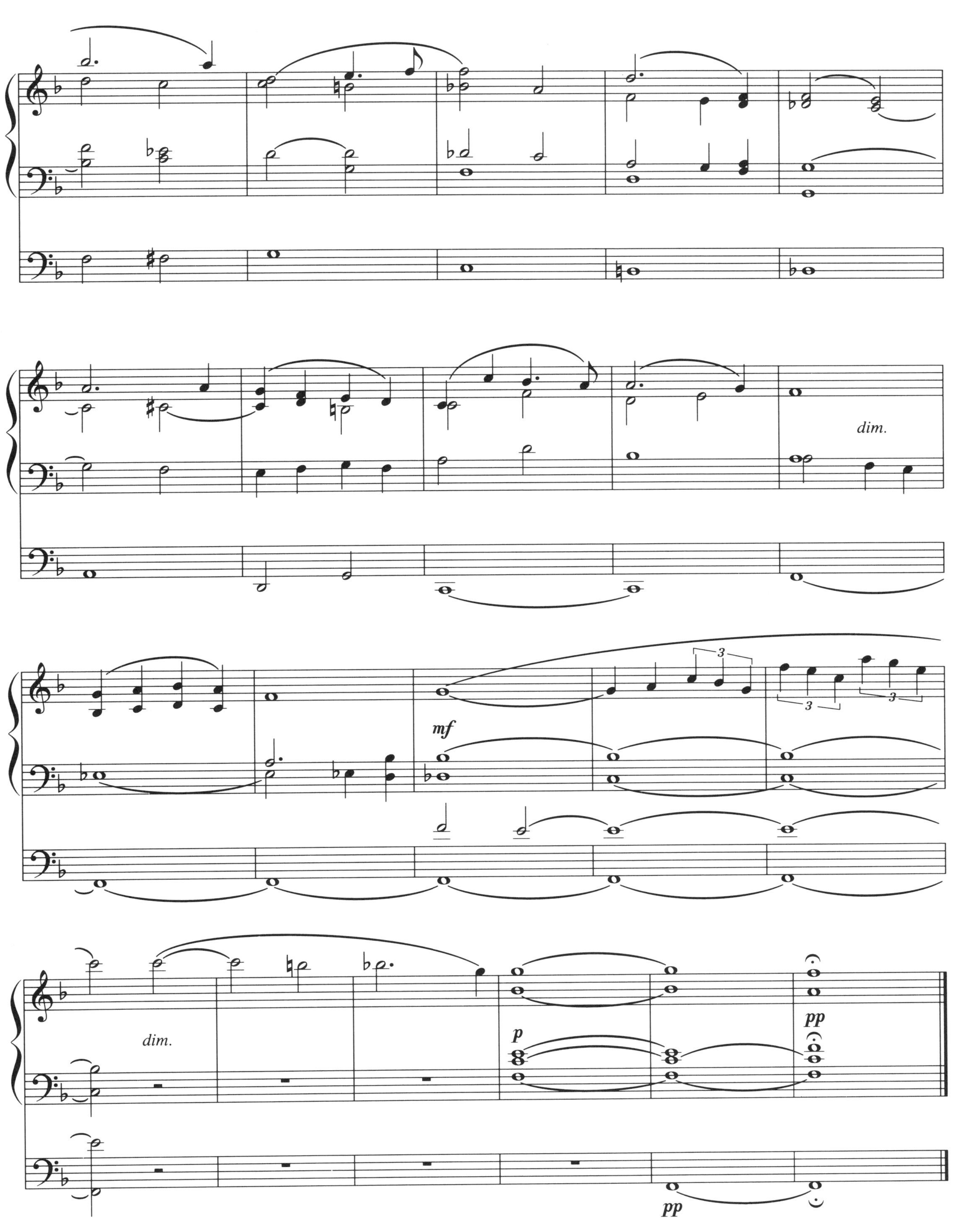
dim.
mf
3
3
3
dim.
p
pp
pp

For Malcolm McKelvey

POSTLUDE

on 'St Columba'
Christopher Tambling (*b.*1964)

Gt. to Mixtures
Sw. to Mixtures

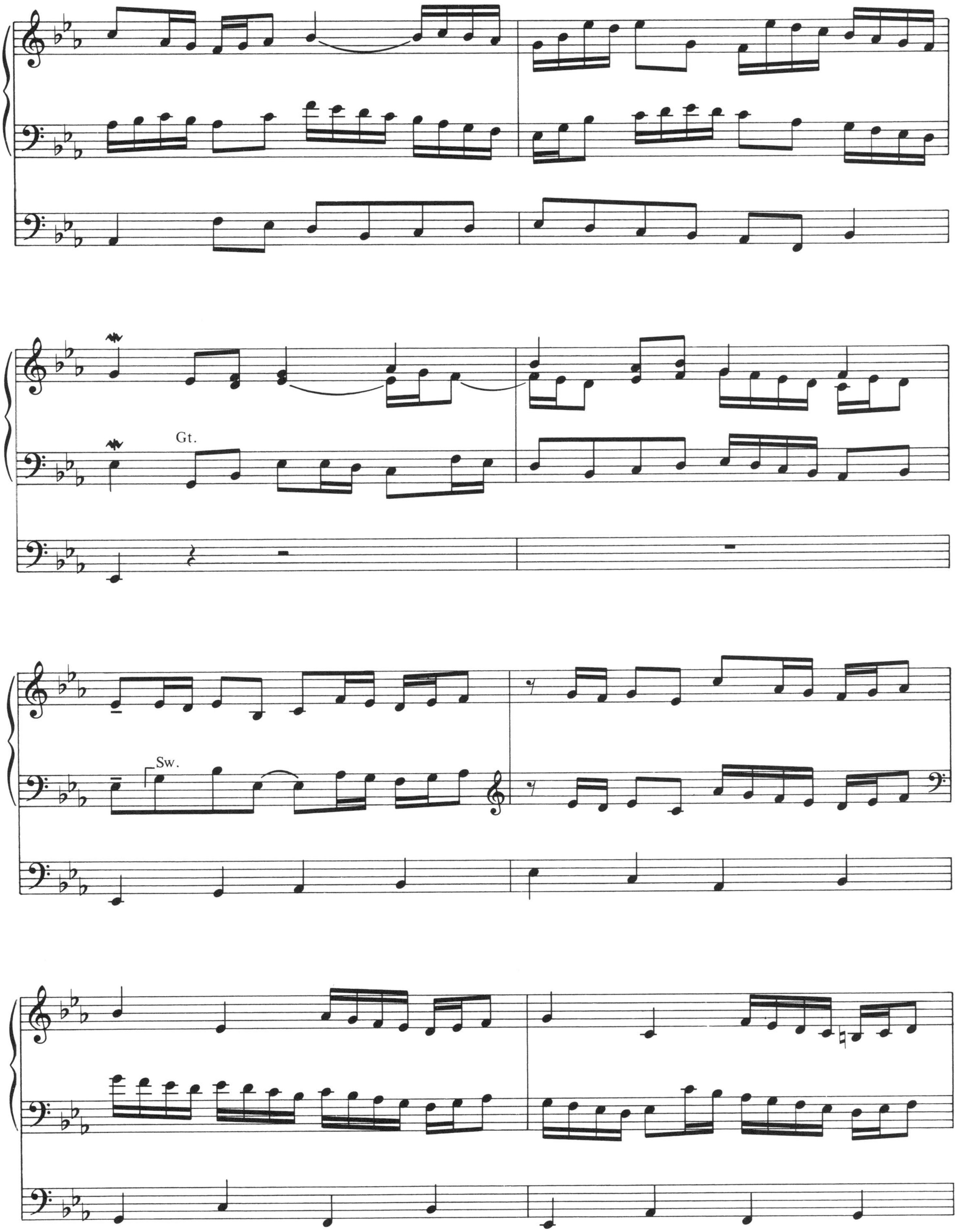
Gt.
Sw.

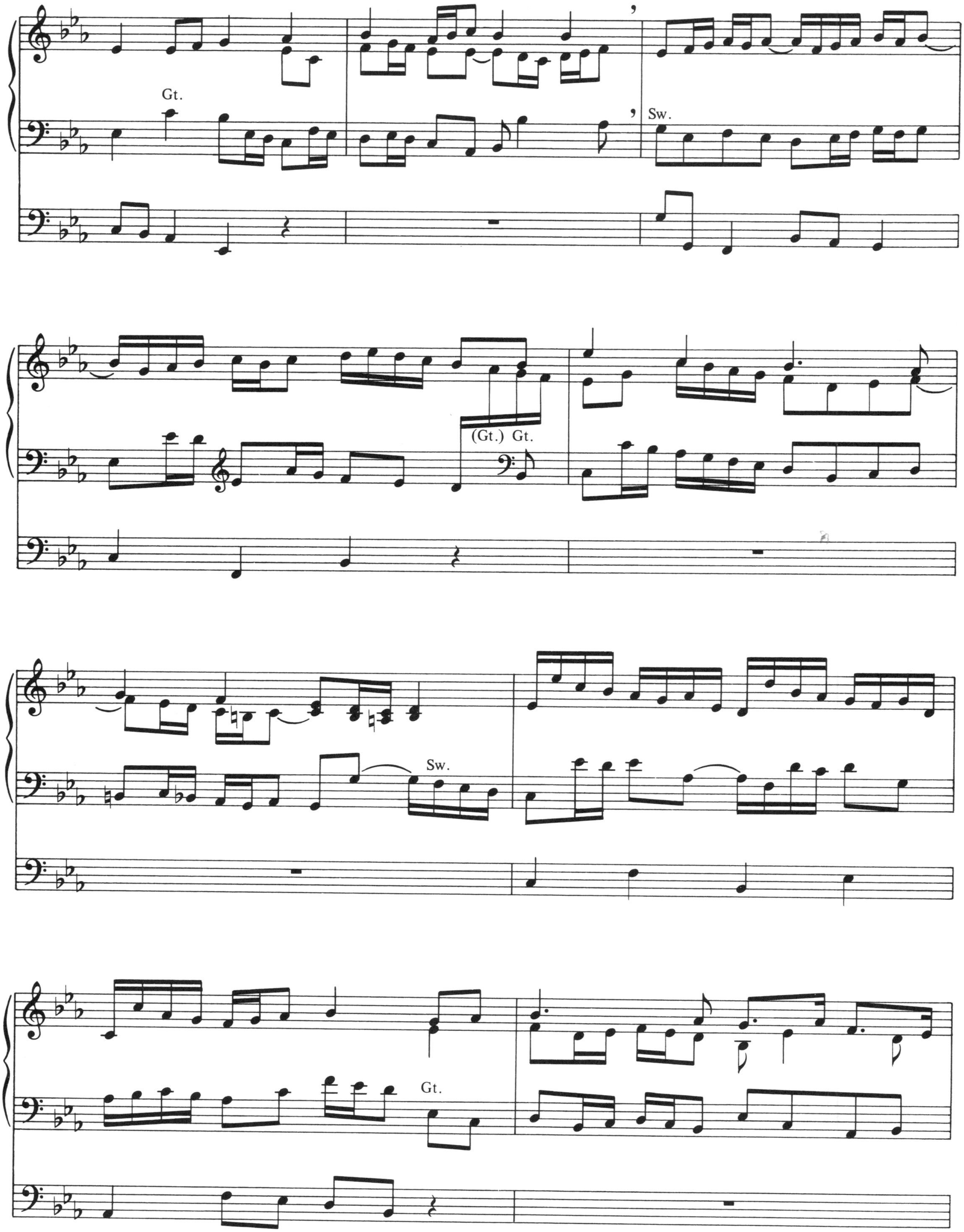
Gt.
Sw.
(Gt.) Gt.
Sw.
Gt.

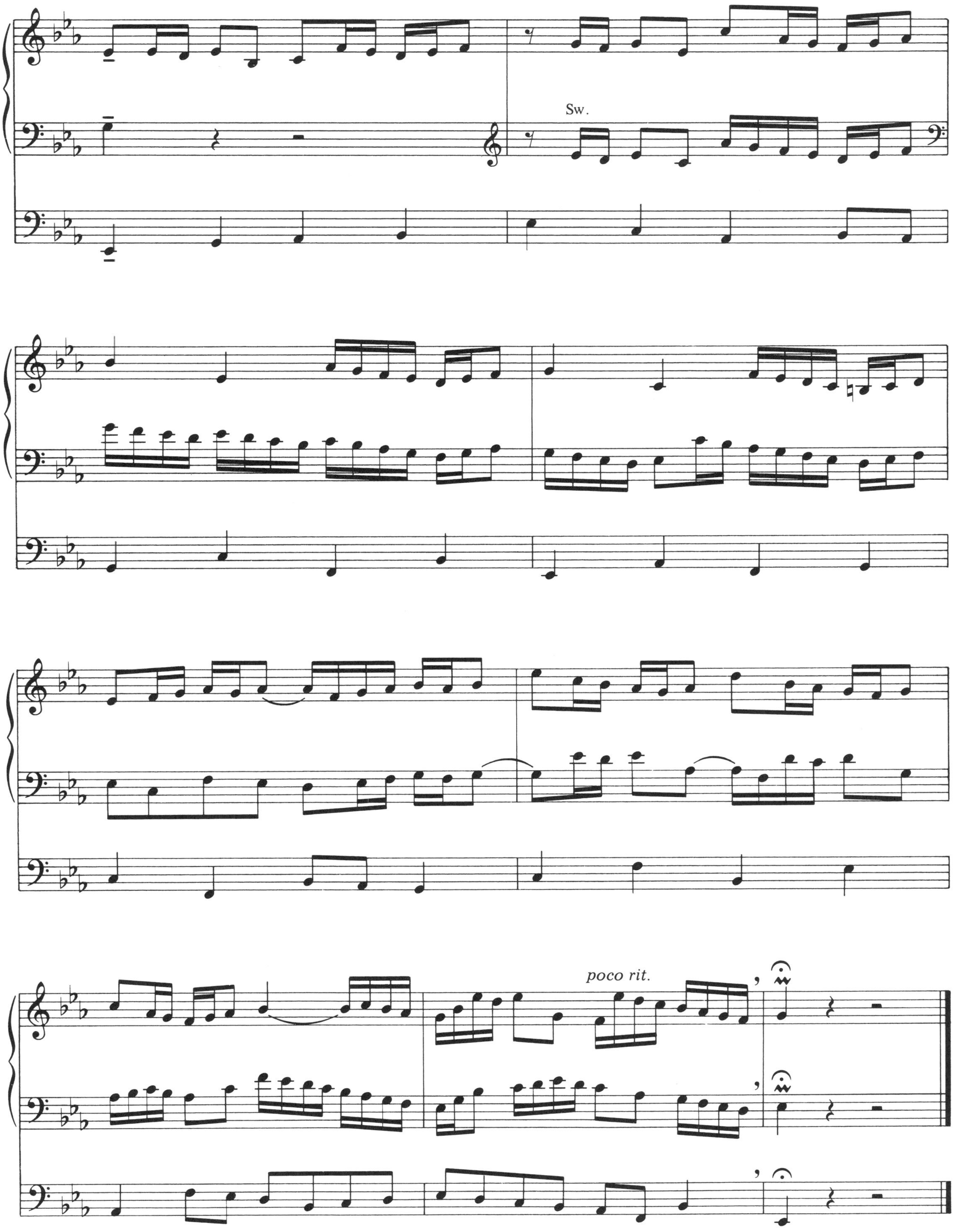
Sw.
poco rit.

PRELUDE in E

Johann Rinck (1770-1846)

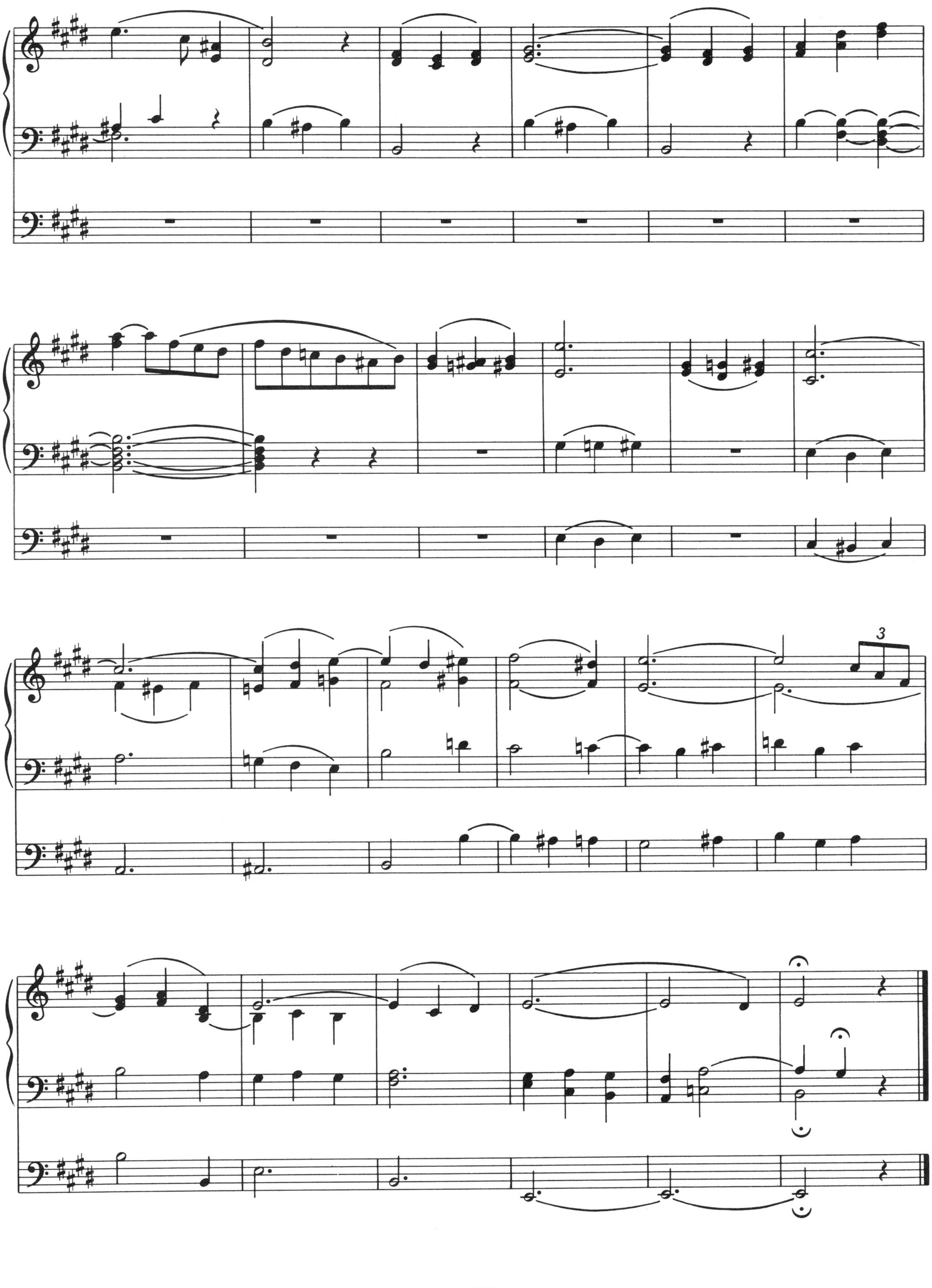
3

ADAGIO

François Verhelst (1853-?)

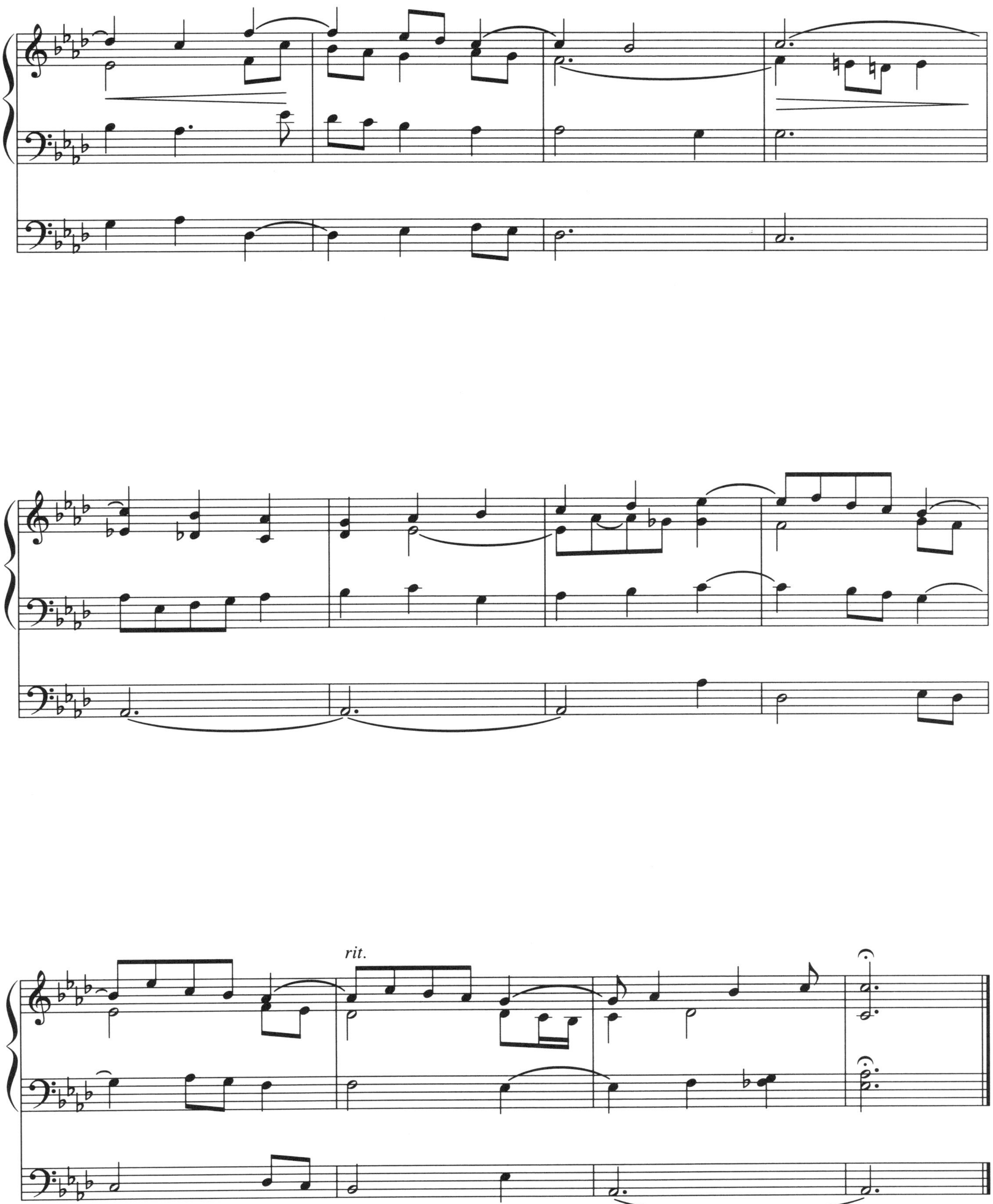
rit.

MARCH in D

Alexandre Guilmant (1837-1911)

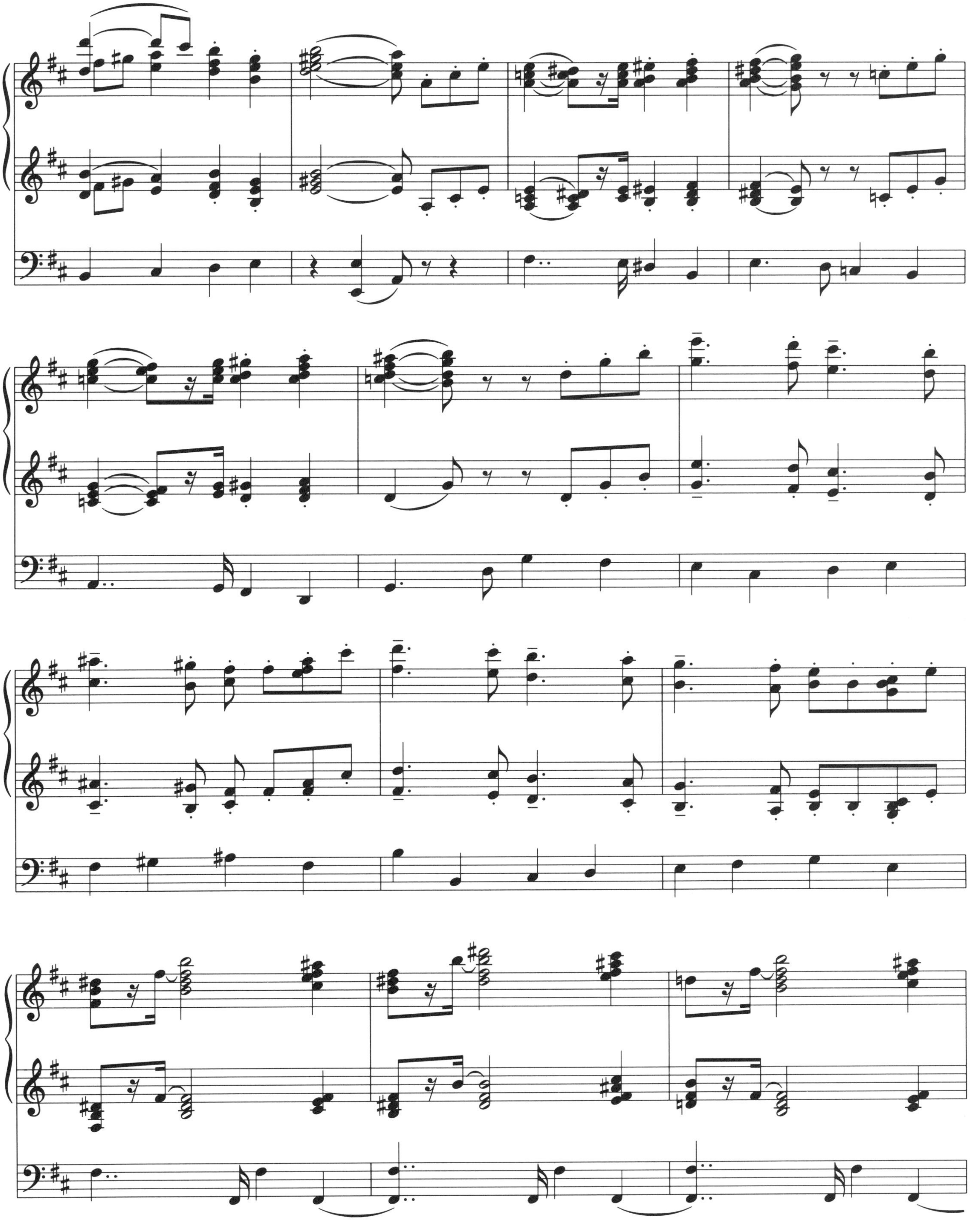

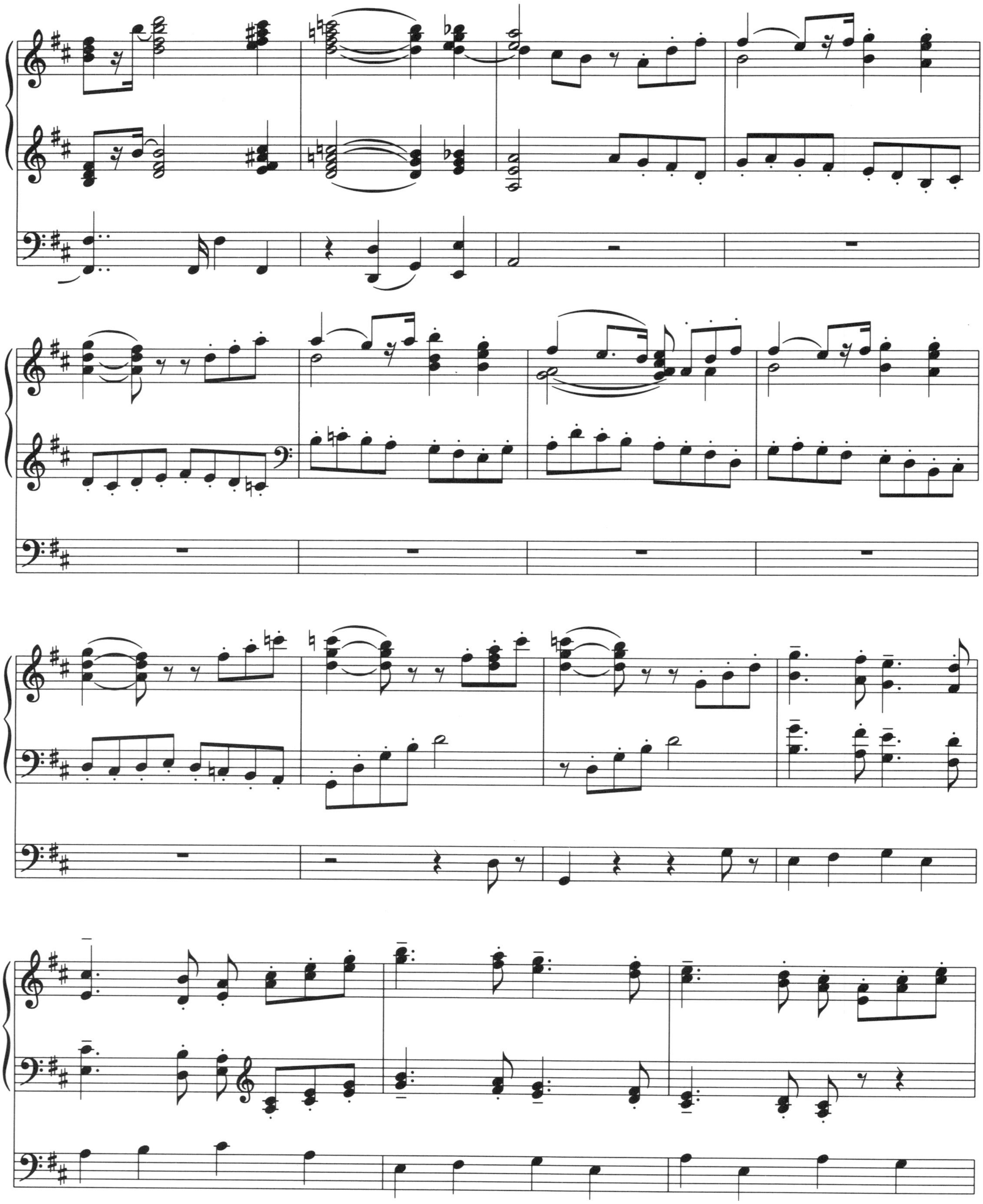

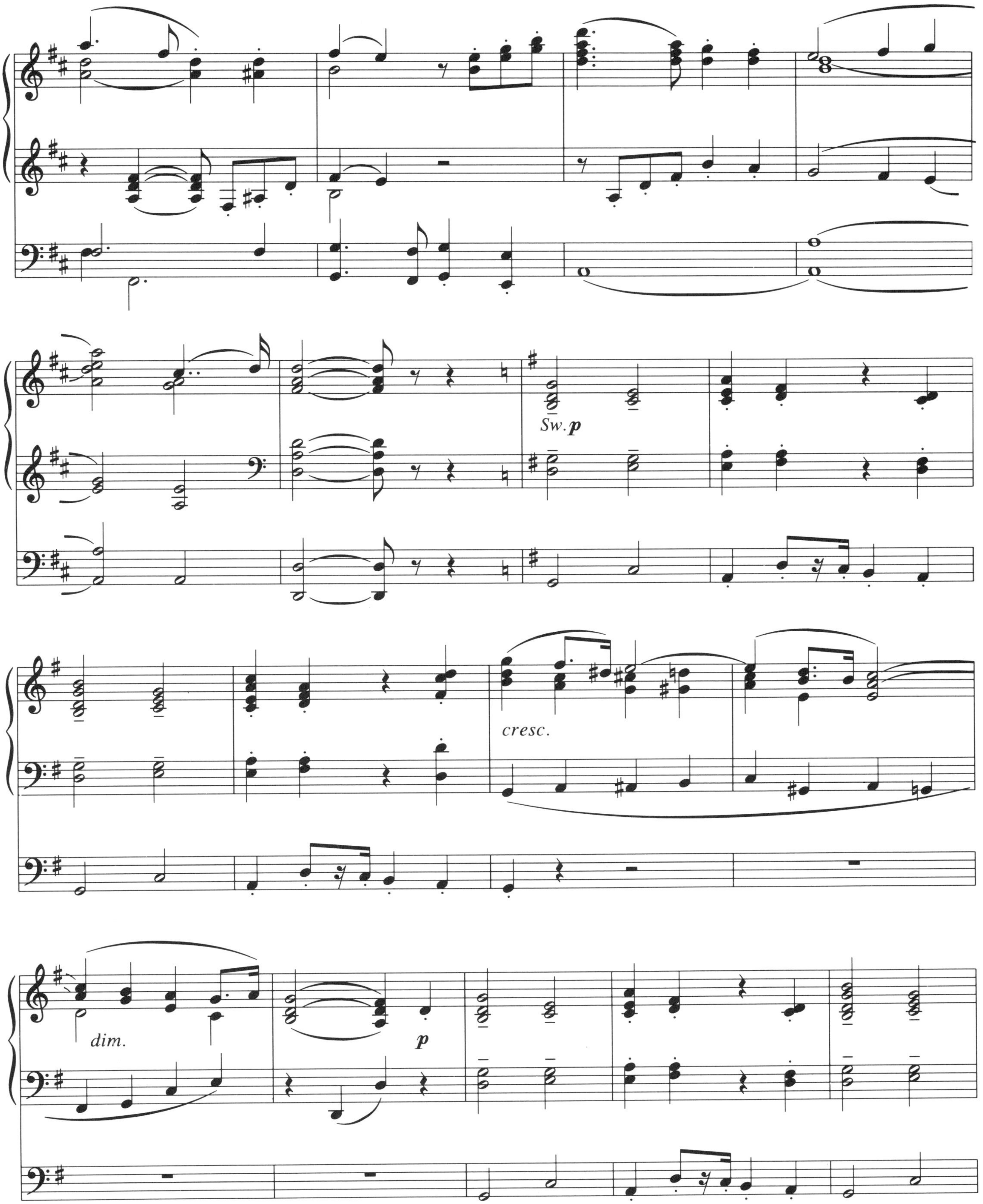
Sw. p
cresc.
dim.
p

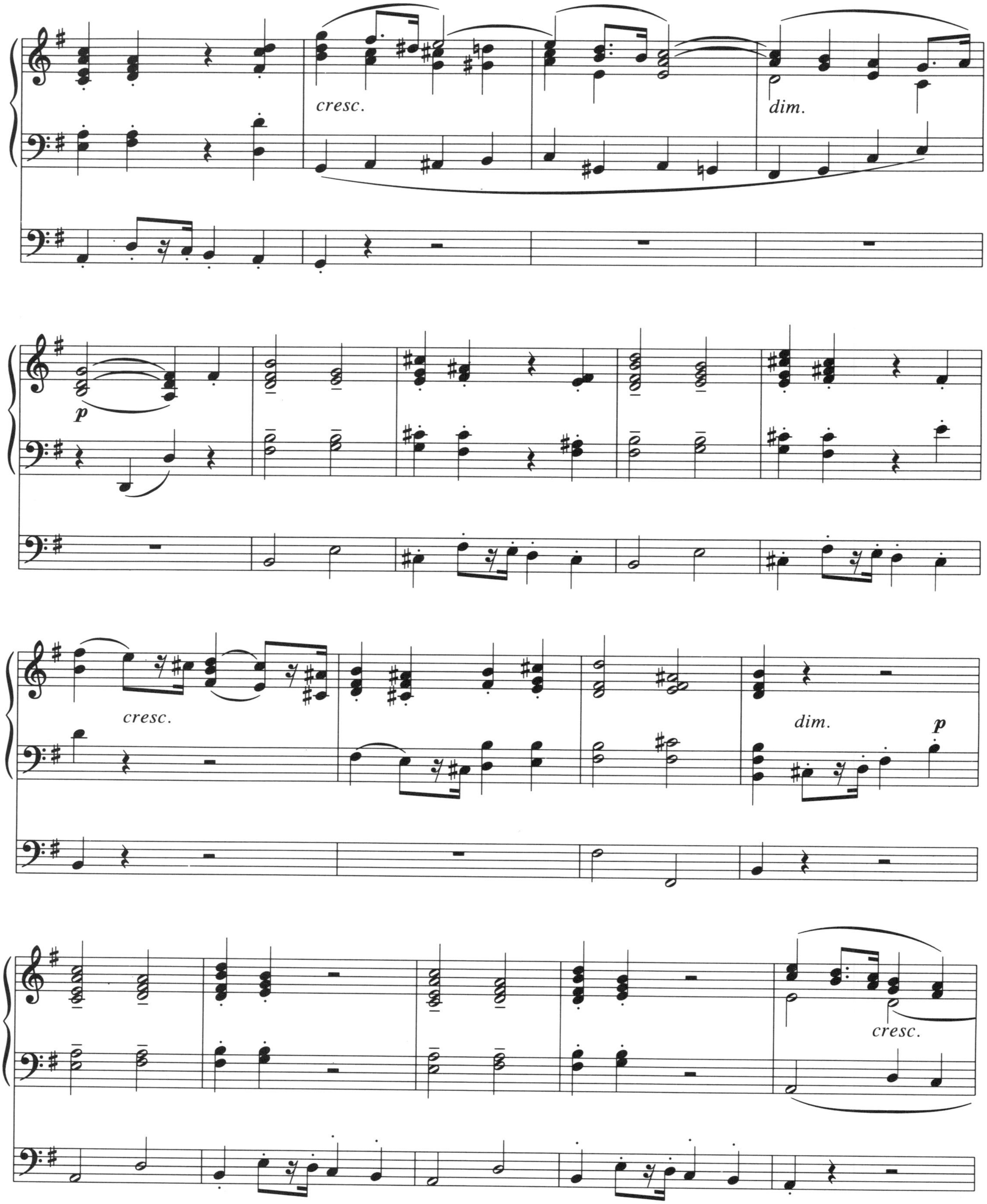
cresc.
dim.
p
cresc.
dim.
p
cresc.

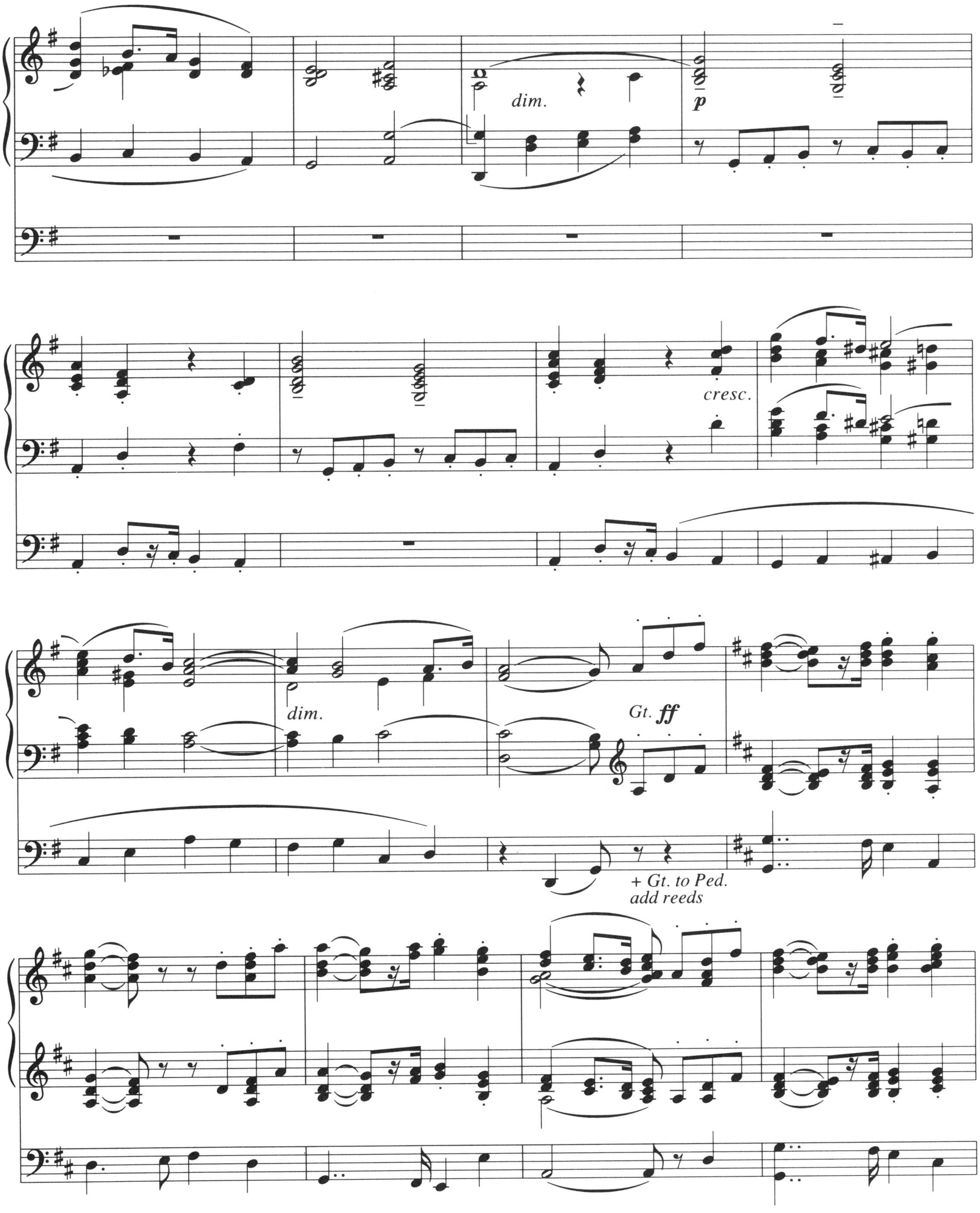
dim.
p
cresc.
dim.
Gt. ff
+ Gt. to Ped.
add reeds

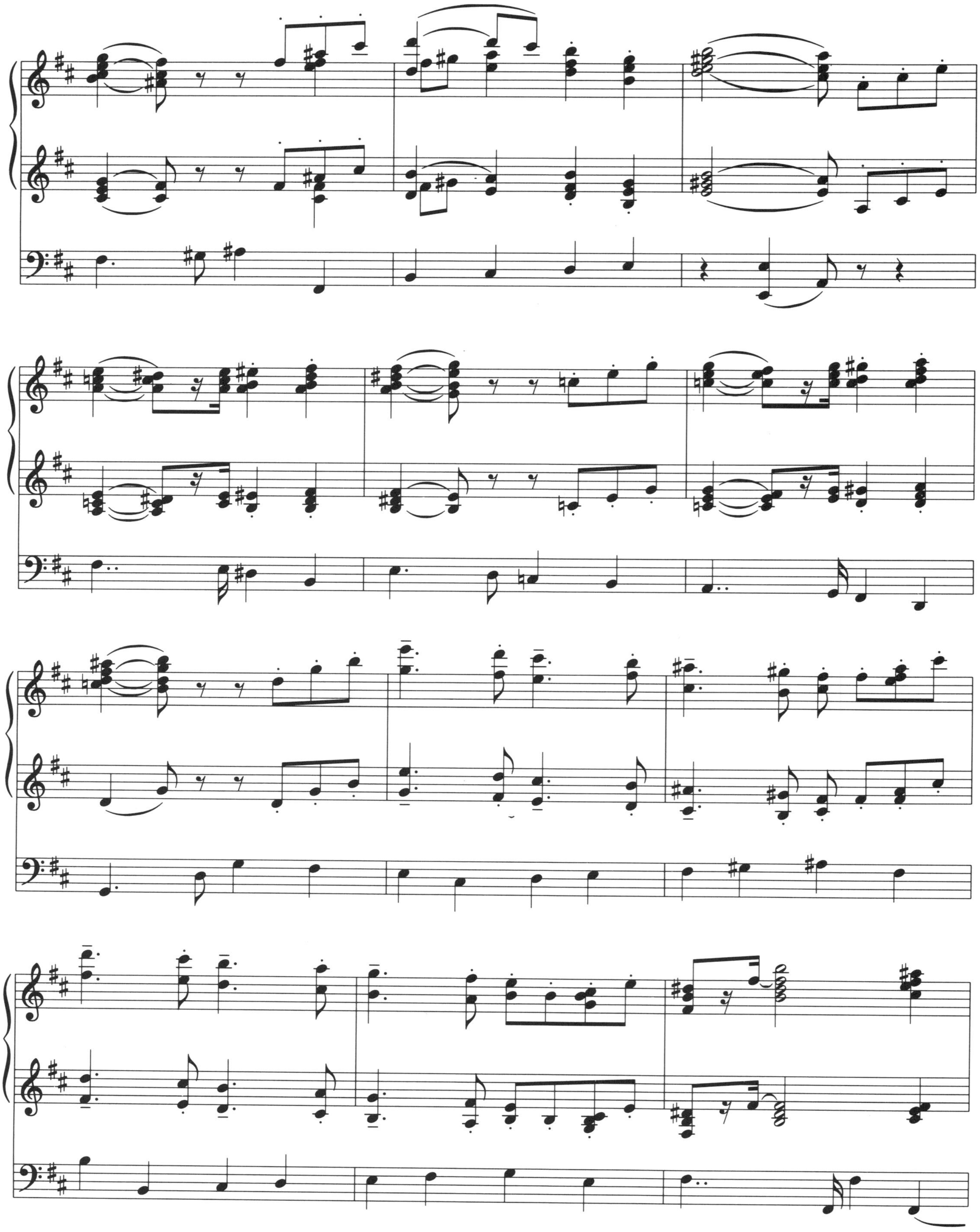

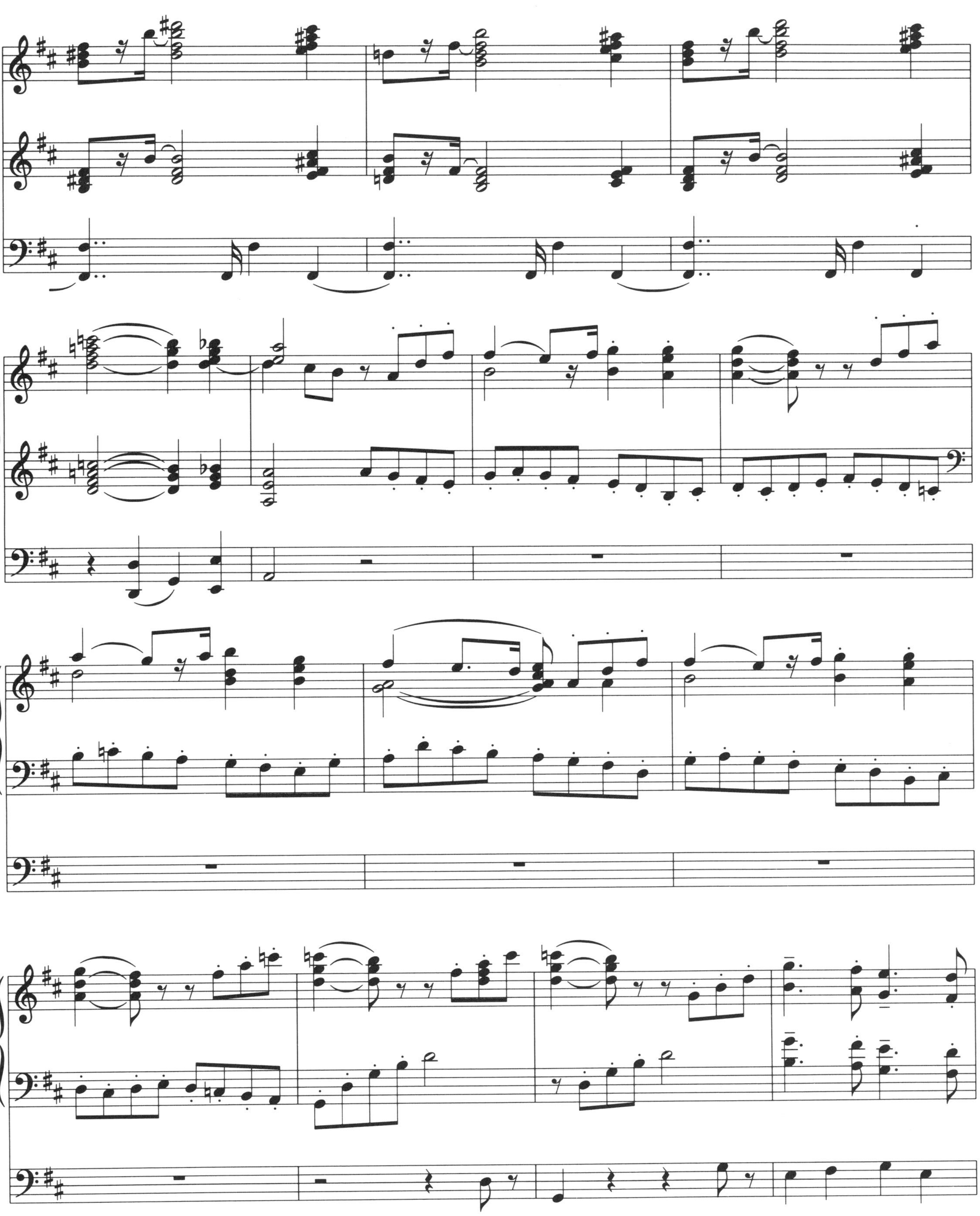

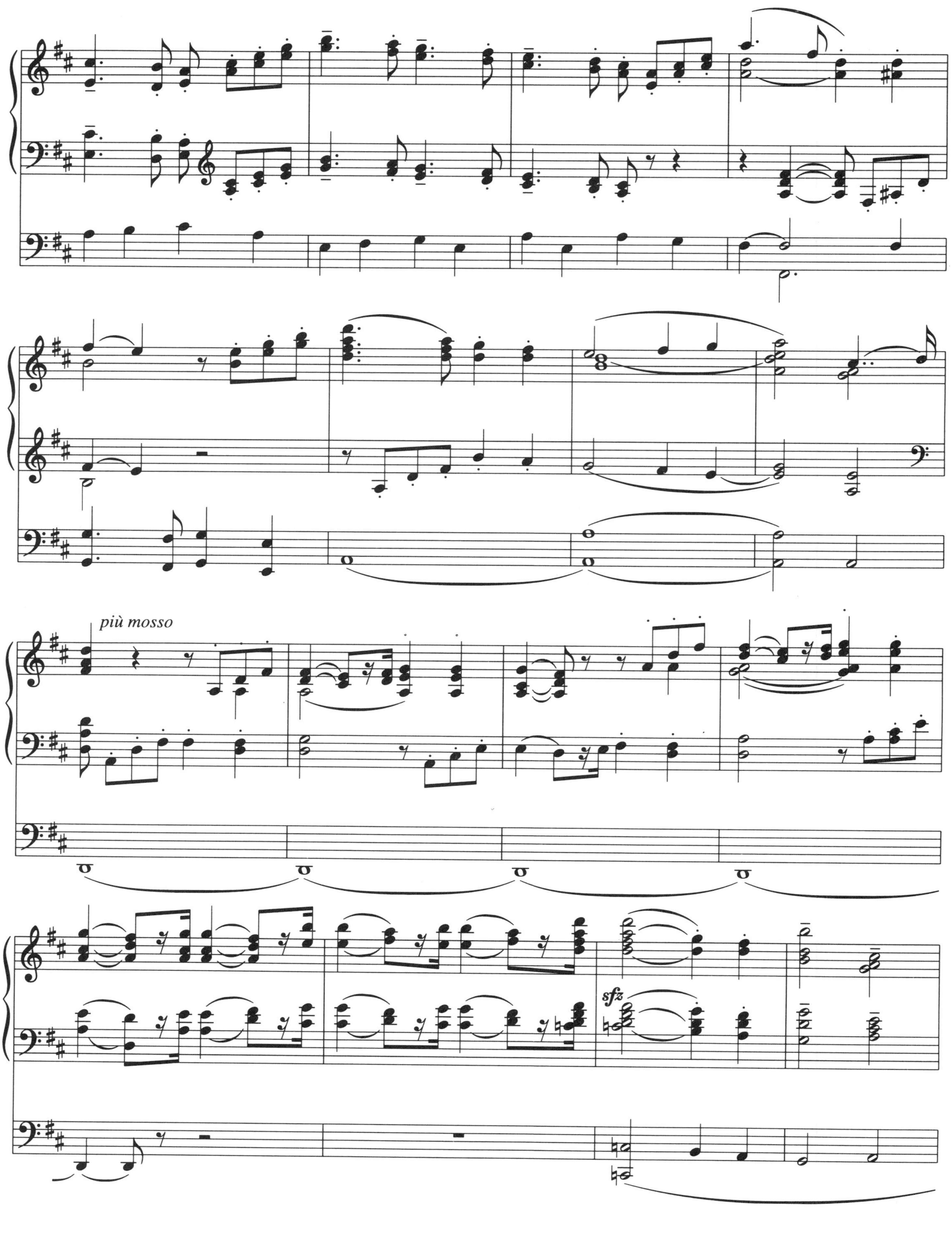
più mosso
sfz

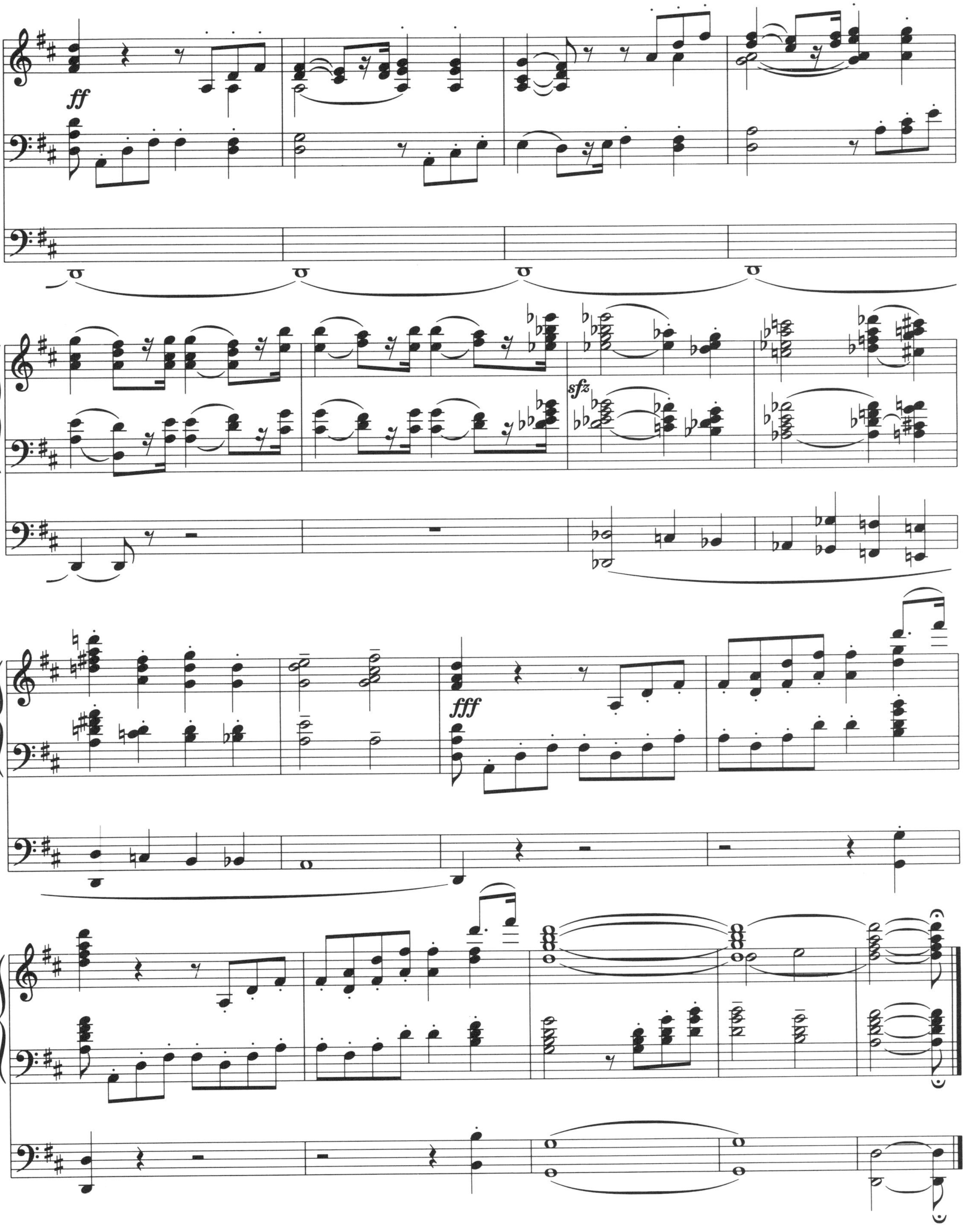
ff
sfz
fff

For Iain McAra

COMMUNION

on 'Dies Dominica'
Christopher Tambling (*b.*1964)

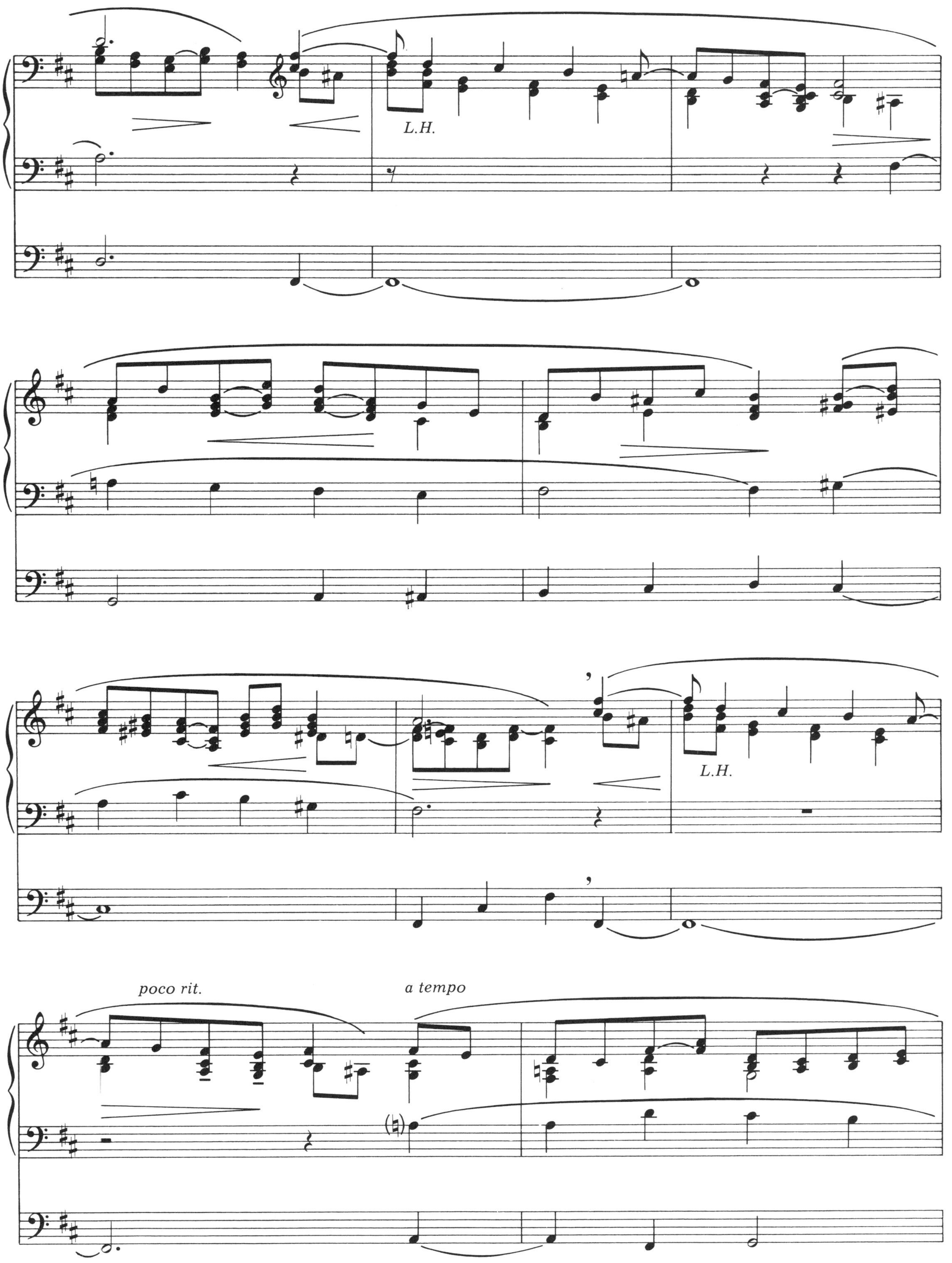
L.H.
L.H.
poco rit.
a tempo

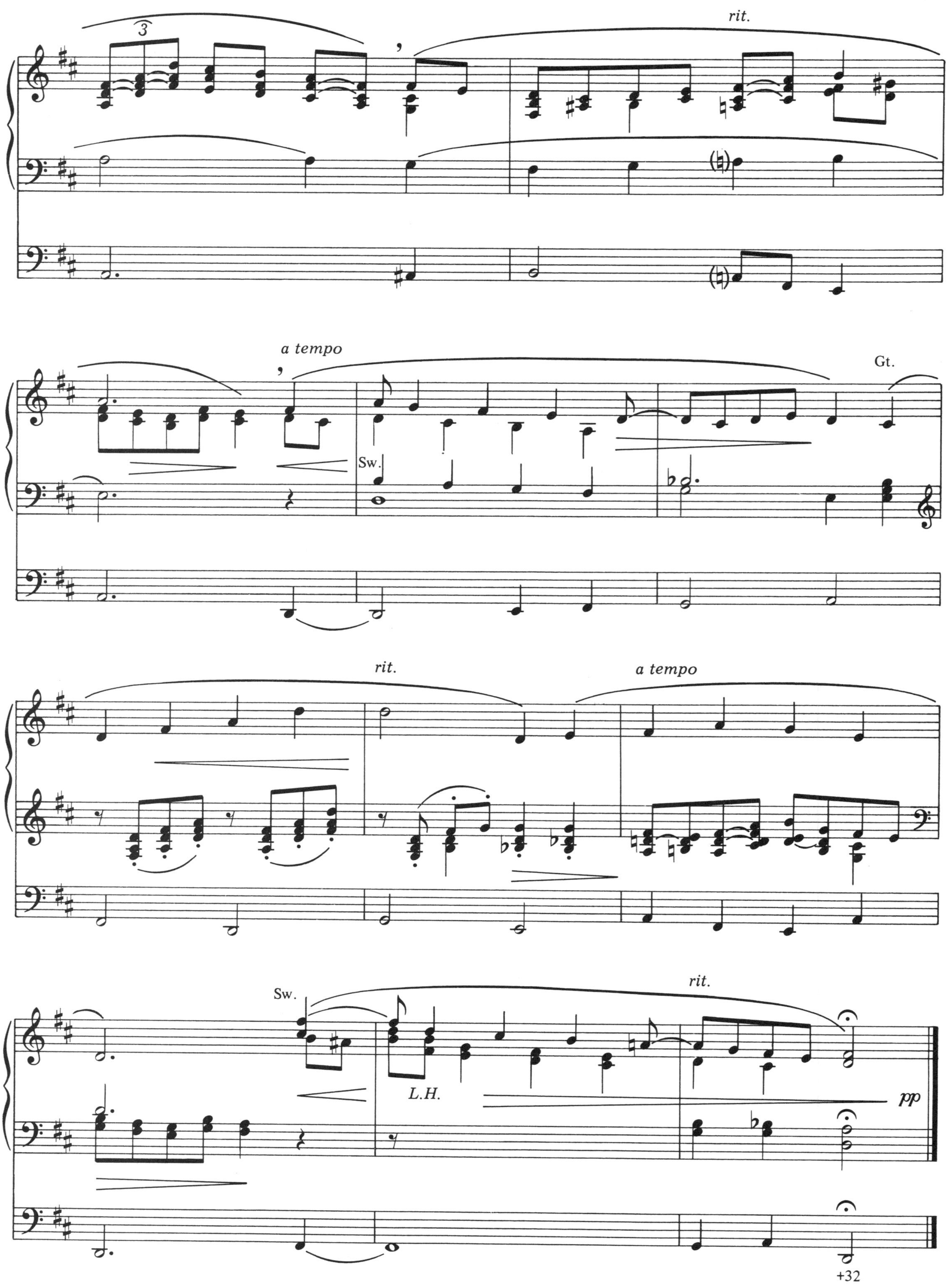
rit.
a tempo
Sw.
Gt.
rit.
a tempo
Sw.
rit.
L.H.
pp
+32

CHORAL PRELUDE on MARIENLIED

Dom Gregory Murray (*b.*1905)

Suggested Registration: Sw. Flute 8' *mp*; Gt. 16' *mf*; Ch. Clarinet 8' *mp*; Ped. 16' *mp* coupled to Sw.

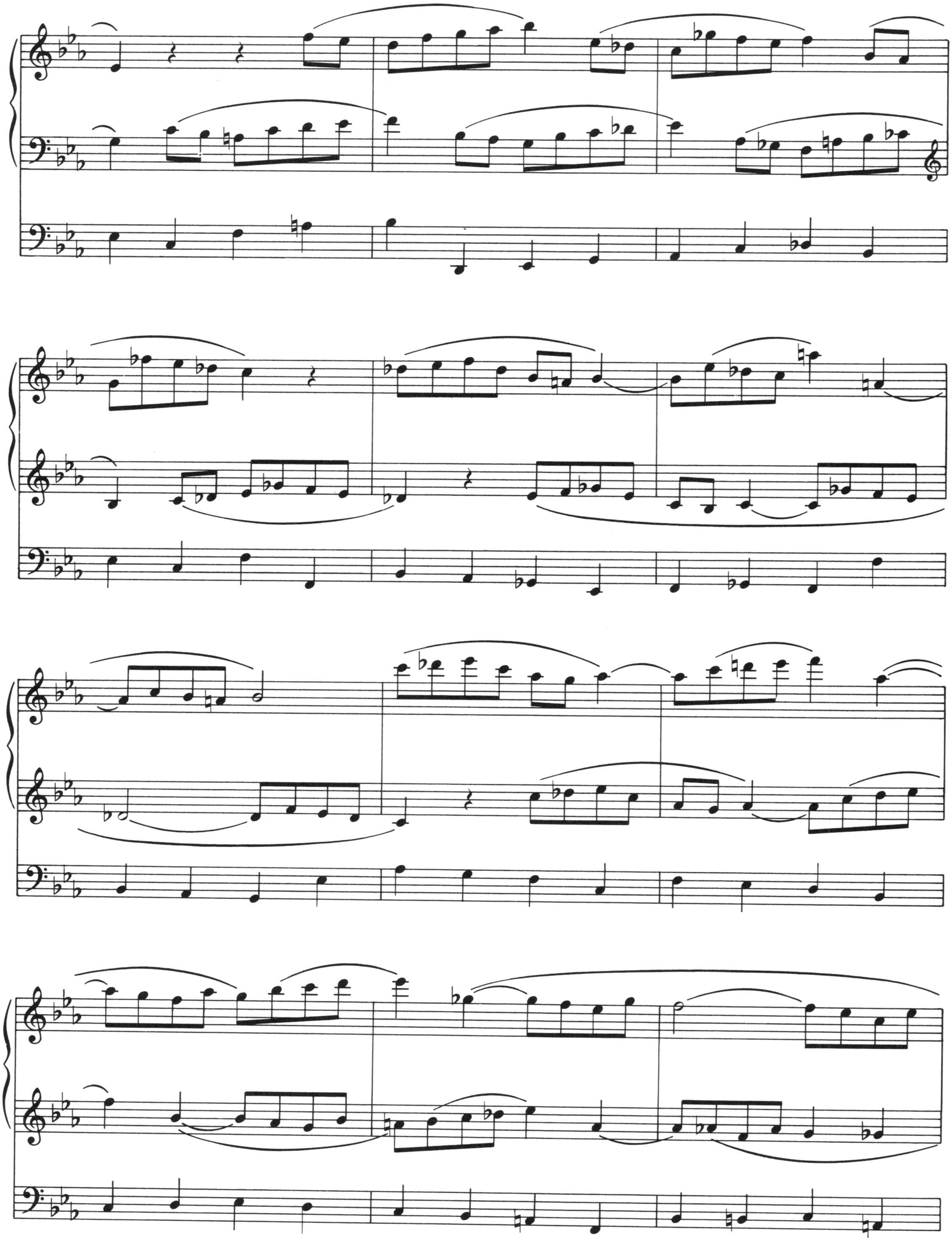

* From this point the Choral melody appears. It should be played by the thumbs on the Great while the contrapuntal accompaniment continues on the Swell.

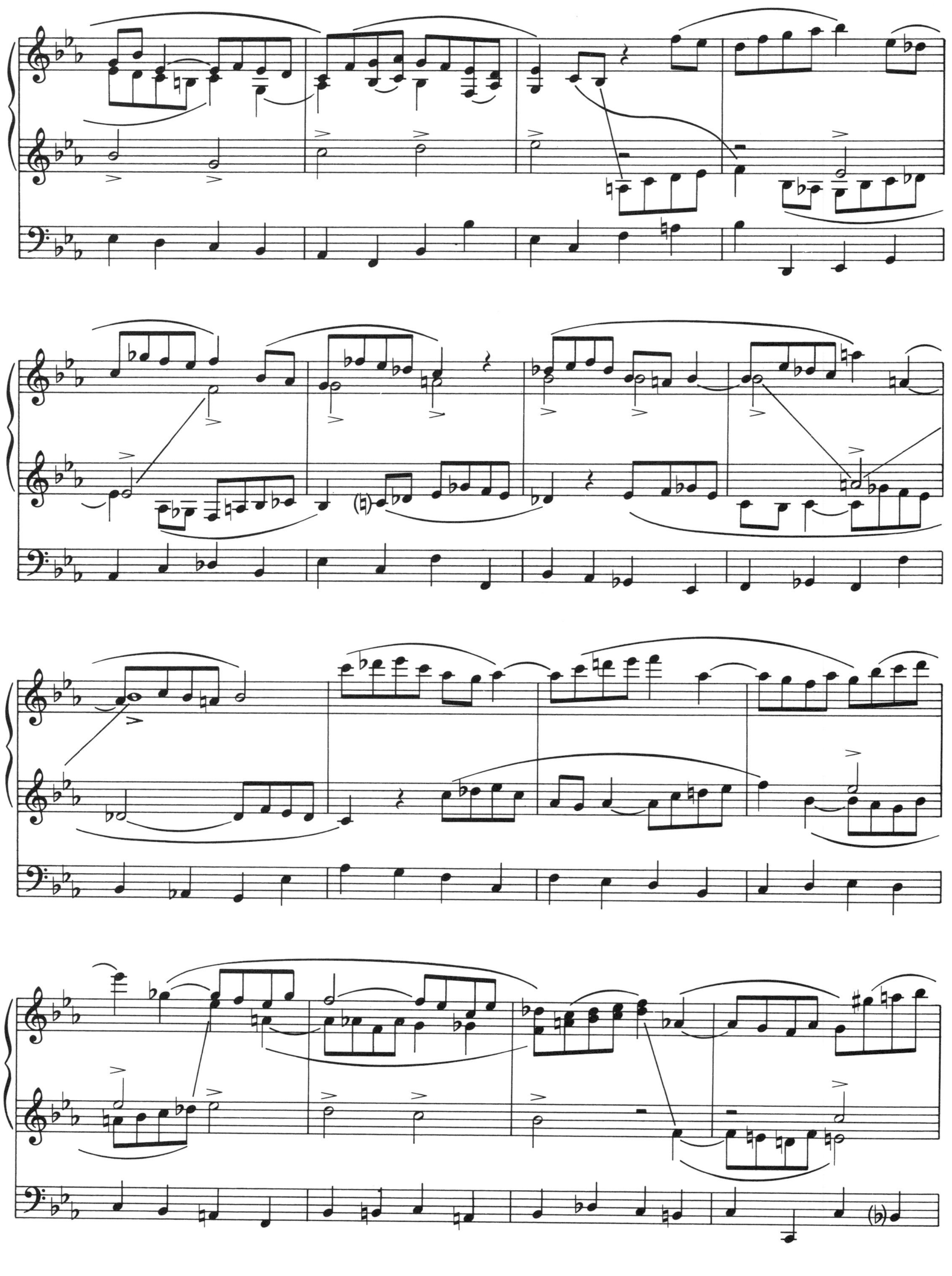

Downside Abbey, 1928

PRELUDE in A MINOR

Johann Rinck (1770-1846)

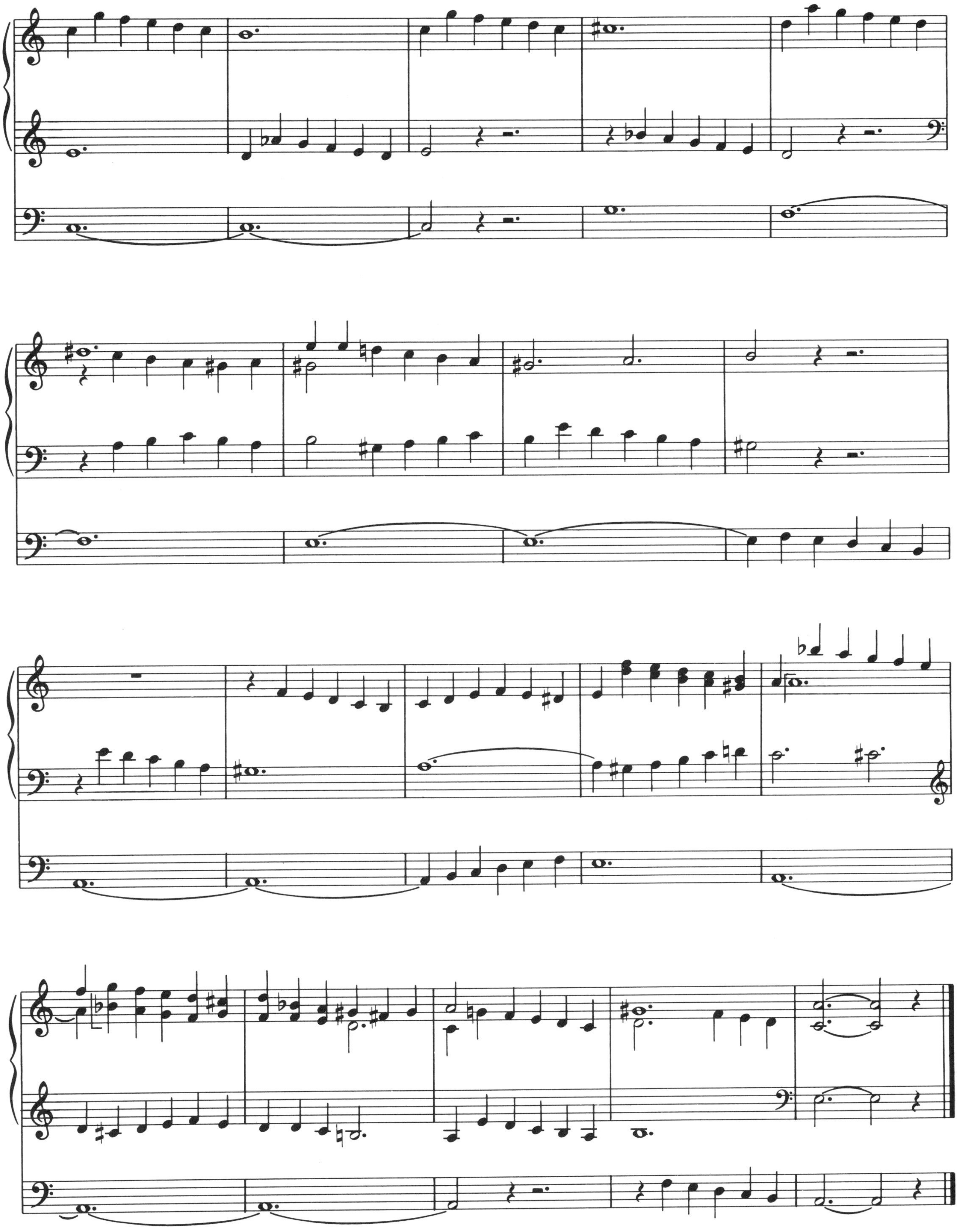

PASTORALE

Walter Battison Haynes (1859-1900)

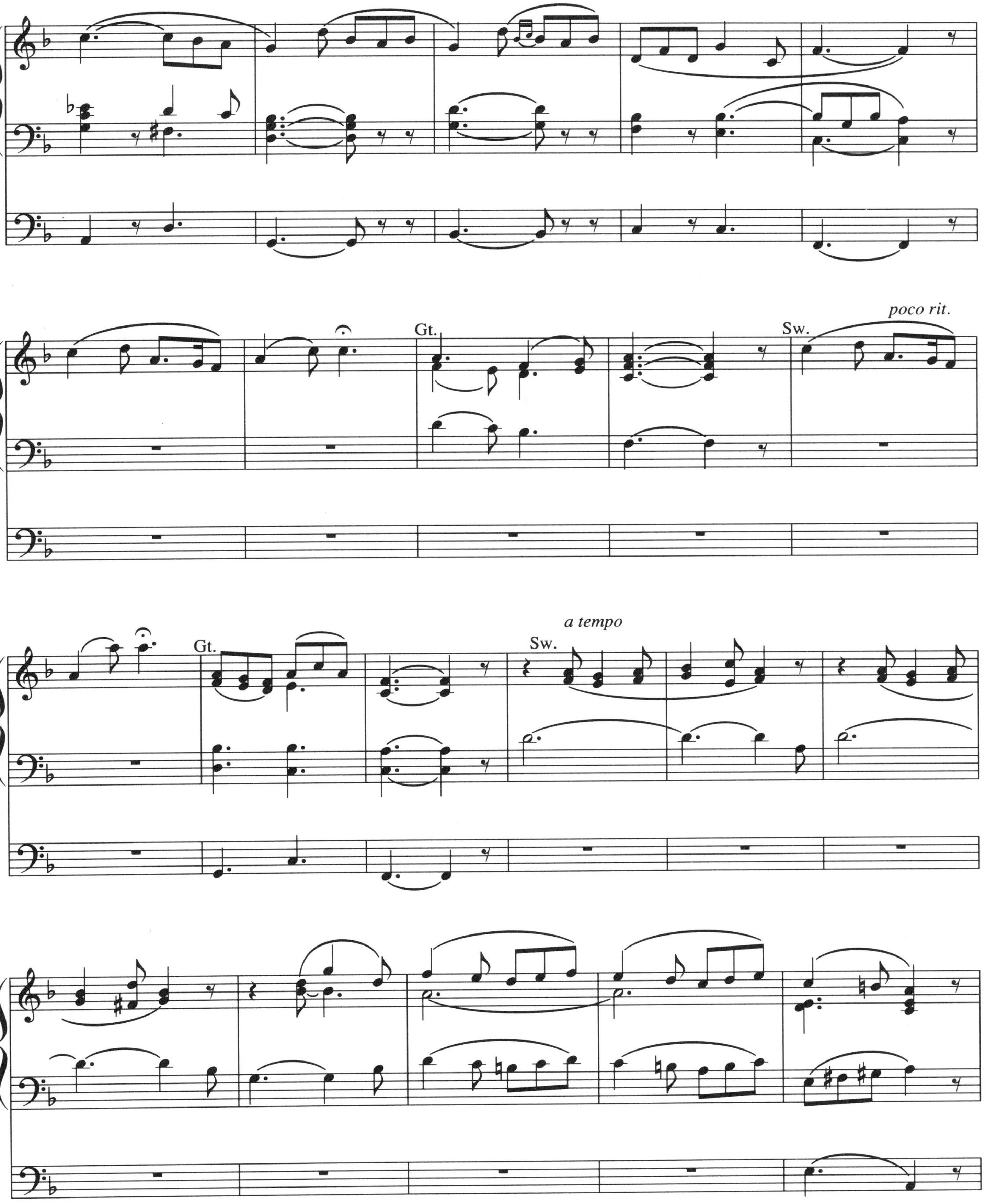
Gt.
Sw.
poco rit.
Gt.
a tempo
Sw.

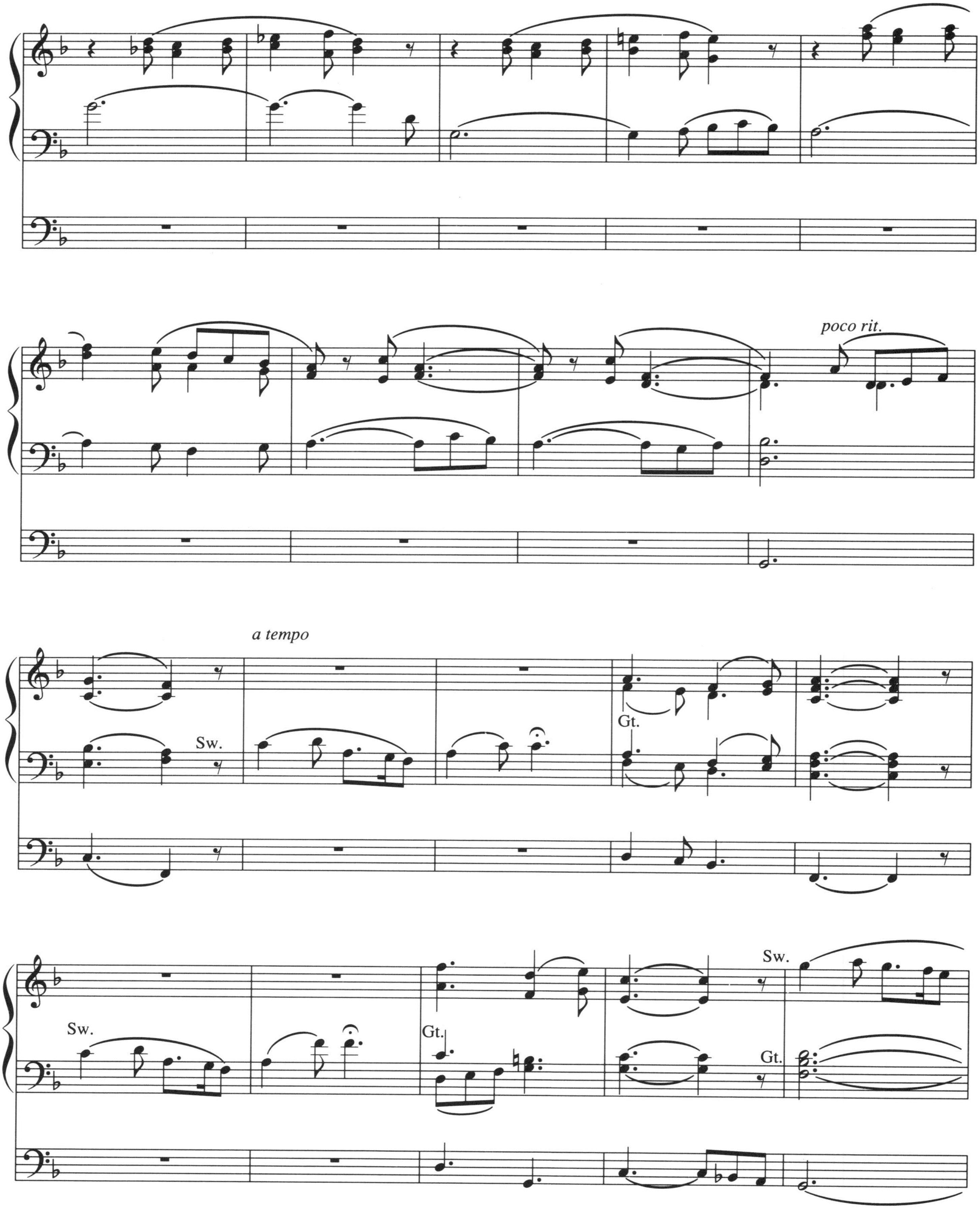
poco rit.
Sw.
a tempo
Gt.
Sw.
Gt.
Sw.
Gt.

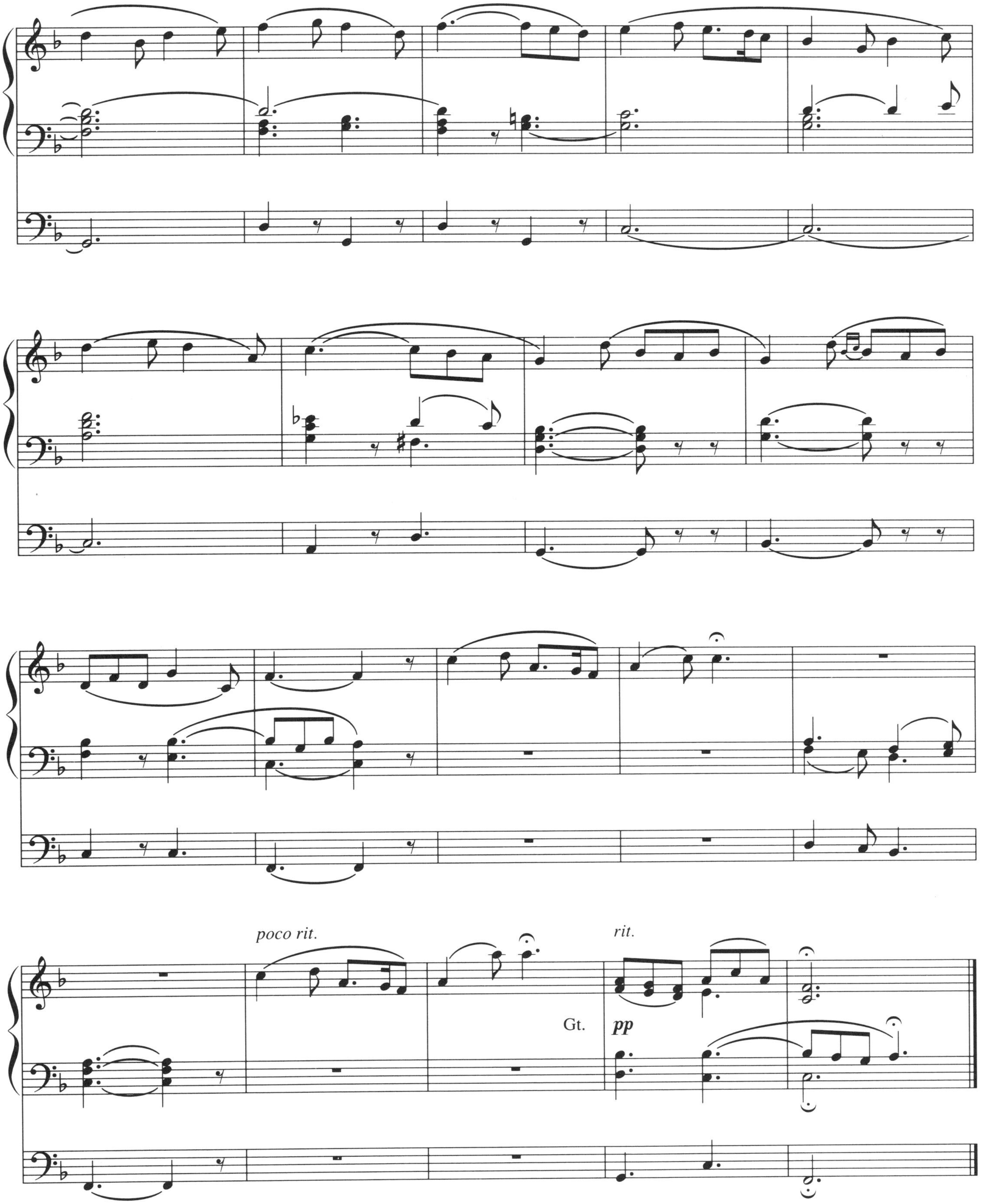
poco rit.
Gt.
pp
rit.

INVOCATION in E♭

Alexandre Guilmant (1837-1911)

– Gt. to Ped.

espressivo

Sw. *p*

cresc.
dim.
p
cresc.
+ Sw. to Gt.
dim.
p
cresc.
rall.
a tempo
dim.
Gt.
p
+ Gt. to Ped.

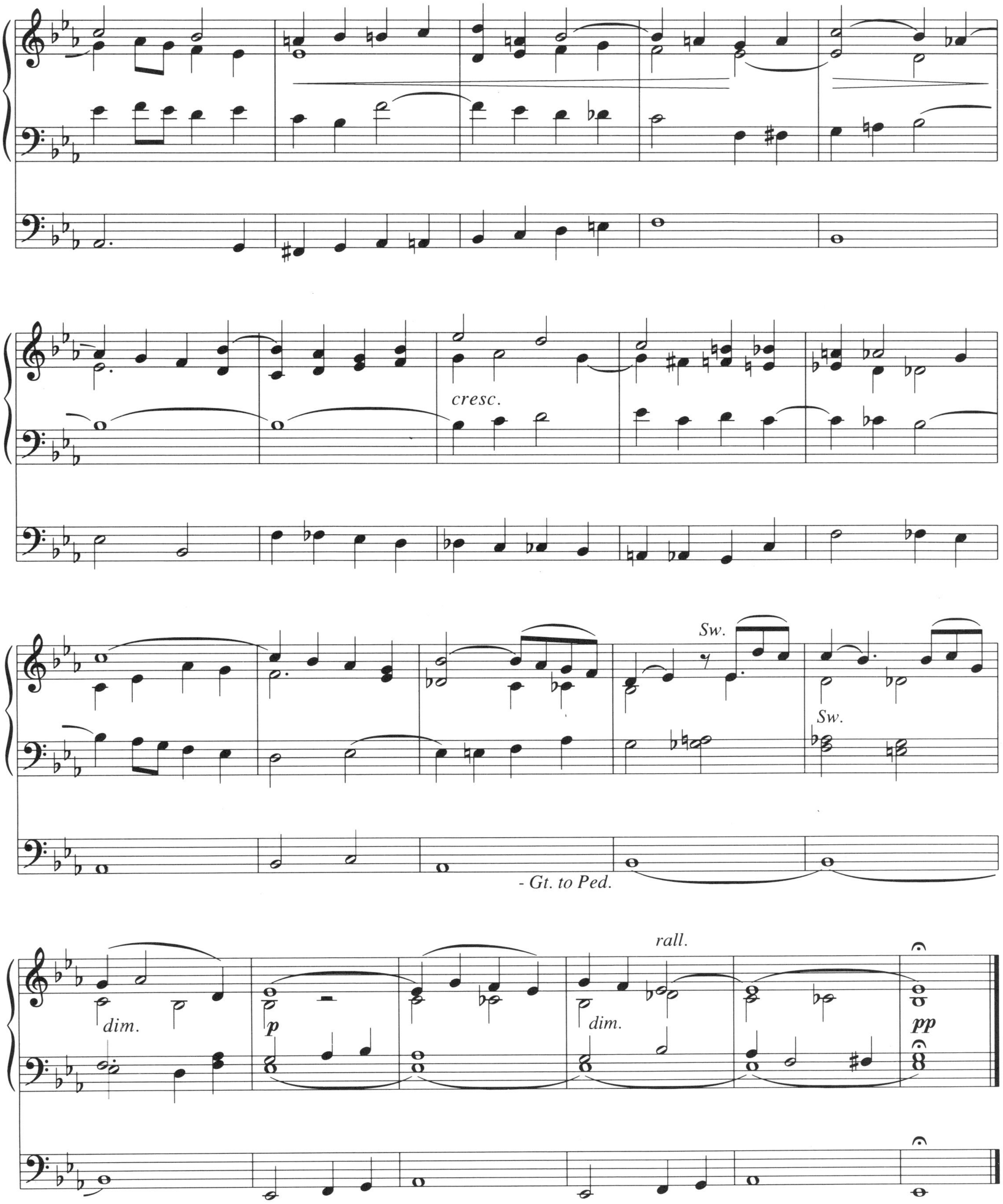
cresc.
Sw.
Sw.
- Gt. to Ped.
rall.
dim.
p
dim.
pp

For W.W. and M.M.

CONCERTINO

Christopher Tambling (*b.*1964)

A tempo ordinario e staccato

tr
mf Largo
rit.
tr
Allegro
(ad lib.)
f Gt. to Mixtures
tr
tr
Sw. 8 + 2
Gt.
Sw.

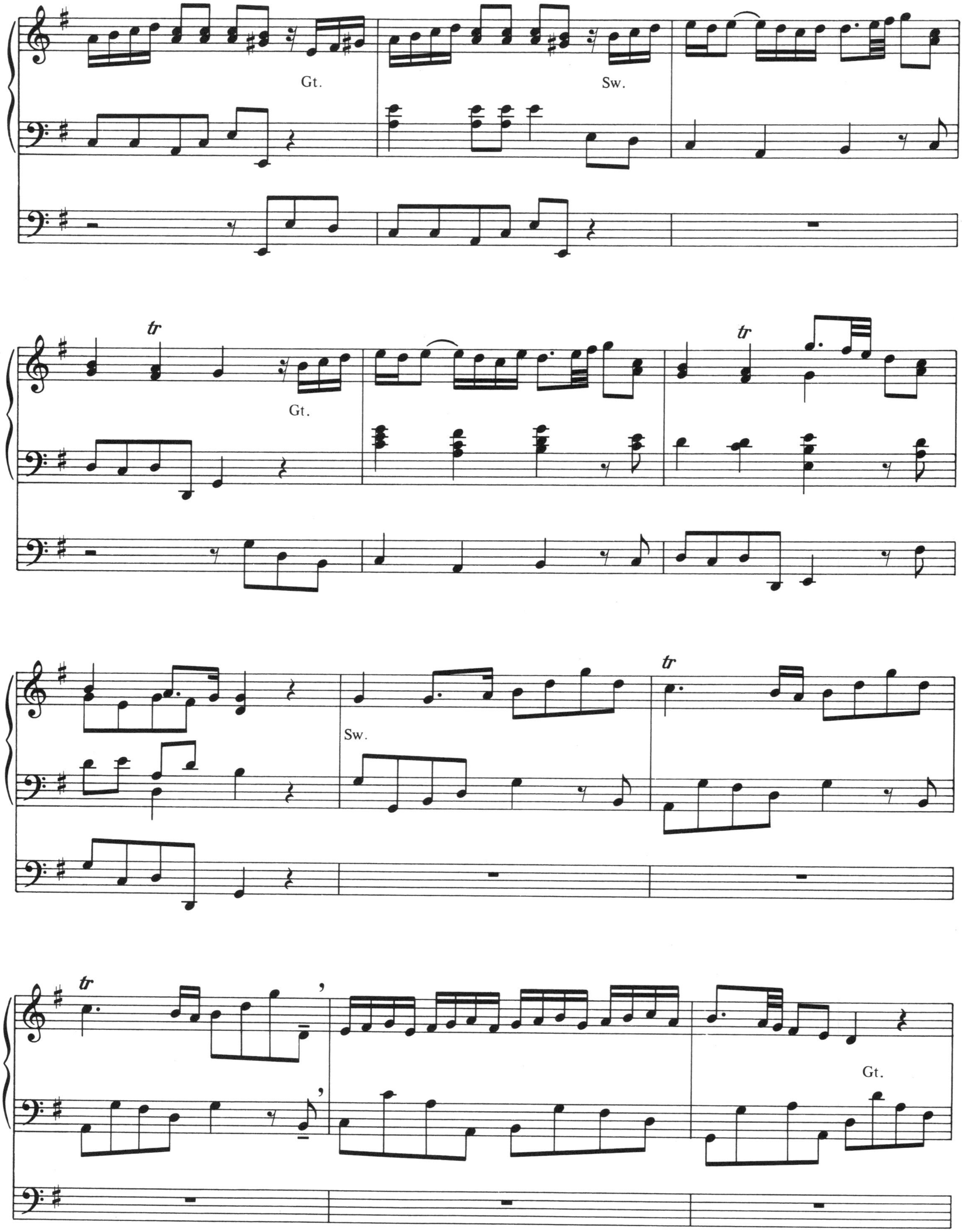
Gt.
Sw.
tr
Gt.
tr
Sw.
tr
tr
Gt.

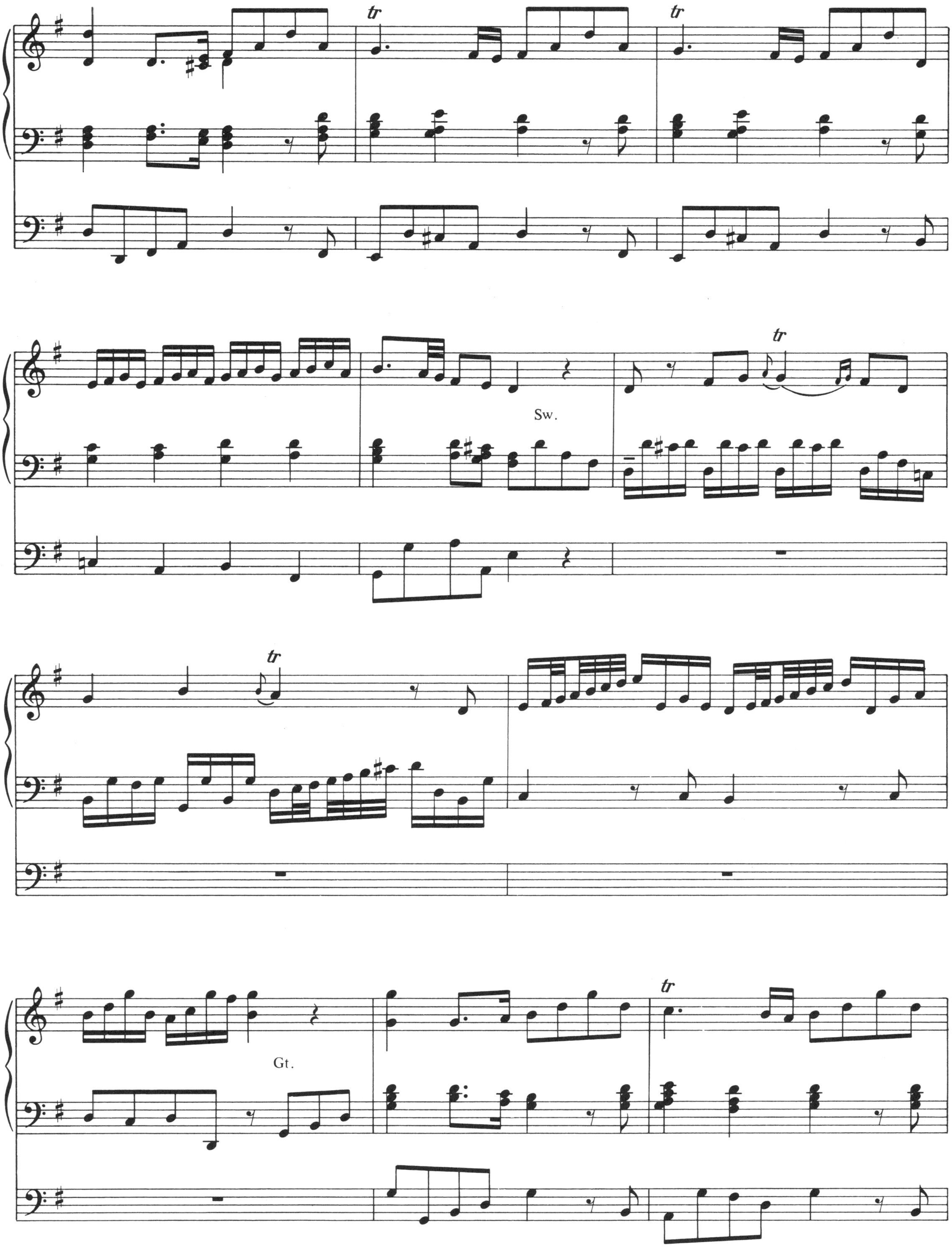
tr
tr
tr
Sw.
tr
tr
Gt.
tr

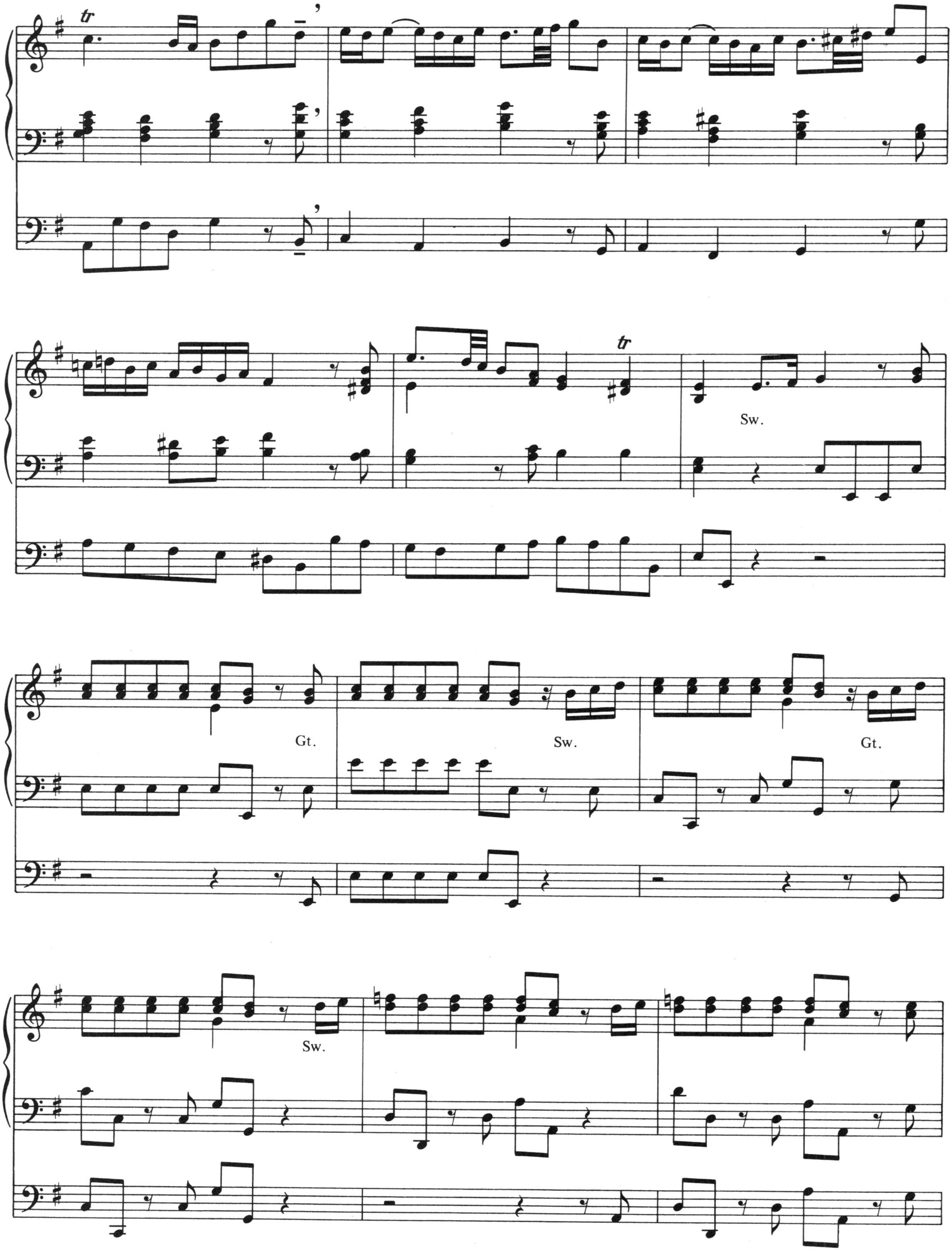
tr
tr
Sw.
Gt.
Sw.
Gt.
Sw.

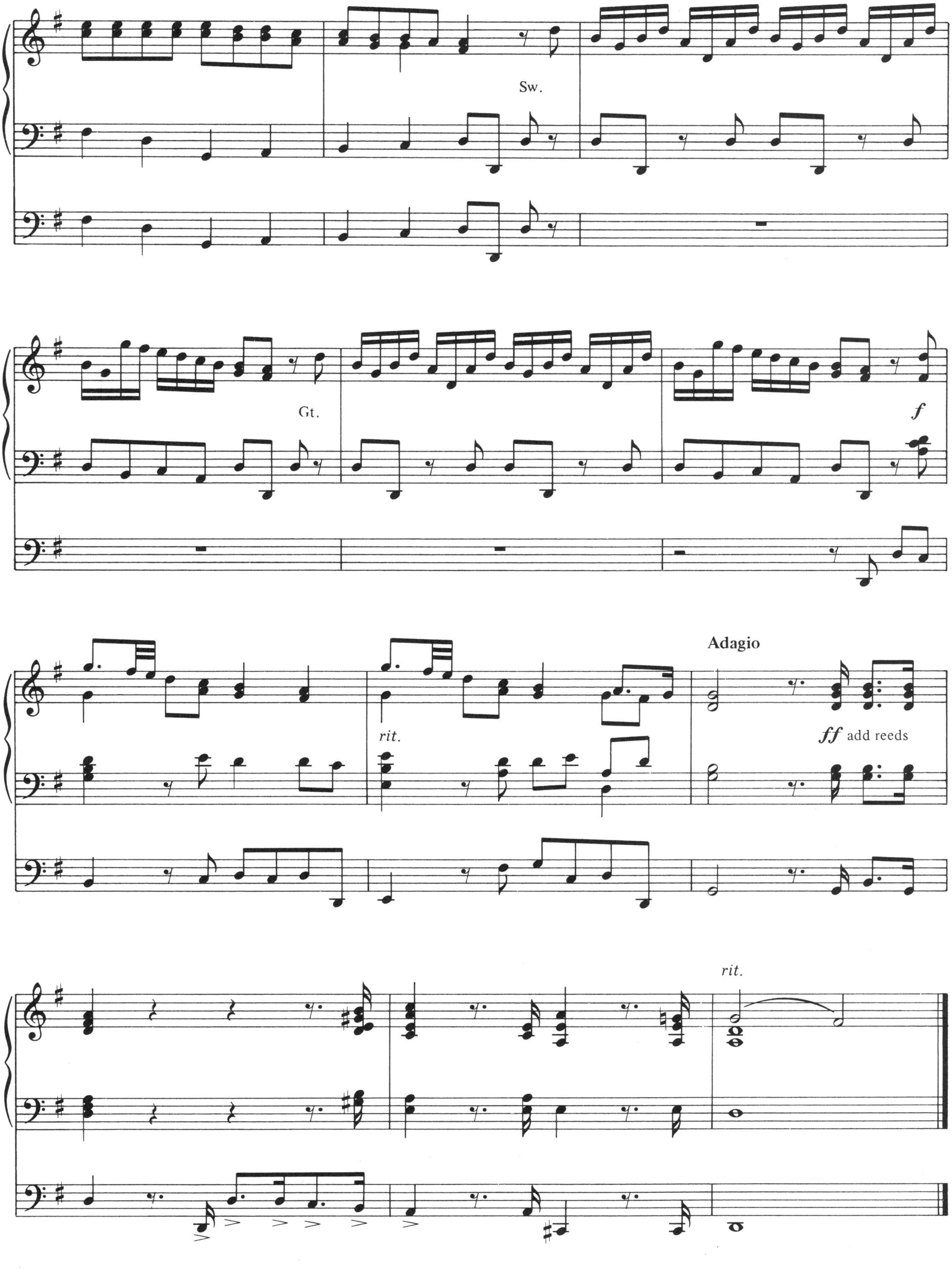
Sw.
Gt.
f
Adagio
rit.
ff add reeds
rit.

SECOND PRELUDE in E MINOR

Johann Rinck (1770-1846)

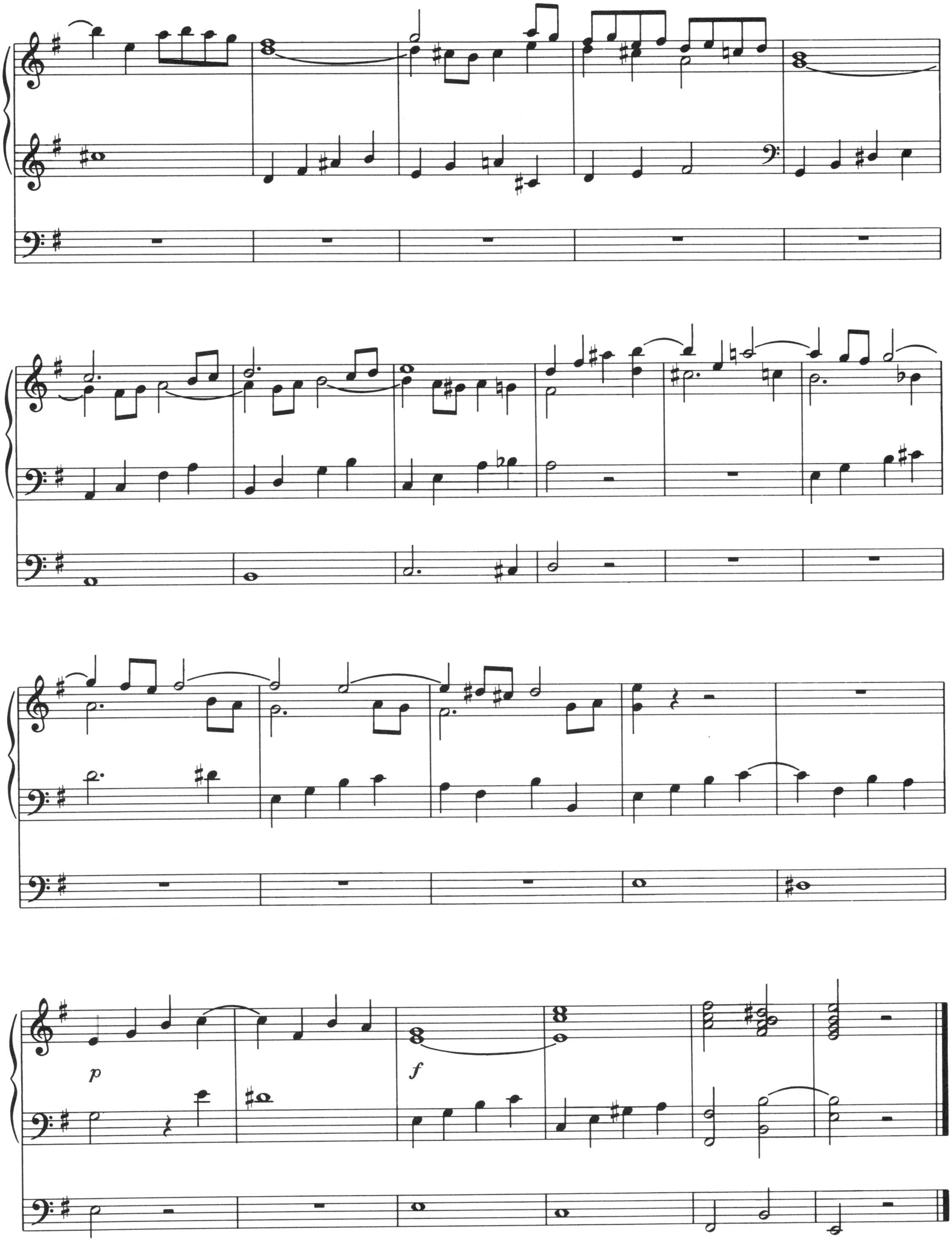
p
f

ELEVATION

Dom Gregory Sergent (1870-?)

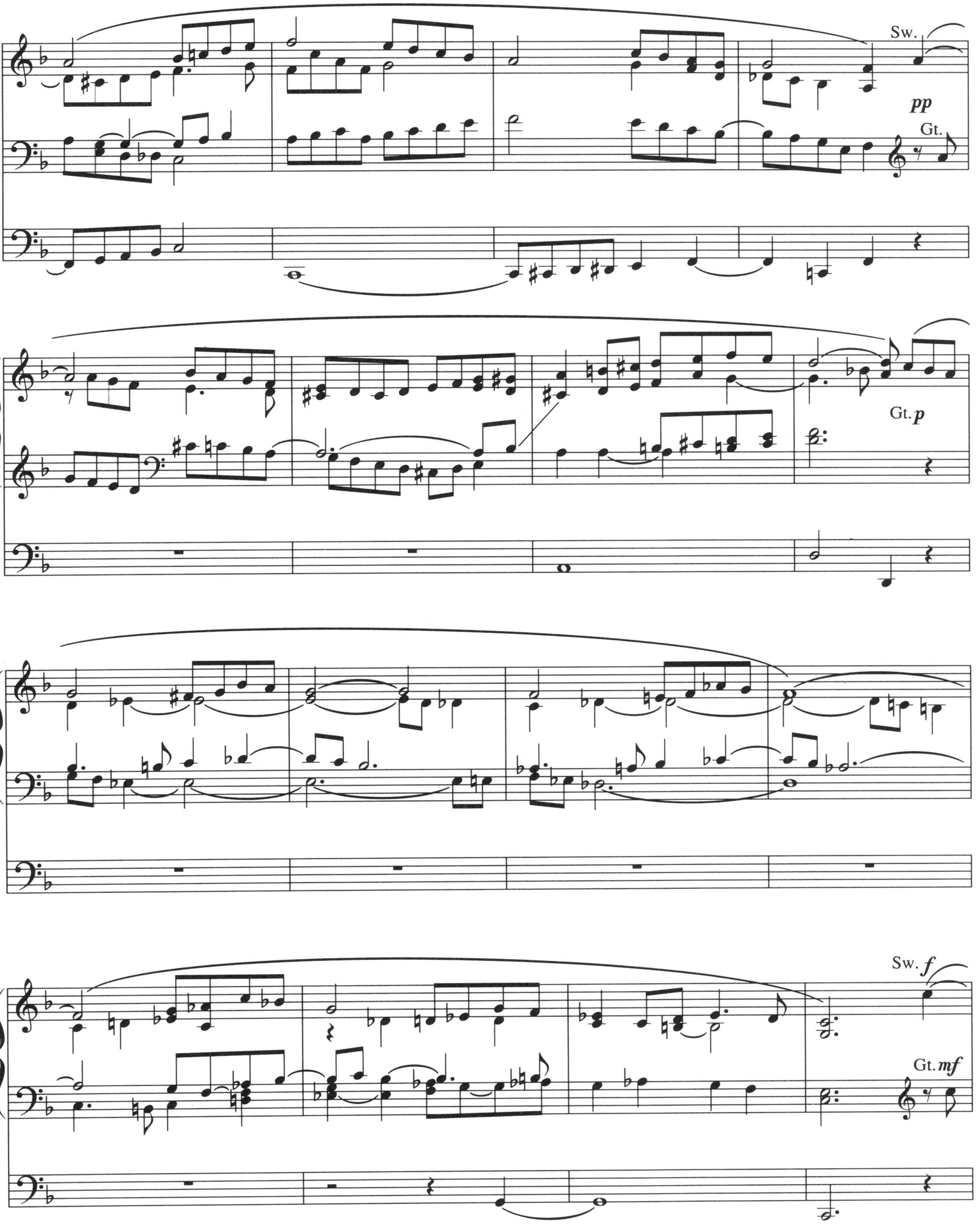
Sw.
pp
Gt.
Gt. p
Sw. f
Gt. mf

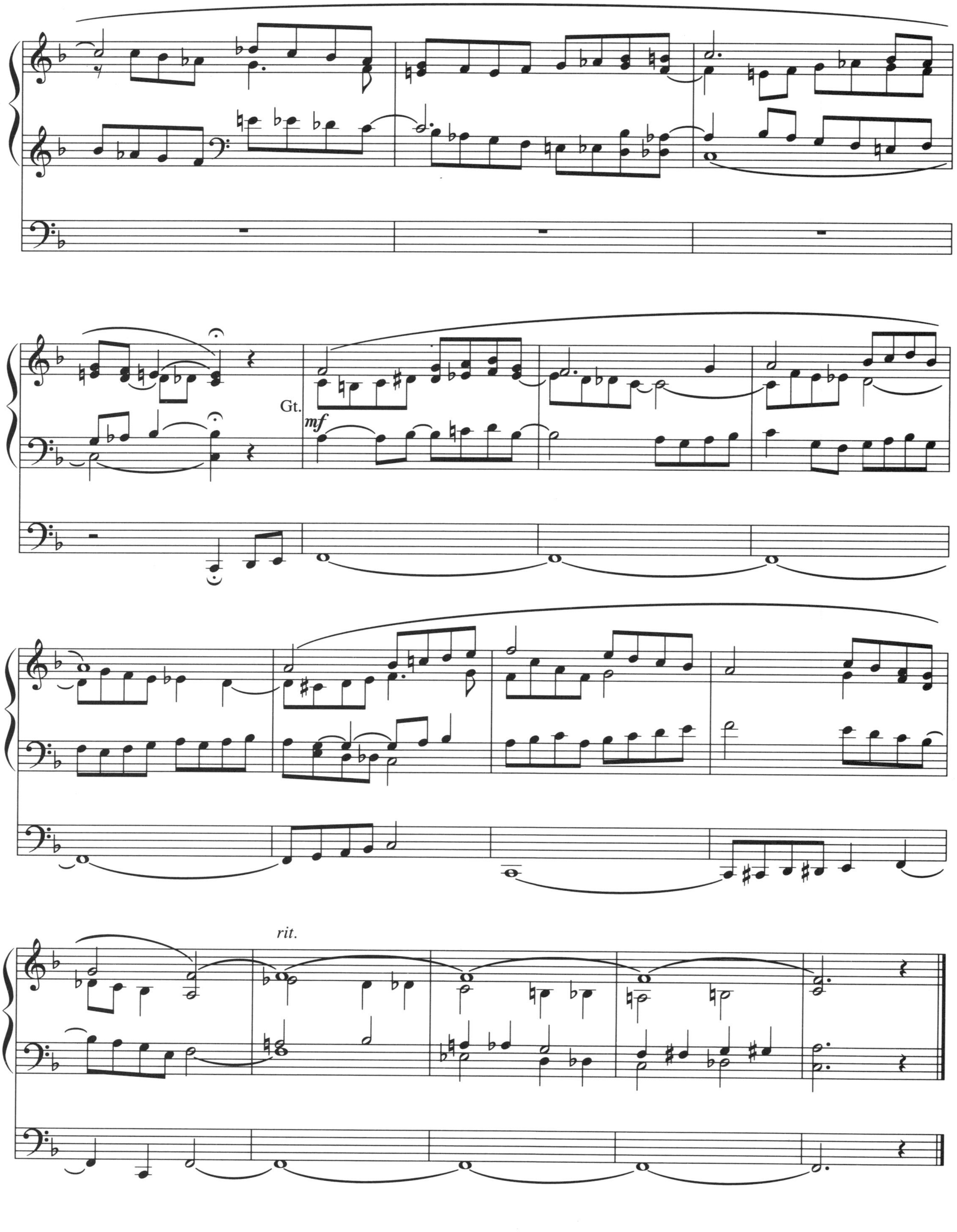
Gt.
mf
rit.

For Darren Oliver

A PLAINTIVE ARIA

Donald Hunt

A little more movement
broader
Gt. f
Gt. to Ped.
Gt. (Flute) p
flexible
At the first tempo
Sw. pp
Gt. to Ped. off
p

215

MINUET

Alexandre Guilmant (1837-1911)

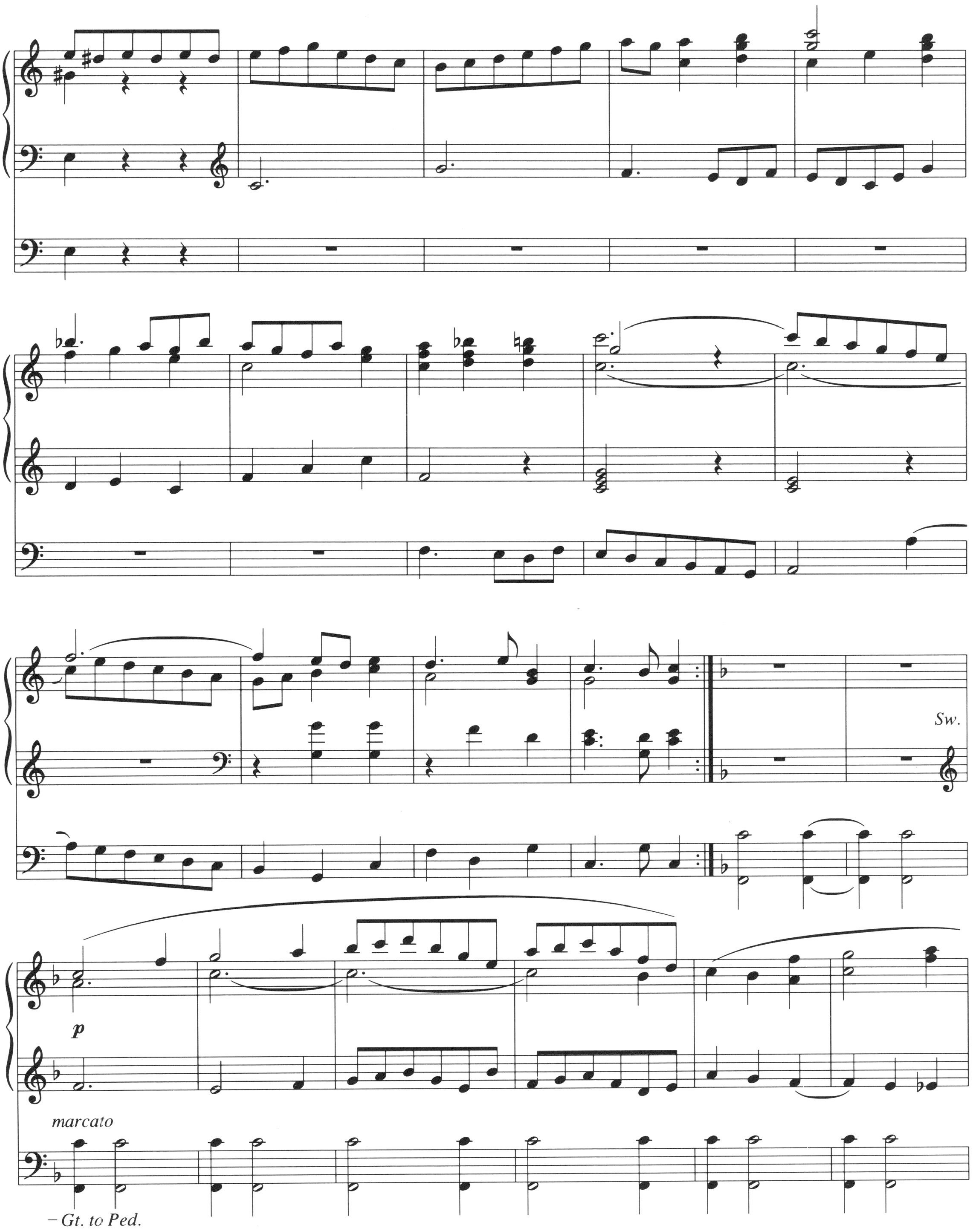
Sw.
p
marcato
– Gt. to Ped.

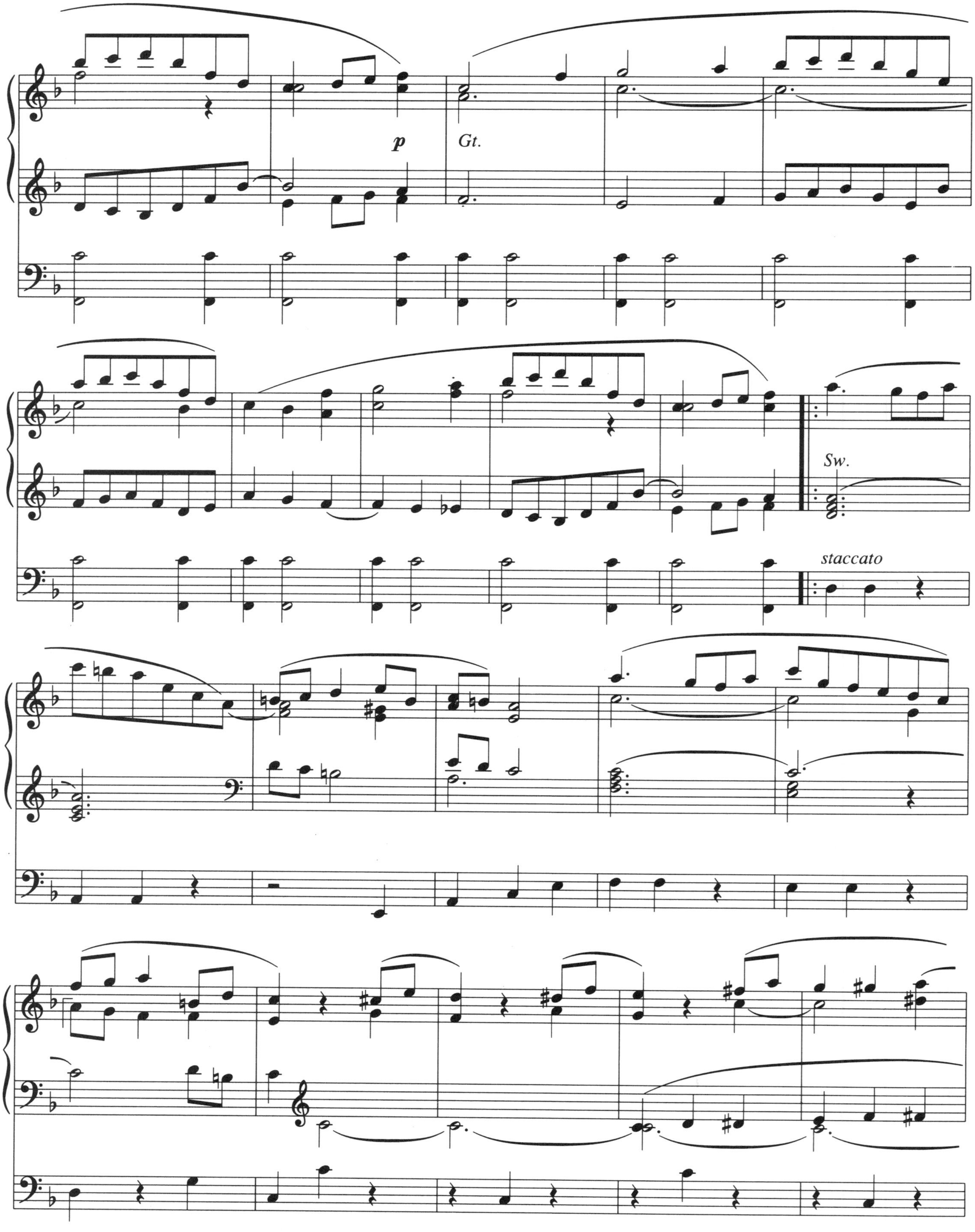
p
Gt.
Sw.
staccato

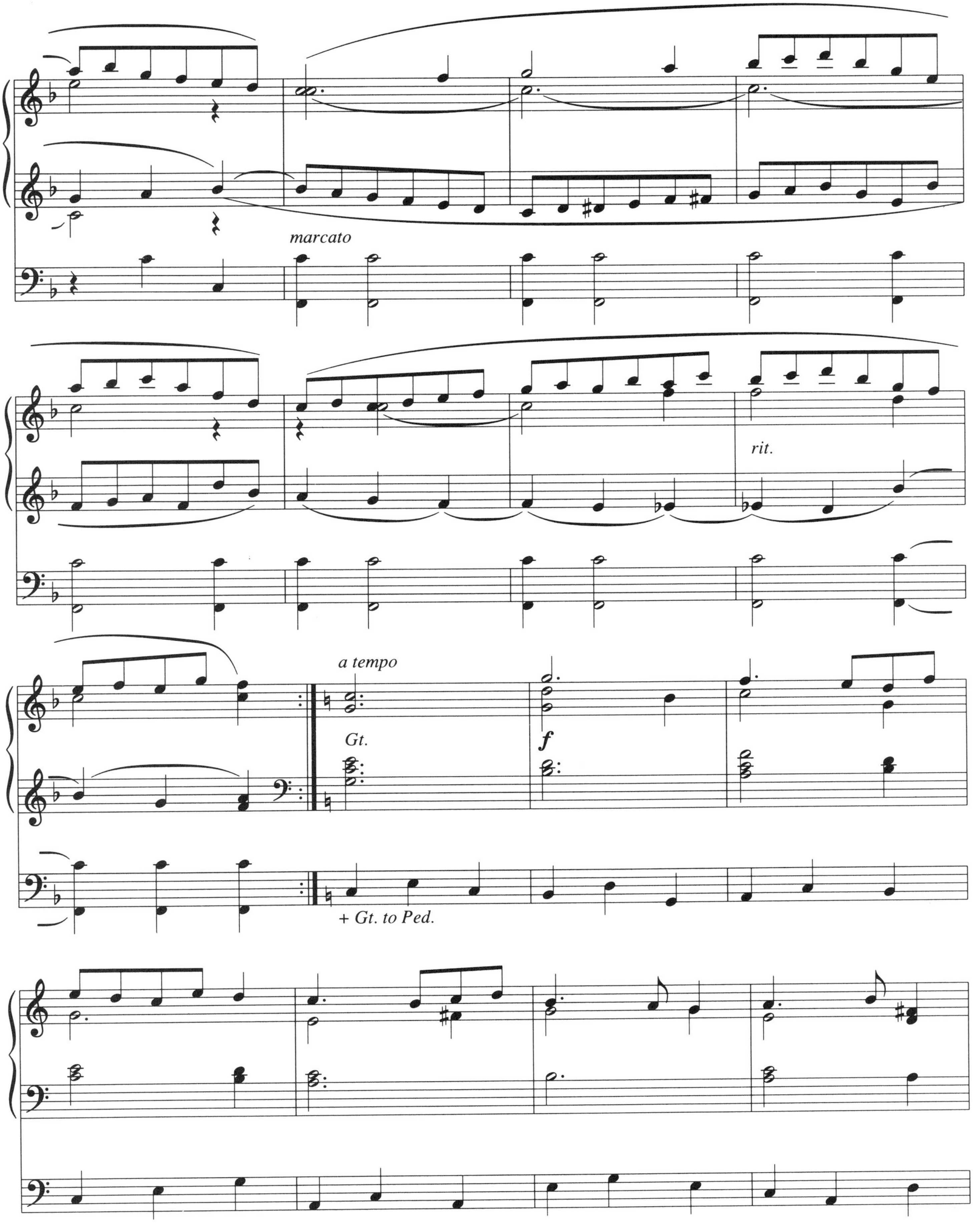
marcato
rit.
a tempo
Gt.
f
+ Gt. to Ped.

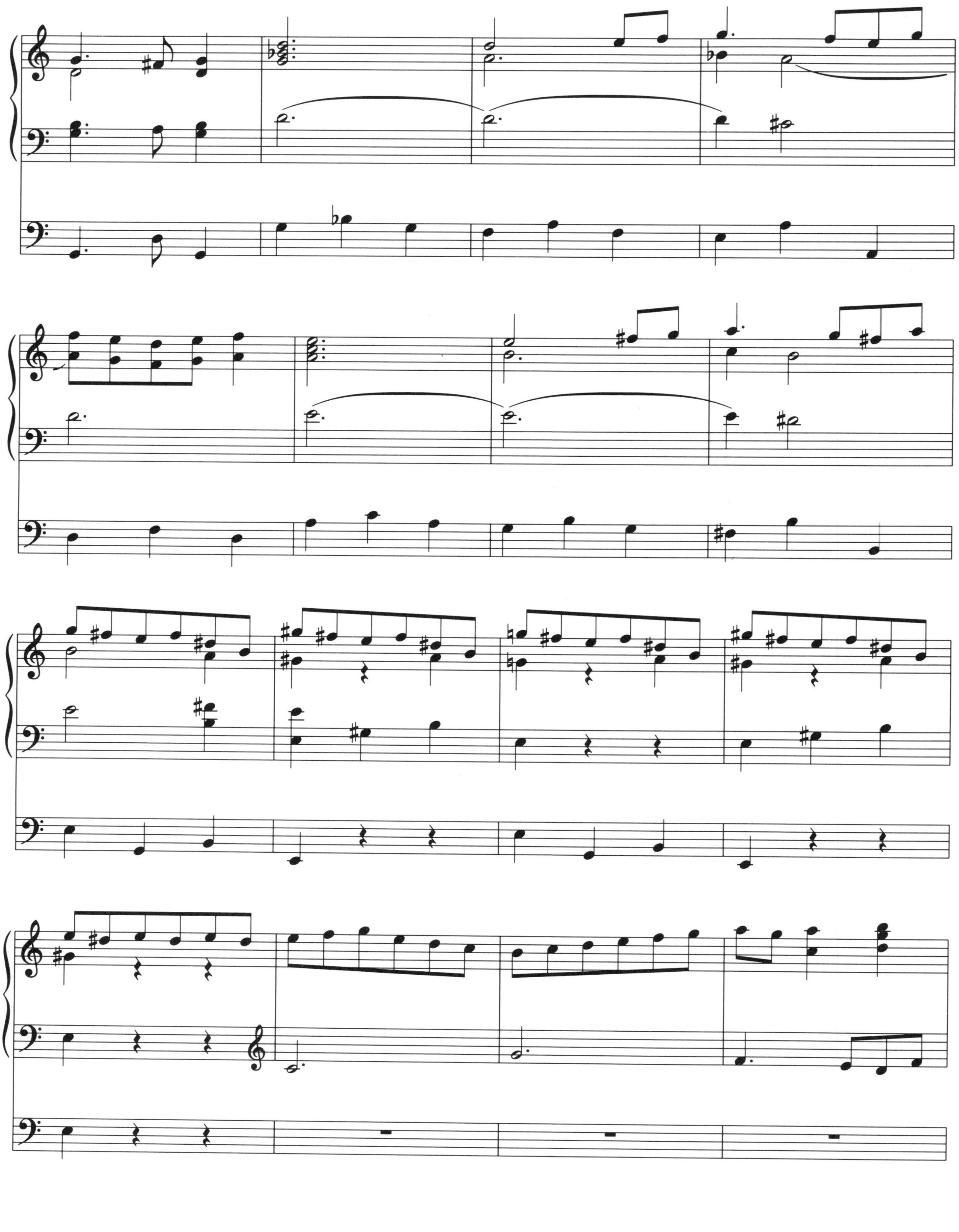

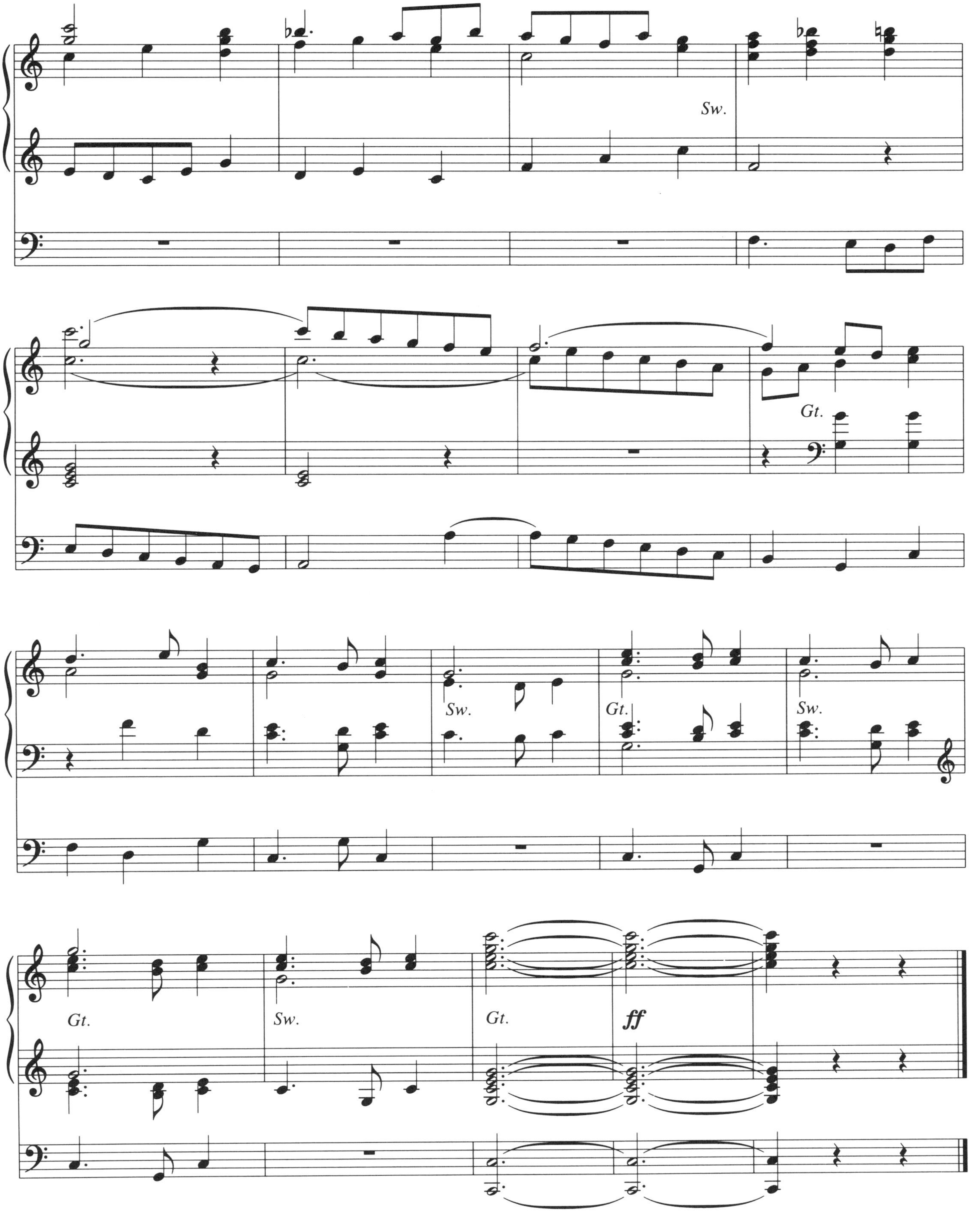
Sw.
Gt.
Sw.
Gt.
Sw.
Gt.
Sw.
Gt.
ff

PRELUDE in A♭

Johann Rinck (1770-1846)

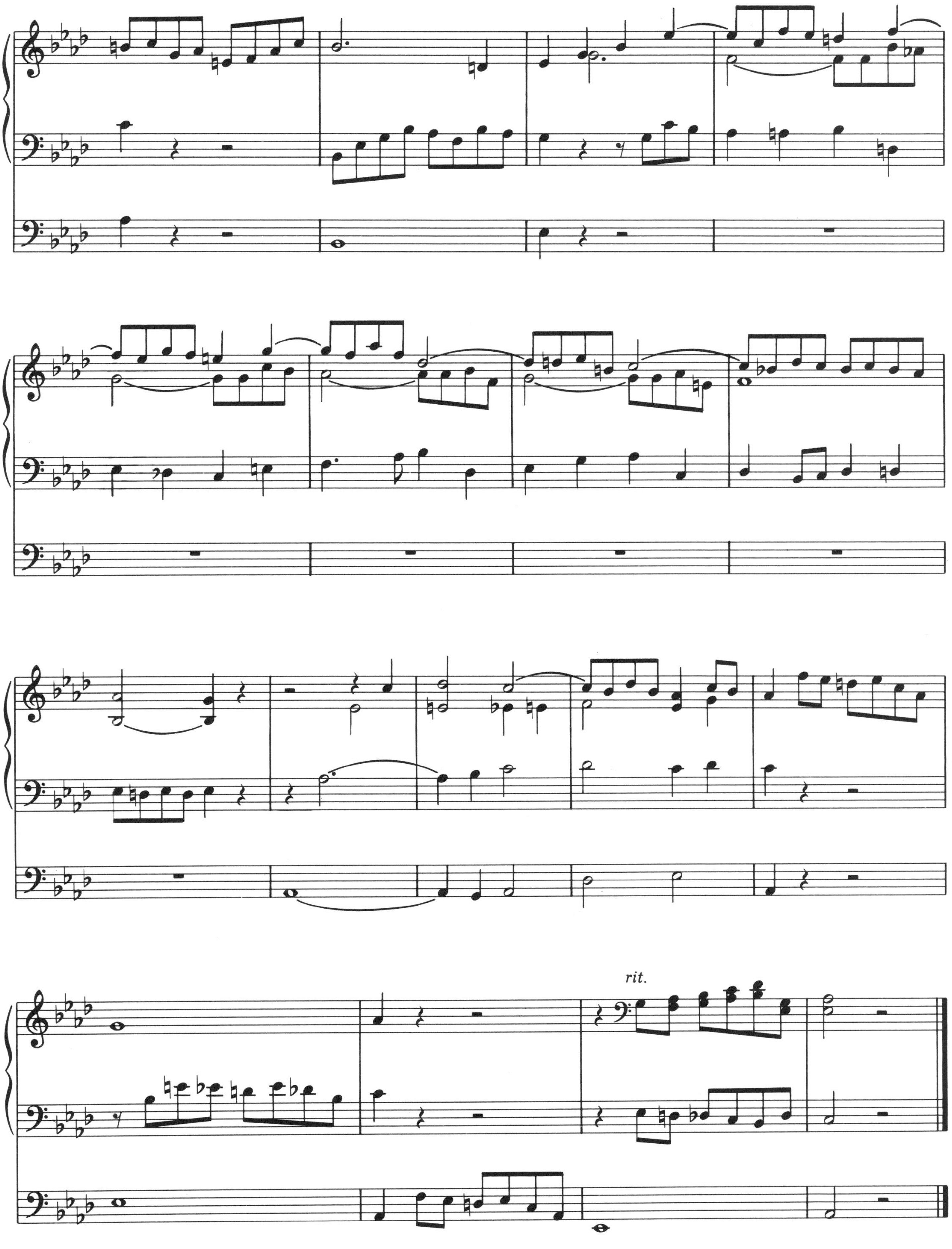
rit.

ANDANTE GRAZIOSO

Henry Smart (1813-1879)

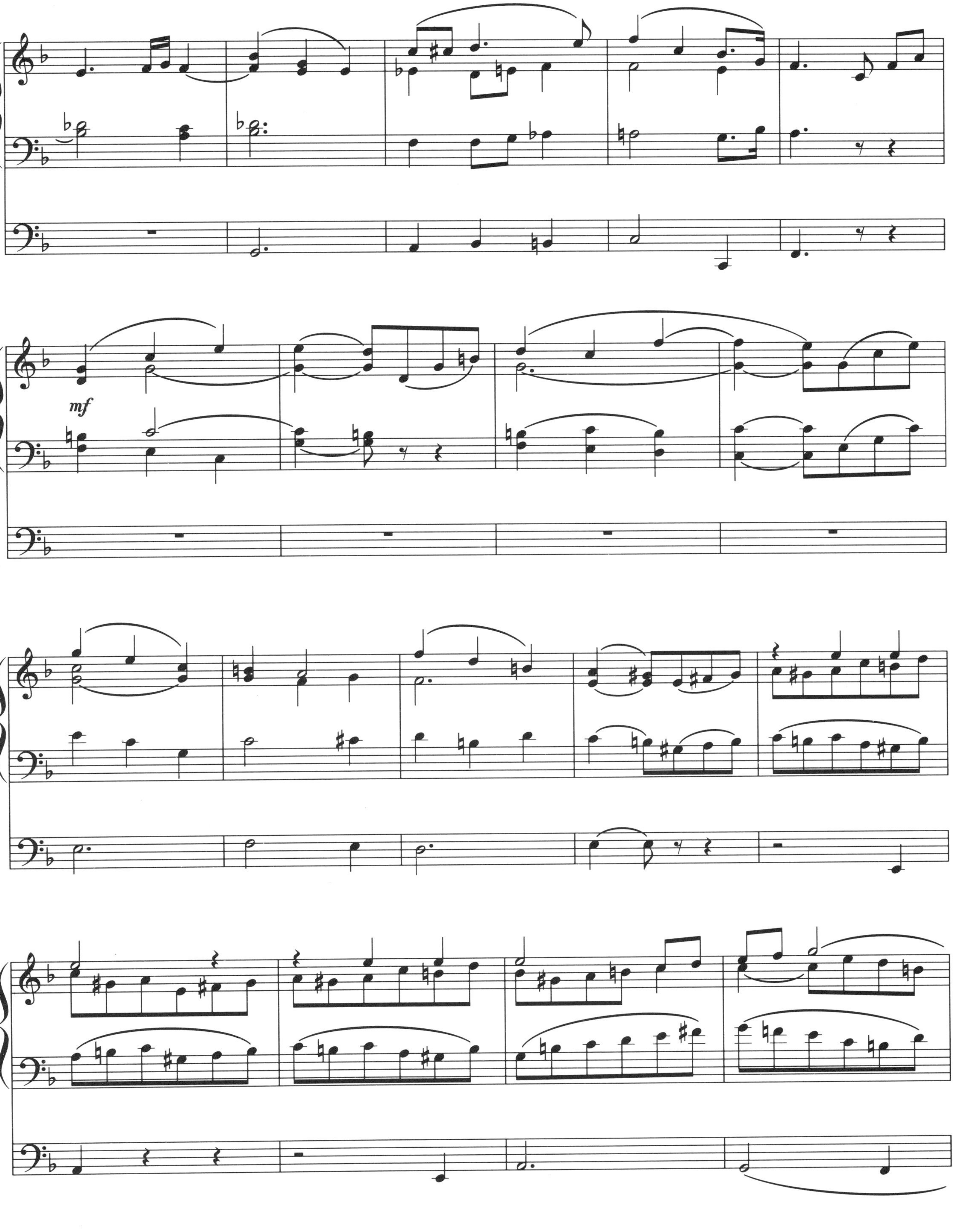
mf

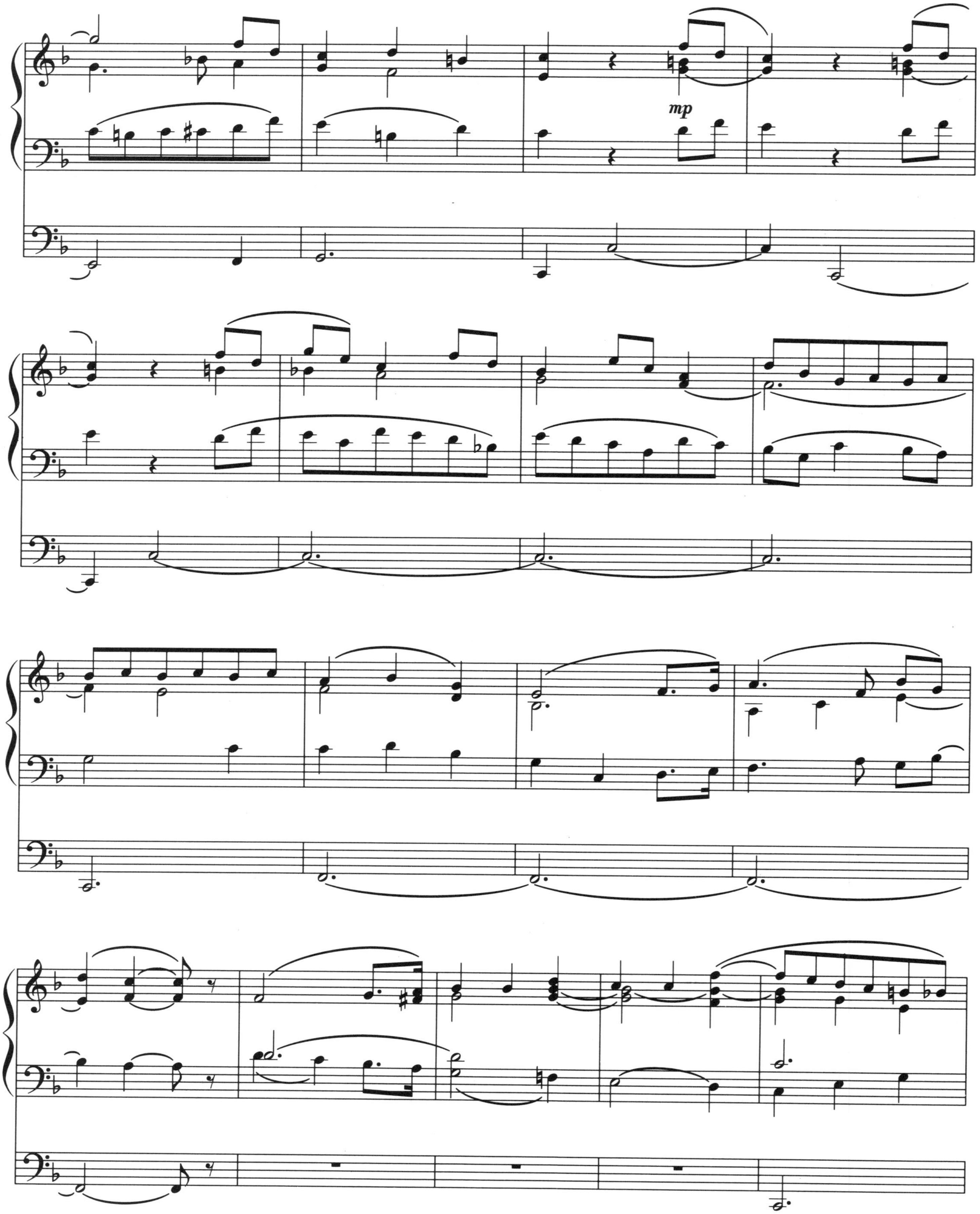
mp

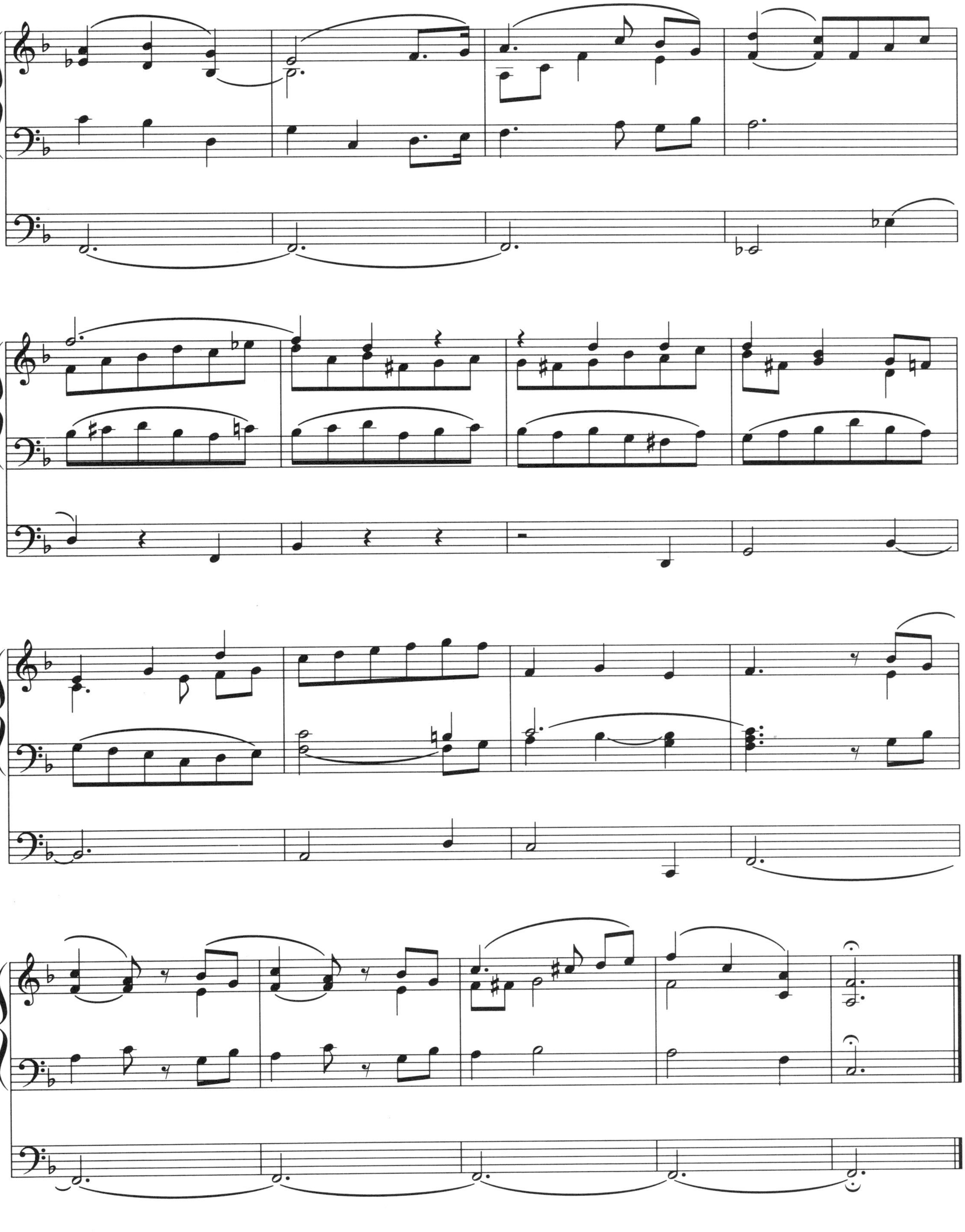

SHORT PRELUDE

Alan Gray (1855-1935)

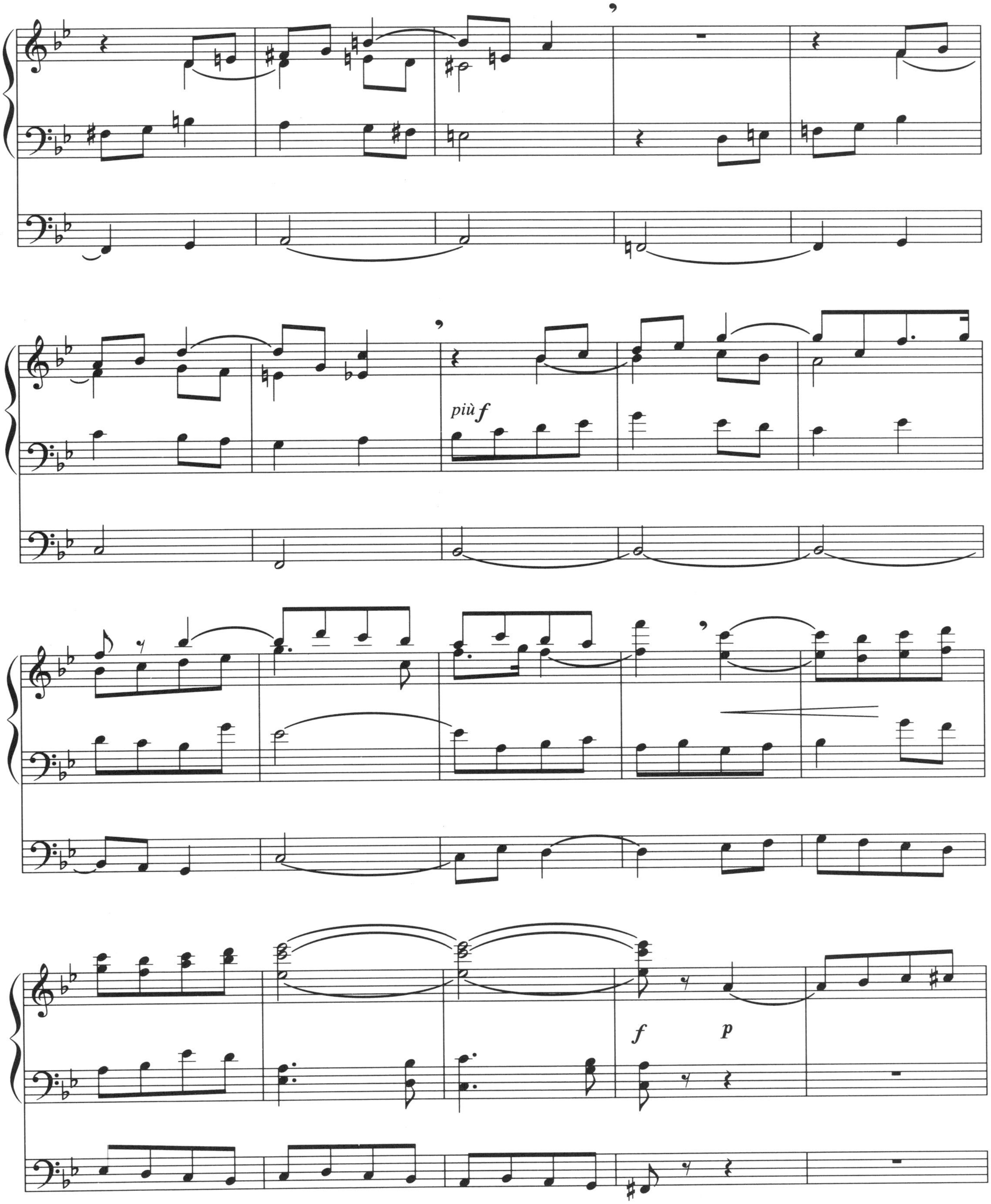
più f
f
p

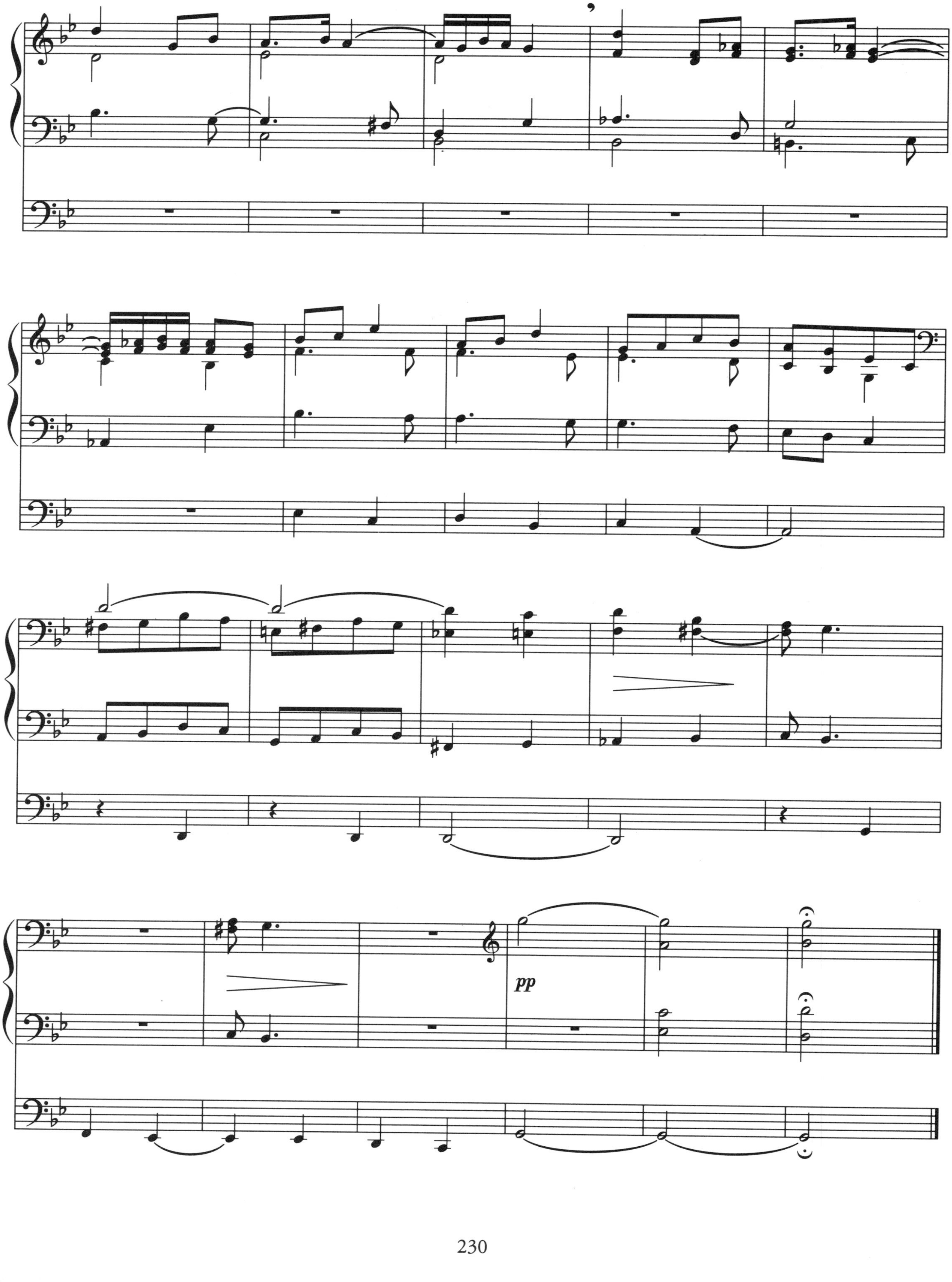
pp

MEDITATION

Norman Warren (*b.*1934)

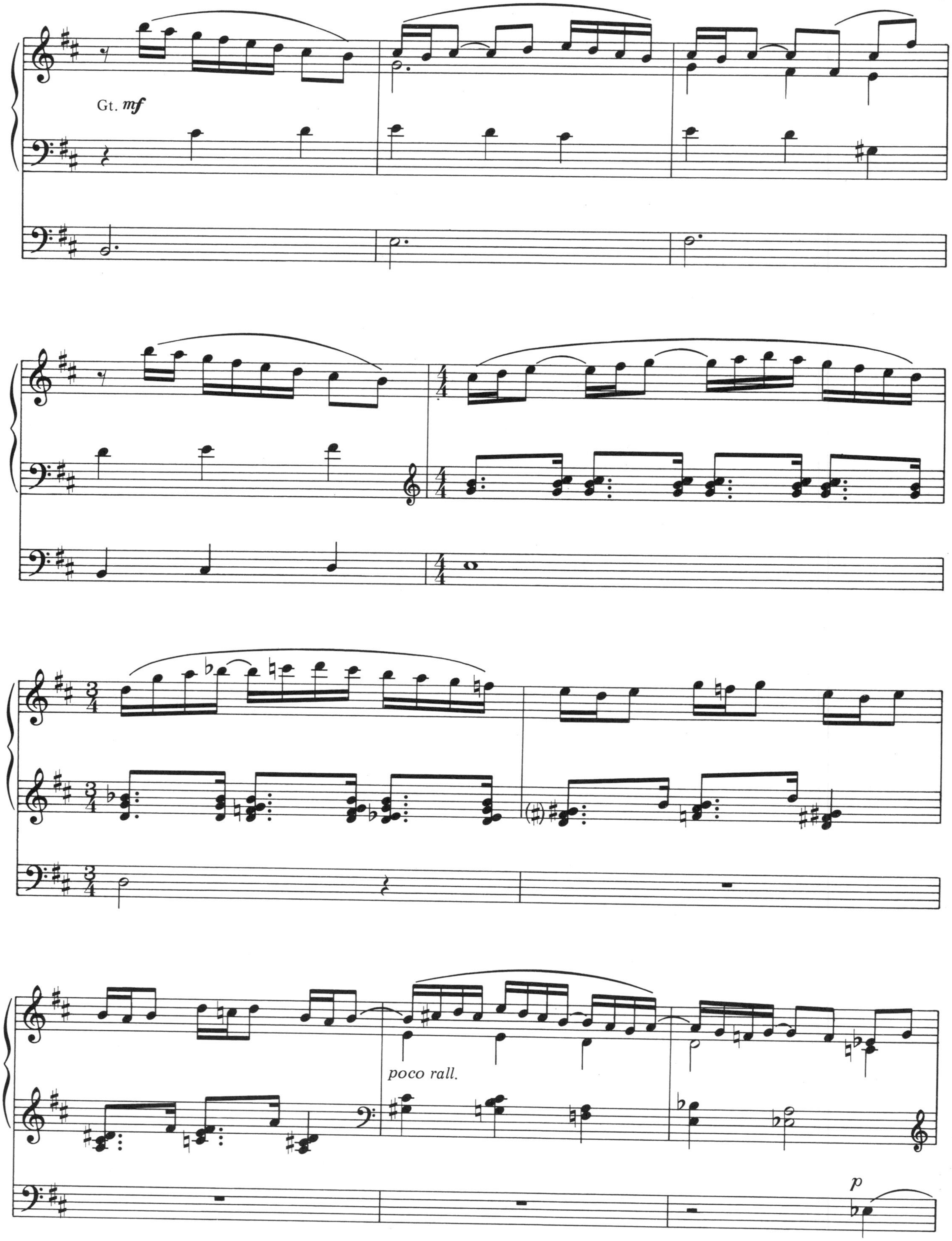

Gt. mf
poco rall.
p

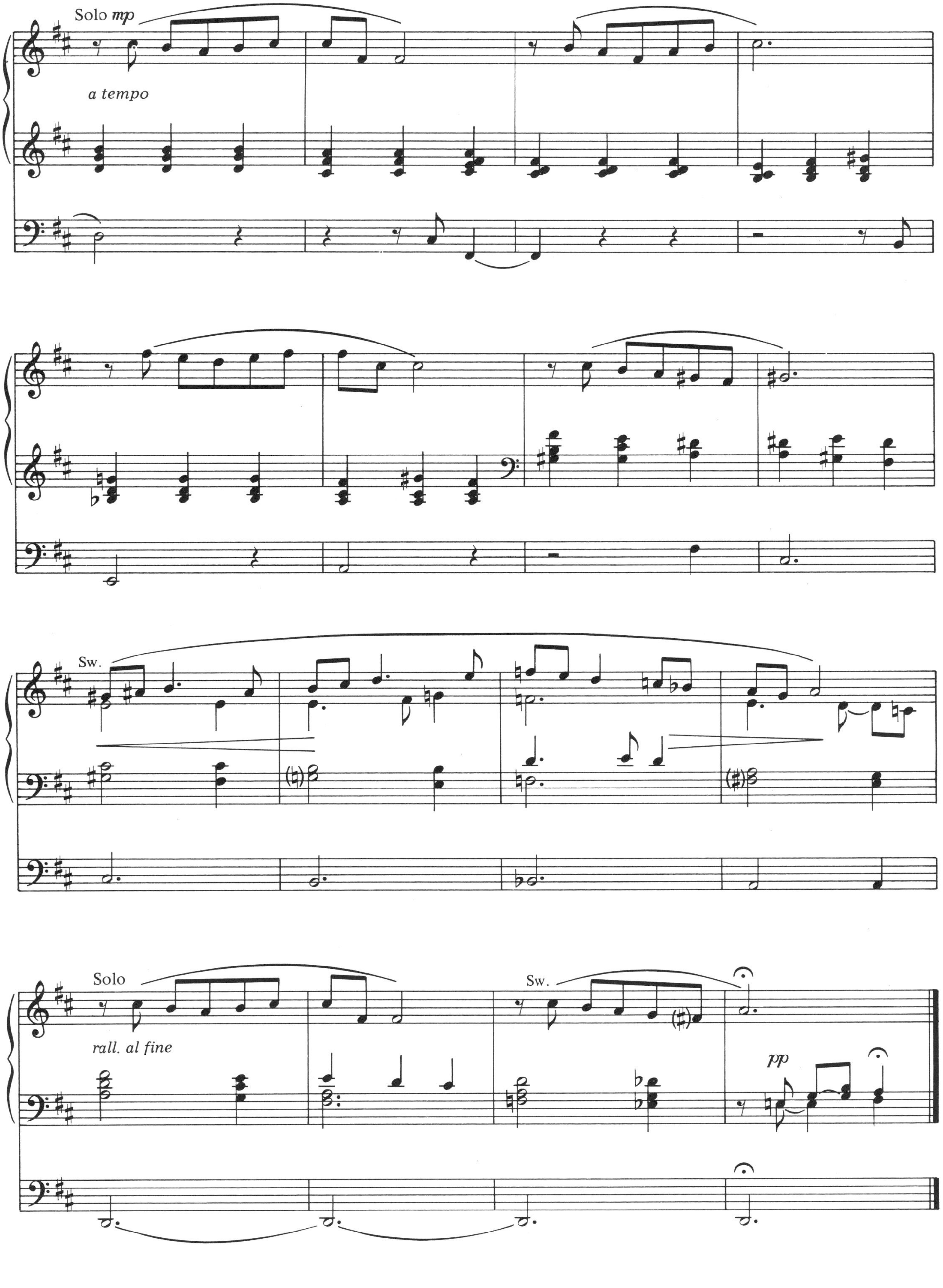
Solo mp
a tempo
Sw.
Solo
rall. al fine
Sw.
pp

For Sara

TRIO

Christopher Tambling (*b.*1964)

Gt. 8 + 4 + 2²⁄₃
Sw. 8 + 4 + 2

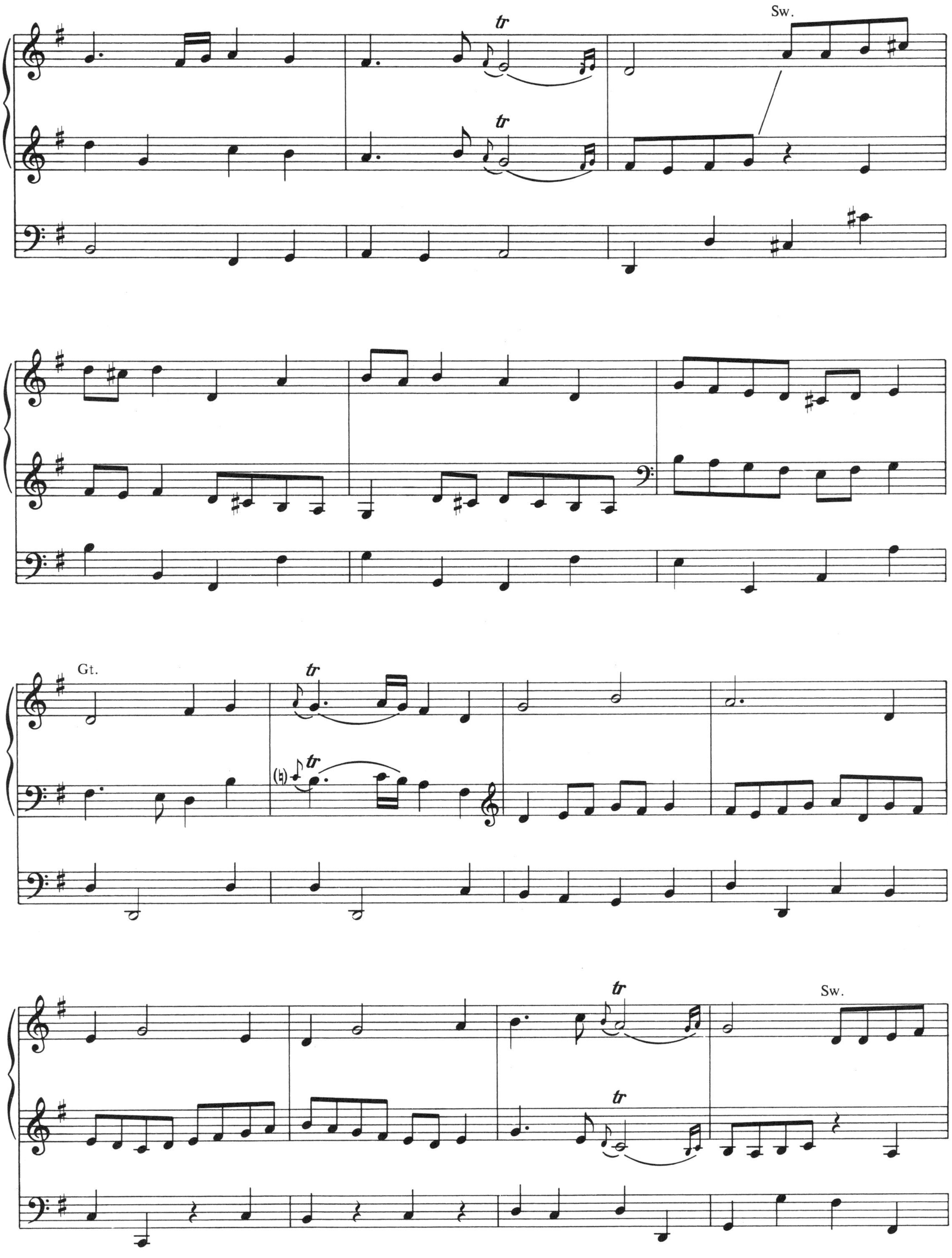
Sw.
Gt.
Sw.

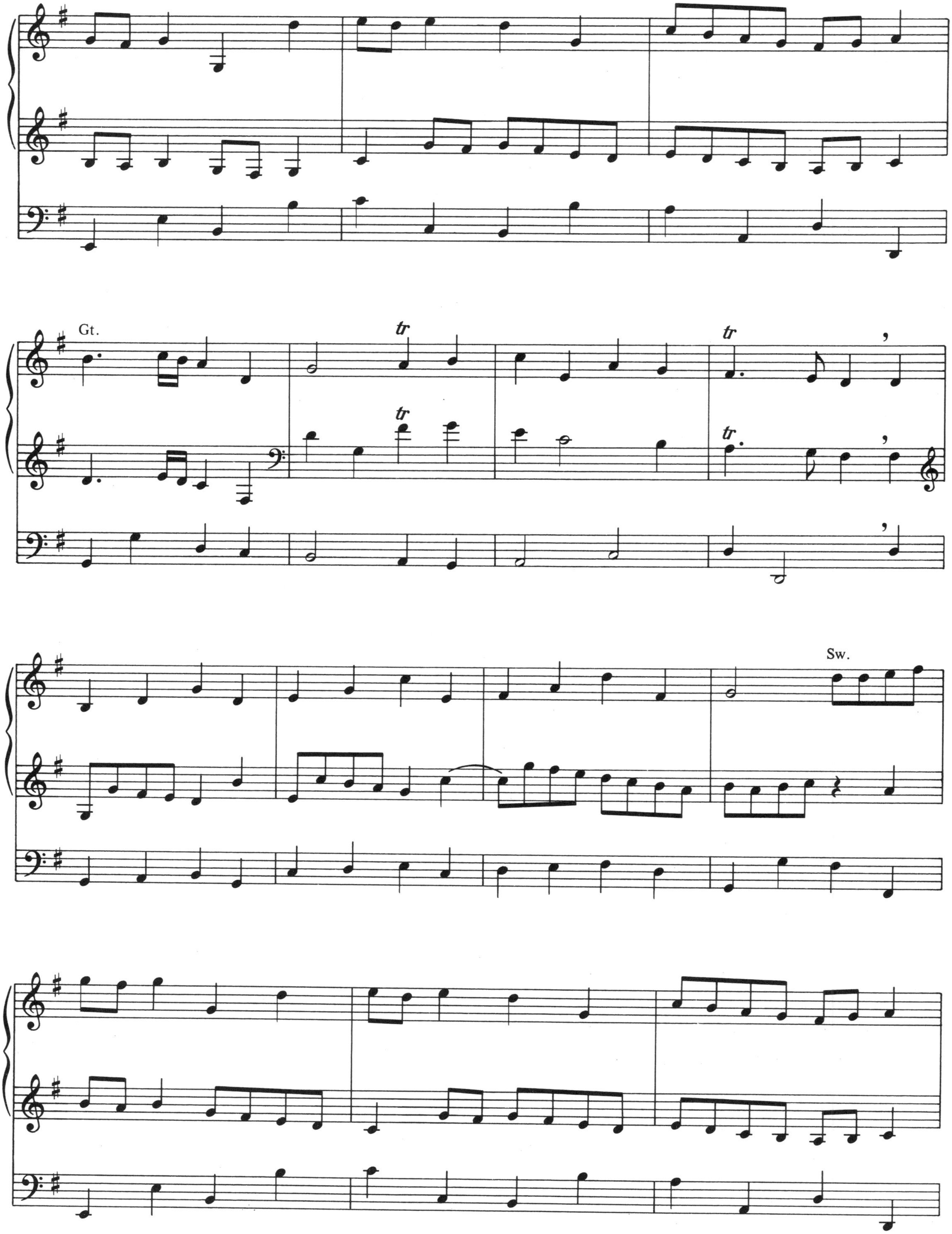
Gt.
Sw.

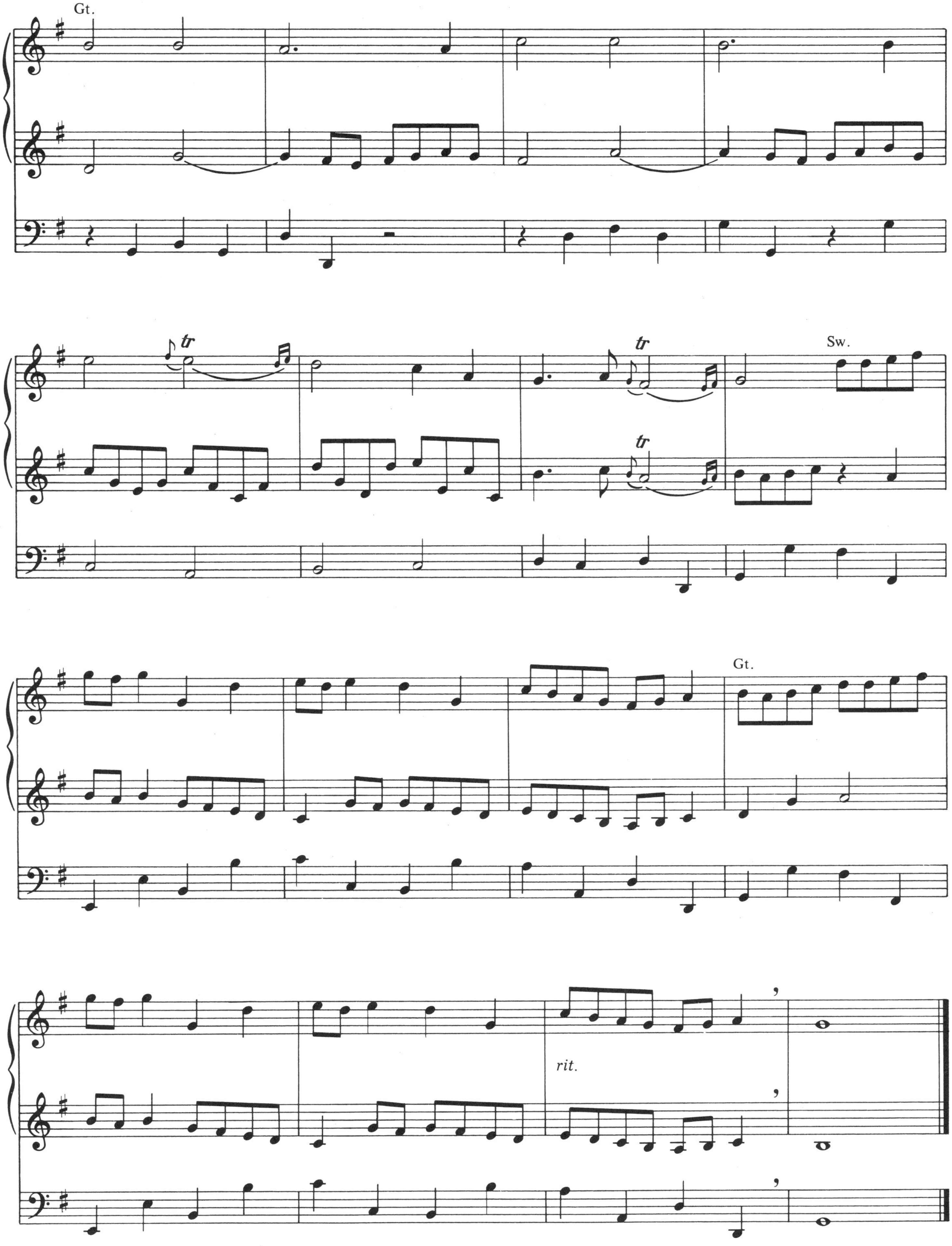
Gt.
tr
tr
tr
Sw.
Gt.
rit.

PRELUDE in F MINOR

Johann Rinck (1770-1846)

Moderato

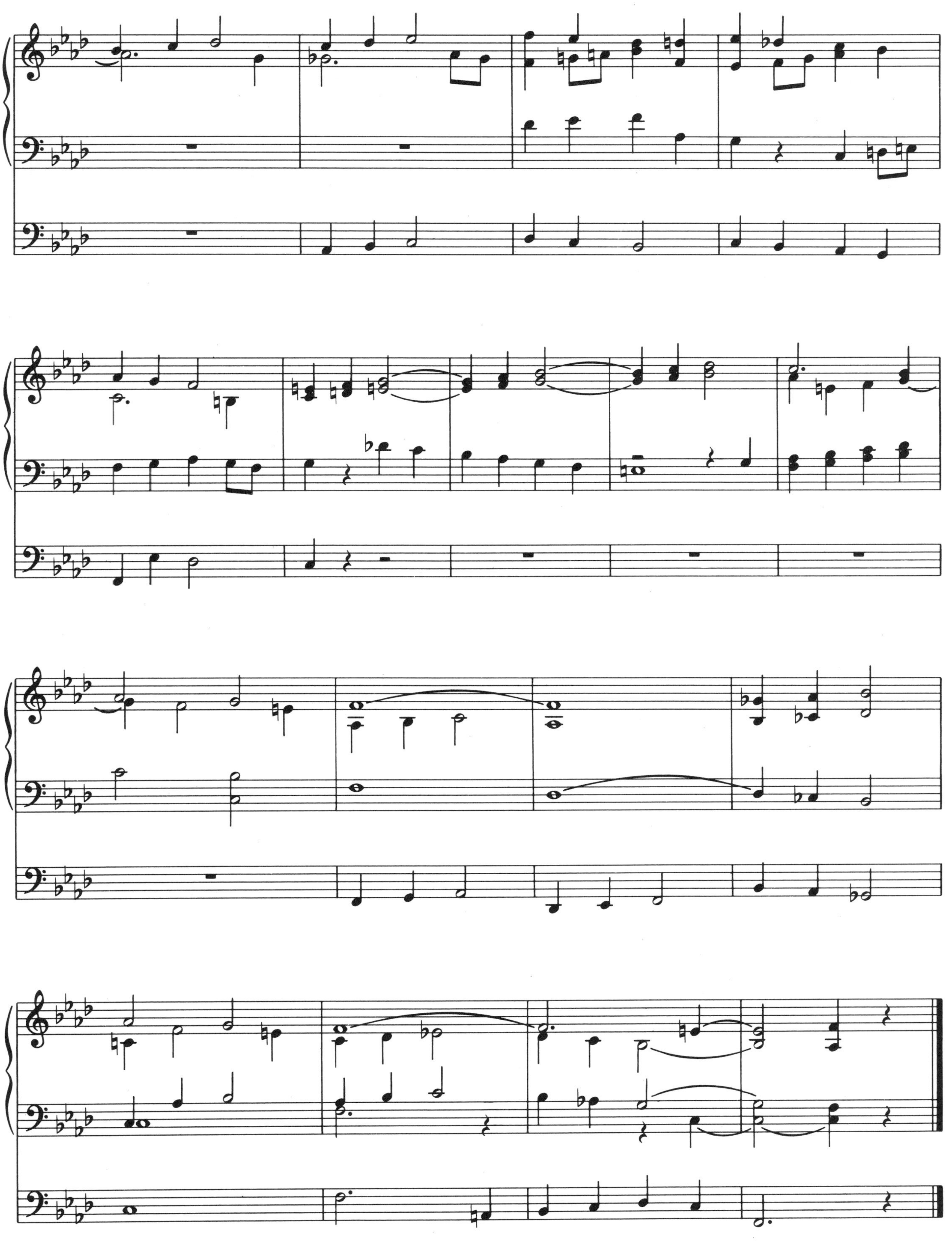

ARIA

Henry Oswald (1852-1931)

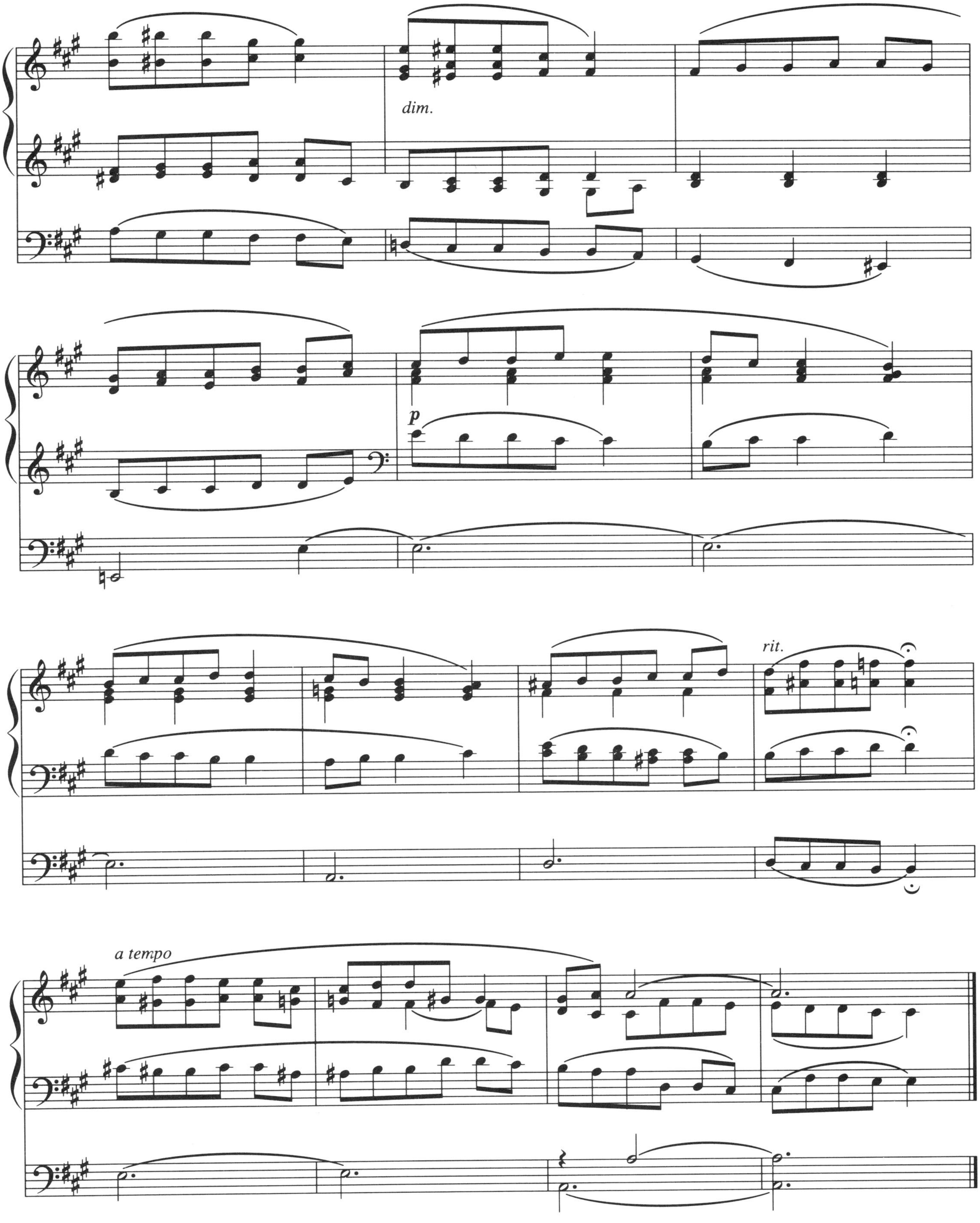
dim.
p
rit.
a tempo

PRAYER II

Alexandre Guilmant (1837-1911)

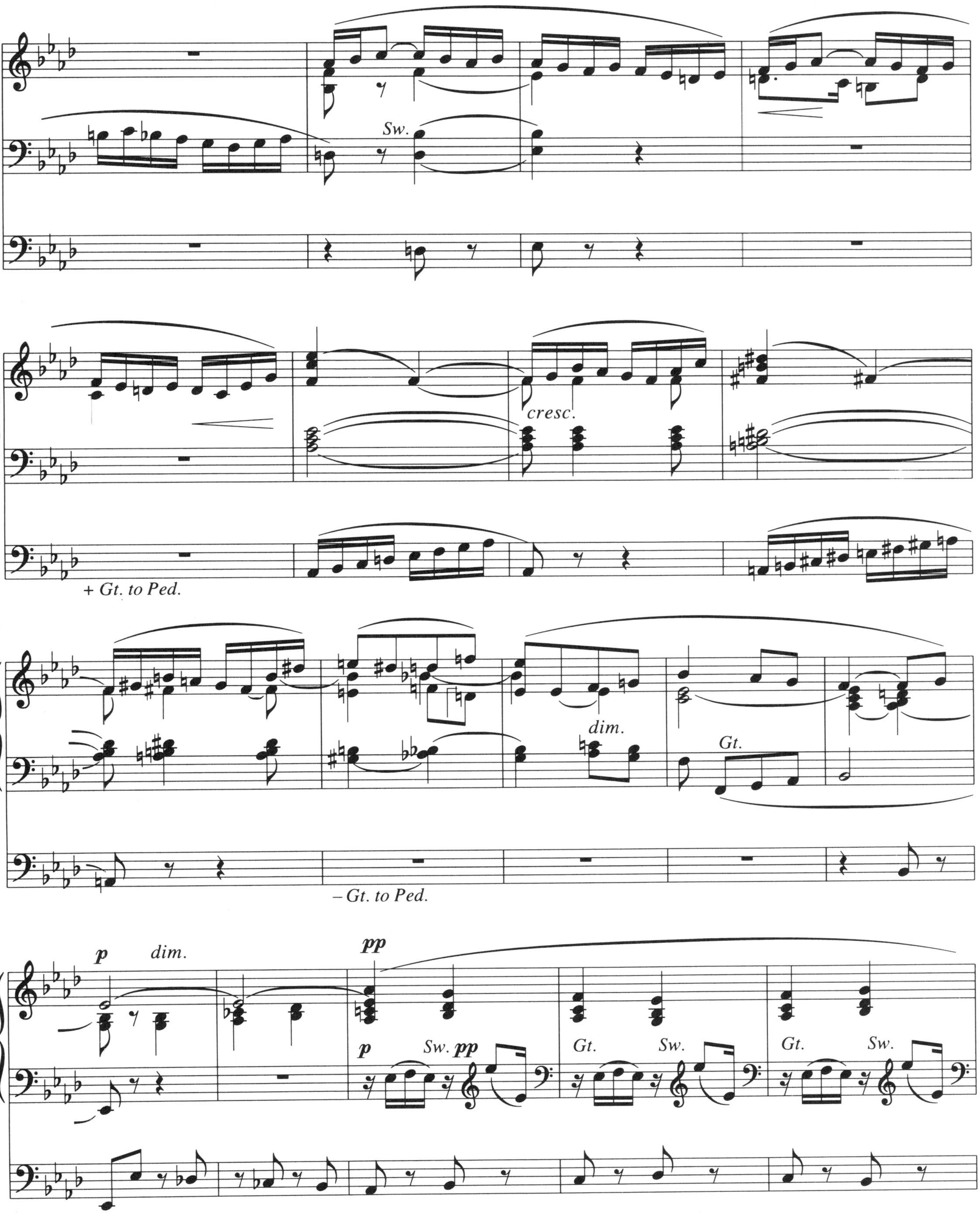

Sw.
cresc.
+ Gt. to Ped.
dim.
Gt.
– Gt. to Ped.
p
dim.
pp
p
Sw. pp
Gt.
Sw.
Gt.
Sw.

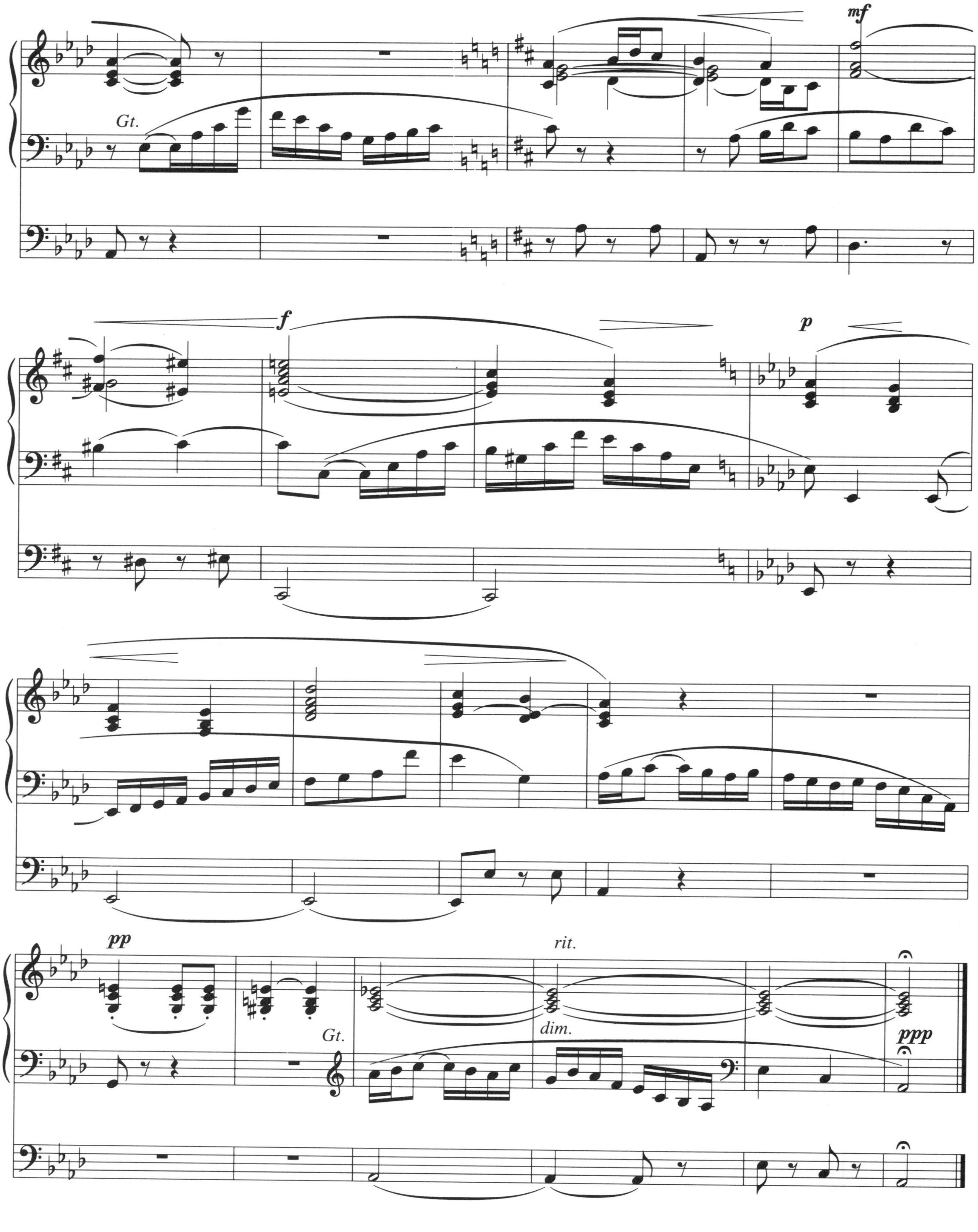
mf
Gt.
f
p
pp
rit.
Gt.
dim.
ppp

PRAELUDIUM

Herbert Brewer (1865-1928)

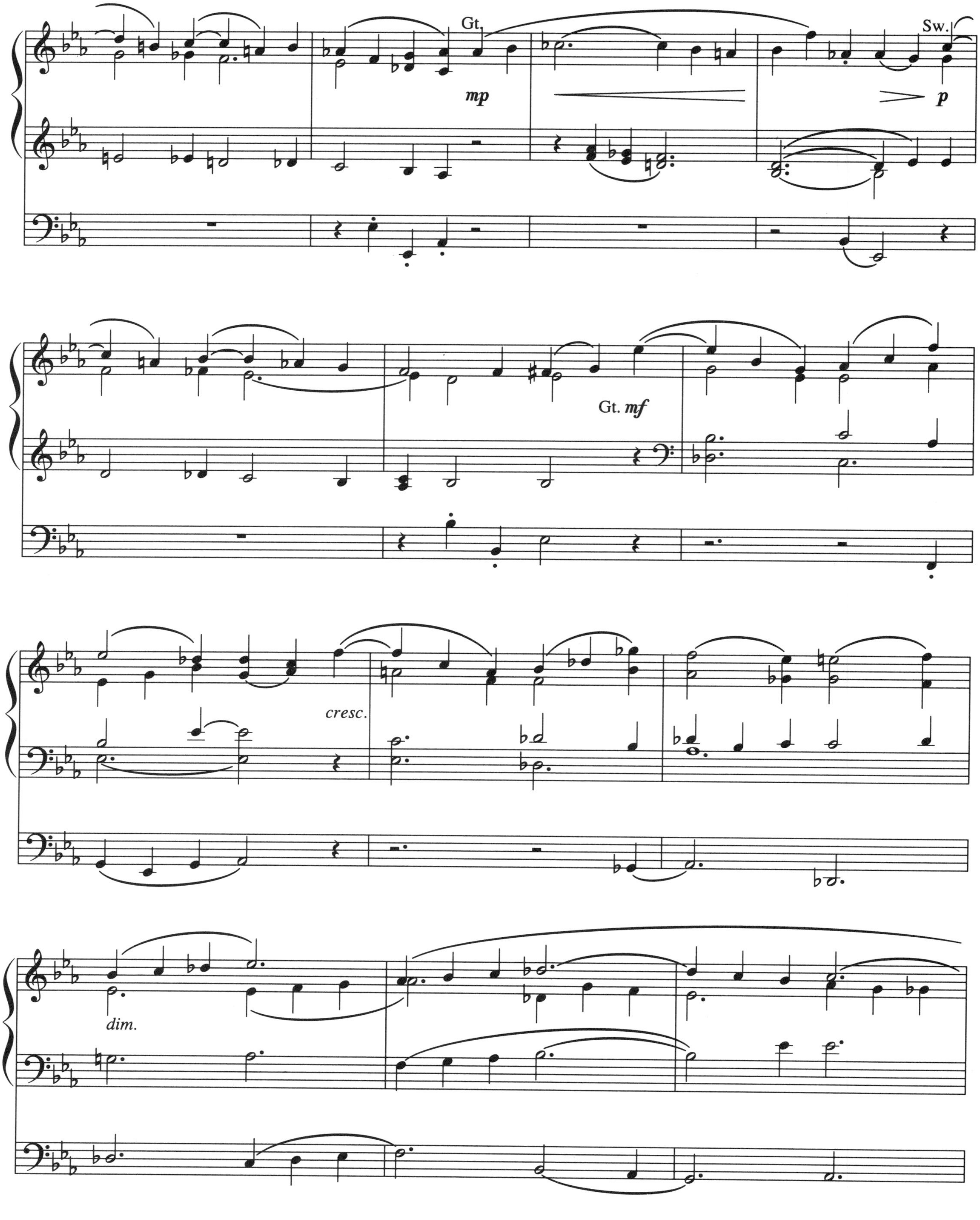
Gt.
mp
Sw.
p
Gt. mf
cresc.
dim.

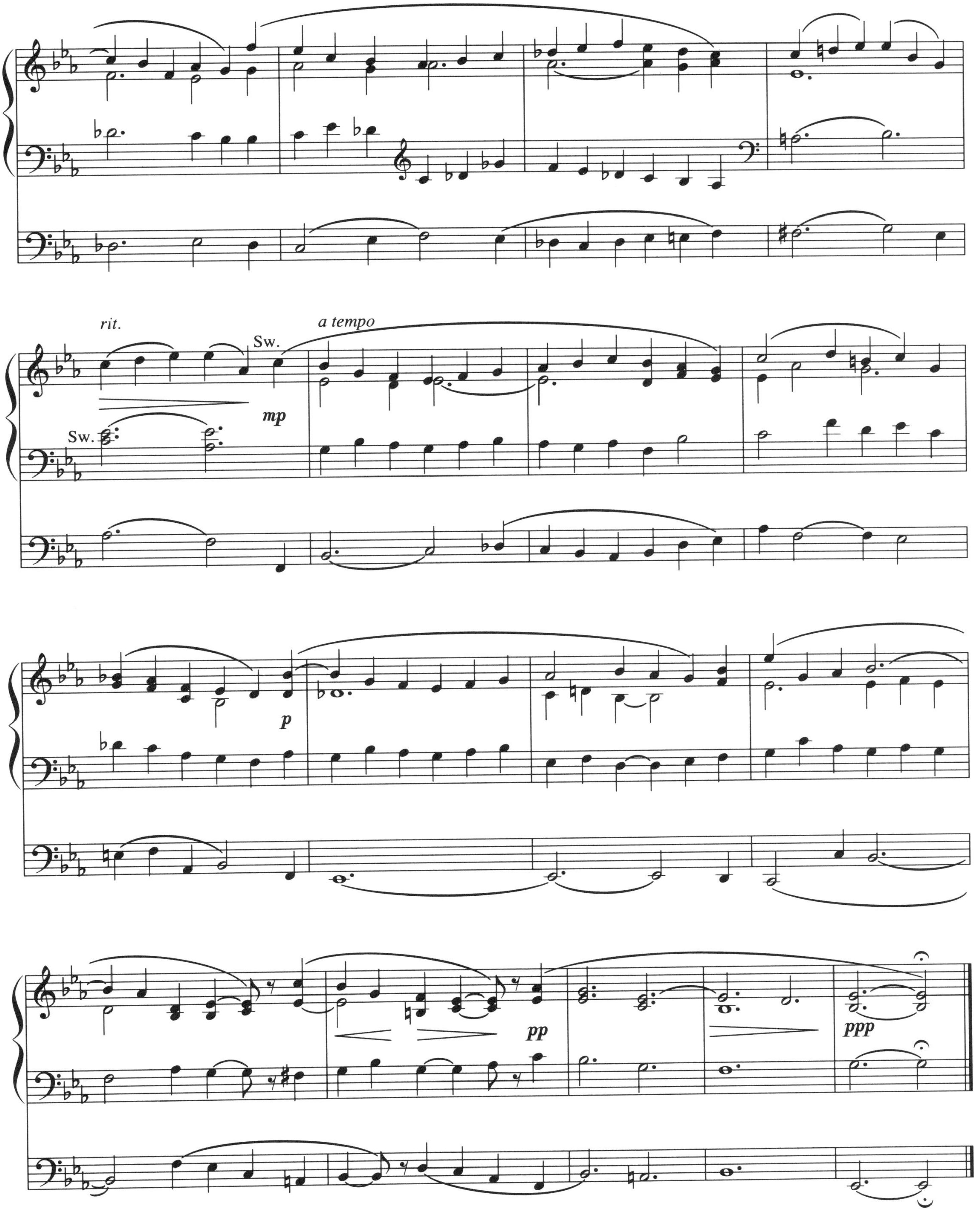
rit.
Sw.
a tempo
mp
Sw.
p
pp
ppp

For David Perry

INTERLUDE

on 'Irish'
Christopher Tambling (*b.*1964)

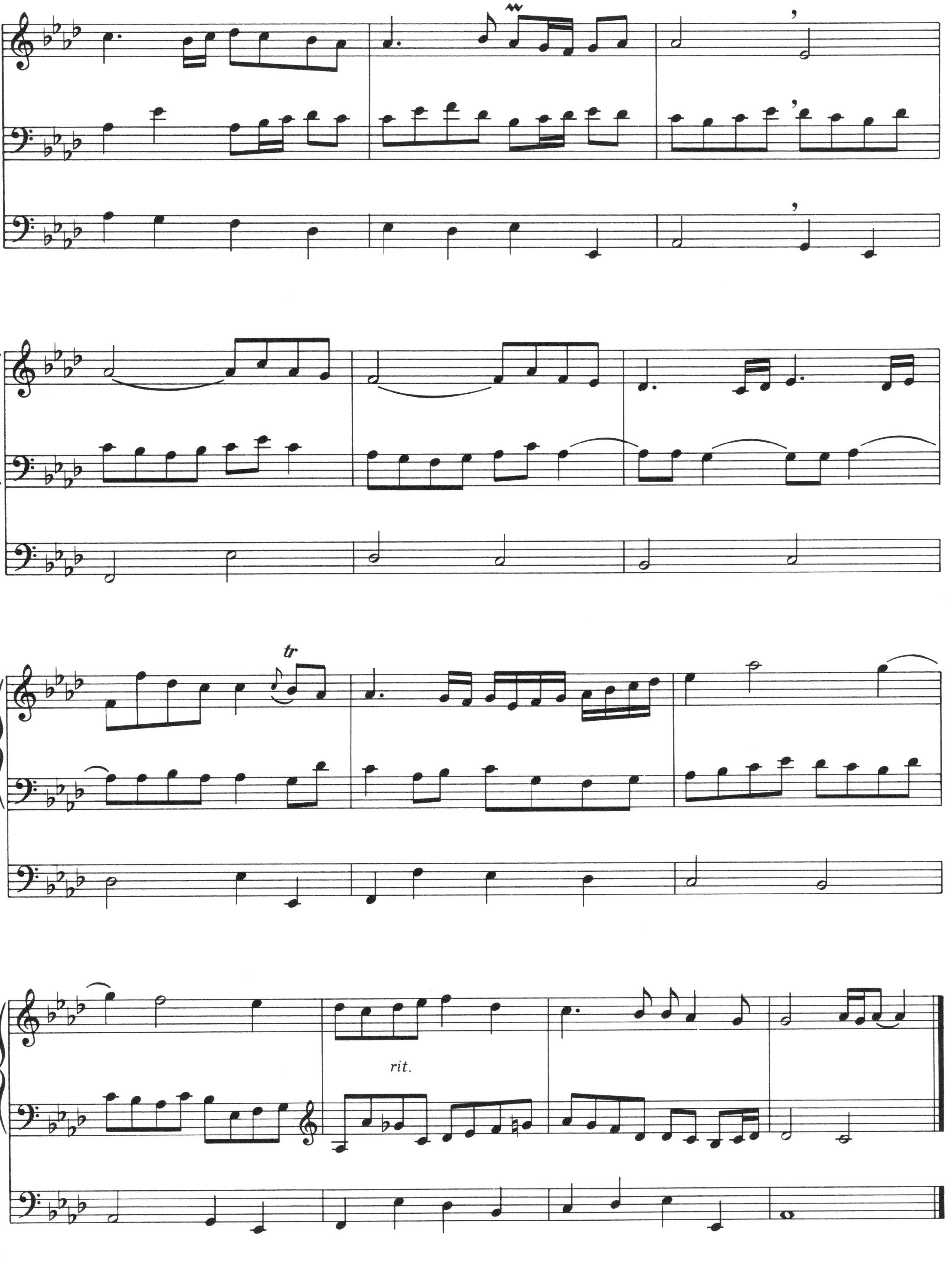

tr
rit.

PRELUDE in F

Johann Rinck (1770-1846)

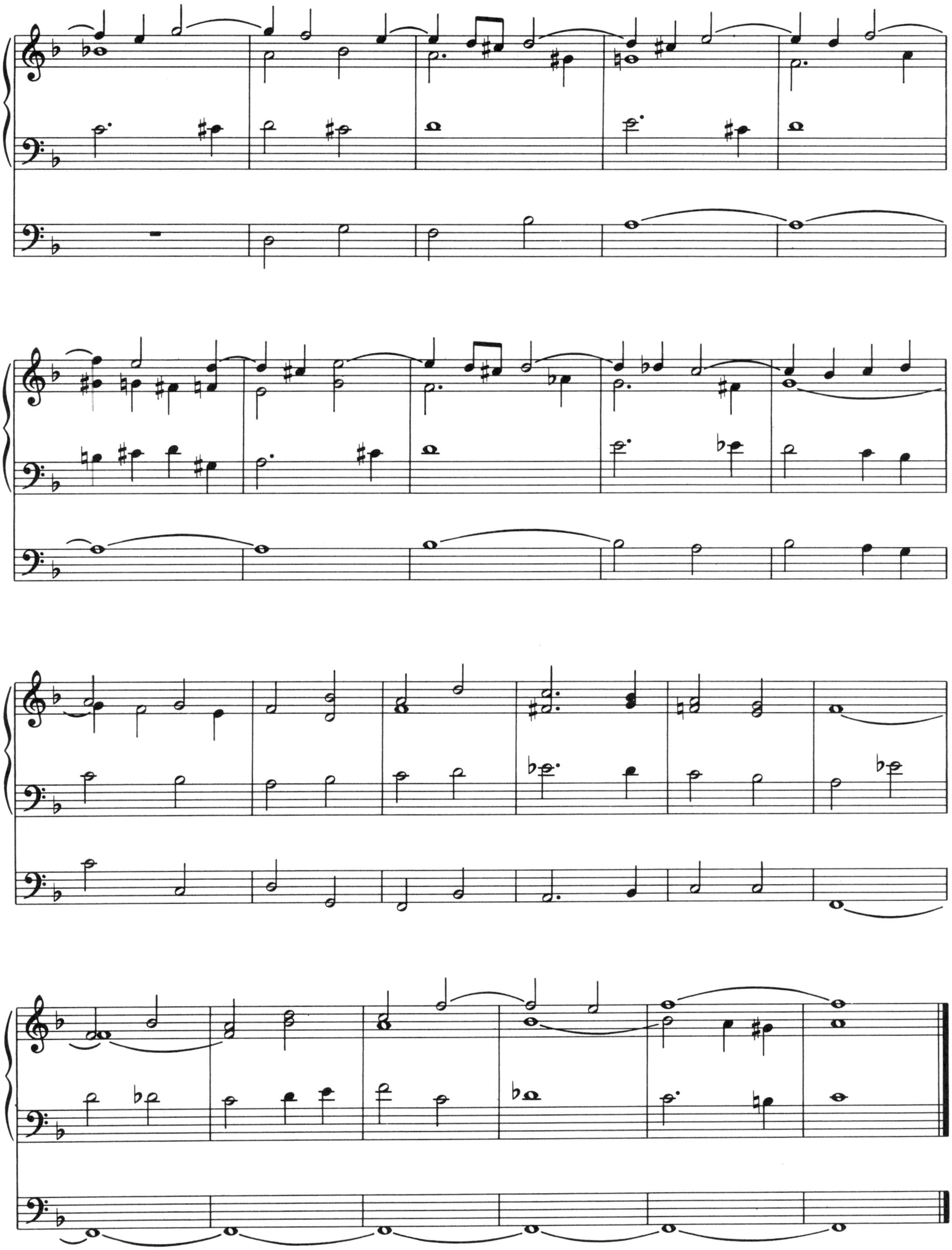

SOFT VOLUNTARY

Harry Alfred Harding (1855-1930)

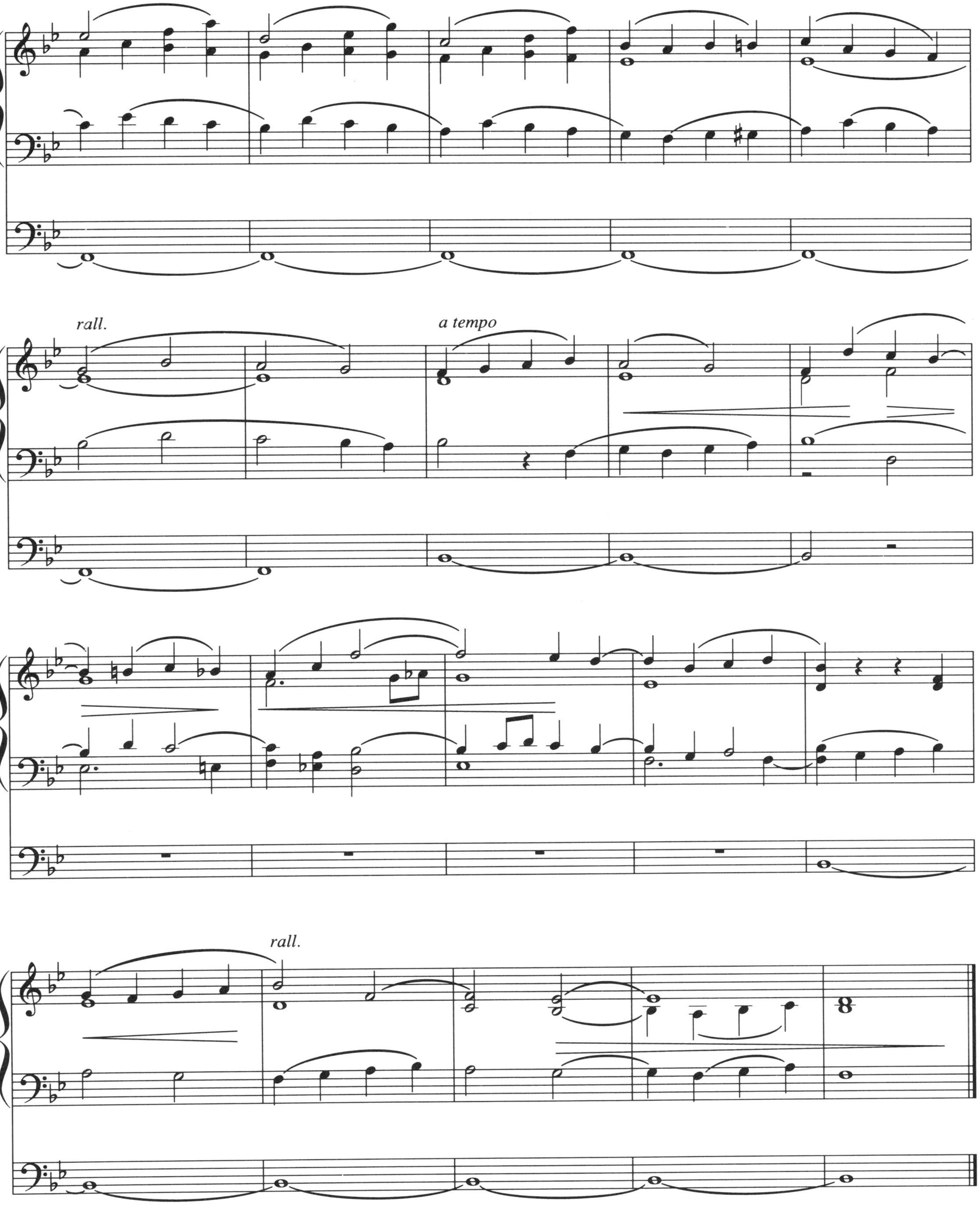
rall.
a tempo
rall.

For Edmond Rose

PRELUDE

on 'Slane'
Christopher Tambling (*b.*1964)

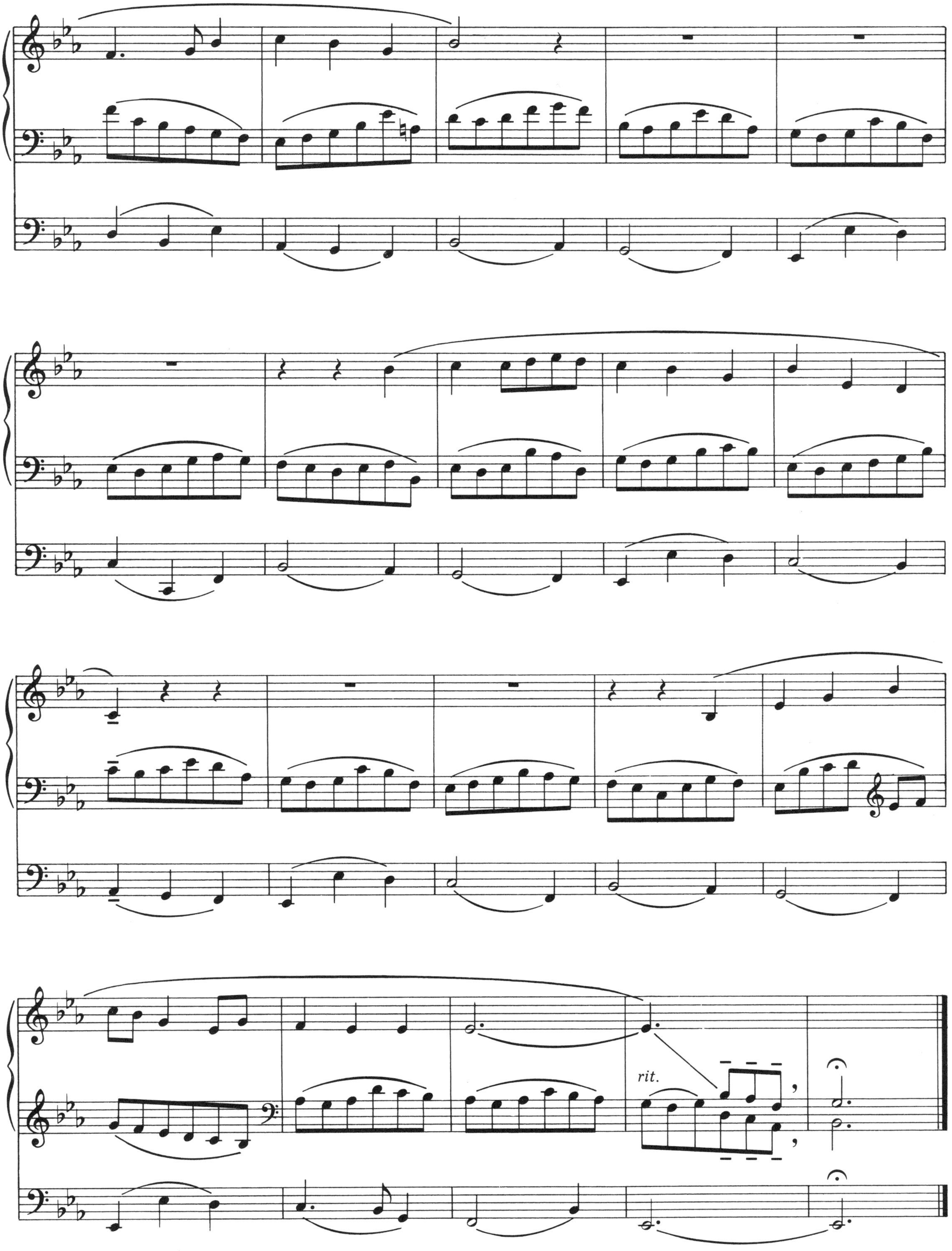
rit.

COMMUNION

William Wolstenholme (1865-1931)

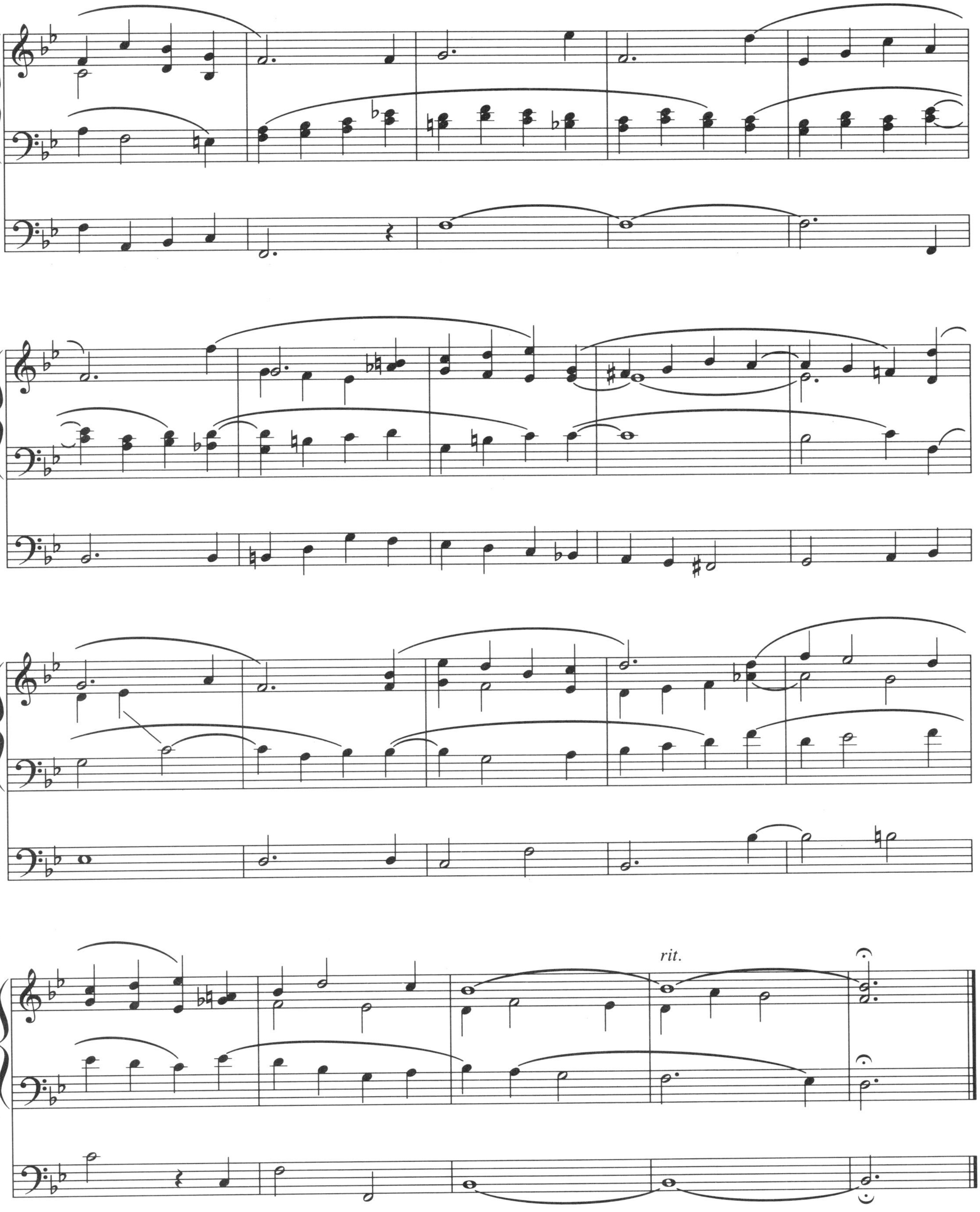
rit.

PRELUDE in G MINOR

Johann Rinck (1770-1846)

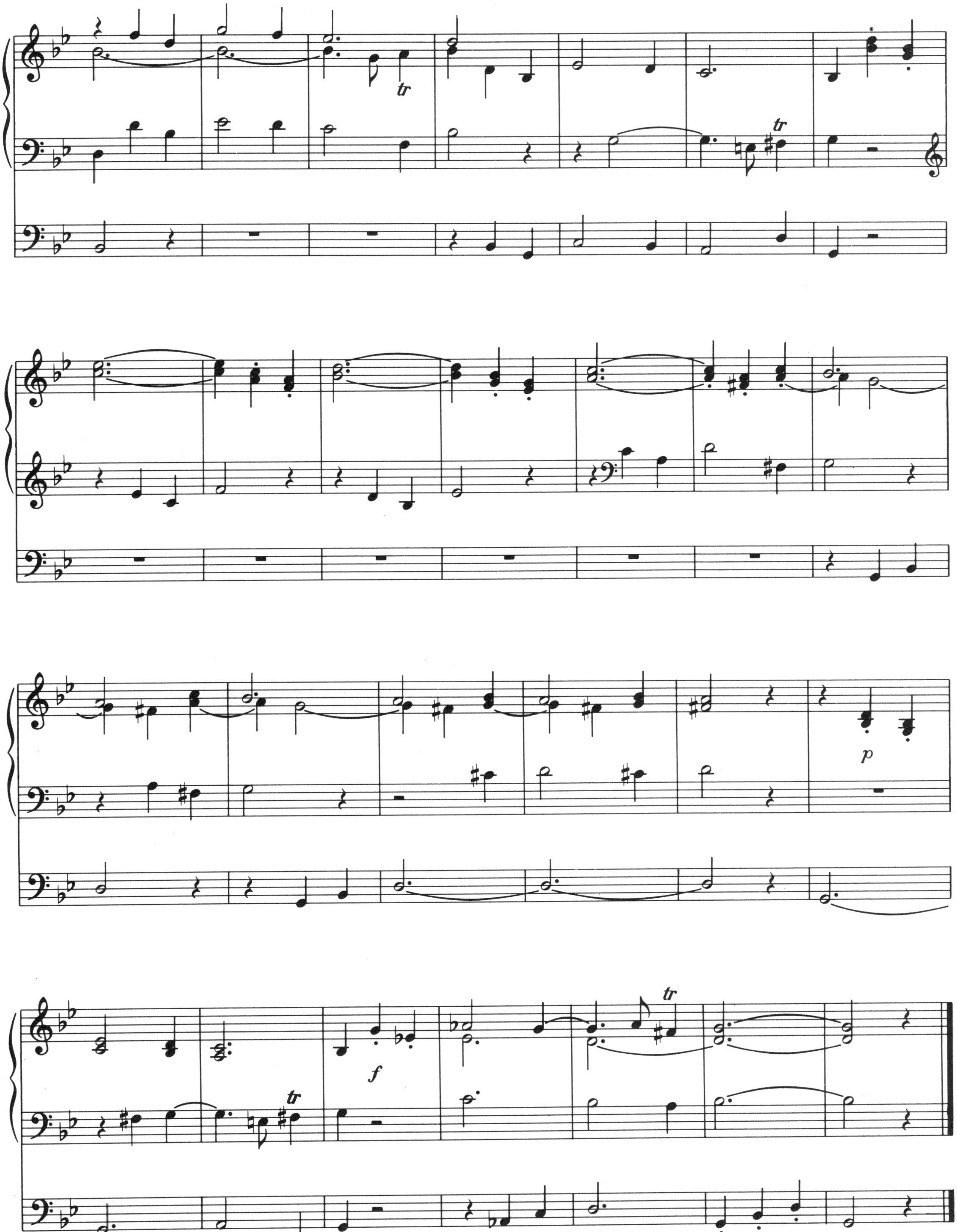
tr
tr
p
tr
f
tr

For Great Aunt Winifred

ARIA

Christopher Tambling (*b.*1964)

Sw. Oboe + Tremulant
Gt. 8

Adagio

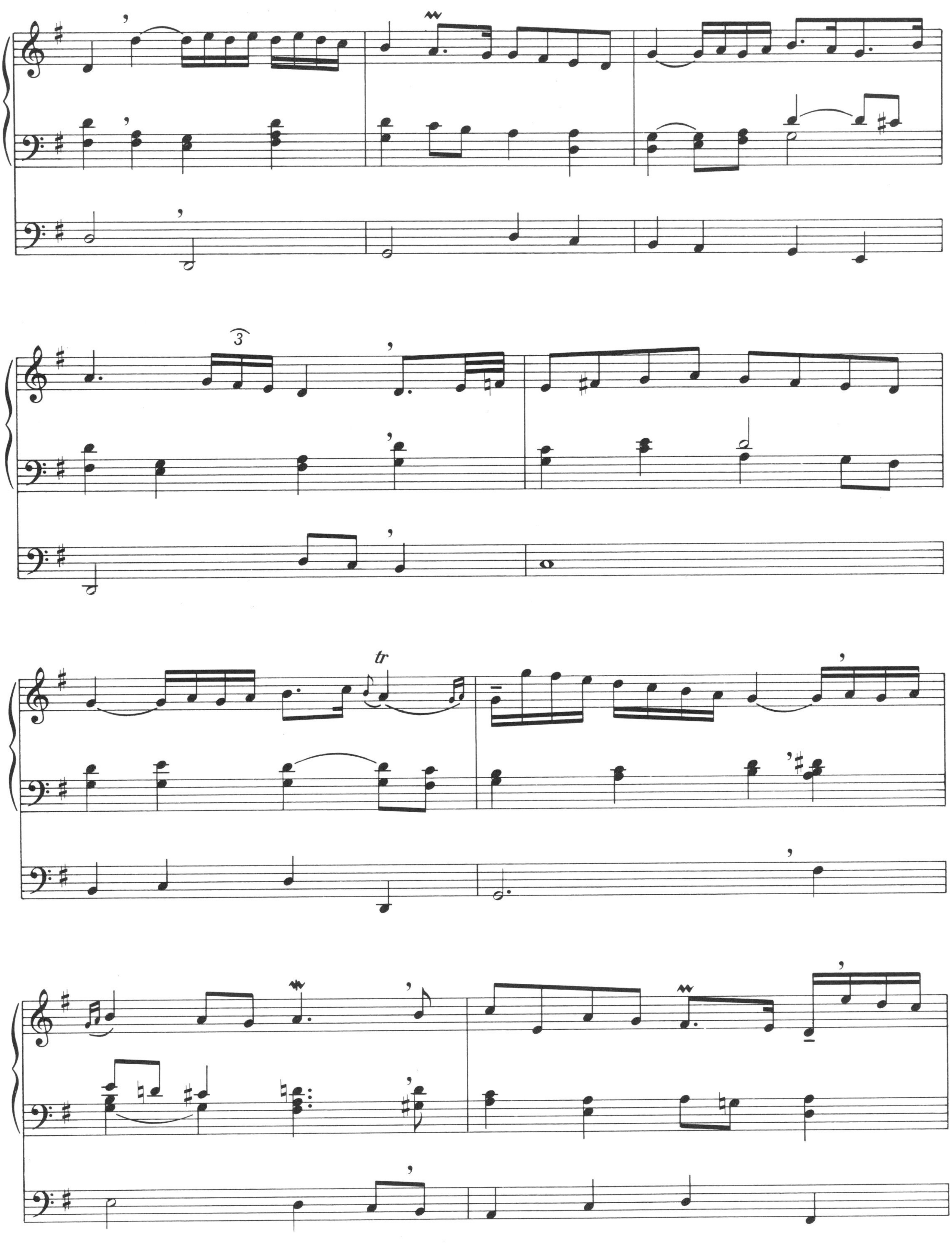

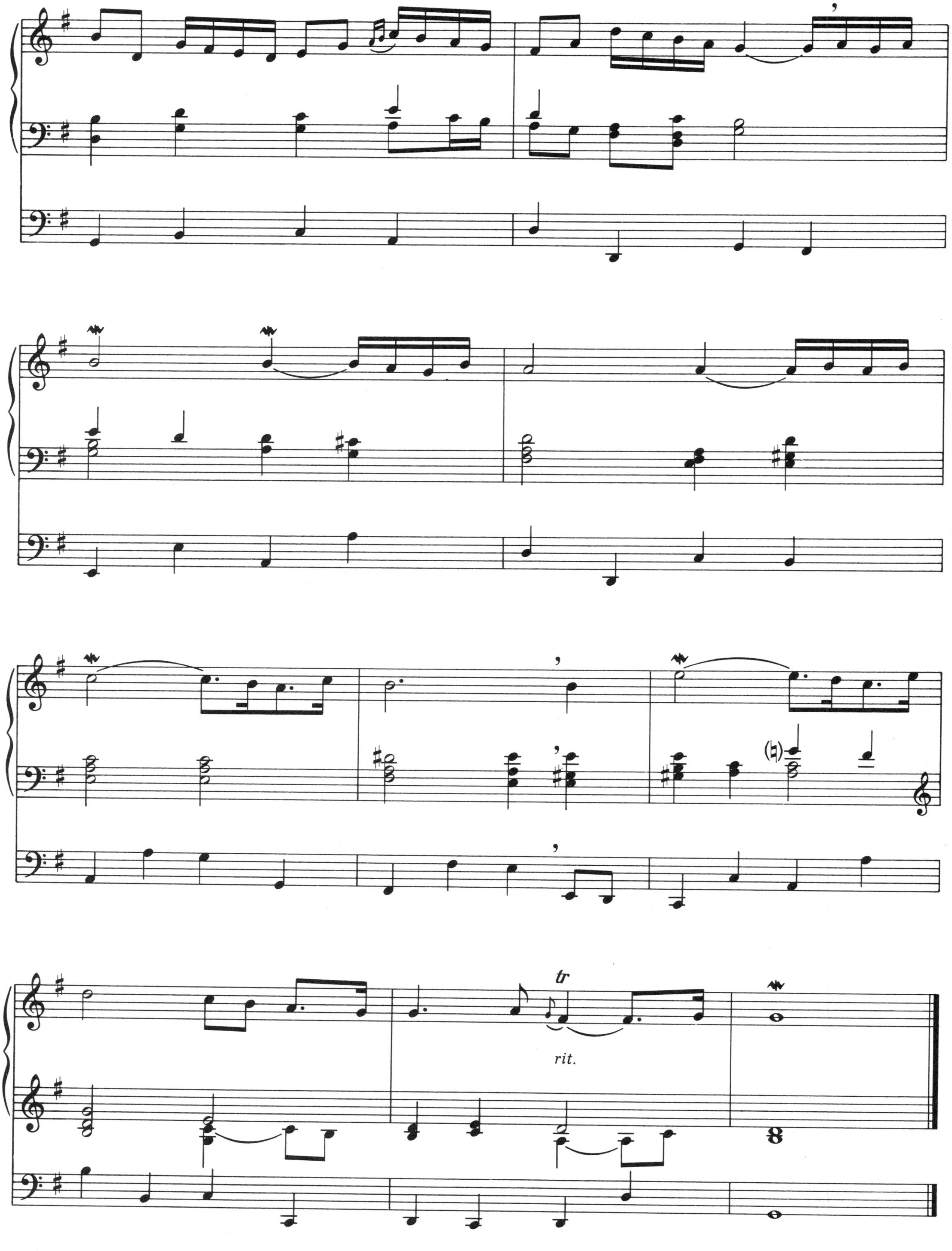
rit.

OFFERTORY in G

Alexandre Guilmant (1837-1911)

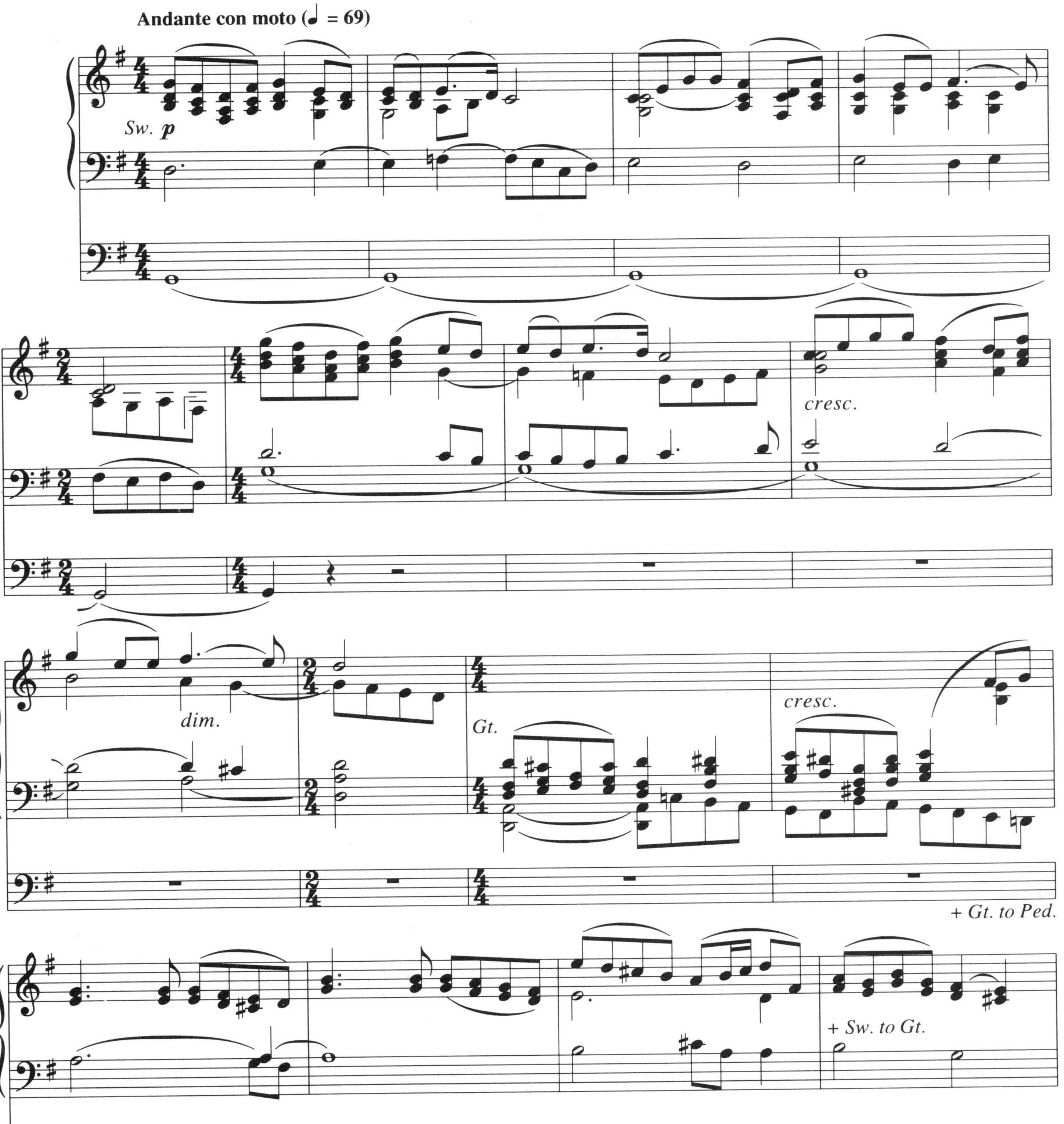

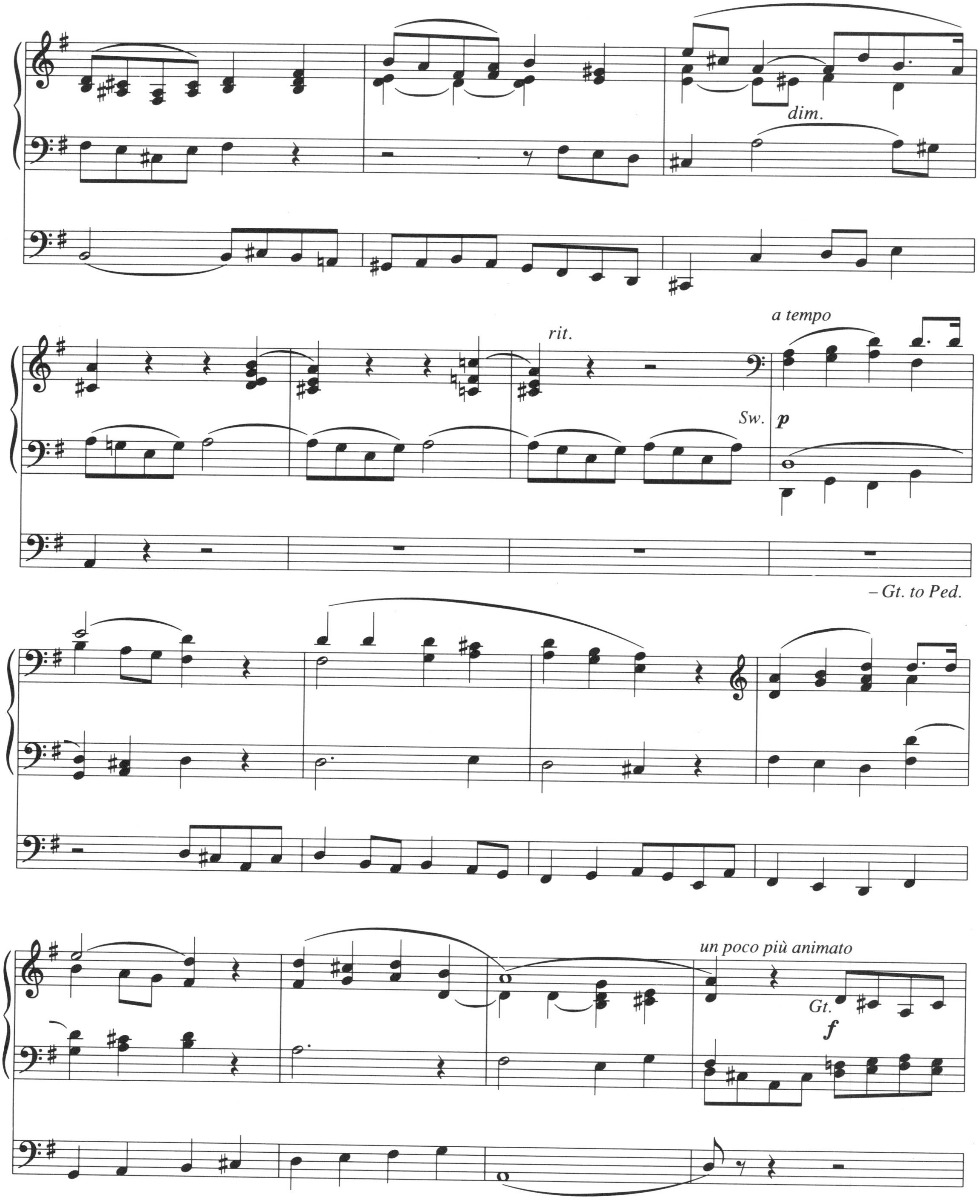
dim.
a tempo
rit.
Sw.
p
– Gt. to Ped.
un poco più animato
Gt.
f

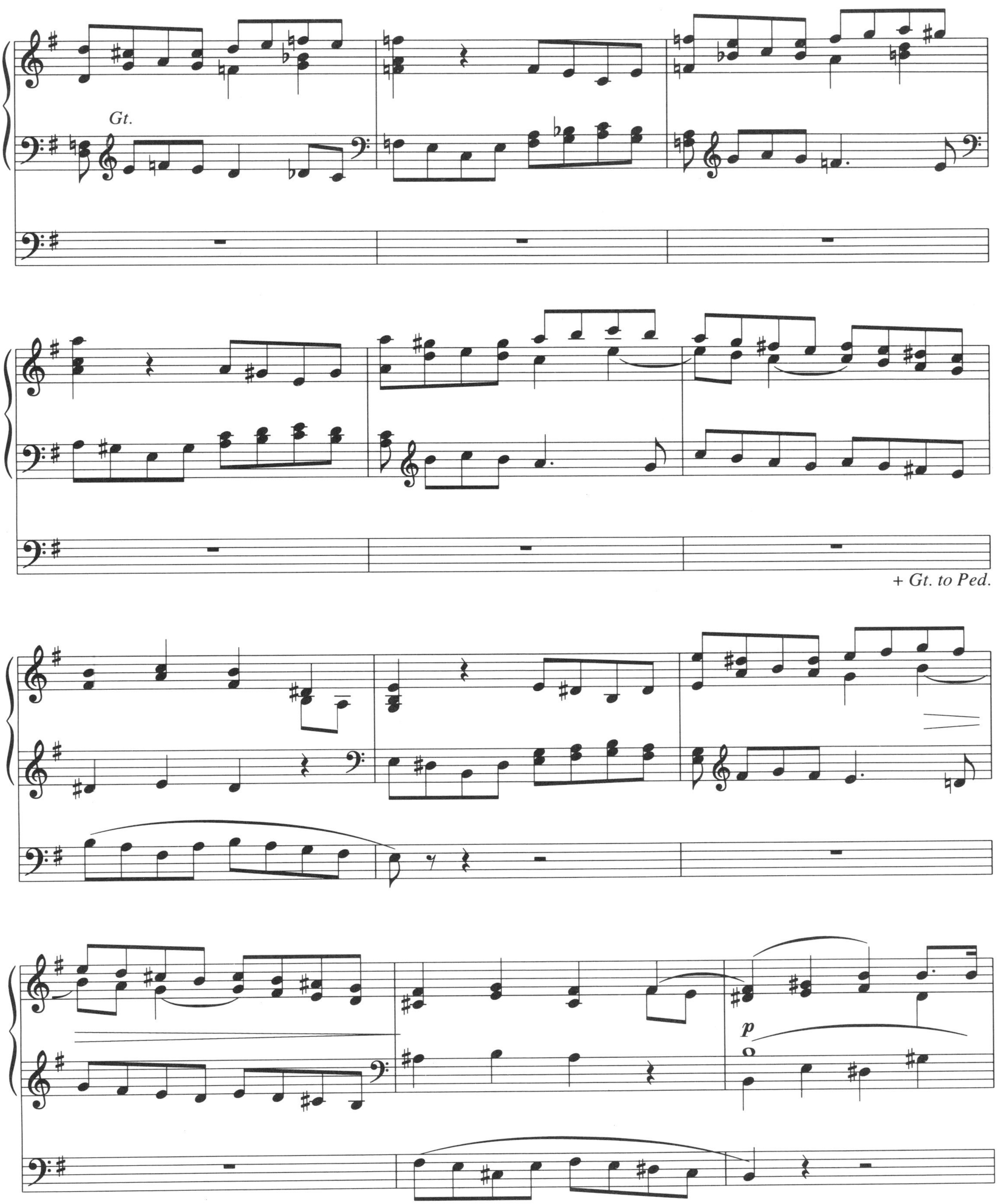
Gt.
+ Gt. to Ped.
p

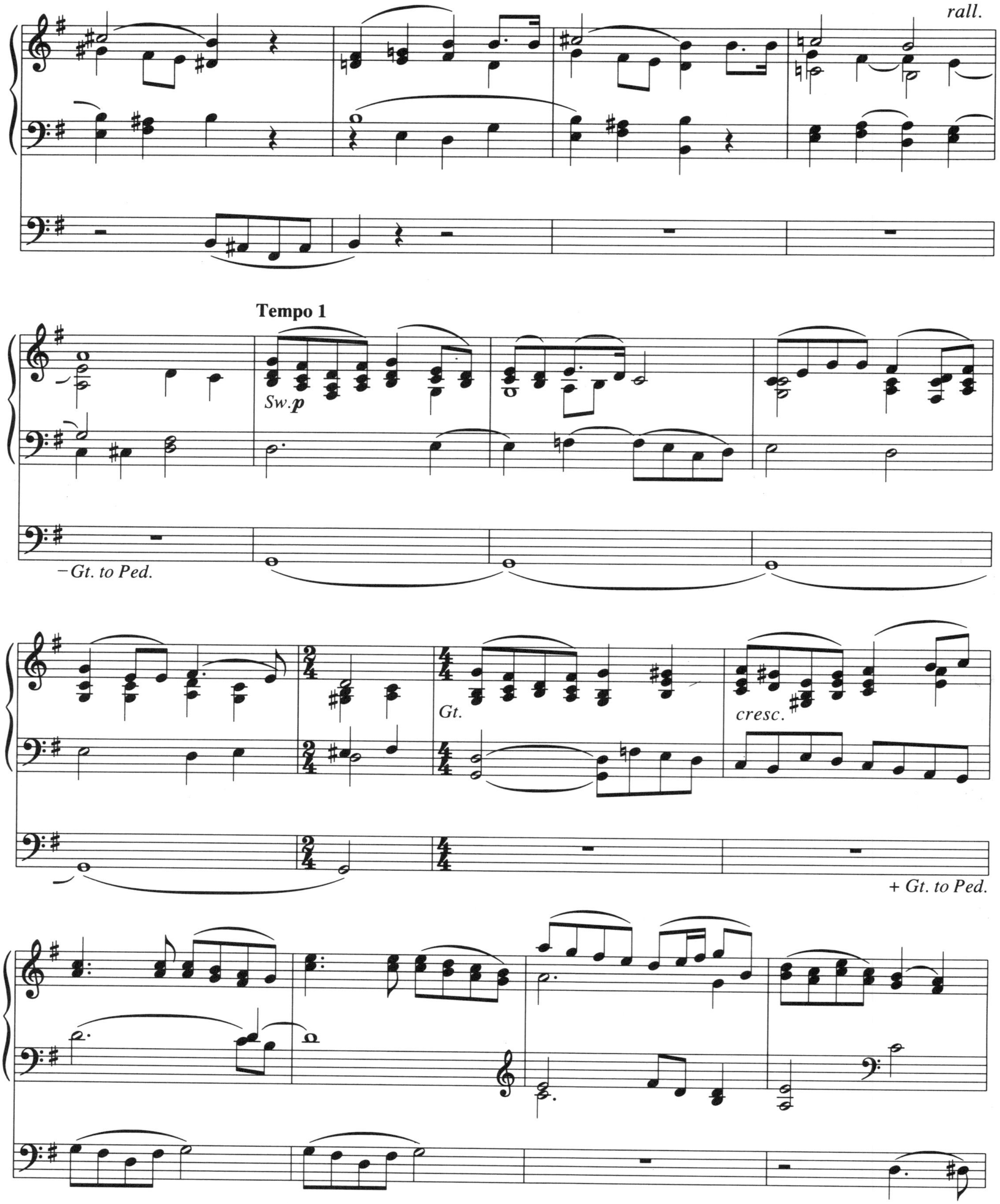
rall.
Tempo 1
Sw. p
−Gt. to Ped.
Gt.
cresc.
+ Gt. to Ped.

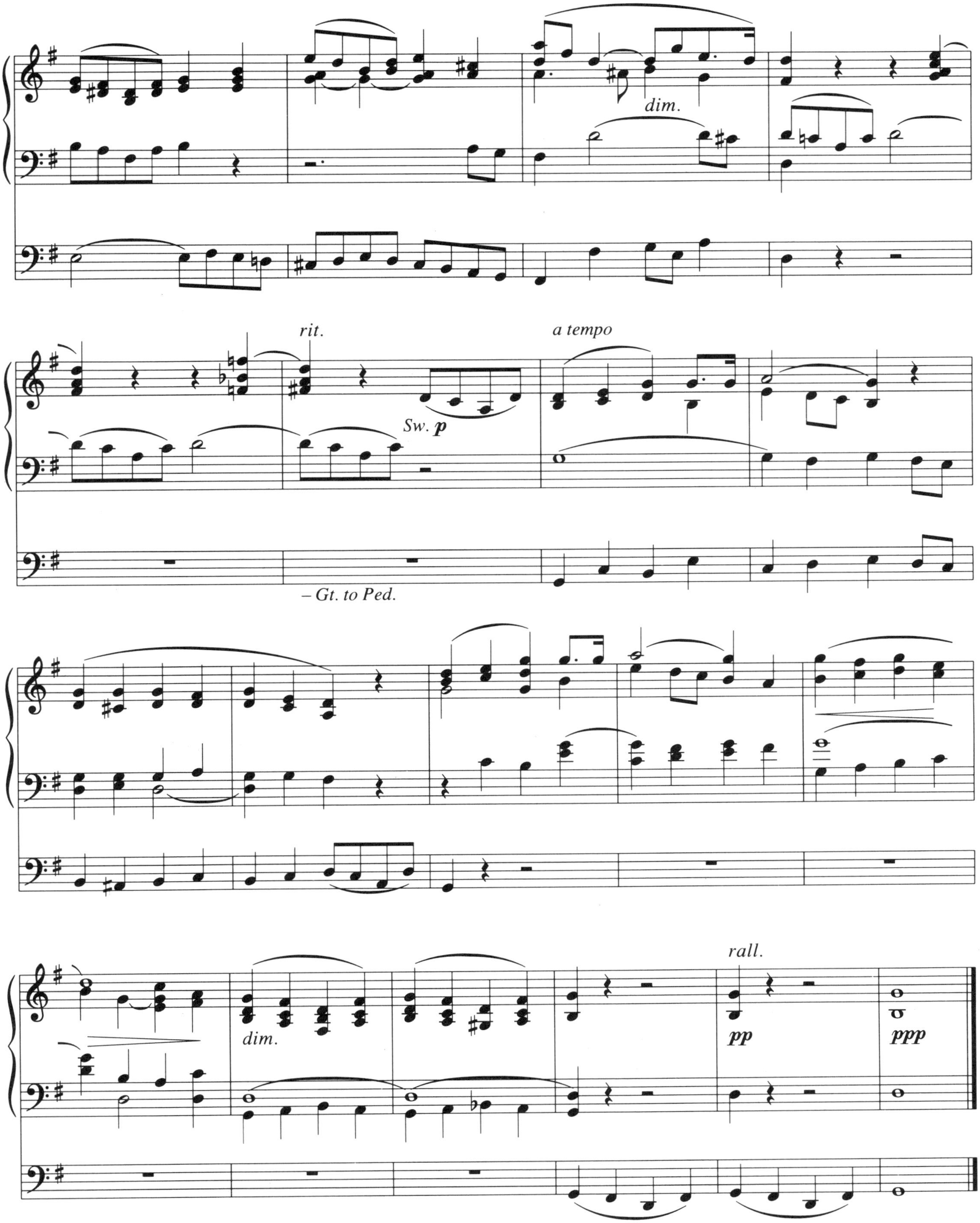
dim.
rit.
a tempo
Sw. p
– Gt. to Ped.
dim.
rall.
pp
ppp

SECOND PRELUDE in A MINOR

Johann Rinck (1770-1846)

ALLEGRETTO

Niels Gade (1817-1890)

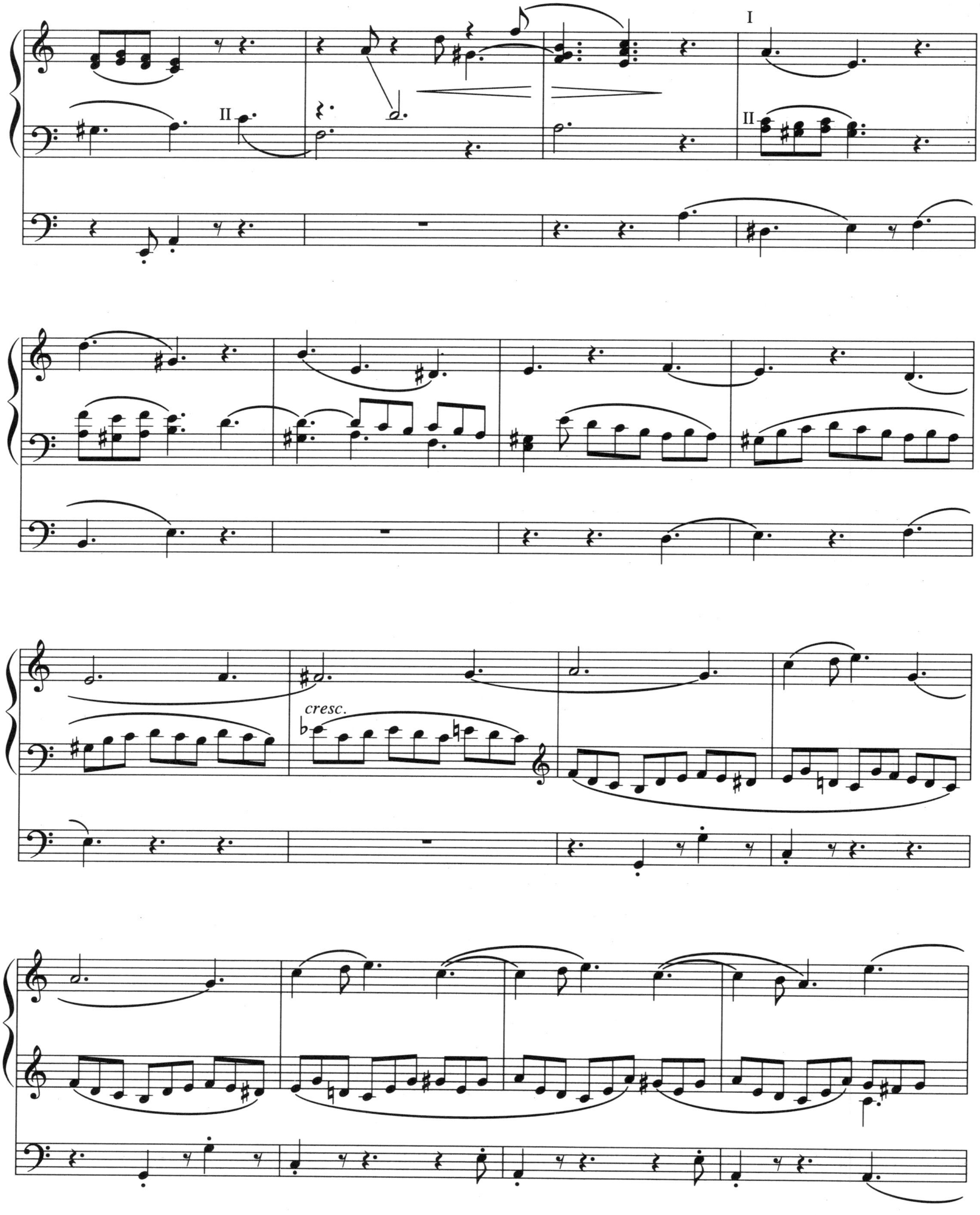
II
I
II
cresc.

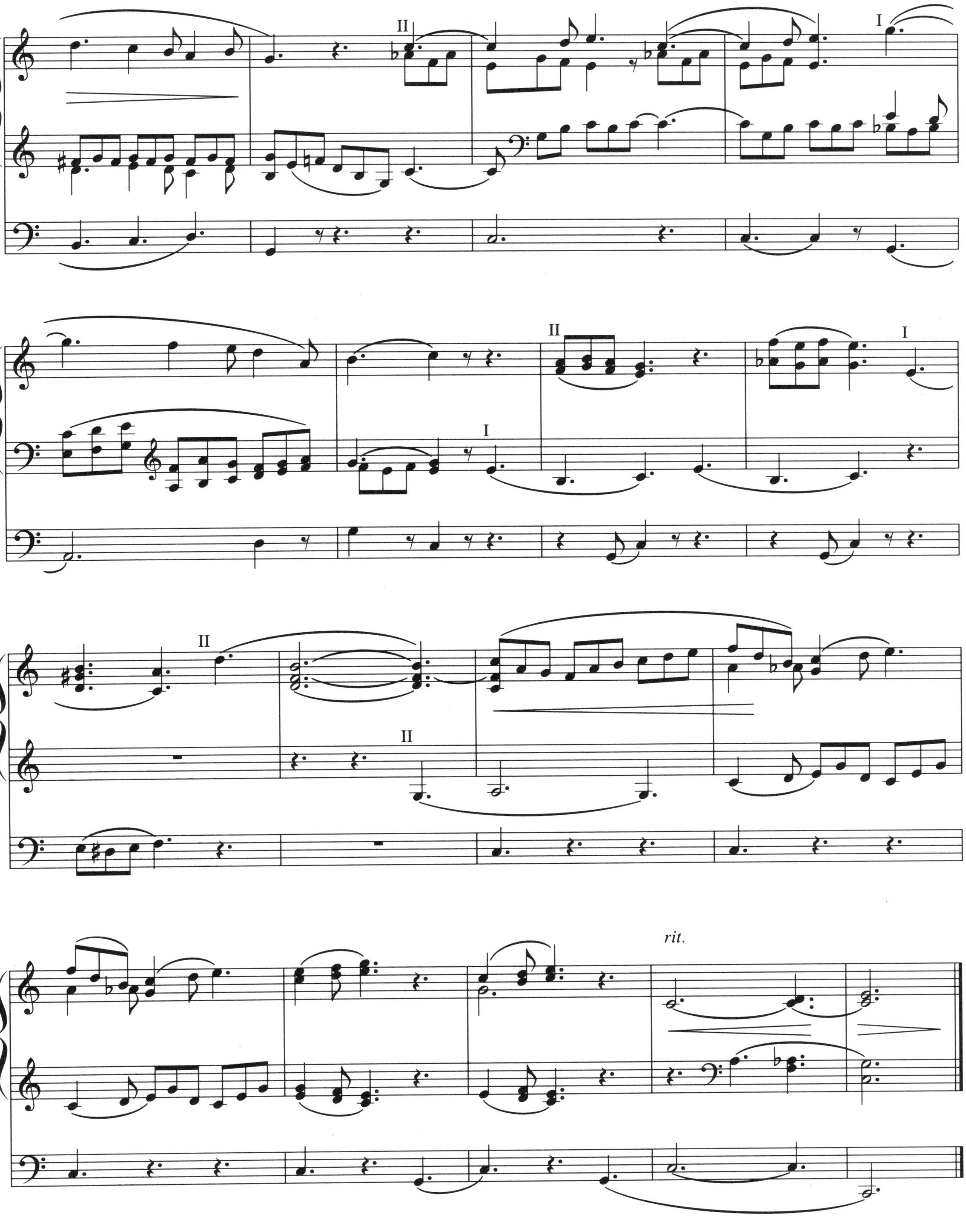
II
I
II
I
II
II
rit.

ANDANTE MODERATO

Henry Smart (1813-1879)

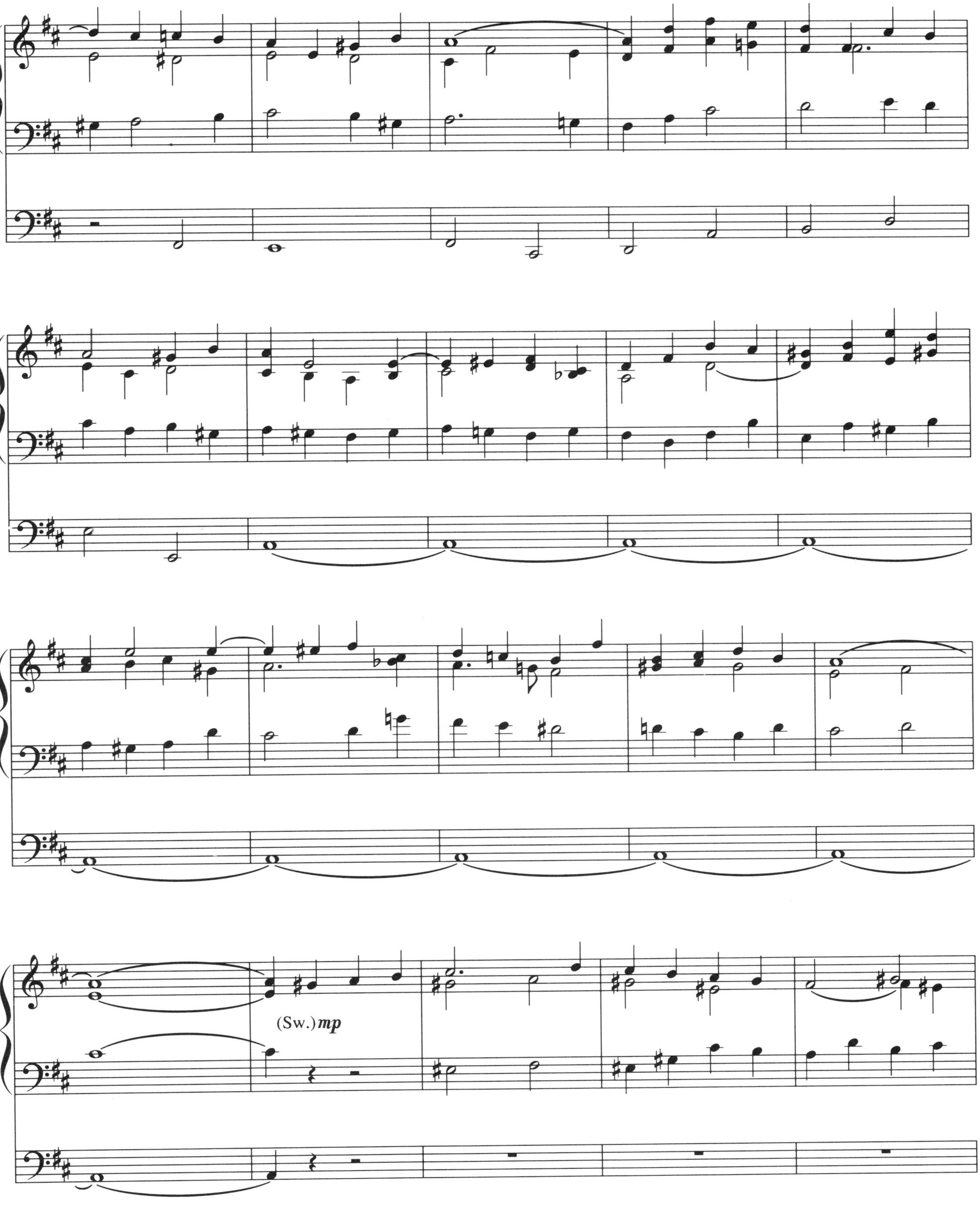
(Sw.) mp

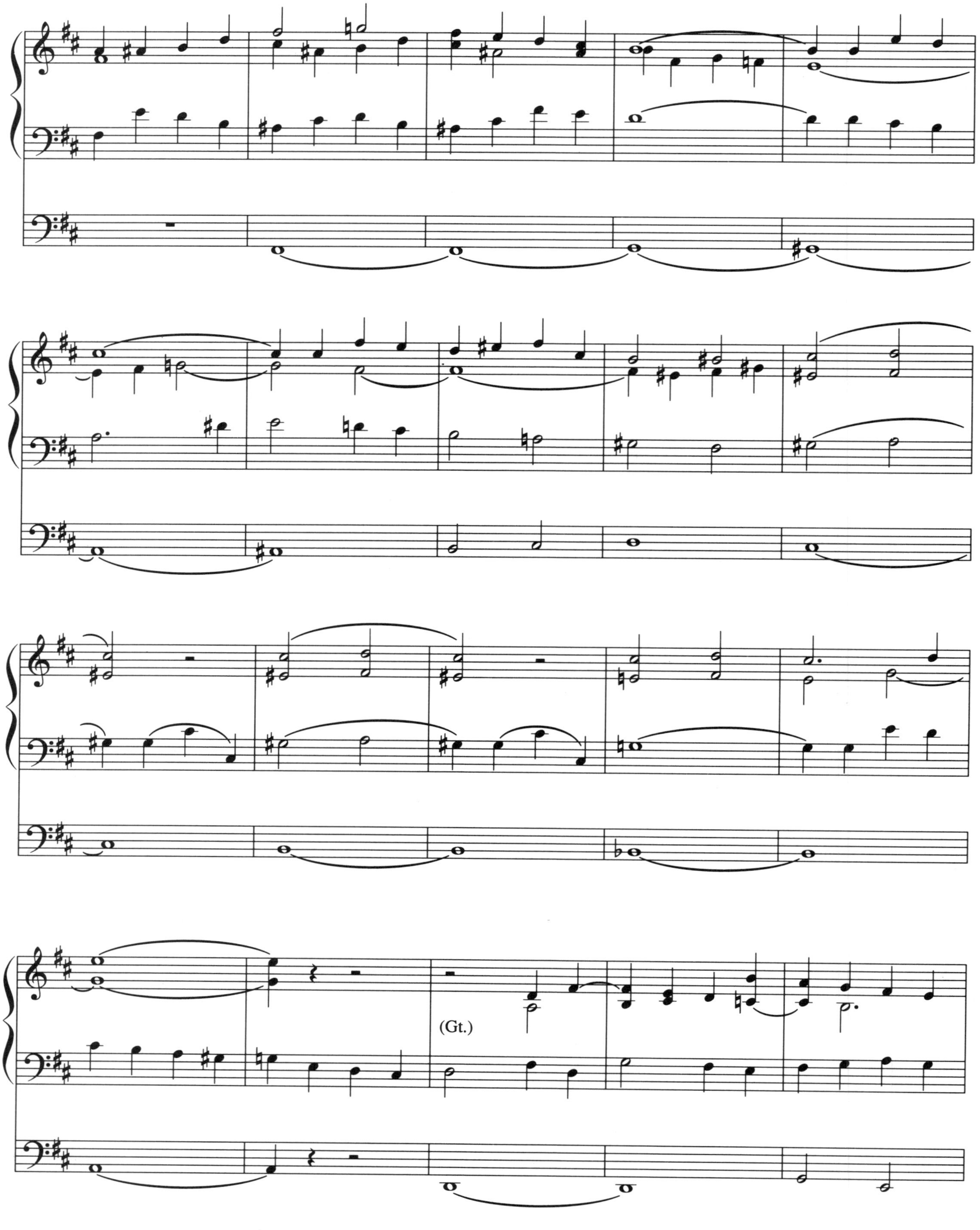
(Gt.)

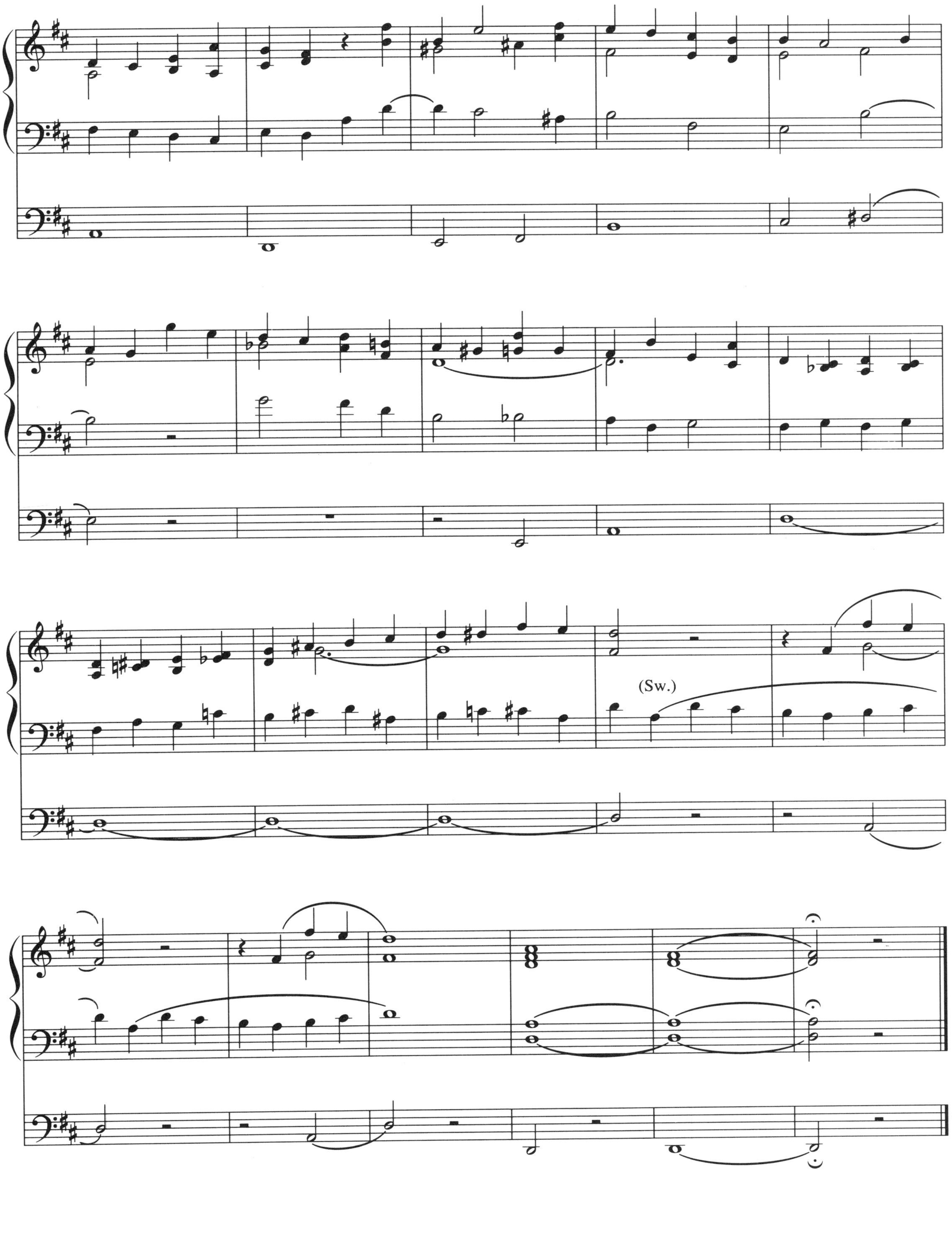
(Sw.)

A STATELY POSTLUDE

Donald Hunt

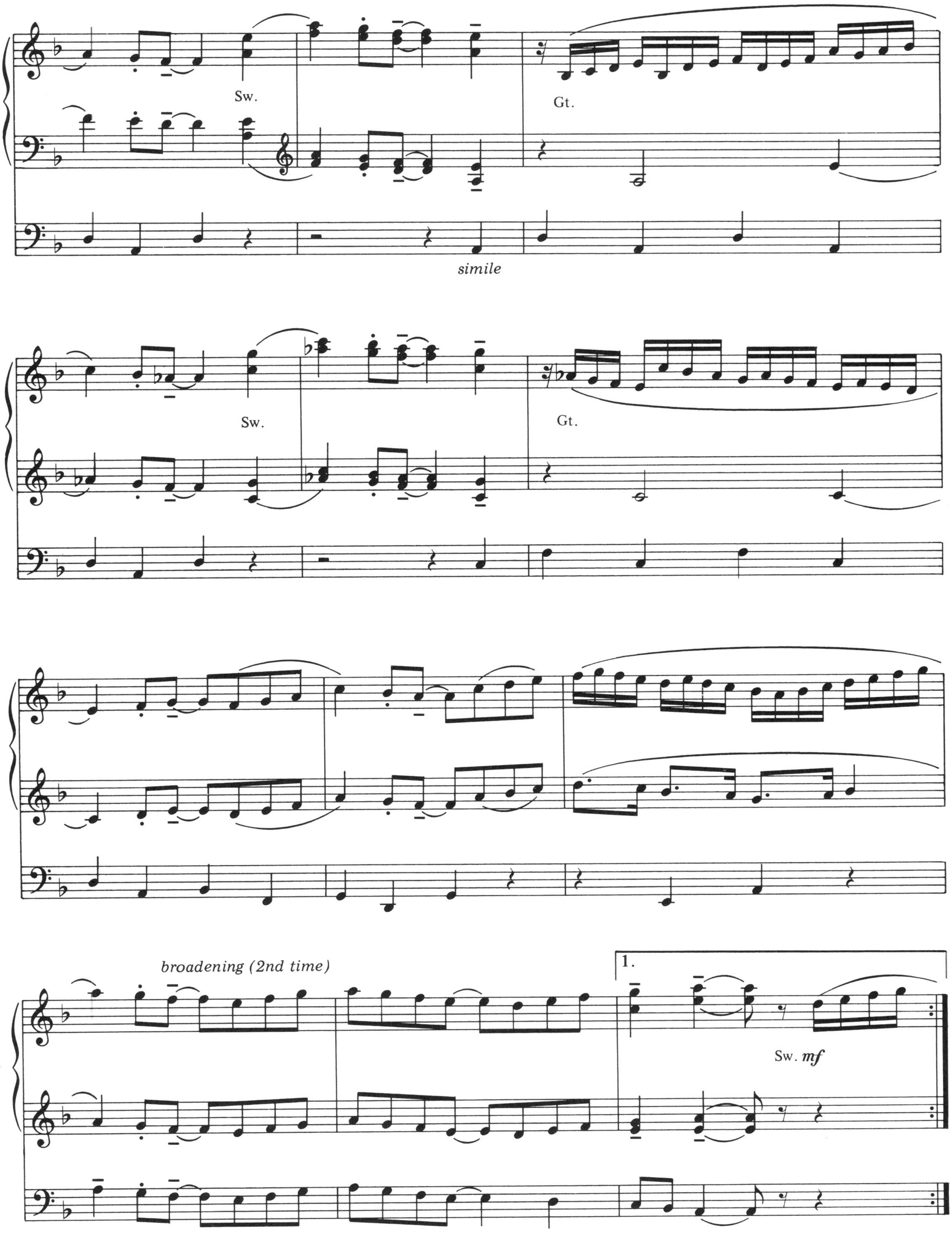
Sw.
Gt.
simile
Sw.
Gt.
broadening (2nd time)
1.
Sw. mf

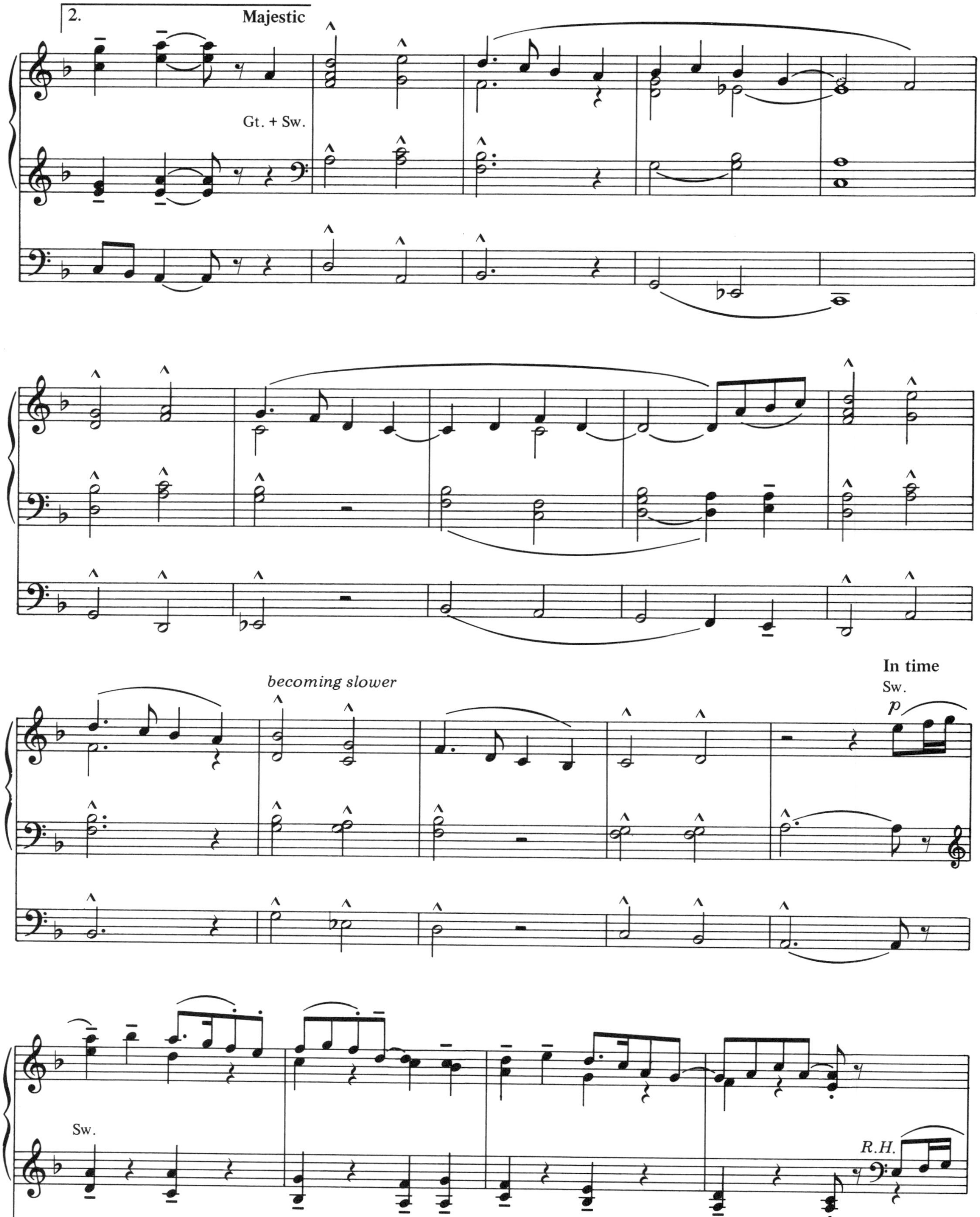
2.
Majestic
Gt. + Sw.
becoming slower
In time
Sw.
p
Sw.
R.H.

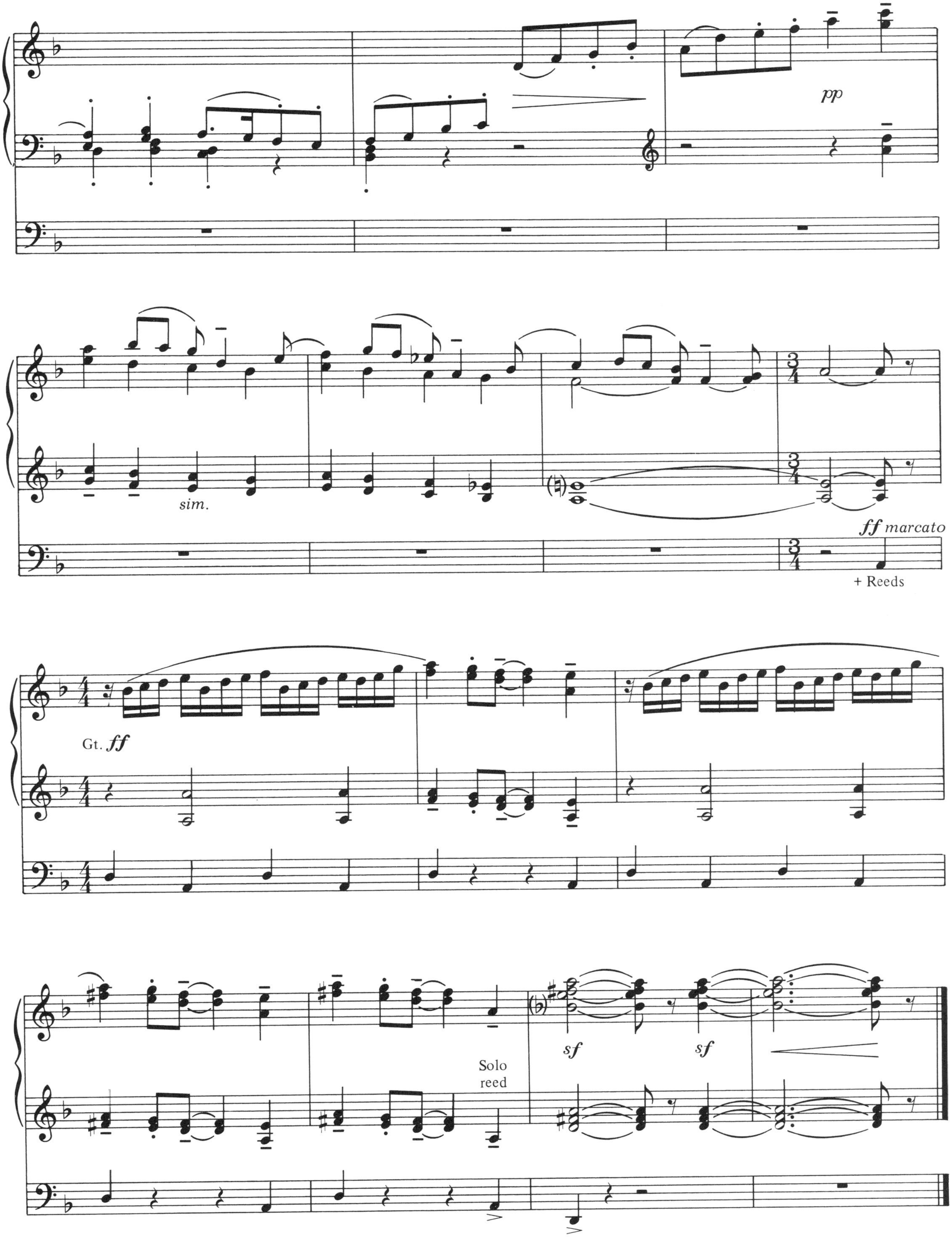
pp
sim.
ff marcato
+ Reeds
Gt. ff
Solo reed
sf
sf

TRUMPET TUNE

Christopher Tambling (*b.*1964)

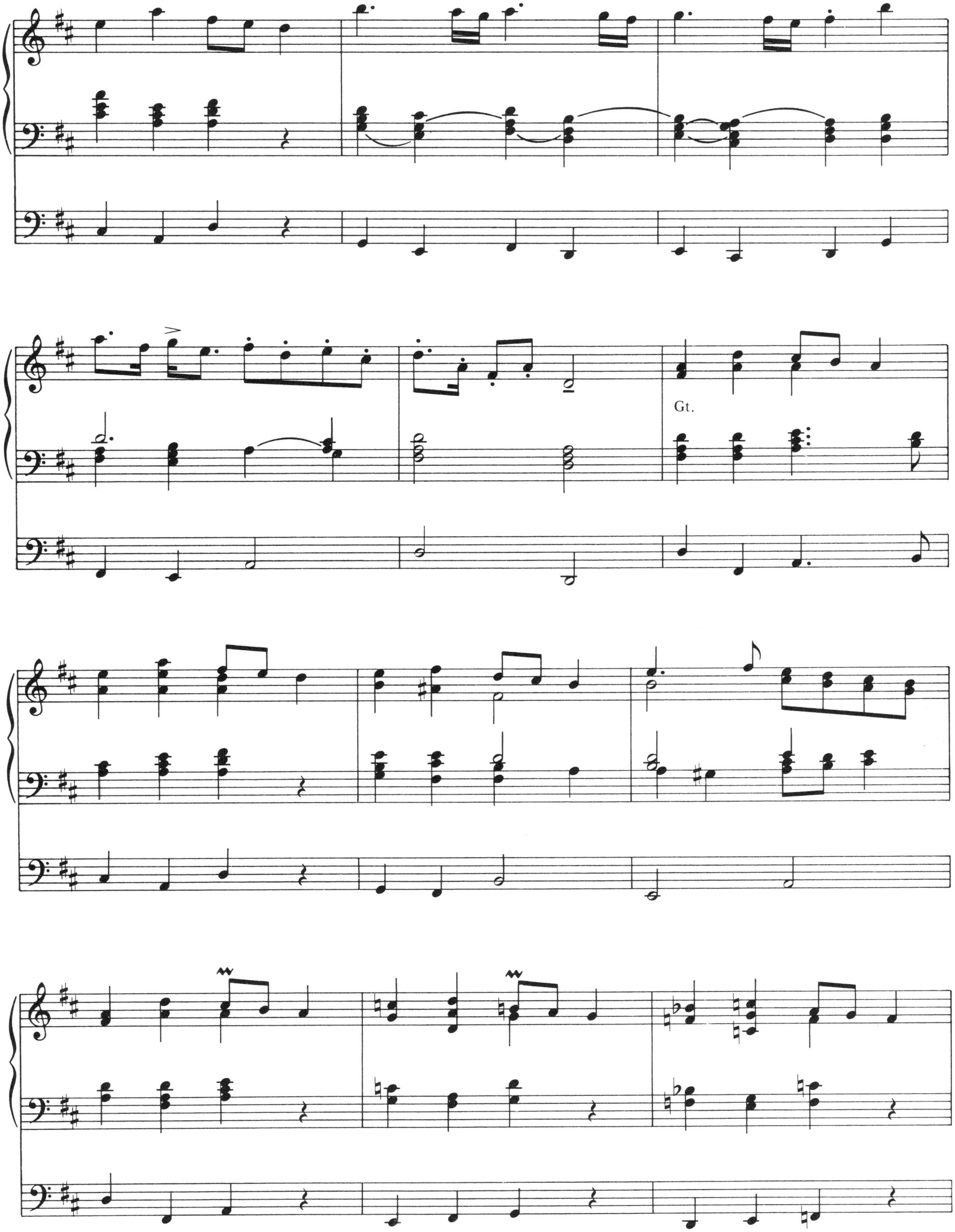
Gt.

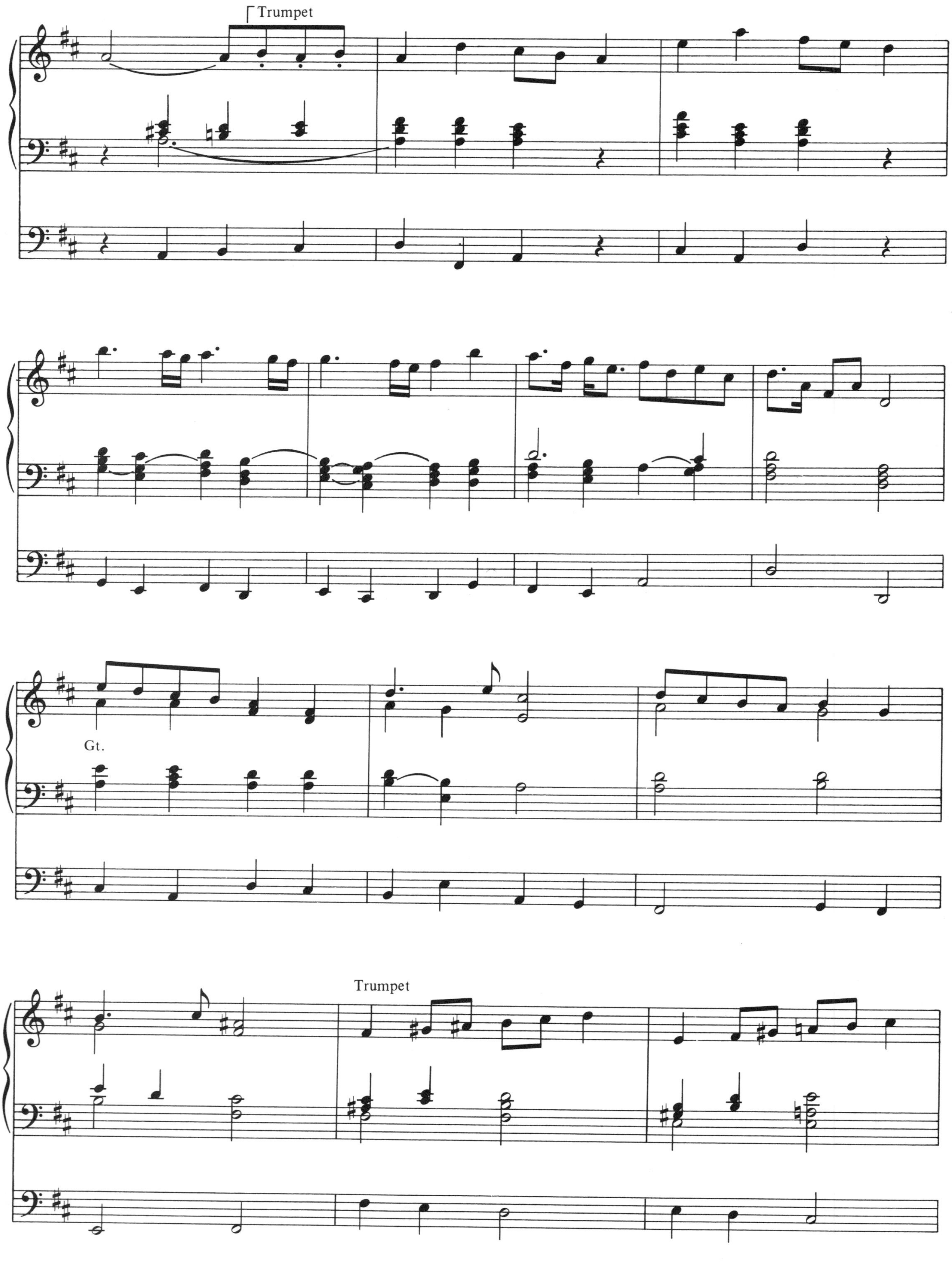
Trumpet
Gt.
Trumpet

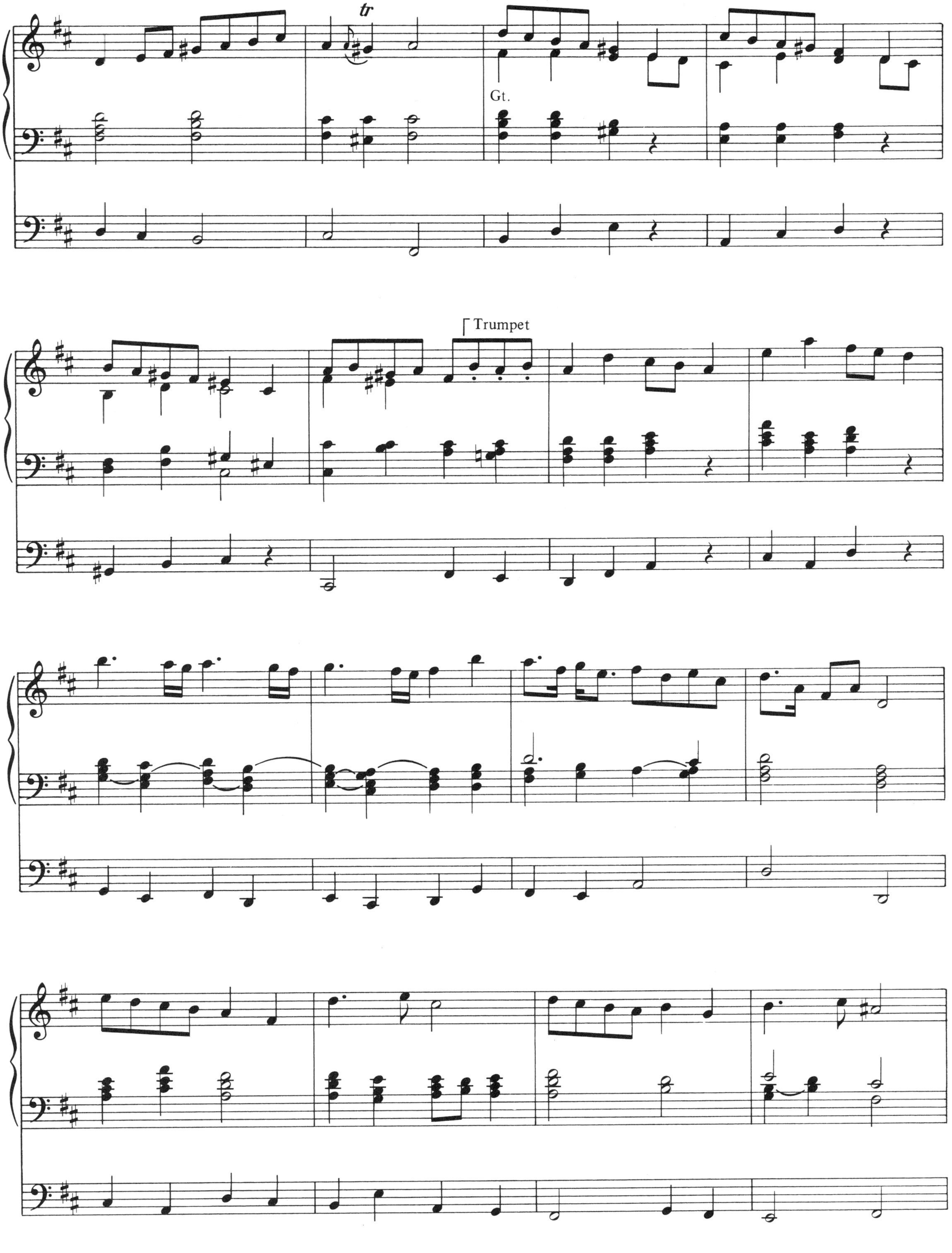
tr
Gt.
Trumpet

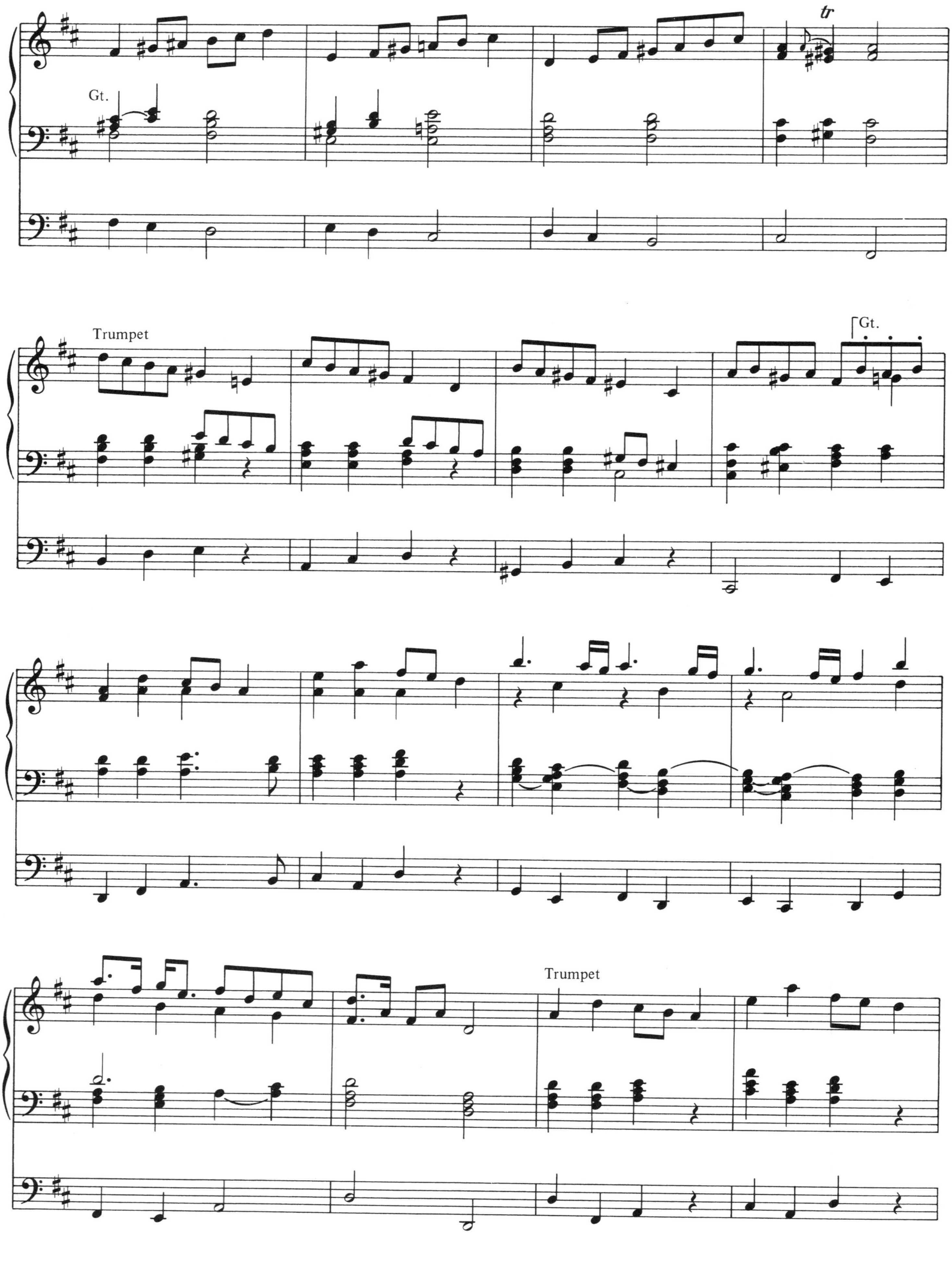
tr
Gt.
Trumpet
Gt.
Trumpet

+ Full Sw. (closed)

cresc.

molto rit.   a tempo   rit.

Gt. *ff*

+32

Christ's Hospital, September 1981

POSTLUDIUM

Gustav Merkel (1827-1885)

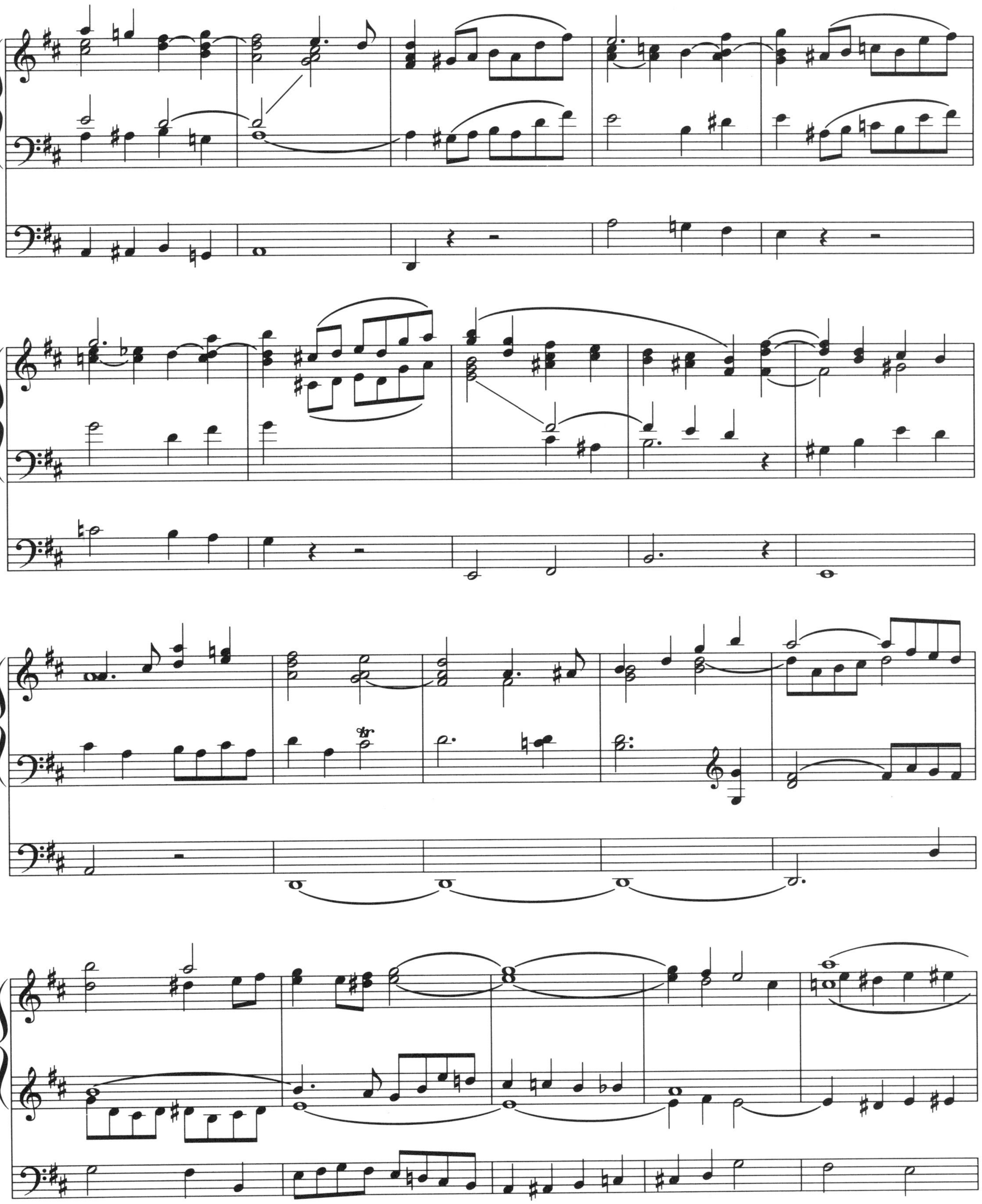

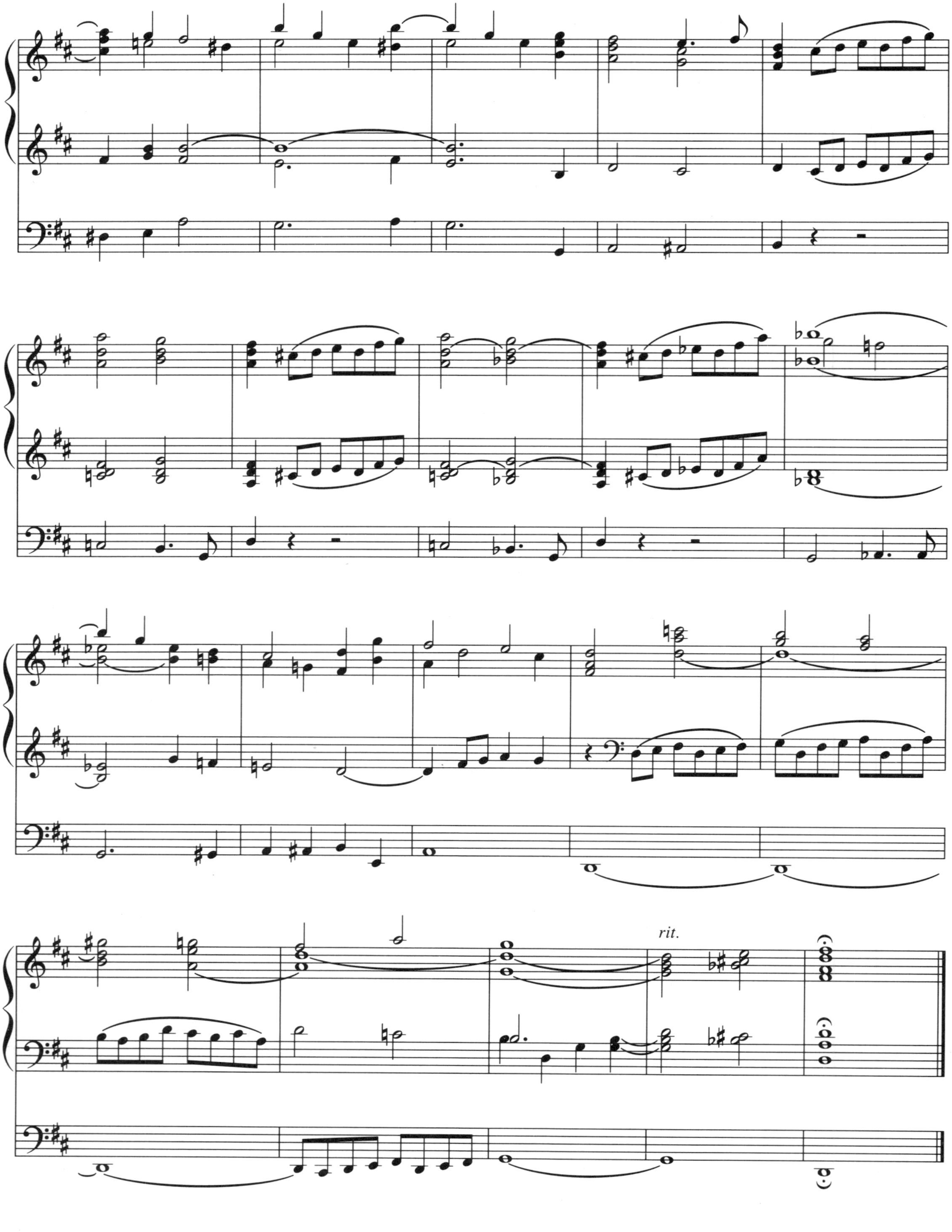
rit.